Demand Forecasting and Order Planning in Supply Chains and Humanitarian Logistics

Atour Taghipour
Normandy University, France

A volume in the Advances in Logistics, Operations, and Management Science (ALOMS) Book Series

IGI Global
PUBLISHER of TIMELY KNOWLEDGE

Published in the United States of America by
IGI Global
Business Science Reference (an imprint of IGI Global)
701 E. Chocolate Avenue
Hershey PA, USA 17033
Tel: 717-533-8845
Fax: 717-533-8661
E-mail: cust@igi-global.com
Web site: http://www.igi-global.com

Library of Congress Cataloging-in-Publication Data

Names: Taghipour, Atour, 1974- editor.
Title: Demand forecasting and order planning in supply chains and humanitarian logistics / Atour Taghipour, editor.
Description: Hershey, PA : Business Science Reference, [2020] | Includes bibliographical references and index. | Summary: "This book focuses on demand anticipation, forecasting, and order planning as well as humanitarian logistics to propose original solutions for existing problems"-- Provided by publisher.
Identifiers: LCCN 2020002818 (print) | LCCN 2020002819 (ebook) | ISBN 9781799838050 (hardcover) | ISBN 9781799853329 (paperback) | ISBN 9781799838067 (ebook)
Subjects: LCSH: Business logistics. | Demand (Economic theory) | Business forecasting.
Classification: LCC HD38.5 .D45 2020 (print) | LCC HD38.5 (ebook) | DDC 658.5/03--dc23
LC record available at https://lccn.loc.gov/2020002818
LC ebook record available at https://lccn.loc.gov/2020002819

This book is published in the IGI Global book series Advances in Logistics, Operations, and Management Science (ALOMS) (ISSN: 2327-350X; eISSN: 2327-3518)

British Cataloguing in Publication Data
A Cataloguing in Publication record for this book is available from the British Library.

For electronic access to this publication, please contact: eresources@igi-global.com.

Advances in Logistics, Operations, and Management Science (ALOMS) Book Series

ISSN:2327-350X
EISSN:2327-3518

Editor-in-Chief: John Wang, Montclair State University, USA

MISSION

Operations research and management science continue to influence business processes, administration, and management information systems, particularly in covering the application methods for decision-making processes. New case studies and applications on management science, operations management, social sciences, and other behavioral sciences have been incorporated into business and organizations real-world objectives.

The **Advances in Logistics, Operations, and Management Science** (ALOMS) Book Series provides a collection of reference publications on the current trends, applications, theories, and practices in the management science field. Providing relevant and current research, this series and its individual publications would be useful for academics, researchers, scholars, and practitioners interested in improving decision making models and business functions.

COVERAGE

- Networks
- Risk Management
- Organizational Behavior
- Finance
- Information Management
- Decision analysis and decision support
- Marketing engineering
- Services management
- Production Management
- Political Science

IGI Global is currently accepting manuscripts for publication within this series. To submit a proposal for a volume in this series, please contact our Acquisition Editors at Acquisitions@igi-global.com or visit: http://www.igi-global.com/publish/.

The Advances in Logistics, Operations, and Management Science (ALOMS) Book Series (ISSN 2327-350X) is published by IGI Global, 701 E. Chocolate Avenue, Hershey, PA 17033-1240, USA, www.igi-global.com. This series is composed of titles available for purchase individually; each title is edited to be contextually exclusive from any other title within the series. For pricing and ordering information please visit http://www.igi-global.com/book-series/advances-logistics-operations-management-science/37170. Postmaster: Send all address changes to above address.

Titles in this Series

For a list of additional titles in this series, please visit:
https://www.igi-global.com/book-series/advances-logistics-operations-management-science/37170

Encyclopedia of Organizational Knowledge, Administration, and Technology
Mehdi Khosrow-Pour D.B.A. (Information Resources Management Association, USA)
Business Science Reference • © 2021 • 4000pp • H/C (ISBN: 9781799834731) • US $3,950.00

Handbook of Research on Sustainable Supply Chain Management for the Global Economy
Ulas Akkucuk (Boğaziçi University, Turkey)
Business Science Reference • © 2020 • 409pp • H/C (ISBN: 9781799846017) • US $265.00

Leadership Strategies for Global Supply Chain Management in Emerging Markets
Ashish Dwivedi (The University of Hull, UK) and Mohammed Saad Alshamrani (King Fahd Naval College, Saudi Arabia)
Business Science Reference • © 2020 • 333pp • H/C (ISBN: 9781799828679) • US $215.00

Managerial Issues in Digital Transformation of Global Modern Corporations
Thangasamy Esakki (Poompuhar College (Autonomous), India)
Business Science Reference • © 2020 • 270pp • H/C (ISBN: 9781799824022) • US $195.00

Contemporary Approaches to Military Operations Research
Mumtaz Karatas (National Defense University, Turkey) and Hakan Tozan (Istanbul Medipol University, Turkey)
Information Science Reference • © 2020 • 300pp • H/C (ISBN: 9781799844051) • US $195.00

Legal, Safety, and Environmental Challenges for Event Management Emerging Research and Opportunities
Vipin Nadda (University of Sunderland, London, UK) Ian Arnott (University of Westminster, London, UK) and Wendy Sealy (University of Chichester, UK)
Business Science Reference • © 2020 • 158pp • H/C (ISBN: 9781799832300) • US $195.00

IGI Global
PUBLISHER of TIMELY KNOWLEDGE

701 East Chocolate Avenue, Hershey, PA 17033, USA
Tel: 717-533-8845 x100 • Fax: 717-533-8661
E-Mail: cust@igi-global.com • www.igi-global.com

Editorial Advisory Board

Table of Contents

Detailed Table of Contents

A coordination approach for forecast operations, known as downstream demand inference, enables an upstream actor to infer the demand information at his formal downstream actor without the need for information sharing. This approach was validated if the downstream actor uses the simple moving average (SMA) forecasting method. To answer an investigative question through other forecasting methods, the authors use the weighted moving average (WMA) method, whose weights are determined in this work thanks to the Newton's optimization of the upstream average inventory level. Starting from a two-level supply chain, the simulation results confirm the ability of the approach to reduce the mean squared error and the average inventory level, compared to a decentralized approach. However, the bullwhip effect is only improved after a certain threshold of the parameter of the forecasting method. Still within the framework of the investigation, they carry out a comparison study between the adoption of the SMA method and the WMA method. Finally, they generalize their results for a multi-level supply chain.

Literature about humanitarian logistics (HL) has developed a lot of innovative decision support systems during the last decades to support decisions such as location, routing, supply, or inventory management. Most of those contributions are based on quantitative models but, generally, are not used by practitioners who are not confident with. This can be explained by the fact that scenarios and datasets used to design and validate those HL models are often too simple compared to the real situations. In this chapter, a scenario-based approach based on a five-step methodology has been developed to bridge this gap by designing a set of valid scenarios able to assess disaster needs in regions subject to recurrent disasters. The contribution, usable by both scholars and practitioners, demonstrates that defining such valid scenario sets is possible for recurrent disasters. Finally, the proposal is validated on a concrete application case based on Peruvian recurrent flood and earthquake disasters.

A supply chain includes several elements such as suppliers, manufacturers, retails, and customers. Forecasting the demands and sales is a challenging task in supply chain management (SCM). The main goal of this research is to create forecasting models for retailers by using artificial neural network (ANN) and to enable them to make accurate business decisions by visualizing future data. Two forecasting models are investigated in this research. One is a sales model that predicts future sales, and the second one is a demand model that predicts future demands. To achieve the mentioned goal, CNN-LSTM model is used for both sales and demand predictions. Based on the obtained results, this hybrid model can learn from very long range of historical data and can predict the future efficiently.

In the home healthcare routing and scheduling problem (HHCRSP), nurses are allocated to a variety of services demanded by clients during a planning horizon. The properties of this problem resemble vehicle routing and nurse scheduling. To propose an efficient solution, the authors consider various issues such as multi-depot, travelling time, time windows, synchronisation, the qualification levels, and other features of nurses and clients. In addition, the continuity of care and work overload should not be ignored in this perspective. First, the authors developed a model in which the continuity of care is redefined by considering connected (synchronous) jobs and the work overload is formulated considering nurse-to-patient staffing ratio. Second, a two-stage solution approach based on a cluster-assign algorithm and variable neighbourhood search (VNS) and variable neighbourhood descent (VND) algorithms are tested on a series of large-scale instances. Computational results present the relations and trade-offs among the aforementioned issues.

Supply chain management (SCM) is a fast growing and largely studied field of research. Forecasting of the required materials and parts is an important task in companies and can have a significant impact on the total cost. To have a reliable forecast, some advanced methods such as deep learning techniques are helpful. The main goal of this chapter is to forecast the unit sales of thousands of items sold at different chain stores located in Ecuador with holistic techniques. Three deep learning approaches including artificial neural network (ANN), convolutional neural network (CNN), and long short-term memory (LSTM) are adopted here for predictions from the Corporación Favorita grocery sales forecasting dataset collected from Kaggle website. Finally, the performances of the applied models are evaluated and compared. The results show that LSTM network tends to outperform the other two approaches in terms of performance. All experiments are conducted using Python's deep learning library and Keras and Tensorflow packages.

Logistics providers have become an important element in completing humanitarian relief work in countries experiencing armed conflict. Delivery aid assistances need to build logistics capacity and critical supply chain functions that help to meet the unconfirmed requirements of beneficiaries at right place, on right date, and with right fees. To reach the research goal, the authors will determine the weights of customer requirements (CRs) using the DEMATEL method, which considers the influences of inconformity and the causal relationship between CRs. This chapter employs quality function deployment (QFD) to integrate the voice of CRs and supplier criteria TRs using house of quality charts. This chapter focuses on case of humanitarian organizations collaborate with logistics service providers (LSPs) to maintain and enhance their performance by identify the crucial factors that effect on LSPs selection and their specified from the perspective of humanitarian relief organizations activated in Syrian humanitarian operation.

Supply chain is a complex system in which most of the activities are inter-related, and changes in one of these activities can affect the performance of the other processes. Thus, integrated management strategies in a supply chain can yield considerable advantages throughout the system as supply chain members and customers become more integrated. In this study, a memetic algorithm is proposed to solve the integrated production-distribution problem. The objective of the problem is to find optimal production quantity, customer delivery quantity, and schedule to minimize the total system cost, which is composed of production setup cost and variable production cost, inventory holding costs, and distribution cost. The effectiveness of the proposed algorithm is tested on the existing data sets. According to test results, the proposed algorithm is a very effective method to solve integrated production-distribution problems. To assess to benefits and applicability of the method on the real-life problems, a case study is conducted in a Turkish water manufacturing company.

Foreword

Demand forecasting and order panning in supply chains and humanitarian logistics is defined as the process of planning, implementing and controlling the efficient, cost-effective flow and storage of goods and materials, as well as related information, from the point of origin to the point of consumption for the purpose of satisfying the customers and more especially for the purpose of alleviating the suffering of vulnerable people. The function encompasses a range of activities, including preparedness, planning, procurement, transport, warehousing, tracking and tracing, and customs clearance.

This book examines the concept of *Demand Forecasting and Order Planning in Supply Chains and Humanitarian Logistics*, which is an answer to a real need expressed by academics and practitioners. Supply chain order planning is now firmly established as a critical business concern. In addition, there is a scarcity of books covering the topic of demand forecasting and order planning in supply chains and humanitarian logistics and this book fills a major gap in this domain. The book analyzes, the concept of demand planning from different aspects. The book deals with different essential processes of supply chains such as demand anticipation, forecasting and order planning. The focus of this book is also on the humanitarian logistics to propose the original solutions for existing problems.

The parts of the book are well-linked and integrated altogether and offer a holistic and overarching perspective of supply chain planning. Hence, readers of this book will benefit extensively from this approach and the intertwined theoretical and applied approach followed when covering various aspects of planning. I am confident that this book will be very popular amongst academics and practitioners. In addition, it will be extremely valuable to both undergraduate and postgraduate students reading for Supply Chain Management. To conclude, this book is a welcome addition. I recommend it highly to anybody interested to the topic of Demand forecasting and order panning in supply chains and humanitarian logistics.

Sharareh Taghipour
Ryerson University, Canada

Preface

AN OVERVIEW OF THE DEMAND FORECASTING AND ORDER PANNING IN SUPPLY CHAINS AND HUMANITARIAN LOGISTICS

A supply chain is two or more agents who work with each other, in order to create and deliver value to final customers. A decentralized supply chain is characterized by independent agents with asymmetric information. In fact, in this form of supply chain, most of supply chain agents may not share information due to confidentiality policies, quality of information or different system's incompatibilities. Every actor holds its own set of information and try to maximize his objective (minimizing costs/minimizing inventory holdings) based on the available settings. Therefore, the agents control their own activities with the objective of improving their own competitiveness, which leads them to make decisions that maximize their local performance by ignoring the other agents or even the final consumer. These decisions are called myopic because they do not consider the performance of all the partners to satisfy this consumer.

In this book, we invest on supply chain demand anticipation, forecasting and order planning. We focus as well on the humanitarian logistics to propose the original solutions for existing problems.

A DESCRIPTION OF THE TOPIC IN THE WORLD TODAY

Supply chain are subject to instability. Small variations in demand can create order oscillations that amplify as one moves up in the supply chain (Forrester, 1961). This phenomenon of amplification of oscillations through the supply chain is also known as the bullwhip effect (Lee et al, 1997). In this context, four main causes of the bullwhip effect are demand signal processing, order batching, rationing game, and price variations. Chen et al (1998) argues that the bullwhip effect is due to the need to forecast the demand. In another study, Sterman (2000) shows that delays inherent within the supply chain together with demand forecasting and distortion can create amplified oscillations. There have been several attempts to perform demand forecasting over last decades. Some researchers tried to use data mining techniques to forecast the demand. Recently, there is a trend to propose the novel methods of forecasting using system dynamics approach to predict demand.

A DESCRIPTION OF THE TARGET AUDIENCE

Demand forecasting and order panning in supply chains and humanitarian logistics is the art of planning and forecasting techniques in the sector of tangible goods and intangible service. In particular, the book provides a comprehensive review and understanding of how these techniques and principles can contribute to the effective and efficient management and planning of supply chain activities and more especially in humanitarian logistics.

A DESCRIPTION OF EACH CHAPTER

Exploring a Downstream Demand Inference Strategy in a Decentralized Two-Level Supply Chain

A coordination approach for forecast operations, known as downstream demand inference, enables an upstream actor to infer the demand information at his formal downstream actor without the need for information sharing. This approach was validated if the downstream actor uses the Simple Moving Average (SMA) forecasting method. To answer an investigative question through other forecasting methods, we use the Weighted Moving Average (WMA) method, whose weights are determined in this work thanks to the Newton's optimization of the upstream average inventory level. Starting from a two-level supply chain, the simulation results confirm the ability of our approach to reduce the mean squared error and the average inventory level, compared to a decentralized approach. However, the bullwhip effect is only improved after a certain threshold of the parameter of the forecasting method. Still within the framework of our investigation, we carry out a comparison study between the adoption of the SMA method and the WMA method. Finally, we generalize our results for a multi-level supply chain.

Designing Valid Humanitarian Logistics Scenario Sets: Application to Recurrent Peruvian Floods and Earthquakes

Literature about Humanitarian Logistics (HL) has developed a lot of innovative decision support systems during the last decades to support decisions such as location, routing, supply or inventory management. Most of those contributions are based on quantitative models but, generally, are not used by practitioners who are not confident with. This can be explained by the fact that scenarios and datasets used to design and validate those HL models are often too simple compared to the real situations. In this chapter, a scenario-based approach based on a five-step methodology has been developed to bridge this gap by designing a set of valid scenarios able to assess disaster needs in regions subject to recurrent disasters. The contribution, usable by both scholars and practitioners, demonstrates that defining such valid scenario sets is possible for recurrent disasters. Finally, the proposal is validated on a concrete application case based on Peruvian recurrent flood and earthquake disasters.

Demands and Sales Forecasting for Retailers by Analyzing Google Trends and Historical Data

A supply chain includes several elements such as suppliers, manufacturers, retails, and customers. Forecasting the demands and sales is a challenging task in Supply Chain Management (SCM). The main goal of this research is to create forecasting models for retailers by using Artificial Neural Network (ANN), and to enable them to make accurate business decisions by visualizing future data. Two forecasting models are investigated in this research. One is a sales model which predicts future sales, and the second one is a demand model which predicts future demands. To achieve the mentioned goal, CNN-LSTM model is used for both sales and demand predictions. Based on the obtained results, this hybrid model can learn from very long range of historical data and can predict the future efficiently.

A Cluster First-Route Second Solution Approach for the Multi-Period Home Healthcare Routing and Scheduling Problem

In the home healthcare routing and scheduling problem (HHCRSP), nurses are allocated to a variety of services demanded by clients during a planning horizon. The properties of this problem resemble vehicle routing and nurse scheduling. To propose an efficient solution, the authors consider various issues such as multi-depot, travelling time, time windows, synchronisation, the qualification levels and other features of nurses and clients. Besides, the continuity of care and work overload should not be ignored in this perspective. First, the authors developed a model in which the continuity of care is redefined by considering connected (synchronous) jobs and the work overload is formulated considering nurse-to-patient staffing ratio. Second, a two-stage solution approach based on a cluster-assign algorithm and variable neighbourhood search (VNS) and variable neighbourhood descent (VND) algorithms are tested on a series of large-scale instances. Computational results present the relations and trade-offs among the aforementioned issues.

Demand Forecasting in Supply Chain Management Using Different Deep Learning Methods

Supply Chain Management (SCM) is a fast growing and largely studied field of research. Forecasting of the required materials and parts is an important task in companies, and can have a significant impact on the total cost. To have a reliable forecast, some advanced methods such as deep learning techniques are helpful. The main goal of this book chapter is to forecast the unit sales of thousands of items sold at different chain stores located in Ecuador with holistic techniques. Three deep learning approaches including Artificial Neural Network (ANN), Convolutional Neural Network (CNN), and Long Short Term Memory (LSTM) are adopted here for predictions from the Corporación Favorita Grocery Sales Forecasting dataset collected from Kaggle website. Finally, the performances of the applied models are evaluated and compared. The results show that LSTM network tends to outperform the other two approaches in terms of performance. All experiments are conducted using Python's deep learning library and Keras and Tensorflow packages.

Logistics Providers in Syria Humanitarian Operations

Logistics providers have become an important element in completing humanitarian relief work in countries experiencing armed conflict. Delivery aid assistances need to build logistics capacity and critical supply chain functions that help to meet the unconfirmed requirements of beneficiaries at right place, on right date, and with right fees. To reach the research goal, the authors will determinant of weights of customer requirements (CRs) using the DEMATEL method, which considers the influences of inconformity and the causal relationship between CRs. This paper employs quality function deployment (QFD) to integrate the voice of CRs and supplier criteria TRs using House of Quality charts. This chapter focuses on case of humanitarian organizations collaborate with logistics service providers (LSPs) to maintain and enhance their performance by identify the crucial factors that effect on LSPs selection and their specified from the perspective of humanitarian relief organizations activated in Syrian humanitarian operation.

A Memetic Algorithm for Integrated Production Distribution Problem in a Supply Chain

Supply chain is a complex system in which most of the activities are inter-related and changes in one of these activities can affect the performance of the other processes. Thus, integrated management strategies in a supply chain can yield considerable advantages throughout the system as supply chain members and customers become more integrated. In this study, a memetic algorithm is proposed to solve the integrated production-distribution problem. The objective of the problem is to find optimal production quantity, customer delivery quantity and schedule to minimize the total system cost which is composed of production setup cost and variable production cost, inventory holding costs and distribution cost. The effectiveness of the proposed algorithm is tested on the existing data sets. According to test results, the proposed algorithm is a very effective method to solve integrated production-distribution problems. To assess to benefits and applicability of the method on the real-life problems, a case study is conducted in a Turkish water manufacturing company.

Mixed Delivery and Pickup Vehicle Routing Problem With Limited Flow and Assignment of Drones in an Urban Network

A new variant of the delivery and pickup transportation problem called mixed delivery and pickup routing problem with unmanned aerial vehicles in case of limited flow is introduced. The objective is to minimize operational costs including total transportation costs and service time at each point. This variant is a solution for the urban congestion and consequently, it is an improvement of the general transport system. First the problem is formulated mathematically. It is considered as NP-hard; therefore, we proposed an iterated local search algorithm to solve the problem of mixed pickup and delivery without Drone. Then, a vehicle first-drone second algorithm is used to solve the mixed delivery and pickup problem with Drone. The performance of the method is compared through numerical experiments based on instance derived from the literature as well as on a set of randomly generated instances. Numerical results have shown that proposed metaheuristic method performs consistently well in terms of both the quality of the solution and the computational time when using drone with vehicle.

Forecasting Sales and Return Products for Retail Corporation and Bridging Among Them

The purpose of this study is to show how we can bridge between sales and return forecasts for every product of a retail store by using the best model among several forecasting models. Managers can utilize this information to improve customer's satisfaction, inventory management, or re-define policy for after sales support for specific products. We investigate multi-product sales and return forecasting by choosing the best forecasting model. To this aim, some machine learning algorithms including ARIMA, Holt-Winters, STLF, Bagged Model, Timetk, and Prophet are utilized. For every product, the best forecasting model is chosen after comparing these models to generate sales and return forecasts. This information is used to classify every product as "Profitable", "Risky", and "Neutral". The experiment has shown that 3% of the total products have been identified as "Risky" items for the future. Managers can utilize this information to take some crucial decisions.

A CONCLUSION OF HOW THE BOOK IMPACTS

The book is written to cover the interests of a wide variety of audiences ranging from academic researchers, students and practitioners. It features numerous methods and technics for Demand forecasting and order panning in supply chains and humanitarian logistics.

This work is an excellent book that pool together the literature related to forecasting and planning, and presents some new methods and algorithms as well. This book is clearly written and makes good use of tables and diagrams to illustrate the forecasting and planning in tangible and intangible supply chains.

I recommend this book for a variety of audiences: professors, researchers, students and practitioners who are interested to obtain a good understanding of the current state of Demand forecasting and order panning in supply chains and humanitarian logistic and to implement them in the service and goods industries.

REFERENCES

Chen, F., Drezner, Z., Ryan, J. K., & Simchi-Levi, D. (1998). The bullwhip effect: Managerial insights on the impact of forecasting and information on variability in a supply chain. In S. Tayur, R. Ganeshan, & M. Magazine (Eds.), *Quantitative Models for Supply Chain Management* (pp. 417–440). Kluwer Academic Publishers.

Forrester, J. W. (1961). *Industrial Dynamics*. MIT Press.

Lee, H. L., Padmanabhan, V., & Whang, S. (1997). The bullwhip effect in supply chains. *Sloan Management Review*, *38*, 93–102.

Sterman, J. D. (1989). Modeling managerial behavior: Misperceptions of feedback in a dynamic decision experiment. *Management Science*, *35*(3), 321–339. doi:10.1287/mnsc.35.3.321

Acknowledgment

The editor would like to acknowledge the help of all the people involved in this project and, more specifically, to the authors and reviewers that took part in the review process. Without their support, this book would not have become a reality.

First, the editor would like to thank each one of the authors for their contributions. Our sincere gratitude goes to the chapter's authors who contributed their time and expertise to this book.

Second, the editor wishes to acknowledge the valuable contributions of the reviewers regarding the improvement of quality, coherence, and content presentation of chapters. Most of the authors also served as referees; we highly appreciate their double task.

Atour Taghipour
Normandy University, France

Chapter 1
Exploring a Downstream Demand Inference Strategy in a Decentralized Two-Level Supply Chain

Youssef Tliche
University of Le Havre Normandie, France

Atour Taghipour
Normandy University, France

Béatrice Canel-Depitre
University of Le Havre Normandie, France

ABSTRACT

A coordination approach for forecast operations, known as downstream demand inference, enables an upstream actor to infer the demand information at his formal downstream actor without the need for information sharing. This approach was validated if the downstream actor uses the simple moving average (SMA) forecasting method. To answer an investigative question through other forecasting methods, the authors use the weighted moving average (WMA) method, whose weights are determined in this work thanks to the Newton's optimization of the upstream average inventory level. Starting from a two-level supply chain, the simulation results confirm the ability of the approach to reduce the mean squared error and the average inventory level, compared to a decentralized approach. However, the bullwhip effect is only improved after a certain threshold of the parameter of the forecasting method. Still within the framework of the investigation, they carry out a comparison study between the adoption of the SMA method and the WMA method. Finally, they generalize their results for a multi-level supply chain.

DOI: 10.4018/978-1-7998-3805-0.ch001

1. INTRODUCTION

The optimal supply chain performance requires the realization of numerous actions. Regrettably, those actions are not always in the best interest of the actors of the same supply chain. The supply chain actors are mainly focused on achieving their own objectives and that self-serving focus often leads to poor performance. However, enhanced performance is achievable if the companies coordinate their operations such that each company's objectives become aligned with the supply chain's performance. Supply chain management (SCM) is one of the most important research areas that aims to improve the overall supply chain performance.

The information sharing policy presents one of the most common managerial solutions in the SCM field. In recent years, numerous studies have highlighted the importance of information sharing within the supply chain (Lambert and Cooper, 2000; La Londe and Ginter, 2003; Trkman et al., 2006). Information-sharing contracts between economic actors in a supply chain can lead to important benefits, such as increased productivity, better policy-making and integrated services. A series of papers have argued that information sharing can reduce inventory levels and associated costs for upstream actors (Cachon and Fisher, 2000; Yu et al., 2001; Sahin and Robinson, 2005). Li (2013) has explored new ways to reduce operational costs in supply chain systems that face uncertainty about shared information. Adopting simulation, the author concluded that information sharing is essential to reduce fluctuations in stock replenishment, thereby improving supply chain performance. The replenishment of companies' inventories depends on customer demand information. To avoid the accumulation of cost-intensive and obsolete inventories, demand information must be frequently updated and shared with transparency and credibility. Trapero et al (2012) studied the impact of information sharing on supplier forecasting performance. The authors concluded that information sharing improves demand forecasting performance. Croson et al. (2014) argued that coordination through information sharing reduces the risk of a very strong demand distortion. In particular, several researchers have shown that sharing end-customer demand information reduces the bullwhip effect and lowers the average inventory level (Chen et al., 2000b; Lee et al., 2000; Cheng and Wu, 2005).

End-customer demand presents crucial information that must be well considered by all actors in the supply chain (Ciancimino et al., 2012; Asgari et al., 2016). Moreover, several researchers have devoted a high importance to customer behavioral studies (Arnould and Thompson, 2005; Badot et al., 2009; Lemoine, 2003). These studies have shown that this demand is fully shaped by consumers' ethnological and environmental components (such as the pleasure felt by the customer in the store, the state of excitement in the store, the time spent at the point of sale, the amount of purchases made, etc.).

If several research studies have focused on the study of the factors that mobilize end-customer demand, it is because there are many motivations in both the academic and entrepreneurial worlds. At the operational level, as the initial demand of the end-customer is the "source-engine" of profits generated for the entire supply chain, a better knowledge of customer demand is then considered as a tool for securing inventory levels and reducing inventory costs. Indeed, if upstream players have access to data from the sales' points, the harmful effect of the distortion of demand is reduced. As downstream actors share their demand information, upstream actors would be aware of the variance of the error terms of customer demand. Then, they could use this variance in their forecasting decisions instead of the amplified variance due to the bullwhip effect (Lee et al., 2000). Disney and Towill (2002) and Ireland and Crum (2006) reported that inventory levels could be reduced by up to 50% and inventory costs reduced by up to 40%, resulting in improved competitiveness in the market. The sharing of demand information is therefore one of the most important catalysts for improving supply chains. This requires, of course, that upstream players have access to customer demand data at the downstream levels. Some researchers (Chen et al., 2000b; Lee et al., 2000; Yu et al. 2002; Raghunathan, 2003) have concluded that downstream actors need to share customer demand information with upstream actors in order to reduce the bullwhip effect. Nevertheless, the need for information retrieval mechanisms has always been a subject of open discussion in the literature. Many researchers (Lee and Whang, 2000; Mendelson, 2000; Fawcett et al., 2007; Forslund and Jonsson, 2007; Klein et al., 2007) have also argued that information sharing has a number of practical limitations, which need to be taken into account before collaboration.

On one side, a stream of papers (Cachon and Fisher, 2000; Yu et al., 2001; Sahin and Robinson 2005) argued that information sharing can reduce the inventory holdings, related costs and bullwhip effect occurring in supply chains. Conversely, many researchers (Lee and Whang, 2000; Mendelson, 2000; Fawcett et al., 2007; Forslund and Jonsson, 2007; Klein et al., 2007) also argued that information sharing has a number of practical limitations, such as confidential policies, data reliability and the lack of information systems' compatibility. Despite all the advantages and benefits of information sharing, the lack of availability of information systems is one of the first and most common barriers to information sharing (Ali et al., 2017). SCM World reports that many companies are hampered by the high investment costs and system implementation problems associated with formal information sharing (Courtin, 2013). As negotiation is the usual challenge to reduce costs for supply chain actors, monetary losses remain the main reason for investment blockages (Klein et al., 2007). Information system costs are composed of initial purchase costs and implementation costs (Fawcett et al., 2007). Although developers are constantly looking for compatibility solutions, companies tend to resist change because of intra-organizational problems. Even when companies succeed in implementing information systems, other problems such as lack of trust and lack of dialogue persist (Mendelson, 2000). In such cases, each partner is wary of the possibility that other partners may abuse information and reap the full benefits of information sharing (Lee and Whang, 2000). Therefore, an established trust is a necessary first pillar for any collaboration. In addition to these inhibitors, even when information technology and trust exist between partners, another type of inhibitor may persist. This is first of all the accuracy of information when decision-makers do not trust the quality of the information shared and believe that the error is relatively high (Forslund and Jonsson, 2007). The information leakage effect can also be a reason for limiting information sharing. Managers are always concerned that the information shared may be obtained or inferred by competitors who will react to the information sharing activity. For example, Ward (wardsauto.com) conducted a survey of 447 car manufacturers. Twenty-eight percent of the respondents reported that their intellectual property had been disclosed by at least one car producer in Detroit and 16% by their manufacturer (Anand and Goyal, 2009). As a result, the reaction of competitors may alter the allocation of benefits to the parties involved in information sharing (Li, 2002).

Vosooghidizaji et al. (2019) considers different scenarios wherein asymmetric information cannot be shared with supply chain partners because of many reasons that include "the fear of losing competitive advantage, getting extra benefits, getting a better price, maintaining one's bargaining power, not being controlled or dictated to by other parties, ensuring compatibility of information systems, and other strategic reasons". An actor not sharing information can affect the whole system of the supply chain. It was also argued that, by revealing sensitive demand information to the upstream manufacturer, a retailer may lose some advantage in future price negotiations (Ha et al., 2010). Wal-Mart announced that it would no longer share its information with other companies like Inc and AC Nielson as Wal-Mart considers data to be a top priority and fears information leakage (Hays, 2004). In fact, depending on the nature and size of supply chains, not sharing information can result to different levels of losses. William Wappler, President of Automotive Technology Leader SURGER, says, "The automotive industry is estimated to lose annually more than 2 billion dollars in the supply chain due to losses in inventory of containers, parts, finished vehicles and logistical inefficiencies, through a notorious lack of visibility and inherent control." He adds: "Most automotive companies struggle to reduce supply chain costs year over year." According to their internal forecasts, the use of the proposed digital platform can help participants achieve double-digit cost savings through highly accurate supply chain visibility and the collaborative power of shared information (Henderson, 2018). Indeed, industries where component suppliers need to build a high capacity in advance due to short lead times, face high inventory costs because of uncertain market demand. Generally, it has been accepted that the demand is a private information of the retailers, that leads to problems of management of the inventory at the upstream levels.

Recently, a new coordination supply chain approach, known as downstream demand inference (DDI), (Ali et al., 2017; Ali and Boylan, 2011; Ali and Boylan, 2012; Tliche et al., 2019) emerged in the supply chain field. The DDI strategy allows the enhancement of decentralized systems without having to go through explicit demand information sharing. Instead of demand information sharing, the upstream actor can infer the demand from the order history. The DDI strategy assumes that the demand process and its parameters are known throughout the two-level supply chain. The first part of the assumptions – that is the retailer facing the customer's demand is able to easily estimate the parameters of the process from his demand history – is evident. The second part of the assumptions – that is the ability of the manufacturer to infer the process of the demand occurring at the retailer – is subject of research and discussion in the literature. Ali and Boylan (2011) showed that DDI cannot be applied with the optimal minimum mean squared error (MMSE) forecast method because the propagation of the demand may not be unique. Ali and Boylan (2012) also showed that DDI is not possible with the single exponential smoothing (SES) method, but only when the downstream actor uses the simple moving average (SMA) method that attaches equal weights to past observations. Ali et al. (2017) showed that DDI generally outperforms the no information sharing strategy in terms of the forecast's mean squared error (MSE) and inventory costs under the assumption of an $AR(1)$ demand model. Under the DDI strategy, Tliche et al. (2019) considered the MSE^{DDI} and average inventory level $\left(\tilde{I}_t^{DDI}\right)$ as upstream supply chain performance metrics and generalized the above results for causal invertible[1] $ARMA(pq,)$ demand processes. In a context of DDI strategy, this chapter aims to further enhance the DDI's results by acquiring further optimized solutions in terms of MSE and average inventory levels.

A first possibility for improvement can be emphasized on the forecasting method adopted in the DDI approach. Since the SMA method is the only method of prediction up to now allowing the inference of the downstream demand, we have thought to introduce a variant of this method while keeping in mind the orientation of improvement of the average inventory levels. The SMA method is characterized by the equal weights associated to the N past observations, to predict the future demand. Every time period, the oldest demand observation is dropped out and exchanged by the last demand observation. A first intuition is to disrupt the weightings of the method in order to improve the performance. In this way, the Weighted Moving Average (WMA) method was selected in order to first investigate its feasibility in the DDI approach, and second to investigate whether any enhancement is achievable in a two-level supply chain. The WMA method is a simple forecasting method, as well as the SMA method. The WMA method attaches different weights/ponderations to the N past demand observations, and in the same way as SMA, the oldest demand observation is dropped out and exchanged by the last demand observation, every time period. The disruption's possibility of the weights in the method was an opening door for exploring potential improvements in different directions. One of these directions is the optimization according to the upstream actor's average inventory levels.

Consequently, acquiring further "optimized" solutions naturally opens the line of our research to other branches of scientific research. Indeed, optimization plays a very important role in several areas of application and especially in supply chain management. Omnipresent since the beginning of time, optimization is a mathematical discipline, that has grown in importance during the 20th century. This is due to the development of industrial sciences, operations planning (economics, management, logistics, scheduling), emerging technologies (automatic, electronic, electrotechnical, etc.) and computer science, which has made previously impassable numerical resolution methods efficient. Mathematically, it consists of minimizing, or maximizing, a function that represents an objective to be achieved on a set called a "domain" or "set of feasible solutions," which is defined as a set of constraints that are to be respected. The objective is to find the best solution belonging to the domain that acquires the optimal value of the objective function. The nature of the objective function and the constraints defining the domain determine the nature of the optimization problem and the difficulty of its resolution.

In this chapter, as discussed, we employ the weighted moving average (WMA) method, which attaches different weights to the N past observations, and then re-establish the manufacturer $MSSE^{DDI}$ and $\tilde{I}^{DDI}$ expressions according to a weighting vector x. Second, we propose two measures to quantify the gap separating the adoption of the NIS strategy with the MMSE method to the adoption of the DDI strategy with the WMA method on one hand, and on the second hand to quantify the gap separating the adoption of the DDI strategy with the SMA method to the adoption of the DDI strategy with the WMA method, in terms of bullwhip effect. Third, we mathematically formalize the manufacturer's forecast optimization problem (MFOP) and propose the application of the well-known Newton's method in order to obtain the optimal weighting vector x^*. To the best of our knowledge, this chapter presents the first attempt to introduce Newton's method into forecasts where the WMA method is adopted. The numerical results of the MSE and $\tilde{I}_t$ optimizations based on the simulated causal invertible $ARMA(p,q)$ demand processes confirm the effectiveness of this approach to produce further-optimized solutions compared to NIS strategy with MMSE method and DDI strategy with SMA method, and consequently to improve the competitiveness in the market. However, the WMA method affects the bullwhip effect since nonequal weights generate higher orders' variability. It is concluded that if the supply chain is initially adopting a NIS strategy where the MMSE method is used in the downstream forecasts, the downstream actor is emphasized to consider a high value of N (beyond a certain break-point) in order to reduce the bullwhip effect. Else, if the supply chain is initially adopting a DDI strategy where the SMA method is used in the downstream forecasts, the upstream actor needs to use a reserve inventory in order to cover the amplified orders variations. Hence, we provide a developed picture of the DDI strategy's adoption when the WMA is used for demand forecasts and where the Newton's method is employed to quantify the weighting vector of the WMA method, according to the minimization of the upstream average inventory levels.

The rest of the chapter is organized as follows. Section 2 is devoted to the literature review. In Section 3, we present the proposed modeling approach. Section 4 is devoted to the implementation, simulation and discussions. Finally, in Section 5, we summarize the contributions, the results, the limitations and perspectives.

2. LITERATURE REVIEW

Collaborative management in decentralized supply chains is therefore about coordinating and synchronizing several activities of different functions from the outset, for example the procurement of raw materials and the distribution of finished products, which may require different coordination mechanisms due to the decentralization of supply chain operations.

Despite a number of studies on coordination of operations, there is no single definition of supply chain coordination (Arshinder et al., 2011). Malone and Crowston (1990) provide an intuitive definition of coordination. According to this definition, when several actors pursue objectives together, they have to do things to organize themselves that an actor pursuing the same objectives could not have done. Coordination is then presented as the processing of additional information when several connected actors pursue objectives that a single actor pursuing the same goals could not have done. An example of this definition can be presented by a computer network with a set of objectives (calculations to be performed) and a set of computer processors of different types that perform the tasks to achieve these objectives. Again according to these authors, coordination can be interpreted as a kind of intelligent behavior, learning, planning and use of languages, which has as its objective organizational development and subsequently the achievement of objectives in common. A more meaningful definition is that given by Richardson et al. (2007) who consider coordination as a "conversation art". Such a definition was inspired by a social experiment analyzing the relationship linking the eye movements of two subjects engaged in a dialogue around a subject. The analysis of cross-recurrence revealed the existence of a coupling between the eye movements of the two subjects. Moreover, this coupling is all the more important if the individuals had previously received common information about the subject. Therefore, by projecting this example to the SCM field, it seems clear that the exchange of information between economic actors in the same supply chain is a key factor that increases the "degree" of coordination of the partners' operations.

The literature is abundant of coordination mechanisms. First of all, we find the coordination contracts: these are mainly wholesale price contracts, volume discount contracts and revenue sharing contracts. Partners coordinate using contracts for better management of the supplier-buyer relationship and mutual risk (Cholez et al., 2017). Contracts specify the parameters (quantity, price, lead time and quality) within which a buyer places orders and a supplier fulfils them. The objectives of contracts can be summarized as increasing the total profit of the supply chain, reducing overstocking and understocking costs, and sharing risk among supply chain partners. Cachon (2003) studied the coordination of supply chains by proposing different models presented according to their complexity. Firms are encouraged to coordinate by adjusting their commercial terms through contracts that establish payment transfer systems. The author defines a number of types of contracts while illustrating their advantages and disadvantages. Giannoccaro and Pontrandolfo (2004) proposed a contract model based on the revenue-sharing mechanism to coordinate a three-stage supply chain. This model makes it possible to achieve the efficiency of the decentralized system while improving the benefits for all actors in the chain by adjusting the parameters of the contract. Cachon and Larivière (2005) studied revenue-sharing contracts in a general supply chain model, with revenues determined by the quantity and purchase price of each retailer. The authors considered demand that can be deterministic or stochastic and revenues that are generated by renting or selling. The authors showed that revenue sharing coordinates a supply chain with a single retailer and arbitrarily distributes the benefits of the supply chain. Second, the authors showed that revenue sharing also coordinates a supply chain with several competing retailers. Sinha and Sarmah (2008) proposed a coordination mechanism for a two-tier supply chain, applying Fuzzy Set Theory (FST) to find the optimal quantity, price and profit for the actors in the chain. The unknown demand and cost are estimated on the basis of subjective judgement using triangular fuzzy numbers. The authors relied on a simulation with 2500 random cases to test the proposed method. The resulting solution is described as "quasi-optimal" which is close to that of a system with complete information. Xu et al. (2013) analyzed the procurement strategy in a system with one manufacturer and two suppliers, one primary supplier and one emergency supplier. The authors proposed a model for formulating the problem and characterizing the contract that allows for careful design of the procurement strategy. To validate the proposed coordination method and optimal values, they perform a sensitivity analysis and provide numerical examples. Lv et al. (2015) proposed capacity reservation contracts in an assembly system with an assembler, who has private market information, and purchases components from two independent suppliers. Zhao and Zhu (2017) proposed a cost-of-service information sharing contract in a two-tier chain. The authors concluded that the performance of the decentralized and coordinated system approaches that of the centralized system. Xie et al. (2017) studied the performance of contract coordination of decentralized dual-channel closed-loop supply chains. The authors compared the centralized decision and the decentralized decision driven by manufacturing by examining the influence of the revenue sharing ratio in the outbound and inbound channels on online/offline prices and on wholesale prices. Ye and Yang (2018) studied three types of coordination contracts, an overproduction risk-sharing contract, an underproduction risk-sharing contract, and a mixed contract with an asymmetric Nash trading model. The authors tested the three contracts with data from the cassava-based biofuel industry in China. The results help practitioners and policy makers understand when and how to implement coordination contracts to achieve sustainable supply of agricultural feedstocks for biofuel production.

Second, information technology is also being used to improve coordination between organizations (Sanders, 2008). The development of new information and communication technologies has shaped by far the new face of working methods in virtually all functions of organizations (Liouville, 2011). Information technology serves as an infrastructural support both within the organization itself and in the upstream and downstream connections of the entire supply chain. Inter-organizational coordination has been shown to have a positive impact on some business performance measures, such as service quality, lead times and production costs (Vickery et al., 2003). Information technology makes it possible to link the point of production with the point of delivery or purchase in a transparent manner. It allows planning, monitoring and estimating lead times based on real-time data. Advances in information technology (Internet, Electronic Data Interchange, ERP, e-business) allow companies to quickly exchange products, information, funds and use collaborative methods to optimize operations throughout the supply chain. Liu et al. (2005) have indicated that the Internet can improve the efficiency of communication, helping stakeholders to review past performance, monitor current performance and forecast the quantity of certain products to be produced in order to manage the workflow system. Jin (2006) studied the relationship between the use of information technology in the US apparel industry and three levels of performance: operational, financial and strategic. The author concluded that only companies with large sales volumes benefit from the use of information technology to increase their performance as measured by turnaround time. Benavent (2016) studied the six mechanisms of the platform economy, such as crowdsourcing, a radical innovation among collaborative approaches that mainly allows the minimization of the operator's inventory costs through outsourcing and decentralization. A well-known example adopting this approach is the American e-commerce giant Amazon.

Another means of coordination is joint decision-making. A joint decision helps to resolve conflicts between partners and to deal with exceptions in case of future uncertainty. Many factors are involved in achieving coordination, such as human relations, technology, strategies, rewards, knowledge sharing, benefit sharing, alignment of objectives, scheduling regular stakeholder meetings for conflict resolution, understanding the nature of intermediaries and knowledge of the concepts, status or power of different actors, and resistance to following instructions from other organizations (Gittell and Weiss, 2004). Vendor-Managed Inventory (VMI) is a coordination initiative through joint decision making, whereby a supplier assumes responsibility for maintaining inventory levels and determining order quantities for its customers. The adoption of VMI has a number of benefits that have been reported in the literature: reduced inventory, shorter order intervals, and more frequent deliveries. VMI typically involves sharing demand forecasts, cost information and timely communications, setting liability levels, risk-sharing parameters, and sharing common objectives between buyer and supplier. VMI can be particularly advantageous for products with high variations in demand and high outsourcing costs (Cheung and Lee, 2002). A second form of coordination by joint decision is the Collaborative Planning, Forecasting, and Replenishment (CPFR), which is a collaborative initiative in which two or more parties in an oversight committee jointly plan a number of decisions and develop synchronized forecasts to determine production and replenishment processes (Larsen et al., 2003). The benefits of the CPFR are summarized as increased sales and service levels, faster response time to orders, lower product inventories, shorter cycle times, reductions in capacity requirements, reductions in the number of stocking centers, improvements in forecast accuracy, and reductions in system-wide expenditures.

Other coordination approaches, based on proposals, negotiations or auctions, have also demonstrated their ability to establish and manage operations between partners in the best possible way. Dudek and Stadtler (2007) propose a negotiation-based process to synchronize plans between a supplier and several buyers with a minimum of information exchange through proposals and counter-proposals. Chu and Leon (2008) propose a heuristic for finding a single supplier's production schedule and replenishment policies in a multi-buyer inventory system that minimizes the cost of ordering and inventorying the system in a restricted information environment. The proposed heuristic presents the process of negotiations between the actors, including some iterations before obtaining the best policy. Li et al (2012) study a supply chain inventory problem for a planning period to find optimal quantities and solve the problem through optimization techniques that minimize costs for the buyer, the supplier and the system as a whole. Mason and Villalobos (2015) propose an auction-based mechanism to coordinate the production of perishable products through a linear scheduling problem in order to estimate the maximum profit of the system. The authors used a set of data collected through a case study, and the results showed that the proposed mechanism coordinates the supply chain by optimizing profit.

The coordination mechanisms mentioned above are all based on information sharing principle. While information sharing can be implicit, supply chain partners coordinate their operations by sharing explicit information about demand, orders, inventory, or store data. In a timely manner, requesting advance information or commitments from downstream customers helps reduce inventory by offering price reductions, and this information can be used as a substitute for delivery time and inventory. The value of sharing information increases as the supplier's service level, supplier inventory costs, demand variability, and clearing time increase, and order cycle time decreases. Qian et al (2012) proposed strategies to encourage multiple retailers to share demand information with a manufacturer with limited production capacity. Zhao and Zhao (2015) conducted an experimental study to analyze the performance of a multi-tiered supply chain over several periods and under different information-sharing scenarios. System performance is examined for two measures: operating cost and the whiplash effect.

One of the most important information as a tool of competition is the demand information or the market information. Sharing customers' demand information requires that upstream actors have access to the demand data of their respective downstream actors. The need for information sharing mechanisms, in order to extract demand information has been an open topic of discussion in the literature. On one hand, some researchers (Chen et al., 2000b; Lee et al., 2000; Yu et al., 2002; Raghunathan, 2003) argued that downstream actors need to share their demand information with upstream actors in order to reduce the bullwhip effect. On the other hand, other researchers (Raghunathan, 2001; Zhang, 2004; Gaur et al., 2005; Gilbert, 2005) relied on some strong arguments to show that the received orders already contain information about the customers' demand process. In a context where actors cannot or don't want to share their demand information (no information sharing policy), DDI appears to be a novel collaboration management approach that allows the upstream actor to infer the demand of his formal downstream actors without the need for information sharing mechanisms. According to the DDI approach, the MSE and the inventory level/cost savings from coordination and negotiation are possible if trust is established between parties (Ali et al., 2017; Tliche et al., 2019). Figure 1 illustrates the principle of demand inference in a two-level supply chain.

The works of Ali and Boylan (2011) and Ali and Boylan (2012) have already shown that "DDI is not possible through SES or optimal MMSE methods, but only

Figure 1. Principle of demand inference in a two-level supply chain

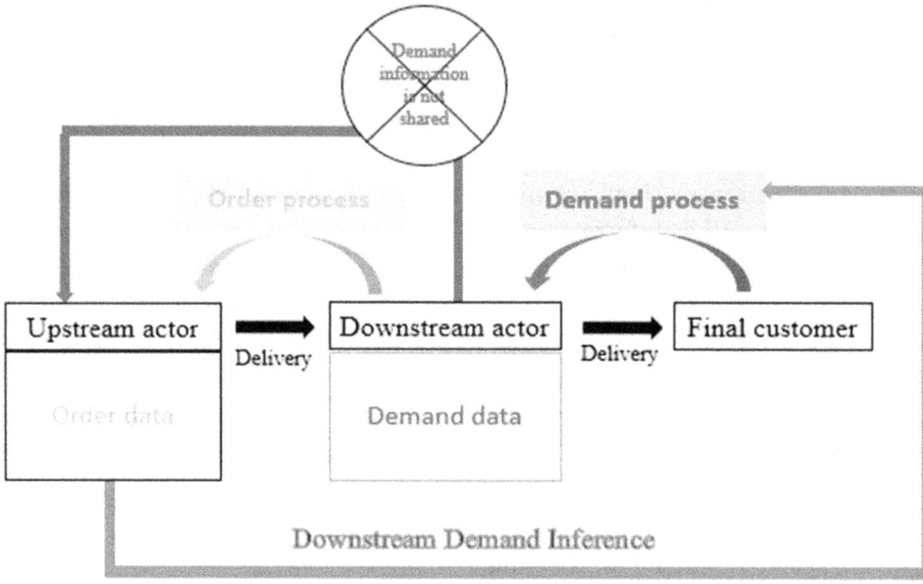

with nonoptimal SMA method". This is due to the nonfeasibility of DDI when the propagation of the demand throughout the supply chain is not unique. Ali et al. (2017) investigated DDI using the SMA method for an $AR(1)$ demand model and conducted numerical analysis based on real data. Ali et al. (2017) were the first to characterize the performance of the DDI approach through an empirical study. The authors studied three different approaches to examine the value of information sharing in a two-tier supply chain, under the assumption of a typical $AR(1)$ application process. The first approach, called No Information Sharing (NIS), is a management strategy that corresponds to a decentralized system, where information on customer demand is not shared between the two actors in the chain, and the upstream actor simply bases its forecasts on the history of orders received from the downstream actor. The second approach, called "Forecast Information Sharing" (FIS), corresponds to the centralized system where the upstream actor has a perfect knowledge of the customer's demand arriving at the level of the downstream actor and thus bases its forecasts on both the history of orders and that of shared demand. The optimal MMSE method was used as a forecasting method both in the decentralized system with "sub-optimal" solutions and in the centralized system with "optimal" solutions. By adopting the DDI approach as a third approach, the authors showed that this coordination approach outperforms the decentralized NIS approach in terms of MSE and in terms of average inventory costs for fairly high values of the autoregressive coefficient of the demand process. It thus makes it possible to raise the performance of the decentralized system of the chain, without going through an explicit exchange of information. The authors also investigated the sensitivity of the DDI approach to the SMA method's N horizon and L delivery time, and found that the DDI approach is especially effective for high values of N and relatively low values of L. In practice, the performance of the DDI approach increases the more the delivery time decreases, and the more decision-makers consider larger historical intervals in the SMA method. The authors found that the improvements (reductions) in the IEM performance indicators and average inventory costs were not proportional. Among other things, the same findings were reported when the application followed a 1st-order Moving Average *MA(1)* or a 1st-order AutoRegressive 1st-order Moving Average *ARMA(1,1)* process. The first reports on the performance results of the DDI approach were therefore promising. Ali et al. (2017) conducted an empirical analysis based on data from a large European market. Out of 557 time series out of 1802, only 30.9% were identified as *AR(1)* type processes, and were selected for analysis. The other data series (69.9%) were therefore not included in their work because they could not be modelled by *AR(1)* processes. Based on simulations, Tliche et al. (2019) generalized DDI's results for causal invertible *ARMA(p,q)* demand models and showed that this strategy reduces also the bullwhip effect, in addition of MSE and average inventory levels. Consequently, it is still natural to explore the feasibility of DDI and the improvement of the results by using other forecasting methods. It's first about the margin of enhancement still existing between the DDI strategy's results and the forecast information sharing FIS strategy's results which corresponds to the centralized system where the demand information is explicitly shared between actors. Therefore, exploring the DDI strategy by adopting simple forecasting methods is still an interesting management research area for both researchers and practitioners.

Thus, in this chapter, we investigate the DDI's performance in a context of an *ARMA(p,q)* demand model. One of the most widespread models in contemporary literature is the *ARMA(p,q)* type process. It is a mathematical model that allows the interdependencies of several observations of a variable to be modelled as a function of time. Many researchers have investigated the dependence of the value of information sharing on the temporal structure of the demand process using an ARMA methodology. Several researchers have argued that demands over consecutive periods of time are rarely statistically independent (Graves, 1999; Lee et al., 2000). Therefore, the demand process (tourism, fuel, food, machinery, etc.) should be modeled as a self-correlated time series, as these are long life cycle goods. This type of process not only allows significant modeling of variations over time, but it also makes it possible to take into account the different peaks (strong variations) that may occur, while keeping a stationary average. Such a model can be useful for large variations in demand over short time intervals, such as an increase in demand for natural gas during the winter seasons (Ervural et al, 2016) or the increase in demand for hotel services during holiday seasons (Chu, 2009; Gustavsson & Nordström, 2001). The ARMA model can also be used to handle demand in several sectors such as the transport sector (Gong, 2010, August), the electricity sector (Pappas et al., 2010), or the automotive sector (Chen et al., 2010, August).

Forecasting in supply chains is an increasingly critical organizational tool (Sanders and Manrodt, 2003) for improving business competitiveness. Ali and Boylan (2012) provided a summary of the highly ranked forecasting methods according to their usage, familiarity and satisfaction among practitioners. Generally, supply chain decision-makers choose a forecasting method based on its simplicity. Especially, the SES, regression analysis (RA) and SMA methods are popular among forecasting managers for familiarity and satisfaction reasons. As reported in the works of Sanders and Manrodt (1994) and Boylan and Johnston (2003), because of their high difficulty and sophistication, optimal forecasting methods are most often considered to be undeserving of extra effort. On the other hand, nonoptimal forecasting methods are more intuitive, especially for those with limited mathematical backgrounds. In addition, Johnston et al. (1999) showed that "the variance of the forecast error for the nonoptimal method SMA was typically 3% higher than the SES method for an $ARIMA(0,1,1)$ ".

In this chapter, we examine the effects of employing a simple nonoptimal forecasting method, namely, the WMA, in the downstream actor's forecasts, where demand follows a causal invertible $ARMA(p,q)$. The WMA is a method that is widely used in the industry literature (Wang and Cheng, 2007; Eckhaus, 2010; Alsultanny, 2012; Kapgate, 2014; Kalaoglu et al., 2015; Wenxia et al., 2015). We selected the WMA method as a method of interest because it belongs to the moving average methods, and more specifically because it is a variant of the SMA method. The narrow difference in weights between the SMA and the WMA methods suggested a potential feasibility (uniqueness of demand process propagation) of the DDI approach in a decentralized supply chain. Such as SMA method, the WMA method is based on the shifting forward of the last N observations in order to predict the future demand. Every time-period, the oldest observation is excluded and the most recent observation is included.

Table. 1 summarizes the experimented forecasting methods in the context a DDI strategy as well as our contribution.

Thus, in this chapter, we first show that demand inference is feasible when the retailer uses the WMA method in his forecasts. The upstream actor is then able to infer the demand arriving at his formal downstream actor as the demand propagation is unique. Next, the consideration of nonequal weights for the N past observations in the WMA method, is achieved through the use of the Newton optimization

Table 1. Forecasting when DDI strategy is adopted

Forecasting method	Mathematical expression	DDI feasibility	Reference
MMSE	$f_{t+1} = E\left(D_{t+1} / \left\{D_t, D_{t-1}, \ldots, D_{t-T}\right\}\right)$ · $\left\{D_t, D_{t-1}, \ldots, D_{t-T}\right\}$ is the available set of demand history	Not feasible	Ali and Boylan (2011) Alwan et al. (2003)
SES	$f_{t+1} = \pm\sum_{j=0}^{T}(1-\pm)^j D_{t-j}$ · $\left\{D_t, D_{t-1}, \ldots, D_{t-T}\right\}$ is the available set of demand history · α is the smoothing constant	Not feasible	Ali and Boylan (2012) Alwan et al. (2003)
SMA	$f_{t+1} = \frac{1}{N}\sum_{j=0}^{N-1} D_{t-j}$ · N is the moving average horizon	Feasible	Ali and Boylan (2012) Ali et al. (2017) Tliche et al. (2019)
WMA	$f_{t+1} = \sum_{i=1}^{N} x_i D_{t+1-i}$ · N is the moving average horizon · $x = \left(x_1, \ldots, x_N\right)$ is the weighted vector which is obtained using Newton's method · $\begin{cases} \sum_{i=1}^{N} x_i = 1 \\ x_i \geq 0 \forall i = 1, \ldots, N \end{cases}$	Feasible	This work

method aligned according to the minimization of the MSE and thus according to the minimization of the upstream actor's average inventory levels.

In this way, this chapter provides a methodology that allows the reduction of the average inventory level at the upstream actor. Since there are no specific "standard approaches" for determining the optimal setting in terms of parameter N and lead-time L, we study the sensitivity of our approach's results in comparison with the NIS strategy through the MMSE method, and in comparison with the DDI strategy through the SMA method. In addition, we present findings on the bullwhip effect in order to obtain a clearer picture of this approach.

3. MODELING APPROACH

We consider a simple two-level supply chain that is formed by a manufacturer (upstream actor) and a retailer (downstream actor) who receives the demand of a final customer. We suppose that a periodic review system is adopted for replenishment in which downstream actors place their orders with upstream actors after examining their respective inventory levels. Indeed, after the realization of demand D_t by the retailer at the beginning of time period$t$ and after checking his own inventory level, the retailer places an order Y_t before the end of the period. Then, the manufacturer prepares the required order Y_t and ships it to the retailer who will receive it at period $t+L+1$. Here, L presents the replenishment time of both production and shipment. Second, it is assumed that there are no order costs. Second, the unit inventory holding costs and shortage costs are constant and respectively denoted by h and s. It is also assumed that both the manufacturer and retailer adopt an order-up-to (OUT) policy, which minimizes the total costs over an infinite time horizon (Lee et al., 2000).

These assumptions were adopted in many papers of this stream of research (Ali et al., 2017; Ali et al., 2012; Hosoda et al., 2008; Hosoda and Disney, 2006; Cheng and Wu., 2005; Alwan et al., 2003; Raghunathan, 2001; Chen et al., 2000b; Lee et al., 2000; Tliche et al., 2019) and we consider our chapter is part of the continuity of this stream of works.

3.1. Customer's Demand Model and Forecast Method

Time-series processes have widely been adopted to model the demand of many products in different fields. Let us assume that the demand at the retailer is a causal invertible *ARMA(p,q)* process. Let D_t be this demand process at period t, which is expressed by Equation (1) as follows:

$$\boldsymbol{D}_t = \boldsymbol{c} + \sum_{j=1}^{p} \phi_j \boldsymbol{D}_{t-j} + ¾ + \sum_{j=1}^{q} ,_j ¾_{-j} \tag{1}$$

where

- $c \geq 0$ is the unconditional mean of the demand process,
- $\phi_j$where $j \in \{1,..,p\}$ is the autoregressive coefficient of the demand process,
- $\theta_j$where $j \in \{1,..,q\}$ is the moving average coefficient of the demand process, and

- $\xi_t \to N\left(0,\sigma_\xi^2\right)$ where $t \in [0,+\infty[$ is the independent and identically distributed error term that follows a normal distribution.

Furthermore, let d_t be the mean-centered demand process, μ_d be the unconditional mean of the demand process D_t and $\gamma_k = Cov\left(D_{t+k}, D_t\right)$ be the covariance between demands at periods t and $t+k$. These definitions are required for the formulas' derivations in this work.

In addition, as mentioned above, we will consider that the retailer adopts the WMA method in the demand forecasts, which, at period $t+1$, is mathematically written as Equation (2):

$$\boldsymbol{f}_{t+1} = \sum_{i=1}^{N} \boldsymbol{x}_i \boldsymbol{D}_{t+1-i} \tag{2}$$

where x_i is the weight that is associated with the customer's demand occurring at time period $t+1-i$, which verifies the set of constraints

$$(C): \begin{cases} \sum_{i=1}^{N} x_i = 1 \\ x_i \geq 0 \forall i \in \{1,\ldots,N\} \end{cases}, \text{ and let } x = \begin{pmatrix} x_1 \\ \vdots \\ x_N \end{pmatrix}$$

be the weighting vector.

To apply DDI strategy, it is first important to check whether the propagation of the demand across the supply chain is unique.

3.2. Downstream Actor's Orders Time-Series Structure

Let Y_t be the order process arriving at the manufacturer at period t, which is expressed by Equation (3) as follows:

$$\boldsymbol{Y}_t = \boldsymbol{c} + \sum_{j=1}^{p} \phi_j \boldsymbol{Y}_{t-j} + \tilde{\tfrac{3}{4}} + \sum_{j=1}^{q} {}_{j}\tilde{\tfrac{3}{4}}_{-j} \tag{3}$$

where

- $c \geq 0$ is the unconditional mean of the order process,

- ϕ_j where $j \in \{1,..,p\}$ is the autoregressive coefficient of the order process,
- θ_j where $j \in \{1,..,q\}$ is the moving average coefficient of the order process, and
- $\tilde{\xi}_t \to N\left(0, \left[L^2\left(x_1^2 + x_N^2 + \sum_{i=1}^{N-1}(x_{i+1} - x_i)^2\right) + 2Lx_1 + 1\right]\sigma_\xi^2\right)$ where $t \in [0, +\infty[$ is the independently and identically distributed error term that follows a normal distribution.

The demand and order processes have the same autoregressive and moving average coefficients, and they differ only by their respective error terms (see Appendix A). Indeed, the order's error terms are amplified by a coefficient

$$\beta = L^2\left(x_1^2 + x_N^2 + \sum_{i=1}^{N-1}(x_{i+1} - x_i)^2\right) + 2Lx_1 + 1$$

such as $\sigma_{\tilde{\xi}}^2 = \beta\sigma_\xi^2$. Consequently, the order process is unique and the upstream actor is able to infer the demand process without the need for demand information sharing. Next, we derive the manufacturer's forecast MSE^{DDI} and $\tilde{I}^{DDI}$ when the WMA method is used in a context of a DDI strategy. The performance metrics MSE^{DDI} and $\tilde{I}^{DDI}$ are considered since they are the first direct measures impacted by demand inference. Indeed, the upstream actor benefits from the DDI strategy that enables the reduction of the MSE and the average inventory level. The next consequence is then the reduction of the inventory costs related to these metrics' enhancements.

3.3. Derivation of the Manufacturer's Mean Squared Error and Average Inventory Level Expressions

Since the forecast expression in Equation (2) is a function of the weights, the MSE^{DDI} and $\tilde{I}_t^{DDI}$ expressions are also functions of these weights. We derive the $MSE^{DDI}(x)$ and $\tilde{I}_t^{DDI}(x)$ expressions as follows:

$$MSE^{DDI} = Var\left[\sum_{i=1}^{L+1}(D_{t+i} - f_{t+i})\right] = Var\left[\sum_{i=1}^{L+1}D_{t+i} - (L+1)f_{t+1}\right]$$

$$\Leftrightarrow MSE^{DDI} = Var\left(\sum_{i=1}^{L+1}D_{t+i}\right) + (L+1)^2 Var(f_{t+1}) - 2(L+1)Cov\left(\sum_{i=1}^{L+1}D_{t+i}, f_{t+1}\right) \tag{4a}$$

We then derive the three components of Equation (4a) (see Appendix B) and obtain the final expression of Equation (4) as follows:

$$MSE^{DDI}\left(x\right)=\left(L+1\right)\gamma_0+2\sum_{i=1}^{L}i\gamma_{L+1-i}$$
$$+\left(L+1\right)^2\left[\gamma_0\sum_{i=1}^{N}x_i^2+2\sum_{j=1}^{N-1}\left(x_j\sum_{i=j+1}^{N}x_i\gamma_{i-j}\right)\right]-2\left(L+1\right)\sum_{i=1}^{L+1}\sum_{j=1}^{N}x_j\gamma_{i+j-1} \quad (4)$$

Next, the general expression of the average inventory level under an OUT policy is given by Ali et al. (2012) and mathematically written as Equation (5a) as follows:

$$\tilde{I}_t=T_t-E\left(\sum_{i=1}^{L+1}Y_{t+i}\right)+\frac{E\left(Y_t\right)}{2} \quad (5a)$$

where Y_t is the order process of the retailer arriving at the manufacturer at time period t; the manufacturer's optimal OUT inventory level T_t is expressed by $T_t=M_t+K\sigma_{\xi}\sqrt{V}$, where M_t and V are respectively the conditional expectation and the conditional variance of the total demand over the lead-time plus one review time unit; and $K=F_{N(0,1)}^{-1}\left(\frac{s}{s+h}\right)$ is the inverse distribution function for the standard normal distribution that is calculated at the ratio point $\frac{s}{s+h}$.

Consequently, under the DDI strategy and using the WMA method for the demand forecasts, we obtain Equation (5b) as follows:

$$\tilde{I}_t^{DDI}\left(x\right)=T_t^{DDI}\left(x\right)-E\left(\sum_{i=1}^{L+1}Y_{t+i}\right)+\frac{E\left(Y_t\right)}{2} \quad (5a)$$

where

$$\tilde{I}_t^{DDI}\left(x\right)=T_t^{DDI}\left(x\right)-E\left(\sum_{i=1}^{L+1}Y_{t+i}\right)+\frac{E\left(Y_t\right)}{2} \quad (5b)$$

Then, the Equation (5b) is equivalent to the following Equation (5c):

$$\tilde{I}_t^{DDI}(x) = M_t^{DDI}(x) + K\sigma_{\xi}\sqrt{V^{DDI}(x)} - E\left(\sum_{i=1}^{L+1} Y_{t+i}\right) + \frac{E(Y_t)}{2} \quad (5c)$$

We then derive the four components of Equation (5c) (see Appendix C), and thus, we obtain the final expression of Equation (5) as follows:

$$\tilde{I}_t^{DDI}(x) = \frac{c}{2\left(1-\sum_{j=1}^{p}\phi_j\right)} + K\tilde{A}_{\xi_4}\sqrt{MSE^{DDI}(x)} \quad (5)$$

We note that $\tilde{I}_t^{DDI}(x)$ in Equation (5) is a nonlinear function of $MSE^{DDI}(x)$, which can explain the nonproportional evolution linking these two performance metrics. Next, we proceed to deriving the resulting bullwhip effect in order to compare the processes variations' evolution with the cases where the NIS strategy with the MMSE is adopted, and then to compare it with the case where the DDI strategy with the SMA method is adopted.

3.4. Bullwhip Effect

In this subsection, we are interested in studying the bullwhip effect occurring in the considered supply chain. Let $\tilde{\psi}_j$, $\tilde{\tilde{\psi}}_j$ and $\tilde{\tilde{\tilde{\psi}}}_j$ be the infinite moving average representation (IMAR) coefficients of the orders processes in the cases where the WMA, SMA and MMSE methods are adopted for the demand forecasts, respectively.

First, when the WMA method is used in order to forecast the customer's demand, the $ARMA(p,q)$ demand process at the retailer where ξ_t is the error term that transforms into an $ARMA(p,q)$ order process at the manufacturer, where $\c{\xi}_t = L\left[\sum_{i=1}^{N} x_i\left(\xi_{t-i-1} - \xi_{t-i}\right) + \xi_t\right]$ is the error term. Considering the lead-time L, the parameter N and the IMAR coefficients ψ_j and $\tilde{\psi}_j$ of the demand and order processes, respectively, the bullwhip effect is measured by Equation (6) as follows:

$$BWeffect^{WMA}(x) = \frac{Var(Y_t)}{Var(D_t)}$$

$$= \left[L^2\left(x_1^2 + x_N^2 + \sum_{i=1}^{N-1}\left(x_{i+1} - x_i\right)^2\right) + 2Lx_1 + 1\right]\left(\frac{\sum_{j=0}^{+\infty}\tilde{\psi}_j^2}{\sum_{j=0}^{+\infty}\psi_j^2}\right) \quad (6)$$

Second, when the SMA forecasting method is adopted, the $ARMA(p,q)$ demand process for the retailer where ξ_t is the error term transforms into an $ARMA(p,q)$ order process at the manufacturer, where $\tilde{\tilde{\xi}}_t = \left(\frac{L}{N}+1\right)\xi_t - \frac{L}{N}\xi_{t-N}$ is the error term (Tliche et al., 2019). Considering the lead-time L the IMAR coefficients ψ_j and $\tilde{\psi}_j$ of the demand and order processes, respectively, the bullwhip effect is measured by Equation (7) as follows:

$$BWeffect^{SMA} = \frac{Var\left(Y_t\right)}{Var\left(D_t\right)} = \frac{2L^2 + N^2 + 2NL}{N^2}\left(\frac{\sum_{j=0}^{+\infty}\tilde{\tilde{\psi}}_j^{\,2}}{\sum_{j=0}^{+\infty}\psi_j^{\,2}}\right) \tag{7}$$

Third, when the MMSE forecasting method is adopted by the retailer, the $ARMA(p,q)$ process at the retailer transforms into an $ARMA(p,\mathrm{Max}(p,q-L))$ process at the producer (Zhang, 2004). Considering the IMAR coefficients of demand and orders processes, respectively, ψ_j and $\tilde{\tilde{\tilde{\psi}}}_j$, the ratio of the unconditional variance of the orders process to that of demand process, namely the Bullwhip effect is measured by Equation (8) as follows:

$$BWeffect^{MMSE} = \frac{Var\left(Y_t\right)}{Var\left(D_t\right)} = \left(\sum_{j=0}^{L}\psi_j\right)^2\left(\frac{\sum_{j=0}^{+\infty}\tilde{\tilde{\psi}}_j^{\,2}}{\sum_{j=0}^{+\infty}\psi_j^{\,2}}\right) \tag{8}$$

Furthermore, considering the obtained expressions of Equations (6), (7) and (8), we simply consider the ratio of $BWeffect^{WMA}$ to $BWeffect^{MMSE}$ and the ratio $BWeffect^{WMA}$ to $BWeffect^{SMA}$. In this manner, we obtain ideas about how the bullwhip effect behaves when switching from a NIS strategy with the MMSE method to a DDI strategy with the WMA method (*case 1*), and when switching from a DDI strategy with the SMA method to a DDI strategy with the WMA method (*case 2*). Let denote the bullwhip effect evolution of the *case 1* by BEE_{MMSE}^{WMA}, which is expressed by Equation (9) as follows:

$$BEE_{MMSE}^{WMA} = \frac{BWeffect^{WMA}\left(x\right)}{BWeffect^{MMSE}} = \frac{\left[L^2\left(x_1^2 + x_N^2 + \sum_{i=1}^{N-1}\left(x_{i+1} - x_i\right)^2\right) + 2Lx_1 + 1\right]}{\left(\sum_{j=0}^{L}\psi_j\right)^2}\left(\frac{\sum_{j=0}^{+\infty}\tilde{\psi}_j^{\,2}}{\sum_{j=0}^{+\infty}\tilde{\tilde{\psi}}_j^{\,2}}\right) \tag{9}$$

Let denote the bullwhip effect evolution of the *case 2* by BEE_{SMA}^{WMA}, which is expressed by Equation (10a) as follows:

$$BEE_{SMA}^{WMA} = \frac{BWeffect^{WMA}}{BWeffect^{SMA}} = \frac{N^2\left[L^2\left(x_1^2 + x_N^2 + \sum_{i=1}^{N-1}(x_{i+1} - x_i)^2\right) + 2Lx_1 + 1\right]}{2L^2 + N^2 + 2NL}\left(\frac{\sum_{j=0}^{+\infty}\tilde{\psi}_j^2}{\sum_{j=0}^{+\infty}\tilde{\tilde{\psi}}_j^2}\right) \tag{10a}$$

We note here that $\tilde{\psi}_j$ are equal to $\tilde{\tilde{\psi}}_j$ since the order processes Y_t keep the same coefficients ϕ_j and θ_j of the demand processes in the cases where WMA and SMA methods are adopted, respectively. Indeed, the only difference between the two structures of Y_t is in the error terms. Hence, Equation (10a) is equivalent to Equation (10):

$$\boldsymbol{BEE_{SMA}^{WMA} = \frac{BWeffect^{WMA}}{BWeffect^{SMA}} = \frac{N^2\left[L^2\left(x_1^2 + x_N^2 + \sum_{i=1}^{N-1}(x_{i+1} - x_i)^2\right) + 2Lx_1 + 1\right]}{2L^2 + N^2 + 2NL}} \tag{10}$$

The mathematical expression of Equation (10) is not a linear function. Studying this equation is not a straightforward task since it does not allow one to understand the domains in which BEE_{SMA}^{WMA} is inferior or superior to 1. Therefore, we suggest some simulations for this metric in Section 4 to have an approximate idea of the gap of the bullwhip effect, such as separating the situations in which WMA and SMA are adopted. Note that BEE_{SMA}^{WMA} will be noted by $BEE_{SMA}^{WMA/Newton}$ since the vector x in the simulation section is the Newton's optimal weighting.

Once the analytical expressions for the different supply chain performance metrics are derived, we proceed to detail the problem model and the resolution method.

3.5. Newton Method for Optimal Weighting

We assume that the manufacturer aims to minimize his average inventory level when forecasting over the time period $L+1$. In this work, this inventory-oriented enhancement is the main engine of the supply chain surplus. Indeed, if the possibility of inventory level minimization still exists, then the value of this gap is convertible to a monetary value that can be shared across the supply chain. To do this, since the inventory expression in Equation (5) is a function of the *MSE*, the manufacturer is recommended to simply determine the weighting vector x^* that minimizes this *MSE*. Then, the expression of the $MSE^{DDI}(x)$ in Equation (4) is replaced by the obtained value $MSe^{DDI}(x^*)$, and the optimal average inventory level $\tilde{I}_t^{DDI}\left(x^*\right)$ is then determined. Let us first define the MFOP, which can be expressed as follows:

$$(MFOP):\begin{cases} \textbf{minimize} MSE^{DDI}(x) \\ subject\ to \begin{cases} \sum_{i=1}^{N} x_i = 1 \\ x_i \geq 0\ \forall i \in \{1,\ldots,N\} \\ x = \begin{pmatrix} x_1 \\ \vdots \\ x_N \end{pmatrix} \end{cases} \end{cases}$$

There are several methods that can be applied to solve such problems. In this chapter, we select the Newton's method, a gradient-based iterative optimization algorithm that is widely used in the literature because of its ease of implementation and quickness of resolution since the convergence is quadratic (Qi and Sun, 1999). For a positive quadratic convex function defined on, the minimum is reached if the derivative function is equal to 0 and the second derivative function is positive on .

We then talk about the 1st order and 2nd order optimality conditions. The Newton's method is suitable for the optimization in this setting because of the mathematical nature of the . Indeed, the is positive and of quadratic convex nature defined on . The 1st optimality conditions (considering the constraints of the weights) are presented by the KKT formulation shown next. The 2nd optimality conditions (always considering the constraints of the weights) are presented by the Hessian matrix also shown next, which must be a semi-definite positive matrix. This statement is not evident because of the complexity of the matrix components. However, a matrix is semi-definite positive if and only if all of its eigenvalues are non-negative (Vandenberghe and Boyd, 1996). In practice, we verified this condition in our simulations.

For the purpose, we go on to state our resolution methodology. We first modify the constraints' form of the MFOP into a matrix form and then the problem is rewritten as follows:

$$(MFOP):\begin{cases} \textbf{minimize} MSE^{DDI}(x) \\ s.t.\begin{cases} x\,e^t \leq 1 \\ -x\,e^t \leq -1 \\ -x_i \leq 0\ \forall i \in \{1,\ldots,N\} \\ e = \begin{pmatrix} 1 \\ \vdots \\ 1 \end{pmatrix}_{[N,1]} \\ x = \begin{pmatrix} x_1 \\ \vdots \\ x_N \end{pmatrix} \end{cases} \end{cases}$$

$$\Leftrightarrow (MFOP):\begin{cases} \textbf{minimize} MSE^{DDI}(x) \\ s.t.\begin{cases} Ax \leq b, A = \begin{pmatrix} \mathrm{e}^t \\ -\mathrm{e}^t \\ -I_N \end{pmatrix}_{[N+2,N]} \quad and\ b = \begin{pmatrix} 1 \\ -1 \\ 0_N \end{pmatrix}_{[N+2,1]} \\ e = \begin{pmatrix} 1 \\ \vdots \\ 1 \end{pmatrix}_{[N,1]}, 0_N = \begin{pmatrix} 0 \\ \vdots \\ 0 \end{pmatrix}_{[N,1]}, I_N = \begin{pmatrix} 1 & 0 & 0 \\ 0 & \ddots & 0 \\ 0 & 0 & 1 \end{pmatrix}_{[N,N]} \\ x = \begin{pmatrix} x_1 \\ \vdots \\ x_N \end{pmatrix} \end{cases} \end{cases}.$$

We first define the necessary Karush-Kuhn-Tucker (KKT) first order optimality conditions that are associated with this problem as follows (Gordon and Tibshirani, 2012):

$$(KKT):\begin{cases}(1):\dfrac{\partial MSE^{DDI}(x)}{\partial x}+A'\lambda=0_N\\(2):\lambda_i(Ax-b)_i=0,i\in\{1,\dots,r\}\\s.t.\begin{cases}Ax\leq b\\\lambda_i\geq 0,i\in\{1,\dots,r\}\\r=N+2\\x=\begin{pmatrix}x_1\\:\\x_N\end{pmatrix}\\\lambda=\begin{pmatrix}\lambda_1\\:\\\lambda_r\end{pmatrix}\end{cases}\end{cases}$$

We note here that λ_i is simply a parameter of the constraints' satisfaction and is not related to our analysis. Next, in order to derive $\dfrac{\partial MSE^{DDI}(x)}{\partial x}$, the $MSE^{DDI}(x)$ function must be rearranged in the following form:

$$MSE^{DDI}(x)=(L+1)^2\gamma_0\sum_{i=1}^{N}x_i^2+2(L+1)^2\sum_{j=1}^{N-1}\left(x_j\sum_{i=j+1}^{N}x_i\gamma_{i-j}\right)-2(L+1)\sum_{i=1}^{L+1}\sum_{j=1}^{N}x_j\gamma_{i+j-1}+(L+1)\gamma_0+2\sum_{i=1}^{L}i\gamma_{L+1-i}$$

We separate the four components of the rearranged $MSE^{DDI}(x)$ expression, and we denote them as follows:

$$C_1(x) = (L+1)^2 \gamma_0 \sum_{i=1}^{N} x_i^{\,2} = (L+1)^2 \gamma_0 x I_N x^t;$$

$$C_2(x) = 2(L+1)^2 \sum_{j=1}^{N-1} \left(x_j \sum_{i=j+1}^{N} x_i \gamma_{i-j} \right);$$

$$C_3(x) = -2(L+1) \sum_{i=1}^{L+1} \sum_{j=1}^{N} x_j \gamma_{i+j-1} = -2(L+1) \left(\sum_{i=1}^{L+1} \yen_i^{\,t} \right) x$$

where

$$\yen_i = \begin{bmatrix} \gamma_i \\ \vdots \\ \vdots \\ \gamma \end{bmatrix}, i = 1, \ldots, L+1$$

$$C_4(x) = (L+1)\gamma_0 + 2 \sum_{i=1}^{L} i \gamma_{L+1-i}$$

We then derive the derivative functions of the four $MSE^{DDI}(x)$ components as follows:

$$\frac{\partial C_1(x)}{\partial x} = 2(L+1)^2 \gamma_0 I_N x,$$

$$\frac{\partial C_2(x)}{\partial x} = 2(L+1)^2 \begin{bmatrix} \sum_{\substack{i=1 \\ i \neq 1}}^{N} x_i \gamma_{|i-1|} \\ \vdots \\ \vdots \\ \sum_{\substack{i=1 \\ i \neq N}}^{N} x_i \gamma_{|i-N|} \end{bmatrix},$$

$$\frac{\partial C_3(x)}{\partial x} = -2(L+1)¥^{t}$$

where $¥ = \begin{bmatrix} \sum_{i=1}^{L+1} \gamma_i \\ \vdots \\ \vdots \\ \sum_{i=N}^{L+N} \gamma_i \end{bmatrix}$, and

$$\frac{\partial C_4(x)}{\partial x} = 0_N .$$

Then, the derivative function of $MSE^{DDI}(x)$ is finally expressed as follows:

$$\frac{\partial MSE^{DDI}(x)}{\partial x} = \begin{bmatrix} 2(L+1)^2 \left(\gamma_0 x_1 + \sum_{\substack{i=1 \\ i\neq 1}}^{N} x_i \gamma_{|i-1|} \right) - 2(L+1) \sum_{i=1}^{L+1} \gamma_i \\ \vdots \\ \vdots \\ \vdots \\ 2(L+1)^2 \left(\gamma_0 x_N + \sum_{\substack{i=1 \\ i\neq N}}^{N} x_i \gamma_{|i-N|} \right) - 2(L+1) \sum_{i=N}^{L+N} \gamma_i \end{bmatrix}_{[N,1]}$$

In a second step, we denote $G(x) = \frac{\partial MSE^{DDI}(x)}{\partial x} + A^{t}\lambda$, and then KKT is equivalent to the following nonlinear equations system (NLS):

$$(NLS): \begin{cases} G(x,\lambda) = 0_N \\ \lambda_i (b - Ax)_i = 0,\ \lambda_i \geq 0, (b - Ax)_i \geq 0, i \in \{1,\ldots,r\} \end{cases}$$

Proposition (Chen et al., 2000a):

If $a \geq 0$ and $b \geq 0$, then $ab = 0 \Leftrightarrow \varphi(a,b) = 0$ with $\varphi(a,b) = a + b - \sqrt{a^2 + b^2}$.

By applying the *Proposition* to (*NLS*), we obtain the following system (NLS'):

$$(NLS'):\begin{cases} G(x,\lambda) = 0_N \\ \psi_i\left(\lambda_i,(b-Ax)_i\right) = \lambda_i + (b-Ax)_i - \sqrt{\lambda_i^2 + (b-Ax)_i^2} = 0, i \in \{1,\ldots,r\} \end{cases}$$

Next, let $g\begin{pmatrix} x \\ \lambda \end{pmatrix} = \begin{pmatrix} G(x,\lambda) \\ \psi(x,\lambda) \end{pmatrix} = 0_{N+r}$. Consequently, solving (NLS') requires solving the following nonlinear Equation (S):

$$(S):\begin{pmatrix} x^{k+1} \\ \lambda^{k+1} \end{pmatrix} = \begin{pmatrix} x^k \\ \lambda^k \end{pmatrix} - \nabla g^{-1}\begin{pmatrix} x^k \\ \lambda^k \end{pmatrix} \cdot g\begin{pmatrix} x^k \\ \lambda^k \end{pmatrix}$$

The resolution of such equation requires the computation of the inverse of the Hessian matrix $\nabla g^{-1}\begin{pmatrix} x^k \\ \lambda^k \end{pmatrix}$ at each iteration *k*, which could be expensive in terms of time and memory. The best solution is then to solve a linear system using the Pivot-Gauss method (Sorensen, 1985). For any linear system of the form $Ax=b$, the Pivot-Gauss method consists of staggering the system by making changes to the rows of matrix *A* of the type $L_i \leftarrow L_i + \alpha L_j$ to obtain the solution at the end a triangular matrix. Finally, solving (S) amounts to solving the following linear equations system (LS):

$$(LS):\nabla g\begin{pmatrix} x^k \\ \lambda^k \end{pmatrix} . \Delta u^k = -g\begin{pmatrix} x^k \\ \lambda^k \end{pmatrix}$$

where

$$\Delta u^k = \begin{pmatrix} \Delta x^k \\ \Delta \lambda^k \end{pmatrix} = \begin{pmatrix} x^{k+1} - x^k \\ \lambda^{k+1} - \lambda^k \end{pmatrix}$$

and

$$\nabla g\begin{pmatrix} x^k \\ \lambda^k \end{pmatrix} = \begin{bmatrix} \dfrac{\partial G(x^k,\lambda^k)}{\partial x} & \dfrac{\partial G(x^k,\lambda^k)}{\partial \lambda} \\ \dfrac{\partial \psi(x^k,\lambda^k)}{\partial x} & \dfrac{\partial \psi(x^k,\lambda^k)}{\partial \lambda} \end{bmatrix}_{[N+r,N+r]}$$

with

$$\frac{\partial G(x^k,\lambda^k)}{\partial x} = \frac{\partial^2 MSE^{DDI}(x^k)}{\partial x^2} = \begin{bmatrix} 2(L+1)^2\gamma_0 & \cdots & 2(L+1)^2\gamma_{|1-N|} \\ \vdots & \ddots & \vdots \\ 2(L+1)^2\gamma_{|N-1|} & \cdots & 2(L+1)^2\gamma_0 \end{bmatrix},$$

$$\frac{\partial G(x^k,\lambda^k)}{\partial \lambda} = A^t,$$

$$\frac{\partial \psi(x^k,\lambda^k)}{\partial x} = -A + \frac{(b-Ax^k)_i A}{\sqrt{(\lambda_i^k)^2 + (b-Ax^k)_i^2}}$$

$$\frac{\partial \psi(x^k,\lambda^k)}{\partial \lambda} = \left(1 - \frac{\lambda_i}{(\lambda_i^k)^2 + (b-Ax^k)_i^2}\right) I_{(r,r)}$$

In this section, we established the transformation of the quadratic problem MFOP into a system of linear equations (LS). The use of the Pivot-Gauss method allows for the reduction of the execution time that is necessary to obtain the Newton's results.

We conclude this section by summarizing the collaborative process in the considered supply chain. The manufacturer signs an income-sharing contract with the retailer. The latter agrees to adopt the WMA/Newton method in his demand forecasting, thus allowing the demand inference at the manufacturer. The manufacturer implements the Newton's method to obtain the optimal allocation vector according to his average inventory level. Once the system (LS) is solved, the manufacturer passes the information on the allocation vector to the retailer who will implement this weighting in his WMA forecasting method. The reduction of the MSE and consequently the average inventory level at the manufacturer, generates savings that will be shared with the retailer.

4. SIMULATION RESULTS AND DISCUSSION

In this section, we carry out some simulated experiments of our implementation, namely, the resolution of some examples that will serve to validate the approach. Then, we discuss the observed results compared to the NIS strategy with the MMSE method and compared to the DDI strategy with the SMA method.

4.1. Implementation of Newton's Method

Using the MATLAB software, we implemented the Newton's method for solving a quadratic problem under linear constraints. We adapted the general form of the quadratic problem to coincide with our MFOP and then conducted simulations by solving some problems using different predefined demand processes. The pseudocode of the Newton's algorithm is shown as follows:

Newton's algorithm:

- Ø Input of the problem data N, L, A, b and γ_i for $i \in \{1, \ldots, N+L\}$
- Ø Input of the algorithm parameters: i_{max} (maximal iterations number) and ε (maximal accepted error)
- Ø Entry of the initial estimates: k=0, $x^0 = \begin{pmatrix} x_1^0 \\ \vdots \\ x_N^0 \end{pmatrix}$ and $\lambda^0 = \begin{pmatrix} \lambda_1^0 \\ \vdots \\ \lambda_r^0 \end{pmatrix}$
- Ø While $g\begin{pmatrix} x^k \\ \lambda^k \end{pmatrix} \geq \varepsilon$ or $\begin{matrix} x^{k+1} - x^k \\ \lambda^{k+1} - \lambda^k \end{matrix} \geq \varepsilon$ or $k < i_{max}$
    - § Compute $g\begin{pmatrix} x^k \\ \lambda^k \end{pmatrix}$ and $\nabla g\begin{pmatrix} x^k \\ \lambda^k \end{pmatrix}$
    - § Solve $\nabla g\begin{pmatrix} x^k \\ \lambda^k \end{pmatrix} . \Delta u^k = -g\begin{pmatrix} x^k \\ \lambda^k \end{pmatrix}$ using the Pivot-Gauss method and deduce

$$\begin{pmatrix} x^{k+1} \\ \lambda^{k+1} \end{pmatrix} = \begin{pmatrix} x^{k} \\ \lambda^{k} \end{pmatrix} + \Delta u^k = \begin{pmatrix} x^{k} \\ \lambda^{k} \end{pmatrix} + \begin{pmatrix} \Delta x^{k} \\ \Delta \lambda^{k} \end{pmatrix}$$

k=k+1

End

Ø If $k = i_{max}$, then the algorithm diverges and it will be necessary to change the initial point x^0.

4.2. Simulation Experiments

In this first part of the simulation, we consider the demand models in Table 2, which are causal invertible *ARMA*(*p,q*) models, and we vary the autoregressive parameters ϕ_j where $j = 1,\ldots,p$ and the moving average parameters θ_j where $j = 1,\ldots,q$. Since it is impossible to infinitely compute the IMAR coefficients, we only compute the first 1000 ψ-weights for all simulated *ARMA*(*p,q*) demand processes. Then, we conduct comparative studies between the cases where NIS with MMSE and DDI with WMA/Newton, and a comparative study between the cases where DDI with WMA/Newton method and DDI with SMA method, for the following fixed parameters: $c = 10, \sigma_\xi^2 = 1, L = 5, N = 12, h = 1,$ and $s = 2$. The optimal ponderation vector is obtained by applying the Newton's method. The chosen parameters of Newton's algorithm are as follows: $\varepsilon = 10^{-5}$ and $i_{max} = 100$. The initial solution can be arbitrarily chosen as long as it is in the realm of feasible solutions. The eigenvalues of the Hessian matrix are positive and for different initial solutions corresponding to multiple simulations on the same problem, the optimal solution is always unique. This ensures the global optimality of the Newton's solution. Finally, the Newton's algorithm does not exceed a dozen iterations and the elapsed time is on the scale of a second using the Windows 7 professional operating system.

4.2.1. Comparative Studies

The following tables present the findings of our simulations on 20 different demand models. We selected 20 different demand models used in the simulation for the simple reason of multiple illustrations, where we variate autoregressive and moving average parameters of the demand processes. Multiple simulations procure more credibility about the robustness of results. Table 2 shows the coefficients of the demand processes and the obtained Newton's optimal weights for the *N* past observations. Table 3 shows the simulation results of the *MSE* and $\tilde{I}_t$, respectively, when the NIS strategy is adopted, when the DDI strategy with the SMA method is adopted, and finally when the DDI strategy with the WMA/Newton method is adopted.

Table 3 reports two important results. The first one is that this table exhibits the effectiveness of the DDI strategy with WMA/Newton compared to the NIS approach. Therefore, the DDI strategy remains valuable when there is no information sharing mechanisms, regardless of the used forecasting method. Besides, based on simulated models in Table 3, the WMA method with the Newton's allocation proves its efficiency by outperforming the SMA method with regards to the two performance metrics. It's about the second result where this table proves that decision-makers in supply chains can enhance their DDI performance and market competitiveness by simply considering the optimal weighting that is generated by Newton's method, rather than considering an equitable weighting of the order of 1 / *N*. As expected, the enhancement of the two metrics is different when we vary the autoregressive and the moving average parameters of the demand processes. This is due to the nonlinear relation mentioned above in Equation (5) that connects the forecast *MSE* to its effective consequence, the average inventory level.

Table 2. Optimal Newton's weights for ARMA(p,q) demand models

Demand model	Autoregressive and moving average coefficients	Newton weights vector
1	ϕ_1=0.400	$\begin{pmatrix} 0.2218;0.0667;0.0667;0.0667;0.0667;0.0667; \\ 0.0667;0.0667;0.0667;0.0667;0.0667;0.1112 \end{pmatrix}$
2	ϕ_1=0.500	$\begin{pmatrix} 0.2835;0.0597;0.0597;0.0597;0.0597;0.0597; \\ 0.0597;0.0597;0.0597;0.0597;0.0597;0.1194 \end{pmatrix}$
3	ϕ_1=0.600	$\begin{pmatrix} 0.3653;0.0508;0.0508;0.0508;0.0508;0.0508; \\ 0.0508;0.0508;0.0508;0.0508;0.0508;0.1269 \end{pmatrix}$
4	θ_1=0.400	$\begin{pmatrix} 0.1727;0.0370;0.0913;0.0696;0.0782;0.0749; \\ 0.0758;0.0764;0.0739;0.0806;0.0636;0.1061 \end{pmatrix}$
5	θ_1=0.500	$\begin{pmatrix} 0.1952;0.0143;0.1046;0.0596;0.0818;0.0714; \\ 0.0753;0.0760;0.0704;0.0837;0.0560;0.1118 \end{pmatrix}$
6	θ_1=0.600	$\begin{pmatrix} 0.2116;0.0000;0.1171;0.0467;0.0880;0.0659; \\ 0.0756;0.0756;0.0659;0.0880;0.0476;0.1171 \end{pmatrix}$

continues on following page

Table 2. Continued

Demand model	Autoregressive and moving average coefficients	Newton weights vector
7	ϕ_1=0.400 θ_1=0.051	$\begin{pmatrix}0.2397;0.0567;0.0661;0.0656;0.0656;0.0656;\\0.0656;0.0656;0.0656;0.0657;0.0631;0.1149\end{pmatrix}$
8	ϕ_1=0.400 θ_1=0.100	$\begin{pmatrix}0.2569;0.0455;0.0666;0.0645;0.0647;0.0647;\\0.0647;0.0647;0.0646;0.0652;0.0593;0.1186\end{pmatrix}$
9	ϕ_1=0.400 θ_1=0.300	$\begin{pmatrix}0.3186;0.0000;0.0752;0.0575;0.0628;0.0613;\\0.0615;0.0621;0.0596;0.0680;0.0400;0.1334\end{pmatrix}$
10	ϕ_1=0.400 θ_1=0.300 θ_2=0.100	$\begin{pmatrix}0.3550;0.0000;0.0449;0.0692;0.0574;0.0586;\\0.0593;0.0585;0.0616;0.0565;0.0413;0.1378\end{pmatrix}$
11	ϕ_1=0.400 θ_1=0.300 θ_2=0.150	$\begin{pmatrix}0.3733;0.0000;0.0271;0.0758;0.0572;0.0557;\\0.0582;0.0578;0.0624;0.0504;0.0420;0.1400\end{pmatrix}$
12	ϕ_1=0.400 θ_1=0.300 θ_2=0.200	$\begin{pmatrix}0.3909;0.0015;0.0068;0.0829;0.0593;0.0514;\\0.0567;0.0583;0.0631;0.0441;0.0428;0.1423\end{pmatrix}$
13	ϕ_1=0.400 θ_1=0.300 θ_2=0.180 θ_3=0.060 θ_4=0.050	$\begin{pmatrix}0.4138;0.0091;0.0259;0.0590;0.0410;0.0602;\\0.0562;0.0493;0.0551;0.0464;0.0425;0.1415\end{pmatrix}$
14	ϕ_1=0.200 ϕ_2=0.150 θ_1=0.100	$\begin{pmatrix}0.2194;0.1045;0.0584;0.0630;0.0626;0.0626;\\0.0626;0.0626;0.0627;0.0614;0.0742;0.1059\end{pmatrix}$
15	ϕ_1=0.200 ϕ_2=0.150 ϕ_3=0.120 ϕ_4=0.100 θ_1=0.100	$\begin{pmatrix}0.2806;0.1607;0.1142;0.0694;0.0308;0.0347;\\0.0344;0.0336;0.0415;0.0509;0.0615;0.0878\end{pmatrix}$
16	ϕ_1=0.200 ϕ_2=0.150 ϕ_3=0.120 ϕ_4=0.100 θ_1=0.100 θ_2=0.065	$\begin{pmatrix}0.3018;0.1767;0.0979;0.0623;0.0261;0.0321;\\0.0335;0.0318;0.0389;0.0463;0.0629;0.0899\end{pmatrix}$

continues on following page

Table 2. Continued

Demand model	Autoregressive and moving average coefficients	Newton weights vector
17	ϕ_1=0.200 ϕ_2=0.150 ϕ_3=0.120 ϕ_4=0.100 θ_1=0.100 θ_2=0.065 θ_3=0.060 θ_4=0.051	$\begin{pmatrix} 0.3293;0.1994;0.1171;0.0501;0.0000;0.0177; \\ 0.0256;0.0257;0.0357;0.0468;0.0629;0.0898 \end{pmatrix}$
18	ϕ_1=0.200 ϕ_2= -0.150 ϕ_3=0.120 ϕ_4= -0.100 ϕ_5=0.080 ϕ_6=0.070 ϕ_7=0.060 ϕ_8= -0.051 θ_1=0.100	$\begin{pmatrix} 0.1484;0.0679;0.1154;0.0721;0.1023;0.0792; \\ 0.0672;0.0589;0.0657;0.0760;0.0606;0.0865 \end{pmatrix}$
19	ϕ_1=0.200 ϕ_2= -0.150 ϕ_3=0.120 ϕ_4= -0.100 ϕ_5=0.080 ϕ_6=0.070 ϕ_7=0.060 ϕ_8= -0.051 θ_1=0.100 θ_2=0.060	$\begin{pmatrix} 0.1614;0.0772;0.1089;0.0709;0.0992;0.0770; \\ 0.0627;0.0550;0.0642;0.0734;0.0617;0.0884 \end{pmatrix}$
20	ϕ_1=0.200 ϕ_2= -0.150 ϕ_3=0.120 ϕ_4= -0.100 ϕ_5=0.080 ϕ_6=0.070 ϕ_7=0.060 ϕ_8= -0.051 θ_1=0.100 θ_2=0.060 θ_3=0.040 θ_4=0.010	$\begin{pmatrix} 0.1712;0.0842;0.1169;0.0648;0.0958;0.0730; \\ 0.0592;0.0499;0.0600;0.0737;0.0627;0.0887 \end{pmatrix}$

Besides, since there are no specific "standard approaches" for determining the best configuration, and for investigation purposes, we study in the next subsection the sensibility of these metrics according to the lead-time L and moving average parameter N values. For illustration purposes, we consider an arbitrary example of an *ARMA* (3, 2) demand process, which is defined as follows:

$$D_t = 10 + 0.6D_{t-1} + 0.4D_{t-1} - 0.3D_{t-1} + \xi_t + 0.1\xi_{t-1} + 0.08\xi_{t-2}$$

4.2.2. Comparison Between the DDI Strategy With WMA/Newton Method and the NIS With MMSE Method With Respect to Lead Time and Moving Average Parameters

Based on the comparison between DDI with WMA/Newton results and NIS with MMSE results, we study the sensibilities of the two performance metrics with respect to the lead-time L and the moving average N. In the cases where the lead-time L is fixed and N varies, Figure 2 presents the simulation results in terms of the MSE^{DDI}

Table 3. MSE and $\tilde{I}_t$ results for ARMA(p,q) demands when NIS, DDI with SMA and DDI with WMA/Newton methods, are adopted

Demand Model	NIS with MMSE method		DDI with SMA method		DDI with WMA/Newton method	
	MSE^{NS}	$\tilde{I}_t^{NIS}$	MSE^{DDI}	$\tilde{I}_t^{DDI}$	MSE^{DDI*}	$\tilde{I}_t^{DDI*}$
1	67.3756	19.6936	20.3867	11.5614	19.4392	11.4855
2	138.3996	33.0452	26.7926	14.3894	24.6456	14.2098
3	300.1029	62.3794	36.5808	18.7090	31.8348	18.2922
4	11.7600	7.8951	16.2400	07.4301	15.8909	7.4038
5	13.5000	8.5608	18.5000	07.7789	17.9541	7.7376
6	15.3600	9.3215	20.9400	08,1536	20.1583	8.0942
7	74.3786	21.3331	22.3074	11.8812	21.0996	11.7838
8	81.4330	23.0569	24.2527	12.2041	22.7645	12.0835
9	113.5408	31.7447	33.2078	13.6816	30.2764	13.4401
10	131.3007	37.0936	37.4282	14.4392	33.4410	14.1049
11	140.6645	40.1215	39.6913	14.8415	35.1010	14.4536
12	150.3507	43.2234	42.0563	15.2594	36.8125	14.8132
13	166.6726	48.7798	44.6284	15.8453	38.2068	15.2839
14	49.8496	17.7593	19.6140	10.8756	18.5583	10.7887
15	82.8049	34.5483	24.1279	15.9735	20.8552	15.6680
16	90.6387	37.3469	26.5067	16.4101	22.4153	16.0256
17	99.4028	41.1695	29.7530	17.0342	23.9784	16.4813
18	14.6534	10.3757	12.8447	8.4158	12.5980	8.3972
19	15.5426	10.5792	13.8480	8.6012	13.5038	8.5747
20	16,4370	10,6580	14.4736	8.7396	14.0079	8.7030

and $\tilde{I}_t^{DDI}$ improvements in percentages. These improvement percentages are computed as follows:

$$MSE^{DDI}\_Improvement = \left|\frac{MSE^{DDI*} - MSE^{NIS}}{MSE^{NIS}}\right| \times 100$$

and

$$\tilde{I}_t^{DDI}\_Improvement = \left|\frac{\tilde{I}_t^{DDI*} - \tilde{I}_t^{NIS}}{\tilde{I}_t^{NIS}}\right| \times 100$$

The obtained results in Figure 2 show that the evolution of the improvements with respect to N is a linear function. This means that the more the parameter N increases, the more the DDI strategy with WMA/Newton is more efficient in comparison with the NIS approach. This result is expected since the parameter N does not interfere in the MMSE method used in the NIS approach. In terms of MSE and average inventories, managers are advised to increase their parameter N as well as possible while their lead-time is constant.

Figure 2. Improvements of adopting DDI strategy with WMA/Newton method rather than adopting NIS strategy according to the moving average parameter N

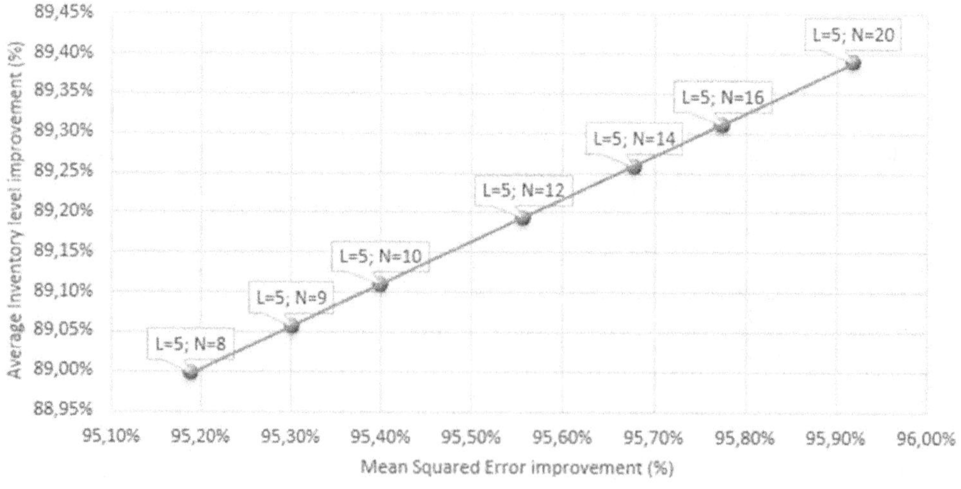

In the same way, Figure 3 schematically presents the simulation results in terms of percentage improvements where the moving average parameter *N* is fixed and the lead-time *L* varies.

Figure 3. Improvements of adopting DDI strategy with WMA/Newton method rather than adopting NIS strategy according to the moving average parameter L

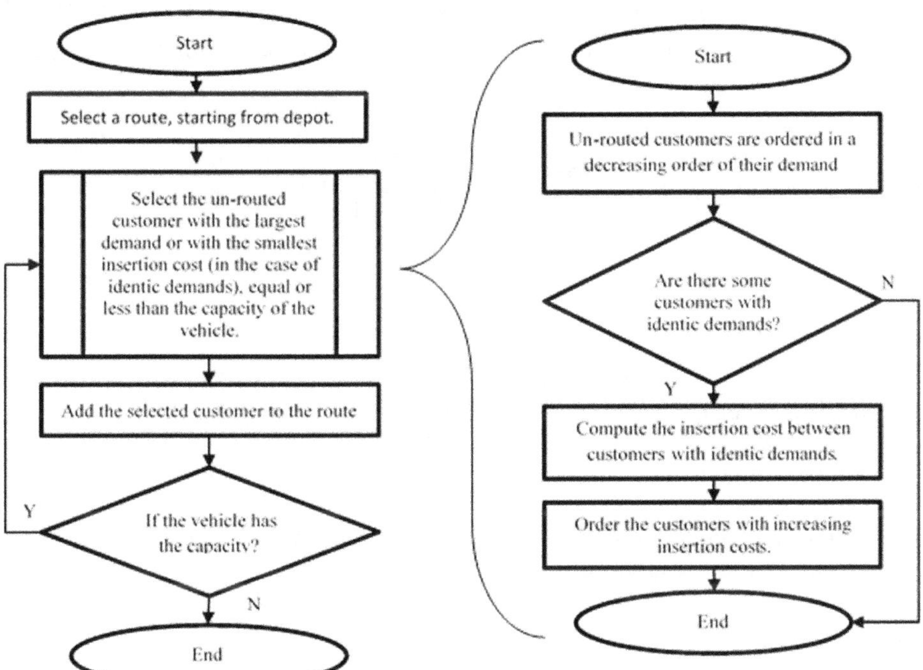

The same reasoning is adopted. The obtained results in Figure 3 show that the evolution according to *L* is a logarithmic function. That is, for a fixed parameter *N*, the evolution of the enhancement in percentage becomes less important as the lead-time *L* becomes more important. Indeed, for low values of *L*, the evolution in performance is important in comparison with cases where the values of *L* are high. This result further confirms that the lead-time value always plays an important role in the performance of the supply chains.

4.2.3. Comparison Between the DDI Strategy With WMA/ Newton Method and the DDI Strategy With SMA Method With Respect to Lead Time and Moving Average Parameters

Based on the comparison between DDI with WMA/Newton results and DDI with SMA results, we study the sensibilities of the two performance metrics with respect to the lead-time *L* and the moving average *N*. In the cases where the lead-time *L* is fixed and *N* varies, Figure 4 presents the simulation results in terms of the MSE^{DDI} and $\tilde{I}_t^{DDI}$ improvements in percentages. These improvement percentages are computed as follows:

$$MSE^{DDI}\_Improvement = \left| \frac{MSE^{DDI*} - MSE^{DDI}}{MSE^{DDI}} \right| \times 100$$

and

$$\tilde{I}_t^{DDI}\_Improvement = \left| \frac{\tilde{I}_t^{DDI*} - \tilde{I}_t^{DDI}}{\tilde{I}_t^{DDI}} \right| \times 100$$

Figure 4. Improvements in terms of the mean squared error and average inventory level according to the moving average parameter N

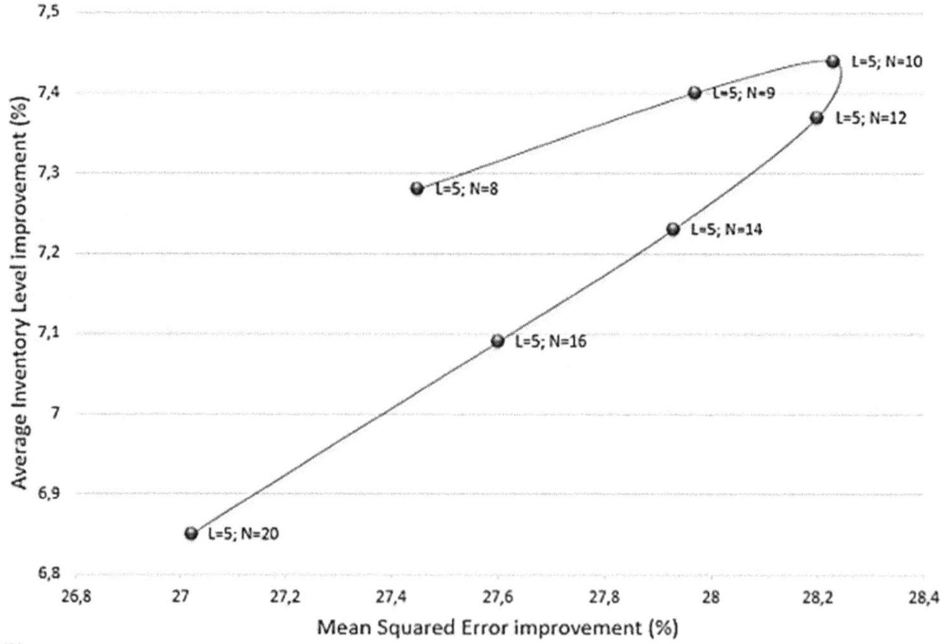

The obtained results in Figure 4 show that the evolution of the improvements with respect to N is a concave function. These numerical results show that this function attains its maximal enhancement at $N = 10$ for $L = 5$. This corresponds to a 7.44% improvement in the average inventory savings. Otherwise, the enhancement is not optimal, but it still exists. In practice, the decision-makers can conduct some

Figure 5. Improvements in terms of the mean squared error and average inventory level according to the lead-time L

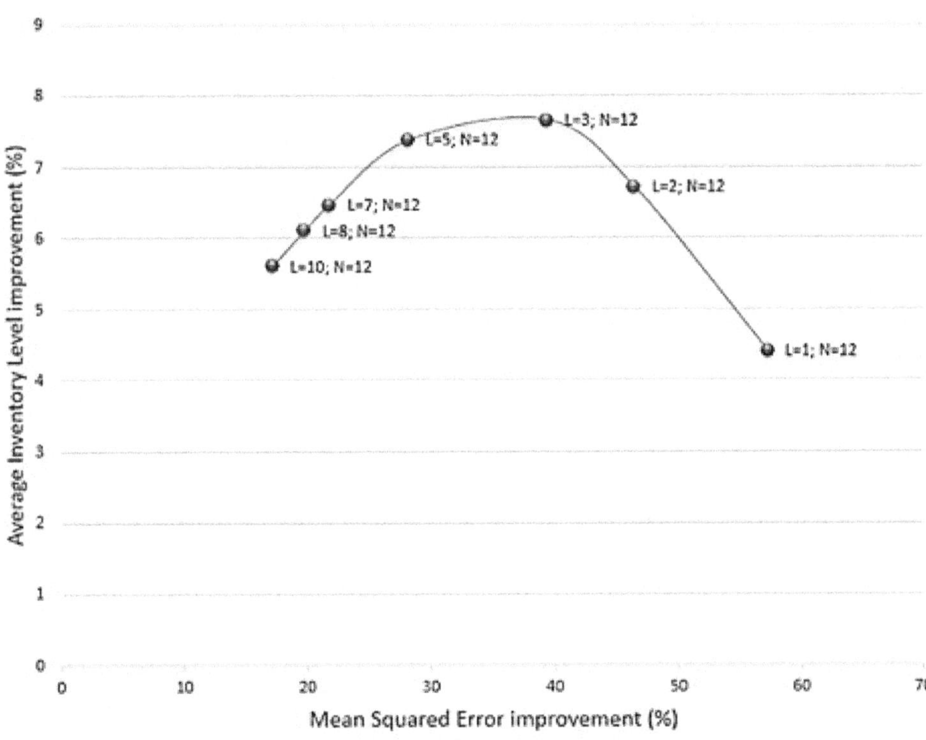

simulations by varying the parameter N over a fixed interval and then by choosing the value that maximizes this enhancement.

In the same way, Figure 5 schematically presents the simulation results in terms of percentage improvements where the moving average parameter N is fixed and the lead-time L varies.

The same reasoning is adopted in Figure 5. The obtained results show that the evolution according to L is also a concave function. These numerical results show that this function attains its maximal enhancement at $L = 3$ for $N = 12$. This corresponds to a 7.65% improvement in the average inventory savings. Generally, the lead-time value does not change since it depends on the transportation and logistics systems, and managers do not truly have the power to easily manipulate its value.

4.2.4. Evolution of the Bullwhip Effect

In this subsection, we study the evolution of the bullwhip effect that is associated with the WMA/Newton forecast method. Thus, we consider an example of an $ARMA(2,2)$ demand process with the following fixed parameters set: $c=10, \phi_1=0.4, \phi_2=0.2, \theta_1=0.15, \theta_2=0.10$ and $\sigma_\xi^2=1$. We mainly compute the $BEE_{MMSE}^{WMA/Newton}$ and $BEE_{SMA}^{WMA/Newton}$ indicators in Equations (9) and (10) in order to approximate the gap of the bullwhip effect, thereby separating on one hand, the DDI strategy with the WMA/Newton method to the NIS strategy with the MMSE method, and on the second hand, the DDI strategy with the WMA/Newton method to the DDI strategy with the SMA method. While these indicators are functions of the moving average *N* and lead-time *L*, we also check the variations according to these two parameters.

Figure 6 illustrates the behavior of the evolution of the bullwhip effect when an actor switches from the MMSE method in a NIS strategy to the WMA/Newton method in a DDI strategy. For a fixed configuration of the parameter *N*, the performance of the WMA/Newton method becomes more important as the lead-time *L* decreases. In this

Figure 6. Simulated $BEE_{MMSE}^{WMA/Newton}$ indicator according to moving average N and lead-time L

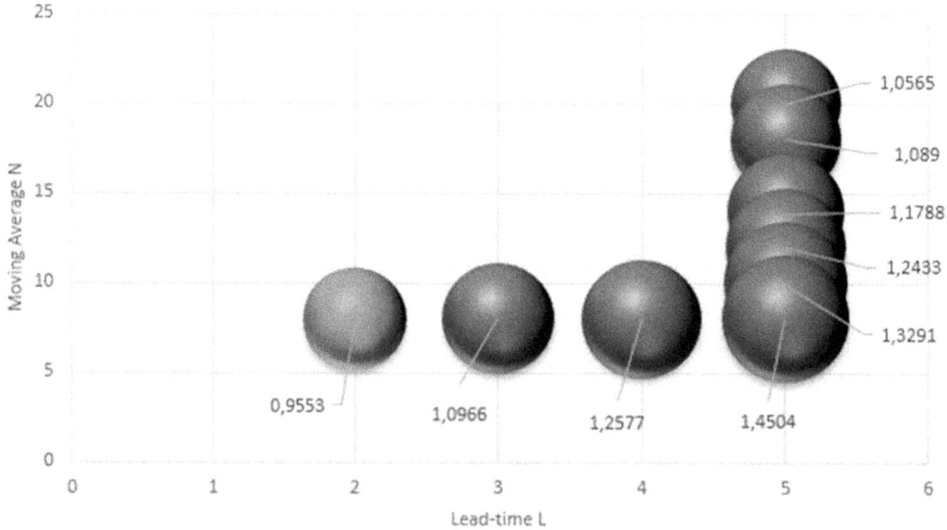

example, for $N = 8$, DDI with WMA/Newton is valuable in terms of bullwhip effect if the lead-time value is less than 3. Next, for a fixed lead-time L, the performance of the WMA/Newton method is more important as the parameter N increases. In terms of L, the results show that the value of the break-point N increases as the lead-time L increases. This is expected as generally, the performance of the MMSE method compared to the WMA/Newton improves with increasing the lead-time value. On the other hand, the results show that the break-point L decreases with the value of N as the performance of WMA/Newton improves with the length of the history being used. We conclude tht for every value of the lead-time L, there exists an increasing threshold of N from which the DDI strategy with the WMA/Newton method is more valuable than the NIS strategy with the MMSE method, in terms of bullwhip effect.

Figure 7 illustrates the behavior of the bullwhip effect when the SMA and WMA/Newton methods are used in the forecasts. There are two important results. The first one is that the SMA method outperforms the WMA/Newton method in terms of bullwhip effect. Indeed, for the simulated data, the $BEE_{SMA}^{WMA/Newton}$ results are always greater than one. This is due to the unequal weights that are associated with the N past observations in Equation (2). This can be argued to be a limitation of the WMA/Newton approach compared to the SMA method, since the SMA method provides lower variability of order processes. The second one is that the $BEE_{SMA}^{WMA/Newton}$ indicator increases with N or L. The results also show that these amplifications

Figure 7. Simulated $BEE_{SMA}^{WMA/Newton}$ indicator according to moving average N and lead-time L

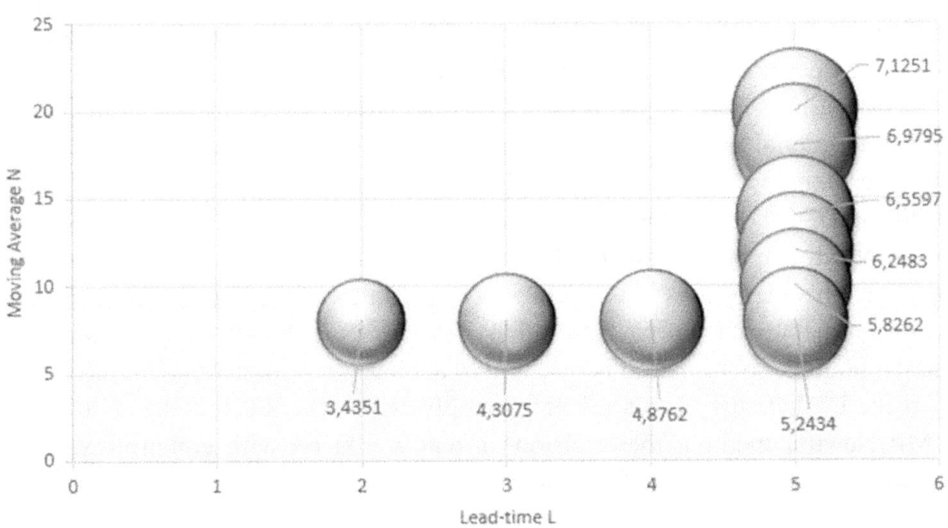

evolve in a quasi-logarithmic manner. That is, the increase in the indicator becomes less important as one of the two parameters increases. Hence, the bullwhip effect amplifies in the case of a DDI strategy where the downstream actor decides to switch from the use of the SMA method to the use of the WMA/Newton method. The amplified bullwhip effect is surely critical if the upstream actor doesn't use a safety stock as a buffer against orders variations. Indeed, excess inventory can result in waste, while insufficient inventory can lead to poor customer experience and lost business. Thus, the upstream actor is emphasized to use a reserve inventory in such context.

4.3. Discussion

In decentralized supply chains, actors often do not want to share their private information, especially in regard to the market demand. This variable is often considered as key data providing competitive power. Even when supply chain actors favor information sharing, other issues (the trust in the shared data, information leakage, high investment costs, systems compatibility, etc.) may still persist.

This work provides an initial attempt to introduce the WMA forecasting method in a decentralized supply chain in which actors favor adopting the DDI strategy. The propagation of demand processes using the WMA forecast method is unique. The introduction of the Newton optimization method allows for the quantification of the weighting of past demand observations with the purpose of minimizing the mean squared error and average inventory. The study of the improvements, according to the parameters, shows that supply chain decision-makers are able to estimate the optimal parameter values. While simulations allow practitioners to obtain general ideas and approximate settings, varying the lead-time is not truly possible. However, they can easily change the moving average while conducting forecasting as long as this value does not exceed the historical time horizon.

It is first important for decision-makers to further reduce inventory levels and gather additional savings. Indeed, the resulting reduction in the manufacturer translates into cost savings over time. These savings are the most important engine leading to DDI adoption. Our work shows through simulations that savings from the WMA/Newton approach exceed the savings from the SMA method. We estimate that Newton's method itself is not expensive in terms of the time implementation. While it is natural to expect a distribution of these savings between the manufacturer and the retailer, coordination is essential to achieve such improvements.

If the DDI strategy is adopted in a supply chain where actors decide to adopt WMA/Newton method, the decision-makers are faced with compromising the two major criteria axes: the forecasted mean squared errors and average inventory levels on one side, and the bullwhip effect amplifications on another side. In this chapter, we have considered the enhancement of the forecast MSE and inventory level metrics since they are directly related to average inventory costs over time. The bullwhip effect is then costly to the supply chain if the upstream actor decides to base his forecasting only on the received orders process. However, in the case of the DDI strategy, the upstream actor bases his forecasting on orders and inferred demand at the same time. The knowledge of the estimated parameters and error variance interfere in the reduction of the MSE and the average inventory level at the upstream actor. If the supply chain is initially adopting a NIS strategy where the MMSE method is used in the downstream forecasts, the downstream actor is emphasized to consider a high value of N (beyond a certain break-point) in order to reduce the bullwhip effect. Else, if the supply chain is initially adopting a DDI strategy where the SMA method is used in the downstream forecasts, the subject of bullwhip effect amplification can be critical if the upstream actor decide to not use a safety stock as a buffer against orders variations. Consequently, the upstream actor needs to use a reserve inventory in order to cover the orders variations.

Except for the optimal weighting information that must be shared between the supply chain actors, this approach does not require further assumptions than those that are required by DDI with the SMA method, namely, the knowledge of the demand process (time-series structure) and its estimated parameters all along the supply chain. Thus, it is also essential to consider the costs of such coordination.

Figure 8. Principle of DDI strategy through a revenue-sharing contract when the WMA/Newton forecasting method is adopted

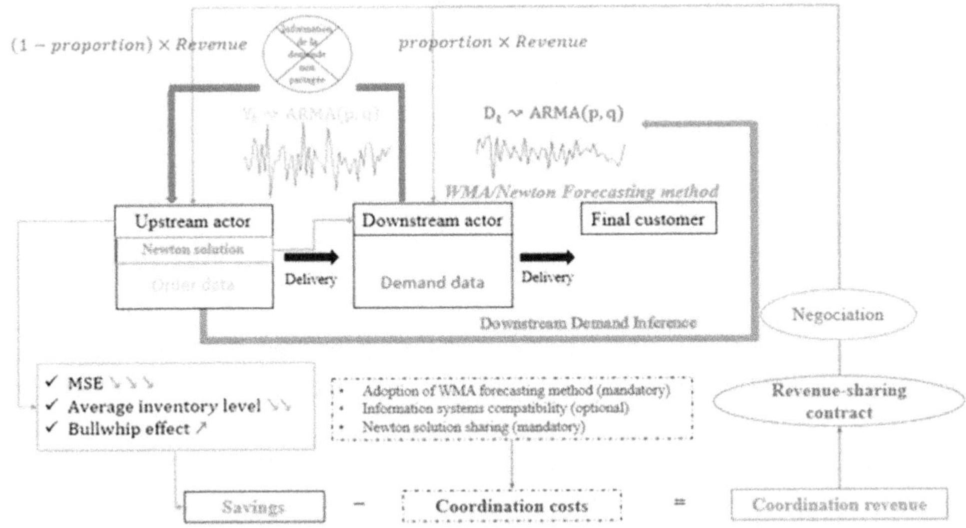

These costs are primarily related to the implementation of the method itself (if another forecast method was adopted) and the weighting information sharing. Figure 8 shows the coordination mechanism in such a DDI strategy.

The WMA/Newton forecasting approach for the DDI strategy can be established through different managerial contracts between the manufacturer and the retailer. The literature on such contracts is abundant. For example, the manufacturer may propose contracts to the retailer based on principal agent relationships (Müller and Turner, 2005), the supply chain actors can negotiate through proposals (Taghipour and Frayret, 2013; Dudek and Stadtler, 2005). Buyback (Chen and Bell, 2011) or price discount (Jain et al., 2011) contracts may also be proposed.

5. GENERALIZATION FOR MULTI-LEVEL SUPPLY CHAINS

The DDI results where the downstream actor adopts the WMA/Newton forecast approach can be extended to multi-level supply chains where there is more than two actors. Let consider a n-level supply chain where each downstream actor places an order to his formal upstream actor after revising his inventory level. We suppose that all actors accept to adopt DDI strategy through the WMA/Newton method. It means that each actor i=2,3,…,n will use the WMA/Newton forecast method by considering the weighting vector of his formal upstream actor i-1. Then every upstream actor

Figure 9. N-level supply chain where actors accept DDI while adopting WMA/ Newton forecasting method

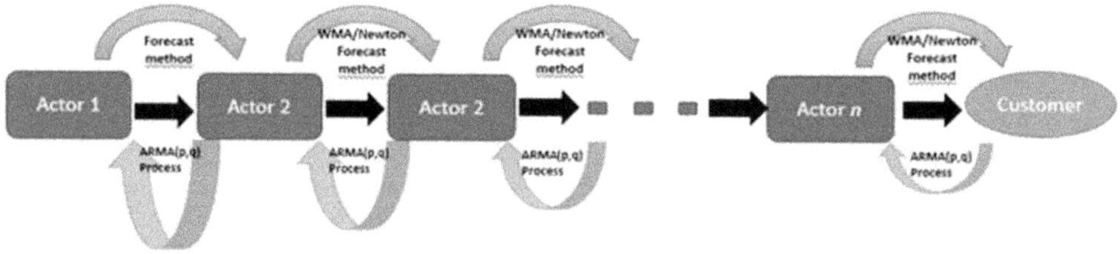

i=1,2,…,n-1 is able to infer the demand occurring at his formal downstream actor i+1. Notice that the first upstream actor is not concerned about a specific forecast approach. Figure 9 shows a demonstration of such a multi-level supply chain.

In a set configuration such as Figure 8, Actor 1 is generally a supplier of raw materials who endures large inventory costs. Let suppose a customer of a single product whose demand follows an $ARMA(p,q)$ process at the actor n. After revising his inventory level, this actor will place an order at the actor n-1. The order process will keep the same autoregressive moving average structure as the demand but it will increase its error variability, as one moves further up the supply chain. Moreover, for illustration, let consider an example of an initial customer's demand model of an *ARMA*(2,1) defined by:

$$D_t = 10 + 0,2D_{t-1} + 0,15D_{t-2} + \xi_t + 0,1\xi_{t-1}$$

where $\xi_t \to N(0,1)$ is the standard normal distributed error at period t. The order process arriving at the actor n-1 is also an *ARMA(p,q)* process defined by:

$$Y_t = 10 + 0,2Y_{t-1} + 0,15Y_{t-2} + \tilde{\xi}_t + 0,1\tilde{\xi}_{t-1}$$

where

$$\xi_t \to N\left(0, \left[L^2\left(x_1^2 + x_N^2 + \sum_{i=1}^{N-1}(x_{i+1} - x_i)^2\right) + 2Lx_1 + 1\right]\right)$$

is the normal error distributed error at period t, and where x_i are the Newton's weights shared by the actor n-1 and used by actor n in his forecasts.

Table 4. NIS and DDI results for ARMA(2,1) demand process

Adopted strategy Metrics	NIS	DDI with SMA forecasting	DDI with WMA/Newton forecasting	% of Reduction when adopting DDI with WMA/Newton rather than NIS	% of Reduction when adopting DDI with WMA/Newton rather than DDI with SMA
MSE	49.8496	19.6140	18.5583	62,7714	5,3823
$\tilde{I}_t$	17.7593	10.8756	10.7887	**39,2504**	**0,7990**

We present in Table 4 the different metrics values at actor n-1 where NIS, DDI with SMA method and DDI with WMA/Newton method are evaluated.

Reductions of MSE and average inventory level at Table 4 is improving when moving from SMA method to WMA/Newton method. In this example, DDI with WMA/Newton allows the actor n-1 to reduce his average inventory level by about

39% compared to NIS and nearly 0,8% compared to DDI with SMA method. Such reductions are translatable into real inventory savings if both actors were favorable to collaborate through a benefit sharing contract. That is, we suppose that the downstream actor is favorable to such contract if he will gain a part of the savings at the upstream actor.

In the same way, let suppose every upstream actor i=1,…,n-1 of a supply chain propose a revenue-sharing contract to his formal downstream actor in order to convince him to adopt WMA/Newton method. Let R_i be the inventory savings of DDI adoption, at actor i. We also assume that the costs of adopting WMA/Newton are related to the Newton's weighting vector information sharing in addition of the implementation costs. Let C_i^{i+1} be the sum of the Newton's weighting information sharing cost at actor i and the implementation cost at actor i+1. The net profit of such collaboration is then expressed by $\pi_i^{i+1} = R_i - C_i^{i+1}$ which will be shared with the downstream actor i+1 according to their contract. Let β_i be the proportion of the net profit π_i^{i+1} shared with the downstream actor i+1, where β_i verifies $0 \leq \beta_i \leq 1$. Then π_i the inventory savings of the actor i, resulting from concluding two contracts of collaboration with actor i-1 and actor i+1 is expressed as follows:

$$\pi_i = \beta_{i-1}\pi_{i-1}^{i} + \left(1-\beta_i\right)\pi_i^{i+1}$$

$$\pi_i = \beta_{i-1}\left(R_{i-1} - C_{i-1}^{i}\right) + \left(1-\beta_i\right)\left(R_i - C_i^{i+1}\right)$$

Note that for actor 1, there is no actor 0 and only one contract can be established with actor 2 which implies β_0=0 and $\pi_0^1 = 0$. Consequently, $\pi_1 = \left(1-\beta_1\right)\left(R_1 - C_1^2\right)$. In the same manner, note that for actor n, there is no actor n+1 and only one contract can be established with actor n-1 which implies β_n=0 and $\pi_n^{n+1} = 0$. Consequently, $\pi_n = \beta_{n-1}\left(R_{n-1} - C_{n-1}^{n}\right)$.

Now if we consider the whole n-level supply chain, the total supply chain inventory savings from adopting DDI strategy with the WMA/Newton method, where a revenue sharing contract is established between every successive couple of actors, is expressed as follows:

$$\pi = \sum_{i=1}^{n}\pi_i = \pi_1 + \sum_{i=2}^{n-1}\pi_i + \pi_n$$

$$\pi = (1-\beta_1)(R_1 - C_1^2) + \sum_{i=2}^{n-1}\left[\beta_{i-1}(R_{i-1} - C_{i-1}^i) + (1-\beta_i)(R_i - C_i^{i+1})\right] + \beta_{n-1}(R_{n-1} - C_{n-1}^n)$$

The last total profit equation proves that the DDI approach with WMA/Newton forecasting improves the performance of the entire decentralized supply chain, as well as DDI with SMA method does. The enhancement is much more considerable compared to NIS strategy and it is more important than DDI with SMA method. Indeed, all the DDI with WMA/Newton forecasts outperforms the DDI results with SMA in terms of average inventory level and consequently in inventory savings. Based on our simulations, we conclude this section by the following statement:

$$\pi^{NIS} <<< \pi_{SMA}^{DDI} < \pi_{WMA/Newton}^{DDI}$$

6. CONCLUSION

Improving the results of supply chains coordination is one of the most important areas for academic researchers and management practitioners. Optimization presents a mathematical branch and an effective tool for collecting better management solutions. In a decentralized supply chain, actors aim to reduce their total costs by applying effective coordination approaches. One of the most cost-effective coordination approaches, namely, DDI, can be set up when actors agree to negotiate and cooperate. DDI allows the upstream actor to infer the demand of his formal downstream actors without the need for information sharing mechanisms. DDI has proved its effectiveness by obtaining almost near-optimal solutions. The literature has shown that the DDI approach cannot be applied through MMSE or SES methods for the downstream actors but only through the SMA method due to the uniqueness of the processes' propagation. Consequently, we found that it is natural to study the feasibility of DDI using other forecasting methods.

This chapter is a follow-up study to previous works with the purpose of improving existing DDI results through the theoretical analysis of inventory models based on some strong assumptions. In a context of the DDI coordination strategy, instead of using the SMA method, we proposed the adoption of the WMA method combined with the well-known Newton optimization method. This chapter thus enriches the existing literature by exploring the feasibility of the DDI approach when the WMA forecasting method is adopted.

We first established the expressions of the manufacturer's forecasting MSE^{DDI} and $\tilde{I}^{DDI}$ and the resulting bullwhip effect. We proposed two measures, namely $BEE_{MMSE}^{WMA/Newton}$, to assess the amplification of the bullwhip effect separating the adoption of the DDI with the WMA method from the adoption of the NIS strategy with the MMSE method, and $BEE_{SMA}^{WMA/Newton}$, to assess the amplification of the bullwhip effect separating the adoption of the DDI strategy with the WMA/Newton method from the adoption of the DDI with the SMA method. Second, we mathematically formalized the MFOP and proposed the application of Newton's method for the resolution. Finally, the results for the MSE^{DDI} and $\tilde{I}^{DDI}$ optimization based on the simulated causal invertible $ARMA(p,q)$ demand processes confirm the effectiveness of the WMA/Newton approach to propose further enhanced supply chain solutions.

The implications of this chapter are as follows. Supply chain managers can introduce the WMA forecast method in the context of the DDI strategy because of the uniqueness of the generated orders process for upstream actors. First, our work provides WMA/Newton as a novel approach for coordination in decentralized supply chains. This approach does not require further assumptions than those required by the DDI strategy with the SMA method, except for the optimal weighting vector, which must be shared between the supply chain. Second, based on the conducted simulations, the chapter confirms that the DDI strategy with the WMA/Newton approach generally outperforms the NIS strategy and the DDI strategy with the SMA method in terms of MSE^{DDI} and $\tilde{I}^{DDI}$. Therefore, our work concludes that the DDI's performance depends on the allocation vector, and especially MSE^{DDI} and $\tilde{I}^{DDI}$ generally improve with the optimal Newton's allocation. The "*generally*" statement is employed here since this work does not provide an exhaustive sensitivity analysis of the performance according to the demand process parameters. Indeed, it is not easy to check the entire sensitivity of the DDI strategy according to the combination of two sets of parameters $\phi_{i\{i=1,\ldots,p\}}$ and $\theta_{j\{j=1,\ldots,q\}}$, especially since they are not fixed in advance. Indeed, in this case, the threshold can take the form of a summation, a product, or any other linear or non-linear relationship, from which we can state a general expression of a yield threshold. Establishing such relation requires a deep study on the sensitivity according to the process parameters. Since the demand models are mathematically discrete and no continuous, there is no way to get through the partial derivative functions. We think this can be a case-by-case study to bring an exhaustive benchmark and then be able to generalize some threshold models.

Reversely, the bullwhip effect is affected. In comparison with the NIS strategy, DDI with WMA/Newton method is valuable if the parameter N is high enough vis-à-vis the lead-time L. As shown in the simulation section, a break-point from which

DDI with WMA/Newton is more valuable than the NIS strategy can be determined by varying the parameter N of the forecast method. In the case of a DDI adoption where the downstream actor is favourable to switch from an initial situation of an SMA method to the WMA/Newton method, the bullwhip effect amplifies. This was predictable because of the non-equitable weights that are associated with the N historical demand observations in the method. However, the fact that the ponderation vector in the downstream actor's forecasts, is determined according to the minimization of the average inventory level of the upstream actor, results into the reduction of the mean inventory costs of the upstream actor over the time. In this case, the bullwhip effect can be costly to the upstream actor of the supply chain if he doesn't use a safety stock as a buffer against orders variations. Indeed, excess inventory can result in waste, while insufficient inventory can lead to poor customer experience and lost business. Thus, the upstream actor is emphasized to use a reserve inventory in such context of methods' change. Third, we conclude that supply chain managers, when the DDI with the WMA/Newton is adopted, can potentially determine the optimal parameters (N,L) in terms of MSE and average inventory levels improvements. The value of the WMA parameter N can be easily manipulated through some simulations, while managers do not truly have a large margin to vary the lead-time L. Indeed, the lead-time is often related to supply chain transportation.

From the point of an upstream actor, the additional merit of going the extra steps of WMA/Newton method is the evident forecast MSE and inventory levels reduction which will be earned over time. The reduction of forecasting error is important because it is directly correlated to the reduction of inventory levels. As shown in Equation 5, the average inventory level is a positive non-linear function of the forecast MSE. The simulated experiments in Table 3 show that all empirical inventory means resulted from adopting WMA/Newton are lower than empirical inventory means resulted from adopting SMA method. This difference may not seem significant. However, the gap percentage separating the two compared methods depends on the size of the enterprise and therefore varies from a small, medium or multinational enterprise. In addition, batch sizing rules and product structure affect the costs of a company's inventory system (Lea and Fredendall, 2002). As example, let suppose a two-level supply chain adopting the NIS strategy where the downstream actor, a retailer, adopts the MMSE method. Moreover, let suppose that the retailer faces an *ARMA(2,1)* demand pattern and the average inventory level at the upstream level, a manufacturer, is equal to 1000 units. By adopting the DDI strategy where the retailer uses the SMA method, the manufacturer earns the reduction of nearly 40% of his average inventory level (Table 4), let's say 400 units, and then the average inventory level is equal to 600 instead of 1000 units. In the same way, by adopting the DDI strategy where the retailer uses the WMA/Newton method, the manufacturer earns an additional average saving of 8 units plus 400 units. Hence, our work provide supplementary inventory reductions based only on the forecasting method. The Newton method's implementation is not an exhausting task. The time and resources needed for such a method depends on the capacity of qualified human resources to implementation. Moreover, the initial implementation cost is unique. We then estimate that the costs associated with the sharing of the Newton weighting vector are negligible, especially when we know that the unit holding costs of some industry products are relatively high. Indeed, if we suppose that a manufacturer produces furniture that is stored in a warehouse and then shipped to retailers, the manufacturer must either lease or purchase warehouse space and pay for utilities, insurance, and security for the location. the company is responsible for paying the salaries of the personnel responsible for moving the goods in and out of the warehouse. In addition, the company is exposed to a certain risk of damage of the goods when moving to trucks or trains for shipping. All these factors are taken into account in the calculation of the unit inventory cost. Therefore, minimizing inventory costs is an important supply-chain management strategy. The inventory presents an asset account that requires significant cash outlays. The importance of this account is then linked to the decisions made by the managers, who must minimize it in order to maintain a reasonable level of liquidity for other purposes. For example, increasing the inventory balance by 20000 dollars means that less cash is available to operate the business each month. This situation is considered an opportunity cost. If a company wants to have more cash, it must sell its products as quickly as possible to reap its profits and move its business forward. The faster the money is raised, the more the company is able to develop its business in the short term. A commonly used indicator is the inventory turnover rate, which is calculated as the cost of goods sold divided by the average inventory (Lee et *al.*, 2015). For example, a company that has 1 million dollars in cost of goods sold and an inventory balance of 250,000 has a turnover ratio of 4. The goal is to increase sales and reduce the required amount of inventory so that the turnover ratio increases. By projecting our results of simulations on this indicator, the turnover ratio of the manufacturer where the retailer uses the WMA/ Newton method, is higher than that where the retailer uses the SMA method, because the average inventory level in the first case is lower than that in the second case $\tilde{I}^{DDI}_{WMA/Newton} \leq \tilde{I}^{DDI}_{SMA}$ for the same fixed cost of goods sold. Consequently, this capability of reducing the average inventory level and increasing the turnover ratio is one of the most important catalysts of an enterprise to enhance productivity and competition. As it was argued in this chapter, some typical contracts can be proposed by the upstream actor to his formal downstream actor, in order to collaborate with the aim of of creating common and shared opportunities of trust, transparency and future coordination.

We conclude our chapter with natural lines for future studies. First, the DDI strategy can still be evaluated using other forecasting methods. Second, it would be interesting to adopt the minimization of the bullwhip effect as the objective function of the WMA/Newton approach. Another direction is the consideration of multiobjective optimization for parallel improvements of the supply chain performance metrics.

REFERENCES

Ali, M. M., Babai, M. Z., Boylan, J. E., & Syntetos, A. A. (2017). Supply chain forecasting when information is not shared. *European Journal of Operational Research*, *260*(3), 984–994. doi:10.1016/j.ejor.2016.11.046

Ali, M. M., & Boylan, J. E. (2012). On the effect of non-optimal forecasting methods on supply chain downstream demand. *IMA Journal of Management Mathematics*, *23*(1), 81–98. doi:10.1093/imaman/dpr005

Ali, M. M., & Boylan, J. E. (2011). Feasibility principles for Downstream Demand Inference in supply chains. *The Journal of the Operational Research Society*, *62*(3), 474–482. doi:10.1057/jors.2010.82

Ali, M. M., Boylan, J. E., & Syntetos, A. A. (2012). Forecast errors and inventory performance under forecast information sharing. *International Journal of Forecasting*, *28*(4), 830–841. doi:10.1016/j.ijforecast.2010.08.003

Alsultanny, Y. (2012, April). Successful forecasting for knowledge discovery by statistical methods. In *2012 Ninth International Conference on Information Technology-New Generations* (pp. 584-588). IEEE. 10.1109/ITNG.2012.160

Alwan, L. C., Liu, J. J., & Yao, D. Q. (2003). Stochastic characterization of upstream demand processes in a supply chain. *IIE Transactions*, *35*(3), 207–219. doi:10.1080/07408170304368

Anand, K. S., & Goyal, M. (2009). Strategic information management under leakage in a supply chain. *Management Science*, *55*(3), 438–452. doi:10.1287/mnsc.1080.0930

Arnould, E. J., & Thompson, C. J. (2005). Consumer culture theory (CCT): Twenty years of research. *The Journal of Consumer Research*, *31*(4), 868–882. doi:10.1086/426626

Arshinder, K., Kanda, A., & Deshmukh, S. G. (2011). A Review on Supply Chain Coordination: Coordination Mechanisms, Managing Uncertainty and Research Directions. In *Supply Chain Coordination Under Uncertainty* (pp. 39–82). Springer. doi:10.1007/978-3-642-19257-9_3

Asgari, N., Nikbakhsh, E., Hill, A., & Farahani, R. Z. (2016). Supply chain management 1982–2015: A review. *IMA Journal of Management Mathematics*.

Badot, O., Carrier, C., Cova, B., Desjeux, D., & Filser, M. (2009). L'ethnomarketing: Un élargissement de la recherche en comportement du consommateur à l'ethnologie. [French Edition]. *Recherche et Applications en Marketing*, *24*(1), 93–111. doi:10.1177/076737010902400105

Benavent, C. (2016). Plateformes. Sites collaboratifs, marketplaces, réseaux sociaux… Comment ils influencent nos choix. FYP editions.

Boylan, J. E., & Johnston, F. R. (2003). Optimality and robustness of combinations of moving averages. *The Journal of the Operational Research Society*, *54*(1), 109–115. doi:10.1057/palgrave.jors.2601472

Cachon, G. P., & Fisher, M. (2000). Supply chain inventory management and the value of shared information. *Management Science*, *46*(8), 1032–1048. doi:10.1287/mnsc.46.8.1032.12029

Cachon, G. P., & Lariviere, M. A. (2005). Supply chain coordination with revenue-sharing contracts: Strengths and limitations. *Management Science*, *51*(1), 30–44. doi:10.1287/mnsc.1040.0215

Chen, J., & Bell, P. (2011). The impact of customer returns on decisions in a newsvendor problem with and without buyback policies. *International Transactions in Operational Research*, *18*(4), 473–491. doi:10.1111/j.1475-3995.2010.00797.x

Chen, B., Chen, X., & Kanzow, C. (2000a). A penalized Fischer-Burmeister NCP-function. *Mathematical Programming*, *88*(1), 211–216. doi:10.1007/PL00011375

Chen, F., Drezner, Z., Ryan, J. K., & Simchi-Levi, D. (2000b). Quantifying the bullwhip effect in a simple supply chain: The impact of forecasting, lead times, and information. *Management Science*, *46*(3), 436–443. doi:10.1287/mnsc.46.3.436.12069

Chen, Y., Zhao, H., & Yu, L. (2010, August). Demand forecasting in automotive aftermarket based on ARMA model. In *2010 International Conference on Management and Service Science* (pp. 1-4). IEEE. 10.1109/ICMSS.2010.5577867

Cheng, T. C. E., & Wu, Y. N. (2005). The impact of information sharing in a two-level supply chain with multiple retailers. *The Journal of the Operational Research Society*, *56*(10), 1159–1165. doi:10.1057/palgrave.jors.2601934

Cheung, K. L., & Lee, H. L. (2002). The inventory benefit of shipment coordination and stock rebalancing in a supply chain. *Management Science*, *48*(2), 300–306. doi:10.1287/mnsc.48.2.300.251

Cholez, C., Magrini, M. B., & Galliano, D. (2017). Les contrats de production en grandes cultures. Coordination et incitations par les coopératives. *Économie rurale. Agricultures, alimentations, territoires*, (360), 65-83.

Chu, C. L., & Leon, V. J. (2008). Power-of-two single-warehouse multi-buyer inventory coordination with private information. *International Journal of Production Economics, 111*(2), 562–574. doi:10.1016/j.ijpe.2006.12.063

Chu, F. L. (2009). Forecasting tourism demand with ARMA-based methods. *Tourism Management, 30*(5), 740–751. doi:10.1016/j.tourman.2008.10.016

Ciancimino, E., Cannella, S., Bruccoleri, M., & Framinan, J. M. (2012). On the bullwhip avoidance phase: The synchronised supply chain. *European Journal of Operational Research, 221*(1), 49–63. doi:10.1016/j.ejor.2012.02.039

Courtin, G. (2013). *Supply chain and the future of applications*. Research Report October 2013 by SCM World.

Croson, R., Donohue, K., Katok, E., & Sterman, J. (2014). Order stability in supply chains: Coordination risk and the role of coordination stock. *Production and Operations Management, 23*(2), 176–196. doi:10.1111/j.1937-5956.2012.01422.x

Disney, S. M., & Towill, D. R. (2002). A discrete transfer function model to determine the dynamic stability of a vendor managed inventory supply chain. *International Journal of Production Research, 40*(1), 179–204. doi:10.1080/00207540110072975

Dudek, G., & Stadtler, H. (2005). Negotiation-based collaborative planning between supply chains partners. *European Journal of Operational Research, 163*(3), 668–687. doi:10.1016/j.ejor.2004.01.014

Eckhaus, E. (2010). *Consumer Demand Forecasting: Popular Techniques, Part 1: Weighted and Unweighted Moving Average*. Academic Press.

Ervural, B. C., Beyca, O. F., & Zaim, S. (2016). Model estimation of ARMA using genetic algorithms: A case study of forecasting natural gas consumption. *Procedia: Social and Behavioral Sciences, 235*, 537–545. doi:10.1016/j.sbspro.2016.11.066

Fawcett, S. E., Osterhaus, P., Magnan, G. M., Brau, J. C., & McCarter, M. W. (2007). Information sharing and supply chain performance: The role of connectivity and willingness. *Supply Chain Management, 12*(5), 358–368. doi:10.1108/13598540710776935

Forslund, H., & Jonsson, P. (2007). The impact of forecast information quality on supply chain performance. *International Journal of Operations & Production Management, 27*(1), 90–107. doi:10.1108/01443570710714556

Gaur, V., Giloni, A., & Seshadri, S. (2005). Information Sharing in a Supply Chain under ARMA Demand. *Management Science*, *51*(6), 961–969. doi:10.1287/mnsc.1050.0385

Gittell, J. H., & Weiss, L. (2004). Coordination networks within and across organizations: A multi-level Framework. *Journal of Management Studies*, *41*(1), 127–153. doi:10.1111/j.1467-6486.2004.00424.x

Giannoccaro, I., & Pontrandolfo, P. (2004). Supply chain coordination by revenue sharing contracts. *International Journal of Production Economics*, *89*(2), 131–139. doi:10.1016/S0925-5273(03)00047-1

Gilbert, K. (2005). An ARIMA supply chain model. *Management Science*, *51*(2), 305–310. doi:10.1287/mnsc.1040.0308

Gong, W. (2010, August). ARMA-GRNN for passenger demand forecasting. In *2010 Sixth International Conference on Natural Computation* (Vol. 3, pp. 1577-1581). IEEE. 10.1109/ICNC.2010.5583711

Gordon, G., & Tibshirani, R. (2012). Karush-kuhn-tucker conditions. *Optimization, 10*(725/36), 725.

Gustavsson, P., & Nordström, J. (2001). The impact of seasonal unit roots and vector ARMA modelling on forecasting monthly tourism flows. *Tourism Economics*, *7*(2), 117–133. doi:10.5367/000000001101297766

Graves, S. C. (1999). A single-item inventory model for a nonstationary demand process. *Manufacturing & Service Operations Management*, *1*(1), 50–61. doi:10.1287/msom.1.1.50

Ha, A. Y., Tong, S., & Zhang, H. (2011). Sharing demand information in competing supply chains with production diseconomies. *Management Science*, *57*(3), 566–581. doi:10.1287/mnsc.1100.1295

Hays, C. L. (2004). What Wal-Mart knows about customers' habits. *The New York Times,* 14.

Henderson, J. (2018). *Supply Chain Digital.* https://www.supplychaindigital.com/scm/nine-automakers-share-supply-chain-data

Hosoda, T., & Disney, S. M. (2006). On variance amplification in a three-echelon supply chain with minimum mean square error forecasting. *Omega*, *34*(4), 344–358. doi:10.1016/j.omega.2004.11.005

Ireland, R. K., & Crum, C. (2005). *Supply chain collaboration: How to implement CPFR and other best collaborative practices*. J. Ross Publishing.

Jain, A., Seshadri, S., & Sohoni, M. (2011). Differential pricing for information sharing under competition. *Production and Operations Management*, *20*(2), 235–252. doi:10.1111/j.1937-5956.2010.01161.x

Jin, B. (2006). Performance implications of information technology implementation in an apparel supply chain. *Supply Chain Management*, *11*(4), 309–316. doi:10.1108/13598540610671752

Johnston, F. R., Boyland, J. E., Meadows, M., & Shale, E. (1999). Some properties of a simple moving average when applied to forecasting a time series. *The Journal of the Operational Research Society*, *50*(12), 1267–1271. doi:10.1057/palgrave.jors.2600823

Kalaoglu, Ö. İ., Akyuz, E. S., Ecemiş, S., & Eryuruk, S. H., Sümen, H., & Kalaoglu, F. (2015). Retail demand forecasting in clothing industry. *Tekstil ve Konfeksiyon*, *25*(2), 172–178.

Kapgate, D. (2014). Weighted moving average forecast model based prediction service broker algorithm for cloud computing. *International Journal of Computer Science and Mobile Computing*, *3*(2), 71–79.

Klein, R., Rai, A., & Straub, D. W. (2007). Competitive and cooperative positioning in supply chain logistics relationships. *Decision Sciences*, *38*(4), 611–646. doi:10.1111/j.1540-5915.2007.00172.x

Lambert, D. M., & Cooper, M. C. (2000). Issues in supply chain management. *Industrial Marketing Management*, *29*(1), 65–83. doi:10.1016/S0019-8501(99)00113-3

Larsen, T. S., Thernoe, C., & Andresen, C. (2003). Supply chain collaboration: Theoretical perspective and empirical evidence. *International Journal of Physical Distribution & Logistics Management*, *33*(6), 531–549. doi:10.1108/09600030310492788

Lea, B. R., & Fredendall, L. D. (2002). The impact of management accounting, product structure, product mix algorithm, and planning horizon on manufacturing performance. *International Journal of Production Economics*, *79*(3), 279–299. doi:10.1016/S0925-5273(02)00253-0

Lee, H. H., Zhou, J., & Hsu, P. H. (2015). The role of innovation in inventory turnover performance. *Decision Support Systems*, *76*, 35–44. doi:10.1016/j.dss.2015.02.010

Lee, H. L., & Whang, S. (2000). Information sharing in a supply chain. *International Journal of Manufacturing Technology and Management*, *1*(1), 79–93. doi:10.1504/IJMTM.2000.001329

Lee, H. L., So, K. C., & Tang, C. S. (2000). The value of information sharing in a two-level supply chain. *Management Science*, *46*(5), 626–643. doi:10.1287/mnsc.46.5.626.12047

Lemoine, J. F. (2003). Vers une approche globale de l'atmosphère du point de vente. *Revue française du marketing*, (194), 83.

Li, C. (2013). Controlling the bullwhip effect in a supply chain system with constrained information flows. *Applied Mathematical Modelling*, *37*(4), 1897–1909. doi:10.1016/j.apm.2012.04.020

Li, L. (2002). Information sharing in a supply chain with horizontal competition. *Management Science*, *48*(9), 1196–1212. doi:10.1287/mnsc.48.9.1196.177

Li, Y., Xu, X., Zhao, X., Yeung, J. H. Y., & Ye, F. (2012). Supply chain coordination with controllable lead time and asymmetric information. *European Journal of Operational Research*, *217*(1), 108–119. doi:10.1016/j.ejor.2011.09.003

Liouville, J. (2011). Enchères électroniques inversées et confiance dans les relations B to B. *REDACTION: Brahim BENABDESLEM Directeur Général de le revue Boualem ALIOUAT Rédacteur en chef*, *1*(1), 68.

Liu, J., Zhang, S., & Hu, J. (2005). A case study of an inter-enterprise workflow-supported supply chain management system. *Information & Management*, *42*(3), 441–454. doi:10.1016/j.im.2004.01.010

Lv, F., Ma, S., & Guan, X. (2015). The implication of capacity reservation contracts in assembly system with asymmetric demand information. *International Journal of Production Research*, *53*(18), 5564–5591. doi:10.1080/00207543.2015.1036150

Malone, T. W., & Crowston, K. (1990, September). What is coordination theory and how can it help design cooperative work systems? In *Proceedings of the 1990 ACM conference on Computer-supported cooperative work* (pp. 357-370). 10.1145/99332.99367

Mason, A. N., & Villalobos, J. R. (2015). Coordination of perishable crop production using auction mechanisms. *Agricultural Systems*, *138*, 18–30. doi:10.1016/j.agsy.2015.04.008

Mendelson, H. (2000). Organizational architecture and success in the information technology industry. *Management Science*, *46*(4), 513–529. doi:10.1287/mnsc.46.4.513.12060

Müller, R., & Turner, J. R. (2005). The impact of principal–agent relationship and contract type on communication between project owner and manager. *International Journal of Project Management*, *23*(5), 398–403. doi:10.1016/j.ijproman.2005.03.001

Pappas, S. S., Ekonomou, L., Karampelas, P., Karamousantas, D. C., Katsikas, S. K., Chatzarakis, G. E., & Skafidas, P. D. (2010). Electricity demand load forecasting of the Hellenic power system using an ARMA model. *Electric Power Systems Research*, *80*(3), 256–264. doi:10.1016/j.epsr.2009.09.006

Qi, L., & Sun, D. (1999). A survey of some nonsmooth Equations and smoothing Newton methods. In Progress in optimization (pp. 121-146). Springer.

Qian, Y., Chen, J., Miao, L., & Zhang, J. (2012). Information sharing in a competitive supply chain with capacity constraint. *Flexible Services and Manufacturing Journal*, *24*(4), 549–574. doi:10.100710696-011-9102-7

Raghunathan, S. (2001). Information sharing in a supply chain: A note on its value when demand is nonstationary. *Management Science*, *47*(4), 605–610. doi:10.1287/mnsc.47.4.605.9833

Raghunathan, S. (2003). Impact of demand correlation on the value of and incentives for information sharing in a supply chain. *European Journal of Operational Research*, *146*(3), 634–649. doi:10.1016/S0377-2217(02)00365-X

Richardson, D. C., Dale, R., & Kirkham, N. Z. (2007). The art of conversation is coordination. *Psychological Science*, *18*(5), 407–413. doi:10.1111/j.1467-9280.2007.01914.x PMID:17576280

Sahin, F., & Robinson, E. P. Jr. (2005). Information sharing and coordination in make-to-order supply chains. *Journal of Operations Management*, *23*(6), 579–598. doi:10.1016/j.jom.2004.08.007

Sanders, N. R. (2008). Pattern of information technology use: The impact on buyer–suppler coordination and performance. *Journal of Operations Management*, *26*(3), 349–367. doi:10.1016/j.jom.2007.07.003

Sanders, N. R., & Manrodt, K. B. (1994). Forecasting practices in US corporations: Survey results. *Interfaces*, *24*(2), 92–100. doi:10.1287/inte.24.2.92

Sanders, N. R., & Manrodt, K. B. (2003). Forecasting software in practice: Use, satisfaction, and performance. *Interfaces, 33*(5), 90–93. doi:10.1287/inte.33.5.90.19251

Shumway, R. H., & Stoffer, D. S. (2011). ARIMA models. In *Time Series Analysis and Its Applications* (pp. 83–171). Springer New York. doi:10.1007/978-1-4419-7865-3_3

Silver, E. A., Pyke, D. F., & Peterson, R. (1998). *Inventory management and production planning and scheduling* (Vol. 3). Wiley.

Sinha, S., & Sarmah, S. P. (2008). An application of fuzzy set theory for supply chain coordination. *International Journal of Management Science and Engineering Management, 3*(1), 19–32. doi:10.1080/17509653.2008.10671033

Sorensen, D. C. (1985). Analysis of pairwise pivoting in Gaussian elimination. *IEEE Transactions on Computers, C-34*(3), 274–278. doi:10.1109/TC.1985.1676570

Taghipour, A., & Frayret, J. M. (2013). Dynamic mutual adjustment search for supply chain operations planning co-ordination. *International Journal of Production Research, 51*(9), 2715–2739. doi:10.1080/00207543.2012.737952

Tliche, Y., Taghipour, A., & Canel-Depitre, B. (2019). Downstream Demand Inference in decentralized supply chains. *European Journal of Operational Research, 274*(1), 65–77. doi:10.1016/j.ejor.2018.09.034

Trapero, J. R., Kourentzes, N., & Fildes, R. (2012). Impact of information exchange on supplier forecasting performance. *Omega, 40*(6), 738–747. doi:10.1016/j.omega.2011.08.009

Trkman, P., Groznik, A., & Koohang, A. (2006). Measurement of supply chain integration benefits. *Interdisciplinary Journal of Information, Knowledge & Management, 1*.

Vandenberghe, L., & Boyd, S. (1996). Semidefinite programming. *SIAM Review, 38*(1), 49–95. doi:10.1137/1038003

Vosooghidizaji, M., Taghipour, A., & Canel-Depitre, B. (2019). Supply chain coordination under information asymmetry: A review. *International Journal of Production Research*, 1–30.

Vickery, S. K., Jayaram, J., Droge, C., & Calantone, R. (2003). The effects of an integrative supply chain strategy on customer service and financial performance: An analysis of direct versus indirect relationships. *Journal of Operations Management, 21*(5), 523–539. doi:10.1016/j.jom.2003.02.002

Wang, J. W., & Cheng, C. H. (2007, August). Information fusion technique for weighted time series model. In *2007 International Conference on Machine Learning and Cybernetics* (Vol. 4, pp. 1860-1865). IEEE. 10.1109/ICMLC.2007.4370451

Wenxia, X., Feijia, L., Shuo, L., Kun, G., & Guodong, L. (2015, August). Design and application for the method of dynamic weighted moving average forecasting. In *2015 Sixth International Conference on Intelligent Systems Design and Engineering Applications (ISDEA)* (pp. 278-280). IEEE. 10.1109/ISDEA.2015.77

Xie, J., Liang, L., Liu, L., & Ieromonachou, P. (2017). Coordination contracts of dual-channel with cooperation advertising in closed-loop supply chains. *International Journal of Production Economics*, *183*, 528–538. doi:10.1016/j.ijpe.2016.07.026

Xu, H., Yao, N., & Tong, S. (2013). Sourcing under cost information asymmetry when facing time-sensitive customers. *International Journal of Production Economics*, *144*(2), 599–609. doi:10.1016/j.ijpe.2013.04.023

Ye, F., Li, Y., & Yang, Q. (2018). Designing coordination contract for biofuel supply chain in China. *Resources, Conservation and Recycling*, *128*, 306–314. doi:10.1016/j.resconrec.2016.11.023

Yu, Z., Yan, H., & Edwin Cheng, T. C. (2001). Benefits of information sharing with supply chain partnerships. *Industrial Management & Data Systems*, *101*(3), 114–121. doi:10.1108/02635570110386625

Yu, Z., Yan, H., & Cheng, T. C. E. (2002). Modelling the benefits of information sharing-based partnerships in a two-level supply chain. *The Journal of the Operational Research Society*, *53*(4), 436–446. doi:10.1057/palgrave.jors.2601255

Zhang, X. (2004). Evolution of ARMA demand in supply chains. *Manufacturing & Service Operations Management*, *6*(2), 195–198. doi:10.1287/msom.1040.0042

Zhao, H. F., & Zhu, C. (2017, June). Service supply chain coordination contract considering advertising level. In *2017 International Conference on Service Systems and Service Management* (pp. 1-5). IEEE. 10.1109/ICSSSM.2017.7996143

Zhao, Y., & Zhao, X. (2015). On human decision behavior in multi-echelon inventory management. *International Journal of Production Economics*, *161*, 116–128. doi:10.1016/j.ijpe.2014.12.005

APPENDIX A. RETAILER'S ORDERS TIME-SERIES STRUCTURE WHEN WMA METHOD IS ADOPTED

Using WMA method, the demand forecast at time period t+1 is written as follows:

$$f_{t+1} = \sum_{i=1}^{N} x_i D_{t+1-i}$$

The lead-time demand forecast f_{t+1}^{L} is given by:

$$f_{t+1}^{L} = L\left(\sum_{i=1}^{N} x_i D_{t+1-i}\right)$$

Now, the OUT level is calculated by:

$$S_t = f_{t+1}^{L} + z\text{£}$$

Where z is the safety factor and Σ is the standard deviation of the noise in the lead-time demand (Silver et *al.*, 1998). The orders from the downstream actor to the upstream actor are calculated by summing the demand at the downstream actor plus any change in the OUT level in the current period.

$$Y_t = S_t - S_{t-1} + D_t$$

$$\Leftrightarrow Y_t = f_{t+1}^{L} + z\text{£} - f_t^{L} - z\text{£} + D_t$$

$$\Leftrightarrow Y_t = f_{t+1}^{L} - f_t^{L} + D_t$$

By substituting f_{t+1}^{L} ad f_t^{L} by their respective expressions, we obtain the following results:

$$Y_t = L\left(\sum_{i=1}^{N} x_i D_{t+1-i}\right) - L\left(\sum_{i=1}^{N} x_i D_{t-i}\right)$$

$$\Leftrightarrow Y_t = L\left(x_1 D_t - x_1 D_{t-1} + x_2 D_{t-1} - x_2 D_{t-2} + \ldots + x_N D_{t-N+1} - x_N D_{t-N}\right) + D_t$$

$$\Leftrightarrow Y_t = c + \phi_1 Y_{t-1} + \ldots + \phi_p Y_{t-p} + \left[L\left(\sum_{i=1}^{N} x_i \left(\xi_{t-i+1} - \xi_{t-i} \right) \right) + \xi_t \right] +$$

$$\theta_1 \left[L\left(\sum_{i=1}^{N} x_i \left(\xi_{t-i} - \xi_{t-i-1} \right) \right) + \xi_{t-1} \right] + \theta_2 \left[L\left(\sum_{i=1}^{N} x_i \left(\xi_{t-i-1} - \xi_{t-i-2} \right) \right) + \xi_{t-2} \right] + \ldots +$$

$$\theta_q \left[L\left(\sum_{i=1}^{N} x_i \left(\xi_{t-i-q+1} - \xi_{t-i-q} \right) \right) + \xi_{t-q} \right].$$

Let consider $\tilde{\xi}_t = L\left(\sum_{i=1}^{N} x_i \left(\xi_{t-i+1} - \xi_{t-i} \right) \right) + \xi_t$, so Y_t can finally be expressed as follows:

$$Y_t = c + \phi_1 Y_{t-1} + \ldots + \phi_p Y_{t-p} + \tilde{\xi}_t + \theta_1 \tilde{\xi}_{t-1} + \theta_2 \tilde{\xi}_{t-2} + \ldots + \theta_q \tilde{\xi}_{t-q}$$

$$\Leftrightarrow Y_t = c + \sum_{j=1}^{p} \phi_j Y_{t-j} + \tilde{\xi}_t + \sum_{j=1}^{q} \theta_j \tilde{\xi}_{t-j}$$

Hence, Y_t follows an $ARMA(p,q)$ process where

$$\tilde{\xi}_t \to N\left(0, \left[L^2 \left(x_1^2 + x_N^2 + \sum_{i=1}^{N-1} \left(x_{i+1} - x_i \right)^2 \right) + 2Lx_1 + 1 \right] \sigma_\xi^2 \right)$$

are the error terms. Indeed, it's easy to check the following errors properties:

$$E\left(\tilde{\xi}_t\right) = E\left(L\left(\sum_{i=1}^{N} x_i \left(\xi_{t-i+1} - \xi_{t-i} \right) \right) + \xi_t \right) = 0$$

And

$$\Leftrightarrow Var\left(\tilde{\xi}_t\right) = L^2 Var\left(\sum_{i=1}^{N} x_i \left(\xi_{t-i+1} - \xi_{t-i} \right) \right) + Var\left(\xi_t\right) + 2cov\left(L\left(\sum_{i=1}^{N} x_i \left(\xi_{t-i+1} - \xi_{t-i} \right) \right), \xi_t \right)$$

$$\Leftrightarrow Var\left(\tilde{\xi}_t\right) = L^2\left[Var\left(x_1\left(\xi_t - \xi_{t-1}\right) + x_2\left(\xi_{t-1} - \xi_{t-2}\right) + \ldots + x_N\left(\xi_{t-N+1} - \xi_{t-N}\right)\right)\right]$$
$$+\sigma_\xi^2 + 2L\, cov\left(\left(\sum_{i=1}^{N} x_i\left(\xi_{t-i+1} - \xi_{t-i}\right)\right), \xi_t\right)$$

$$\Leftrightarrow Var\left(\tilde{\xi}_t\right) = L^2\left[Var\left(x_1\xi_t - x_1\xi_{t-1} + x_2\xi_{t-1} - x_2\xi_{t-2} + \ldots + x_N\xi_{t-N-1} - x_N\xi_{t-N}\right)\right]$$
$$+\sigma_\xi^2 + 2L\, cov\left(\left(\sum_{i=1}^{N} x_i\left(\xi_{t-i+1} - \xi_{t-i}\right)\right), \xi_t\right)$$

$$\Leftrightarrow Var\left(\tilde{\xi}_t\right) = \left[L^2\left(x_1^2 + x_N^2 + \sum_{i=1}^{N-1}\left(x_{i+1} - x_i\right)^2\right) + 2Lx_1 + 1\right]\sigma_\xi^2$$

As all the parameters of Y_t, namely, the constant c, ϕ_j and θ_j are unique, the order process Y_t arriving at the upstream actor is also unique and thus, the upstream actor is able to infer the demand arriving at his formal downstream actor.

APPENDIX B. DERIVATION OF THE MEAN SQUARED ERROR EXPRESSION WHEN WMA METHOD IS ADOPTED

We derive the three components of equation (4a). The first term of equation (4a) is given by Tliche et *al.*, (2019) as follows:

$$Var\left(\sum_{i=1}^{L+1} D_{t+i}\right) = \left(L+1\right)\gamma_0 + 2\sum_{i=1}^{L} i\gamma_{L+1-i}$$

We go on to calculate the second term of equation (4a):

$$Var\left(f_{t+1}\right) = Var\left(\sum_{i=1}^{N} x_i D_{t+1-i}\right) = \sum_{i=1}^{N} x_i^2 Var\left(D_{t+1-i}\right) + 2\sum_{i=1}^{N-1}\sum_{j=i+1}^{N} Cov(x_i D_{t+1-i}, x_j D_{t+1-j}).$$

$$\Leftrightarrow Var\left(f_{t+1}\right) = \gamma_0 \sum_{i=1}^{N} x_i^2 + 2\sum_{i=1}^{N-1}\left[Cov\left(x_i D_{t+1-i}, x_{i+1} D_{t-i}\right) + \ldots + Cov\left(x_i D_{t+1-i}, x_N D_{t+1-N}\right)\right]$$

$$\Leftrightarrow Var\left(f_{t+1}\right)=\gamma_0\sum_{i=1}^{N}x_i^2+2\Big[\Big[Cov\left(x_1D_t,x_2D_{t-1}\right)+\ldots+Cov\left(x_1D_t,x_ND_{t+1-N}\right)\Big]$$
$$+\Big[Cov\left(x_2D_{t-1},x_3D_{t-2}\right)+\ldots+Cov\left(x_2D_{t-1},x_ND_{t+1-N}\right)\Big]+\ldots+Cov\left(x_{N-1}D_{t+2-N},x_ND_{t+1-N}\right)\Big]$$

$$\Leftrightarrow Var\left(f_{t+1}\right)=\gamma_0\sum_{i=1}^{N}x_i^2+2\Big[\left[x_1x_2\gamma_1+\ldots+x_1x_N\gamma_{N-1}\right]+\left[x_2x_3\gamma_1+\ldots+x_2x_N\gamma_{N-2}\right]+\ldots+x_{N-1}x_N\gamma_1\Big]$$

$$\Leftrightarrow Var\left(f_{t+1}\right)=\gamma_0\sum_{i=1}^{N}x_i^2+2\left[x_1\sum_{i=2}^{N}x_i\gamma_{i-1}+x_2\sum_{i=3}^{N}x_i\gamma_{i-2}+\ldots+x_{N-1}\sum_{i=N}^{N}x_i\gamma_{i-(N-1)}\right]$$

$$\Leftrightarrow Var\left(f_{t+1}\right)=\gamma_0\sum_{i=1}^{N}x_i^2+2\sum_{j=1}^{N-1}\left(x_j\sum_{i=j+1}^{N}x_i\gamma_{i-j}\right)$$

Consequently,

$$\left(L+1\right)^2 Var\left(f_{t+1}\right)=\left(L+1\right)^2\left[\gamma_0\sum_{i=1}^{N}x_i^2+2\sum_{j=1}^{N-1}\left(x_j\sum_{i=j+1}^{N}x_i\gamma_{i-j}\right)\right]$$

We go on to calculate the third term of equation (4a):

$$Cov\left(\sum_{i=1}^{L+1}D_{t+i},f_{t+1}\right)=Cov\left(\sum_{i=1}^{L+1}D_{t+i},\sum_{i=1}^{N}x_iD_{t+1-i}\right)=\sum_{i=1}^{L+1}\sum_{j=1}^{N}x_jCov\left(D_{t+i},D_{t+1-j}\right)$$

$$\Leftrightarrow Cov\left(\sum_{i=1}^{L+1}D_{t+i},f_{t+1}\right)=\sum_{i=1}^{L+1}\sum_{j=1}^{N}x_jCov\left(D_t,D_{t+1-i-j}\right)=\sum_{i=1}^{L+1}\sum_{j=1}^{N}x_j\gamma_{i+j-1}$$

Consequently,

$$-2\left(L+1\right)Cov\left(\sum_{i=1}^{L+1}D_{t+i},f_{t+1}\right)=-2\left(L+1\right)\sum_{i=1}^{L+1}\sum_{j=1}^{N}x_j\gamma_{i+j-1}$$

Finally, summing the three obtained components leads us to obtain equation (4).

APPENDIX C. DERIVATION OF THE AVERAGE INVENTORY LEVEL EXPRESSION WHEN WMA METHOD IS ADOPTED

We derive the four components of equation (5c). The first term is expressed as follows:

$$M_t^{DDI}(x) = E\left(\sum_{i=1}^{L+1} f_{t+i}\right) = E\left(\sum_{i=1}^{L+1}\sum_{j=1}^{N} x_j D_{t+i-j}\right) = E\left(\sum_{j=1}^{N} x_j \left(D_{t+1-j} + \ldots + D_{t+L+1-j}\right)\right)$$

$$\Leftrightarrow M_t^{DDI}(x) = E\left(x_1\left(D_t + \ldots + D_{t+L}\right) + x_2\left(D_{t-1} + \ldots + D_{t+L-1}\right) + \ldots + x_N\left(D_{t+1-N} + \ldots + D_{t+L+1-N}\right)\right)$$

$$\Leftrightarrow M_t^{DDI}(x) = x_1(L+1)E(D_t) + x_2(L+1)E(D_t) + \ldots + x_N(L+1)E(D_t) = (L+1)\left(\sum_{i=1}^{N} x_i\right)\mu_d$$

$$\Leftrightarrow M_t^{DDI}(x) = \frac{c(L+1)}{\left(1-\sum_{j=1}^{p}\phi_j\right)}\left(\sum_{i=1}^{N} x_i\right) = \frac{c(L+1)}{\left(1-\sum_{j=1}^{p}\phi_j\right)}$$

The second term is expressed as follows:

$$K\sigma_{\xi}\sqrt{V^{DDI}(x)} = K\sigma_{\xi}\sqrt{MSE^{DDI}(x)}$$

Let y_t be the mean-centered order process at the manufacturer. The third term is expressed as follows:

$$-E\left(\sum_{i=1}^{L+1} Y_{t+i}\right) = -(L+1)\mu_y - E\left(\sum_{i=1}^{L+1} y_{t+i}\right)$$

$$\Leftrightarrow -E\left(\sum_{i=1}^{L+1} Y_{t+i}\right) = -(L+1)\mu_y - E\left(\sum_{i=1}^{L+1}\sum_{j=0}^{+\infty} \tilde{\psi}_j \tilde{\xi}_{t+i-j}\right) = -(L+1)\mu_y$$

$$\Leftrightarrow -E\left(\sum_{i=1}^{L+1} Y_{t+i}\right) = -c(L+1)\left(1-\sum_{j=1}^{p}\phi_j\right)^{-1}$$

The fourth term is expressed as follows:

$$E(Y_t) = \mu_y = \mu_d = \frac{c}{\phi_0 - \sum_{j=1}^{p} \phi_j} = c\left(1 - \sum_{j=1}^{p} \phi_j\right)^{-1}$$

Finally, substituting the four components by their respective expressions in equation (5c), we obtain the equation (5).

[1] Please refer to Shumway and Stoffer (2011) for more details on *ARMA* models, causality and invertibility.

Chapter 2
Designing Valid Humanitarian Logistics Scenario Sets:
Application to Recurrent Peruvian Floods and Earthquakes

Jorge Vargas-Florez
Pontifical Catholic University of Peru, Peru

Matthieu Lauras
Industrial Engineering Center, IMT Mines Albi, University of Toulouse, France

Tina Comes
Delft University of Technology, The Netherlands

ABSTRACT

Literature about humanitarian logistics (HL) has developed a lot of innovative decision support systems during the last decades to support decisions such as location, routing, supply, or inventory management. Most of those contributions are based on quantitative models but, generally, are not used by practitioners who are not confident with. This can be explained by the fact that scenarios and datasets used to design and validate those HL models are often too simple compared to the real situations. In this chapter, a scenario-based approach based on a five-step methodology has been developed to bridge this gap by designing a set of valid scenarios able to assess disaster needs in regions subject to recurrent disasters. The contribution, usable by both scholars and practitioners, demonstrates that defining such valid scenario sets is possible for recurrent disasters. Finally, the proposal is validated on a concrete application case based on Peruvian recurrent flood and earthquake disasters.

DOI: 10.4018/978-1-7998-3805-0.ch002

INTRODUCTION

A variety of approaches, ranging from analytical models and theories to case studies, have been considered to manage risks during disaster operations. In the field of Humanitarian Logistics (HL), mathematical programming is the most frequently used research methodology (Galindo and Batta, 2013). While the use of optimization tools and algorithms has been shown to have a great potential to improve disaster management practices, they are rarely used in the field (Laguna Salvadó *et al.*, 2015; Laguna Salvadó *et al.*, 2016). Hence, the lack of an easy-to-use and established approach to risk assessment means that in practice, decision-makers often refer to their experience and intuition, which can lead to a range of biases and loss of performance (Comes, 2016). As demonstrated by (Charles et al., 2016), this statement is mainly due to research works that frequently use fictitious scenarios and data compensating for the lack of information. This approach fails to validate whether decision support systems can be successfully applied in the actual context of disaster relief (Charles et al., 2016). Real cases, or at least realistic ones, with accurate data are necessary to enable practitioners to be confident with the results of scholar and to start to use them concretely in the field. This chapter tackles this issue by suggesting an innovative methodology able to generate valid and realistic scenario sets on future disaster trends as suggested by (Galindo and Batta, 2013; Pedraza-Martinez and Van Wassenhove, 2013). We therefore develop a series of requirements that are designed to support researchers in producing valid and plausible scenarios for their quantitative decision support systems that are tailored to fit the needs and standards of field-based decision-makers. Basically, such systems should be able to support HL decisions such as location-allocation, routing or inventory management for instance.

When referring to disasters, most of us will intuitively refer to mega-disasters such as Indonesia's tsunami in 2004, Haiti's earthquake in 2010, Japan's earthquake / tsunami in 2011 or Nepal's earthquake in 2015. Although all those cases have had dramatic consequences, they are far from typical for disaster response. Ferris *et al.* (2013) define the notion of "recurrent disaster" as "*the repeated occurrence of a unique natural hazard in the same geographical region*". Since 2000, each year, more than 400 disasters have been recorded in the disaster database EM-DAT (http://www.emdat.be). More than 90% of those disasters recur in the same regions: cyclones in the Caribbean, earthquakes in the Pacific Ring of Fire or floods in South-Eastern Asia. In this chapter, we focus on recurrent disasters, which constitute the great majority of disasters.

To conduct empirically grounded work that enables HL practitioners to analyse the implications of their HL decisions (such as planning, routing, allocating…), we suggest using a scenario-based approach. Scenario based reasoning has been advocated for its flexibility and appeal to the user, particularly in complex situations (Comes *et al.*, 2015). Scenarios are understood as a means for exploring eventualities before they occur. They support users to think through a variety of different situations, and as such are well-positioned for HL decisions support. We here propose an approach that avoids some of the most common pitfalls of a too narrow or biased set of scenarios, which reflects opinions of a small number of experts, or is subject to groupthink (Wright *et al.*, 2009; Comes *et al.*, 2012). Our approach guarantees that each individual scenario is sufficiently plausible (i.e. a good assessment of truth (Bosch, 2010)) and relevant for feeding HL decision support systems.

The remainder of this chapter is divided into four parts. The subsequent section will present a literature review and overview of research statements. The third section will describe the proposed scenario method and its associated tools. The fourth section will develop an application case based on real data on HL preparedness for Peruvian recurrent disasters. The final section will then discuss the limitations of the approach and derive implications for research and practice.

BACKGROUND

Scenario-Based Hazard Prediction

With increasing digitalization and the growing involvement of affected populations and volunteer & technical communities in the response to disasters, there is henceforth no shortage in information about disasters (Van de Walle and Comes, 2015). Disaster databases focus on few core data sets and facilitate analyses across countries, regions or over time. EM-DAT, the most prominent example of such a database, provides data on over 18,000 disasters worldwide from 1900 to present. An open question is how to exploit this wealth of information to provide support to HL decision-makers in practice.

Most authors working on disaster forecasts track past occurrences to characterize recurrent disasters. Predictive methods have been developed for various natural hazards such as floods (Braman *et al.*, 2013; Ndille and Belle, 2014), cyclones (Tatham *et al.*, 2012) or earthquakes (WGCEP, 2008). Most of these models aim to specify the time, location, and magnitude of a future hazard with a probability of occurrence. Historic data enables analyses of trends and developments. In the context of the Climate Change prediction, it is widely expected that there will be more disasters, many of which will be of small or medium scale.

Charles *et al.* (2016) analysed African casualties' patterns (seasonality, location and affected population), and showed that future occurrences, though highly uncertain, *can* be predicted. Vargas *et al.* (2016) confirmed this by studying South

American recurrent disasters. Other researchers (Kovács *et al.*, 2007; Peres *et al.*, 2012) consider that for small and medium disasters, future occurrences will be globally like previous ones.

From Assessing Disaster Risks to Forecasting

Although they are cyclical in nature, individual instances of recurrent disasters are not easily anticipated in terms of their exact time, location, frequency, or magnitude. Driven by an ever more quickly changing socio-economic environment and migrating populations, the disaster needs at local level are even harder to predict (Vitoriano *et al.*, 2013).

In the context of disaster risk reduction, most predictive approaches focus on a combination of hazard (event), exposure (elements at risk) and vulnerability or resilience (Djalante et al., 2011; Merz *et al.*, 2013). The hazard dimension is typically modelled through dedicated meteorological, geological, seismic etc. models, which provide an assessment about the magnitude of specific events that have a given likelihood of occurrence (Karimi and Höllermeier, 2007). The exposure dimension is determined by the topography, demographic and socio-economic structure of a country or region, typically measured in terms of the value of social capital, infrastructure and assets affected by the hazard event (Birkmann *et al.*, 2013).

The vulnerability dimension is defined as "*the characteristics and circumstances of a community, system or asset that make it susceptible to the damaging effects of a hazard*" (UNDP, 2004). While vulnerability is fundamental in explaining disaster impact, it is not sufficient. The importance of resilience as counterpart of vulnerability was highlighted by many authors, as shown by Djalante *et al.* (2011), Peres *et al.* (2012), Vitoriano *et al.* (2013) or Aldunce *et al.* (2014). There is, today, a plethora of resilience definitions, which focus on different systems or aspects of resilience. In this chapter, we follow Peres *et al.* (2012), understanding resilience as the "*capacity to resist and to recover after exposition of a system, community or society, to hazards*".

Based on those elements our ambition is to make the step from disaster impact to needs assessment, and thus close the gap in the sequence of assessing *damage – impact – needs*. Disaster impact is defined by (UNISDR, 2009) as, "*the potential disaster losses, in lives, health status, livelihoods, assets and services, which could occur to a particular community or a society over some specified future time*". While Wisner *et al.* (2004) showed that disaster impact is a function of vulnerability, UNESCAP (2008) indicates that disaster impact is a function of both resilience and vulnerability.

The question of assessing the impact of disasters *a priori* has not yet received sufficient attention in literature. Most work in the disaster-risk domain focuses on modelling the direct impact and damage resulting from a disaster, not on the resulting disaster needs. Recently, a prediction and demand forecasting model was presented for longer term disaster projects of a single organization (van der Laan *et al.*, 2016). However, their forecasts relied on clearly defined project aims that are typical for long-term response to slow-onset disasters or conflicts. Similarly, in a study for the International Federation of Red Cross that has received much attention in disaster practice, (Dieckhaus *et al.*, 2011) present a global framework for assessing demands. This approach enables better sourcing strategies and positioning of warehouses in a context, in which risks can be pooled over longer periods of time or geographical regions.

In contrast, in the context of the national or local response to sudden onset disasters most authors assume that "*urgent needs related to sudden and unpredictable disasters with shifting demand*" (Balcik *et al.*, 2015) need to be met. Many authors therefore circumvent the planning problem and focus on responsiveness of supply chains (Balcik *et al.*, 2015), or their agility (Charles and Lauras, 2011; Charles *et al.*, 2010; Oloruntoba and Gray, 2006). Some further research has also been done on the assessment of needs *a posteriori* (Xu *et al.*, 2010; Zhang *et al.*, 2012), but there are no studies that forecast disaster needs in recurrent sudden-onset disasters that provide an overview of the disaster needs across clusters or organizations before a disaster occurs.

Designing Relevant and Valid Scenarios

Scenarios used in scientific approaches can perform two fundamentally different representational functions (Frigg and Hartmann, 2012): a scenario can be a representation of a selected part of the world (model of data) or a scenario can simulate the consequences of implementing the theory, policy or decision (model of theory). Since our objective is creating valid scenario sets to feed HL quantitative models, we understand scenarios here as "models of data".

Numerous such models of data have been developed over the last decades, many of them in the context of stochastic programming and Monte-Carlo simulations (Dupačová *et al.*, 2000; Di Domenica *et al.*, 2007; Klibi and Martel, 2012). More recently, researchers adapted scenarios for use in HL models, particularly in the context of disaster aid (Peres *et al.*, 2012; Galindo and Batta, 2013). Although those models are interesting from a mathematical programming standpoint, they are usually not implemented through a valid model of real data. Consequently, these proposals need to be reconsidered as they are not meeting the requirements of plausibility.

HL Scenario Definition

Respecting previous comments and scenario requirements (Comes *et al.*, 2015), we define a HL scenario by:

- A trigger event (disaster characteristics) and its probability of occurrence.
- A period: time horizon (overall duration) and frequency (intervals).
- A set of geographical regions potentially affected.
- A set of sourcing capacities: inventory of sourcing options that exist or might exist in the network. Each potential source should be defined through its existing or expected capabilities (types of products that can be delivered) and capacities (volume of products that can be delivered).
- A set of disaster needs (demand): expected number of victims per region affected and per period. Disaster practitioners can then translate this into product needs by considering international standards (e.g. http://www.SphereProject.org) or internal rules and practices.
- A set of HL capacities: assessment of required capacities (HL facilities, transportation infrastructures, etc.). These losses of capacities can be defined as percentages of the normal ones (i.e. 100% means that the HL capacity is fully available while 50% means that the available capacity is only half of the usual one). Those should be expressed per region and per period.

Such a scenario represents a *minimal set* of data and information that is required to inform properly HL decision-makers.

HL Scenario Creation

There is a wealth of methods that has been used in practice and research to create scenarios (Carter *et al.*, 2004; Comes *et al.*, 2014). But none of those methods completely meets the requirements of field-based practitioners in terms of content (see above), computation time, scope, granularity, update frequency and transparency / ease of understanding. Lacking a suitable formal method that is quick and easy to use, disasters will most often rely on their own expertise or experience (Mendonca *et al.*, 2006) – leading to inefficiencies and misallocations.

A suitable scenario creation technique for the HL context thus requires the definition of plausible scenarios and to assign them reliable probabilities. For operational decision-making, a relatively small number of scenarios needs to be identified as a basis for reasoning. As resources are typically short in the heat of a disaster requirement, the run-time needs to be minimized of both the scenario creation and the mathematical model. Based on (Tietje, 2005; Comes *et al.*, 2015), we conclude that the creation of valid scenario sets should include two complementary steps:

- The generation of a large set of accurate and representative scenarios;
- The selection of a covering sub-set able to answer the question asked.

Proposal

Our research objective is to generate a covering set of valid scenarios for improving HL performance. To reach this goal, we have defined a five-step methodology, as described in Figure 1:

Figure 1. Five-step methodology to define valid scenario sets

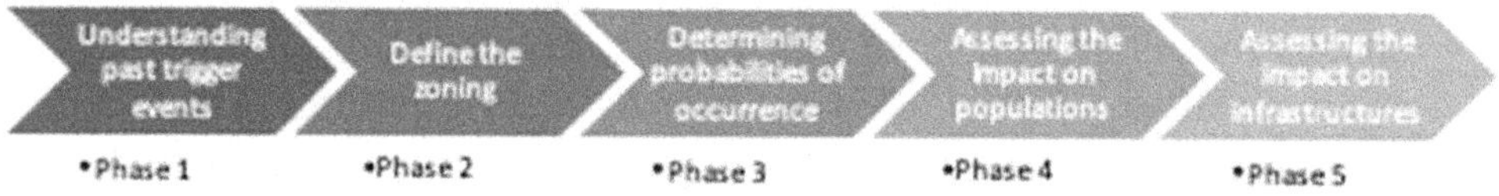

Phase 1. Understanding past trigger events.

This first phase consists in analysing past disaster characteristics through a review of past disasters. Dedicated databases provide a lot of information on past events: date; localization; phenomenon typology; geomorphology; intensity; impacts on different areas and duration of the phenomenon. In our study, we assume that the quality and the exhaustiveness of the databases are sufficiently rich for data-based analyses and forecasting.

Since we study recurrent disasters, the time frame needs to be sufficiently large to be representative. Data needed can be provided by specific national or topical databases or by generic ones such as the OFDA/CRED International Disaster Database (EM-DAT, http://www.emdat.be/database).

Phase 2. Defining the zoning

This phase consists in proposing a geographical grid of the territory concerned. This division should be coherent with the natural phenomena, but also with the administrative and organizational boundaries. To reach this goal, socio-demographic, geomorphological, climatological or administrative information is used. Experts (on floods, earthquakes, landslides or local politics for instance) should be solicited.

In addition to zoning, this phase must allow the characterization of how spreads a hazard. The analysis of data gathered during step 1 should allow an understanding of the cause-effects relationships that exist between the different zones. In simple cases, a correlation matrix between each zone will be defined. In more complex cases, specific functions should be established with dedicated experts. Usually, those experts / institutions can establish the sensitivity that exists between two regions regarding such or such a phenomenon and formulate the propagation function of this sensitivity. As an example, for an earthquake, the border region between two regions could be considered as a Sensitive Zone (SZ) if the seismic wave will propagate strongly into it, or a Non-Sensitive Zone (NSZ) if a geological barrier, such as a mountain or sea, will alleviate the intensity of the seismic wave.

Phase 3. Determining probabilities of occurrence

The aim of this phase is to build a set of scenarios, with an estimation of their probabilities of occurrence. For this purpose, we assume that there is a quasi-periodical value for disasters per fixed time. This assumption is only valid because we are working on "recurrent disasters". In practice, we use here the data gathered in phase 1. To determine the region where the epicentre of the disaster is located, we calculate the percentage of past disasters in each region determined in phase 2.

A disaster event is defined by both its occurrence and its intensity. Consequently, a scenario must include a probability of occurrence of a given intensity. For instance, it could indicate that 45% of the earthquakes of a given region (see Phase #2) have a magnitude between 6 and 7 on the Richter scale. To reach this goal, we decided to consider intensity through intervals. In the case of earthquakes for instance, a scenario might be defined through 5 classes of intensity (magnitude below 5.5; between 5.5 and 6; between 6 and 7; between 7 and 8, and above 8). Then, based on data gathered in Phase #1, we calculate the percentage of earthquakes belonging to each class. As we focus on "recurrent" disasters, extreme events are excluded from our statistics.

Finally, the number of scenarios generated can vary from 0 to n, in which n is the number of intervals of intensity. The phenomenon-oriented zoning (Phase #2) associated to the impact-oriented definition of scenarios (phase 3) allow defining a set of scenarios that is representative and manageable as the number of intervals is necessarily limited. Since extreme events are discarded, in some cases less than 100% of the gathered data during phase 1 will be kept. We suggest verifying that at least 75% of the whole data recorded in phase 1 is represented. If it is less than 75%, it means that the region is not mainly affected by recurrent phenomena but by chaotic ones. In that case, we do not respect our assumptions. It is obvious that this threshold is not absolute and can be discussed for each case.

Phase 4. Assessing the impact on populations

In this research, in accordance with the background discussed in previous sections, we assumed that the disaster-occurrence forecasts are like the previous recorded disasters. Consequently, disaster-demand forecasts will depend only on the future-disaster impact assessment. Based on these hypotheses, we propose the following approach to assess future disaster demand.

The first step consists in identifying the influencing factors that allow us qualifying the vulnerability and resilience of a potentially affected area. A literature review based on (Weichselgartner, 2001; UNDP, 2004; Alinovi *et al.*, 2009; Tveiten *et al.*, 2012; Aldunce *et al.*, 2014) allows us identifying 81 generic factors that could characterize the vulnerability and the resilience of impacted areas (see Tables 1 and 2).

Table 1. Influencing factors that can explain vulnerability in a territory.

Income and Food Access: Average per person daily income (local currency/person/day); Average per person daily expenditure (local currency / person/day); Household food insecurity access score; Dietary diversity and food frequency score, Dietary energy consumption (Kcal/person/day).
Access to Basic Services: Physical access to health services; Quality score of health services; Quality of educational system; Perception of security; Mobility and transport constraints; Water, electricity and phone networks.
Social Safety Nets: Amount of cash and in-kind assistance (local currency/person/day); Quality evaluation of assistance; Job assistance; Frequency of assistance (number of times assistance received last 6 months); Overall opinion of targeting.
Assets: Housing (number of rooms owned); Housing equipment index (TV, Car, etc.); Tropical livestock unit (TLU) equivalent to 25 K; Land owned (in hectares).
Adaptive Capacity: Diversity of incomes sources; Educational level (household average); Employment ratio (ratio, number of employed divided by household size); Available coping strategies; Food consumption ratio (by expenditure).
Stability: Number of household members that have lost their job; Income change; Expenditure change; Capacity to maintain stability in the future; Net safety dependency (share of transfers on the total income); Education system stability, the Human de Development Index (IDH).

The second step consists in selecting a subset of significant independent variables among influencing factors identified in step one. To support this step, we propose to use a Principal Component Analysis (PCA) (Jolliffe, 2002) to identify the discriminating variables associated with a given type of disaster. The objective consists in reducing the size of the problem and finding the discriminating variables that will be used in step three. In the following stage, only the discriminating variables will be used.

Table 2. Influencing factors that can explain resilience in a territory.

Exposure of resources: Zoning by seismic exposition, also inundation zones due to tsunami hazards.
Access to resources: Accessibility of resources in emergency situation.
Functional and vulnerability structures: Structural vulnerability; major bridges, interchanges; Structural function & vulnerability key health facilities.
Access to resources and vulnerability of the population: Access to resources (rate resource / population); Population by age; Population by access to services; Population without access to any services; Average population by households by room; Population without potable water; Population without drainage system; Population without electricity; Households with average people per room; Population living with dirt floors; Population settlements resulting from land's invasion; % Population that are newcomers to the district; % Population with low education; Accessibility due to urban design; Exposure to Hazards.
Vulnerability humanitarian response: Governance humanitarian response system; Quality of system, processes, services and tasks; Maturity and expertise humanitarian institutions; Decision and intervention centers available; Water supply hubs available; Food supply available; Health care available; Energy supply available; Transport, roads and accessibility available; Telecommunications available; Shelters area available; Waste dumps disposable areas available; Economic and finance support; Keep permanent measure system population vulnerability updated; Keep measure system hazard seismic updated; Keep measure system tsunami threat updated; Keep a database robustness and updated base

The third step consists in modelling the correlation formula that allows the future demand to be assessed, using a multivariate regression analysis (Hair *et al.*, 2006). For the occurrence of any given disaster, two different areas would not record the same impact due to their own vulnerability and resilience characteristics. Considering the previous frame, we define for each region impacted in the past, the following association:

$$\text{Past Disaster Impact} = f(V_1, V_2, \ldots, V_m; R_1, R_2, \ldots, R_n) \tag{1}$$

In which:

{V1, ..., Vm} are the vulnerability discriminating variables identified during the PCA analysis.

{R1, ..., Rn} are the resilience discriminating variables identified during the PCA analysis.

Based on these equations, we estimate, for a potential impacted localization and for a given period *t*, an expected gravity using a multivariate regression model. Following Sopipan *et al.* (2012), if explanatory independent variables have multi-collinearity, the forecasting calculation can be defined as:

Future Disaster impact= f_(t=1,…,T) (X_1,…,X_k,…,X_mxn) (2)

In which:

X_k is an independent variable composed of *{m x n}* values recorded in each period *t,* from a database which carries a total of *T* periods.

The fourth step consists in validating the relevance of the proposed regression models. To support this step, we propose carrying out a comparative analysis to measure the deviation between the forecast calculated by the model and the real needs that have been recorded in the field. This is defined as Ratio. We should note that the objective is to obtain a valid forecast that constitutes a rough estimate and not necessarily a very accurate estimate. The following deviation ratio criteria are proposed:

- If Ratio < 50% then the model is considered as "good";
- If Ratio < 100% then the model is considered as "admissible";
- If Ratio > 100% then the model is considered as "irrelevant".

Of course, those thresholds might appear quite high compared with commercial supply chain context, in which a Ratio of more than 80% is generally considered as irrelevant. But the standards of forecast accuracy differ from one sector to another. Due to the high level of uncertainty in disaster world, new thresholds must be defined. Of course, those ratios can be adapted for each case study in function of the targeted precision level.

Phase 5. Assessing the impact on infrastructures

To help those who need assistance after the disaster, disaster workers use available HL resources. Local infrastructures may have suffered from the disaster. An estimation of available capacity, together with an estimation of the impacts of the disaster on local infrastructures is therefore needed to evaluate the potential difficulty of aid delivery.

This phase starts with a review of the information on available infrastructures. This step must be based on HL database in which all the existing resources are identified. All these resources must be characterized through their capacities.

The second step of this phase consists in assessing the potential impact of a disaster on HL infrastructures in terms of transportation and warehousing capability limitations. Practically, we suggest building a propagation tree that describes all the cause-effect links that could exist between the regions. Let us consider an earthquake with a magnitude of 7.5 in region R1. This region is geographically connected with regions R2 and R3 represented by 2 branches of the propagation tree. R2 is a sensitive zone regarding earthquakes (big impact expected) whereas R3 is a non-sensitive zone (low impact expected). Based on geological and territorial expertise, we can estimate the potential impact on HL infrastructure in R2 and R3 in case of an earthquake of 7.5-magnitude earthquake in R1. This could be for instance that the warehousing capabilities could be reduced by 40% in region R2 and 10% in R3. Of course, this estimate is not deterministic and is subject to a high level of uncertainty. However, it provides an indication to decision-makers where to expect and prepare for damage to infrastructure.

At the end of these five phases, a plausible set of scenarios is defined. This set provides figures on the number of expected affected families and capacities of HL resources. The defined set of scenarios can be used to feed any kind of HL decision support systems. To illustrate benefits and limits of this proposal, an application on the recurrent impact of floods and earthquakes in Peru is provided in the following section.

Designing Post-Disaster Scenarios for HL in Peru

Peru is a country prone to natural hazards, including earthquakes, flooding, landslides and climatic shifts. In the following example, we applied the proposed methodology to define a set of valid scenarios that will, in future works, provide accurate and relevant information to feed HL decision-support systems dedicated to this context. The recurrent disasters considered in this study are only floods and earthquakes.

Phase 1: Gathering data on past disasters in Peru

The database used to generate plausible scenarios was built from Geophysical Institute of Peru (IGP) database. This database is considered as the most complete and reliable in the opinion of local experts. For earthquakes, more than 2500 events recorded in this database have been used for this study, with a period of data collection from 1970 to 2012. Regarding flooding events, National Institute of Civil Defence of Peru (INDECI) statistical reports were used on a ten-years period (2002 – 2012) to gather data. All information on localization, time, nature and intensity of past events has been recorded and analysed over those periods for both floods and earthquake disasters.

Phase 2: Defining the zoning of Peru

To define which area may suffer from the recurrent disasters given in the list of scenarios, specialized cartographies from IGP and INDECI were analysed respectively related to seismic and flooding zones. Based on this knowledge, it was possible to consider 24 regions as significant in terms of the natural phenomena studied (earthquakes and floods).

It is important to fully understand the topology of the territory because geographic and geological factors can influence the propagation of the wave of the disaster and can have a great incidence on HL. For example, an earthquake striking Lima will also affect the Ancash and Ica regions, because the seismic fault line follows the coast. However, it will not affect the Pasco and Junin regions though, as they are protected by the Andes Mountains. In this way, regarding an earthquake with its epicentre in Lima region, the Ancash and Ica regions will be considered as Sensitive Zones (SZ) whereas Pasco and Junin will be considered as Non-Sensitive Zones (NSZ).

Phase 3. Defining occurrences of recurrent disasters in Peru

The key parameters, such as magnitude, peak intensity, epicentre, time duration, and occurrence period can be correlated by means of simple functions (Corbi, 2013). For each region, we use past disaster occurrences to evaluate the probability of occurrence of a new disaster in the future, and its magnitude. For example, in the region around Lima, the probability of the occurrence of an earthquake is p=0.1 and If a disaster occurs, its magnitude is either low (p=0.96 of having a disaster with a magnitude M<6) or very high (p=0.04 of having an earthquake with a magnitude above 8 in this region). Table 3 provides the probabilities of occurrence for earthquakes and their intensity for each region, as defined in the previous phase.

To define a consistent list of scenarios, we select the most representative earthquakes. Every earthquake with a magnitude below 5.5 is discarded, because values below this range are related to seismic movements without an important disaster impact (such as Moquegua and Puno regions into as shown in Table 3). A new scenario is built for each non-empty class (value >0% in the last four column of the database). At the end of this phase, a list of 27 potential valid scenarios including "intensity" and "probability of occurrence" is built (see grey cells on Table 3). At this stage, the scenarios should be completed with an assessment of the quantity of victims, which is the main cause of uncertainty and discrepancy between researchers and practitioners. That is the purpose of the next phase.

Phase 4. Estimation of the amount of post-disaster victims

According to the methodology developed in the previous section, we applied a Principal Component Analysis (PCA) on the value of the Peru influencing factors for

Table 3. Probability of earthquakes' occurrences by Peruvian region.

No	Regions	M mean	M max	M critical	%	<5,5	5,5 - 6,0	6,0 - 7,0	7,0 - 8,0	8,0 - 9,0
1	Amazonas	4,8	4,8	7,3	1,3%	50%	0%	0%	50%	0%
2	Ancash	5,2	5,2	8,2	10,0%	75%	0%	0%	0%	25%
3	Apurimac	3,9	6,1	6,0	1,3%	86%	0%	14%	0%	0%
4	Arequipa	4,5	5,9	8,0	10,0%	93%	0%	0%	0%	7%
5	Ayacucho	5,6	5,9	6,7	1,3%	67%	0%	33%	0%	0%
6	Cajamarca	4,3	4,3	7,0	1,3%	88%	0%	0%	12%	0%
7	Cusco	4,6	6,3	7,2	1,3%	93%	0%	0%	7%	0%
8	Huancavelica	3,8	6,0	6,0	1,3%	89%	0%	11%	0%	0%
9	Huanuco	5,7	5,9	5,9	1,3%	60%	40%	0%	0%	0%
10	Ica	4,5	5,7	8,4	10,0%	86%	0%	0%	0%	14%
11	Junin	4,7	5,8	7,5	1,3%	82%	0%	0%	18%	0%
12	La Libertad	4,8	6,1	7,8	10,0%	86%	0%	0%	14%	0%
13	Lambayeque	4,5	6,3	6,3	1,3%	83%	0%	17%	0%	0%
14	Lima	4,2	6,3	8,4	10,0%	0%	96%	0%	0%	4%
15	Loreto	6,0	6,0	7,0	1,3%	0%	0%	75%	25%	0%
16	Madre de Dios	5,8	5,8	6,4	1,3%	0%	50%	50%	0%	0%
17	Moquegua	4,7	4,7	4,7	10,0%	100%	0%	0%	0%	0%
18	Pasco	5,5	5,6	5,6	1,3%	60%	40%	0%	0%	0%
19	Piura	4,5	7,1	6,7	1,3%	0%	0%	80%	20%	0%
20	Puno	4,8	4,8	4,8	1,3%	100%	0%	0%	0%	0%
21	San Martin	5,3	7,5	7,0	1,3%	0%	0%	80%	20%	0%
22	Tacna	5,4	5,4	8,6	10,0%	80%	0%	0%	0%	20%
23	Tumbes	5,0	5,0	7,7	10,0%	66%	0%	0%	34%	0%
24	Ucayali	5,2	5,2	6,7	1,3%	66%	0%	34%	0%	0%
					100,0%					

the years 1993 to 2007. Concerning our problem, it appears that three of them were particularly discriminating (more than 85% of the variance): Human Development Index (IDH), Precariousness of Buildings (or Vulnerability Construction to Seism: VCS), and Insecurity (or Number of Crimes and Delinquency: NCD). Of course, this result is only valid for this country and cannot be generalized for other territories.

Based on this result, and on the historical data on the number of victims associated with past disasters since 1993, we established the equations of regression for each one of the 24 regions (see Table 4). These equations explain the relationships that exist between the number of victims per year and per region and the values of the three discriminating influence factors. The overall significant dependencies between variables were tested and validated through the Fischer test. The numerical

Table 4. Multivariate regression models for each one of the 24 Peruvian regions.

No	Regions	Multivariate Equations
1	Amazonas	+38035,515*IDH+0,857*NCD+30227,91*VCS-40410,026
2	Ancash	+16826,995*IDH+0,686*NCD-2581,551*VCS-11168,97
3	Apurímac	+34299,477*IDH-5,995*NCD+91063,601*VCS-91550,67
4	Arequipa	+348649*IDH-10,623*NCD+814492,233*VCS-240522,978
5	Ayacucho	+621533,227*IDH+0,597*NCD+258270,109*VCS-479974,519
6	Cajamarca	-882137,69*IDH-0,699*NCD-1311377,424*VCS+1600535,042
7	Cusco	+220593,116*IDH +1,856*NCD-13987,094*VCS-112461,426
8	Huancavelica	+289253,681*IDH-8,676*NCD+570179,879*VCS-646952,953
9	Huánuco	-43062,933*IDH+0,893*NCD-64148,197*VCS+66515,424
10	Ica	+161046,558*IDH-13,451*NCD-895759,802*VCS+580042,954
11	Junín	+4118,794*IDH-0,022*NCD-12083,176*VCS+6633,609
12	La Libertad	+203718,006 *IDH+2,687*NCD-38391,946*VDC-128032,081
13	Lambayeque	+51480,326*IDH +1,779*NCD-7484,189*VCS-42826,641
14	Lima-Callao	+174323,153*IDH+0,44*QNCD-1450525,446*VCS+23054,334
15	Loreto	-8188822,64*IDH-14,17*NCD-6864768,675*VCS+4943835,767
16	Madre de Dios	+58615,818*IDH+0,022*NCD+103031,332*VCS-37854,745
17	Moquegua	+47548,176*IDH+0,026*NCD+8636,842*VCS-33671,117
18	Pasco	+43953,669*IDH-0,217*NCD+36170,662*VCS-42454,652
19	Piura	+21014,559*IDH-0,134*NCD+16910,62*VCS-18383,037
20	Puno	+75221,765*IDH+0,089*NCD+27714,244*VCS-57515,927
21	San Martin	-3418533,812*IDH-55,448*NCD-445324,247*VCS+2248853,148
22	Tacna	-38427,373*IDH+0,268*NCD+26868,258*VCS+21099,831
23	Tumbes	+11223,028*IDH+0,071*NCD+6190,019*VCS-10253,339
24	Ucayali	+39359,878*IDH+1,838*NCD+102590,051*VCS-28361,224

results indicate that only 12 regions out of 24 meet the assumptions of recurrence (Amazonas, Ancash, Cajamarca, Huanuco, Junin, Madre de Dios, Pasco, Piura, Puno, San Martin, Tacna and Tumbes). The other regions are more chaotic with many years without any significant disasters and some years with major events (Moquegua for instance). Consequently, we focused the next steps only on these 12 regions. In this way, it will be possible to forecast the impact that a new recurrent disaster will have if it occurs in a given region. In Table 5, we can see the results obtained for the year 2012 by means of multivariate regression models and the real number of victims recorded for this year for the regions in which recurrent disasters occur. The results show that:

- 25% of the results (3 regions: Ancash, Huanuco and Junin) can be judged as very reliable with a deviation ratio lower than 50%;
- 33% of the results (4 regions: Amazonas, Piura, Puno, Tacna) can be judged as admissible with a deviation ratio lower than 100%.
- 41% of the results (5 regions: Cajamarca, Madre de Dios, San Martin, Pasco and Tumbes) can be judged as doubtful with a deviation ratio higher than 100%. Among these, two regions were hit by major events in 2012 (San Martin and Madre de Dios). Our models are not able to forecast these exceptional events. If we do not take into consideration the number of victims due to these events, the model becomes reliable. For the three other regions, the problem is because the disaster occurrences are not yearly but have a frequency of several years. The current models are consequently not relevant for these regions. It is important to remark that our approach could be applied successfully to these three regions, and potentially to the twelve regions that did not meet the recurrence assumptions, by changing the periodicity and the time horizon (respectively ten years and one century for instance).

Table 5. Gap analysis between regression-model results and real observations for the year 2012.

No	Regions	Model validation		
		2012 Forecast	**2012 Observation**	**Valid?**
1	Amazonas	4138	1 364	Admisible
2	Ancash	2566	2 193	Reliable
6	Cajamarca	12870	745	Doubtfull
9	Huánuco	5013	5 284	Reliable
11	Junín	3909	2 790	Reliable
16	Madre de Dios	-	231 827	Doubtfull
18	Pasco	64	2 051	Doubtfull
19	Piura	1627	649	Admisible
20	Puno	6491	12 453	Admisible
21	San Martin	-	26 011	Doubtfull
22	Tacna	411	1 701	Admisible
23	Tumbes	155	4 655	Doubtfull

Phase 5. Impact on local HL capabilities

After important disruptive events, such as an earthquake, HL capacity is drastically reduced due to the total or partial destruction of vehicles, infrastructures and facilities. Following the methodology described before, we made a set of experts' interviews from INDECI and IGP to assess the potential impact on HL infrastructures that a disaster may have. These interviews have allowed defining if a Region can be considered as a Sensitive Zone or a Non-Sensitive Zone. Then, a deep analysis of previous disasters from 1993 to 2012 was made to assess the impact of a given earthquake on HL infrastructures. This impact is both assess for the epicentre region and for border regions depending of their sensitivity. Finally, we obtained the following Table that shows the estimated capacity reduction (following an earthquake) between two regions as a function of both the intensity of the disaster, and the sensitivity of the region. This shows the last dimension of the valid scenarios we obtained for the Peruvian HL.

CONCLUSION AND PERSPECTIVES

Although a plethora of HL decision support systems has been proposed during the last decade, scientific innovation has not yet led to considerable improvement in practice. This is particularly true for quantitative approaches and risk management. The scenario approaches frequently suggested in academic literature, are often too complex and time-consuming, while rapid heuristics and experienced based decisions lead are prone to bias. Designing valid scenarios that meet requirements of field-based practitioners is of prime importance in ensuring that quantitative models that can be implemented and used by practitioners.

In this chapter, a methodology has been developed to design a set of valid scenarios able to assess disaster needs in regions subject to recurrent disasters. The proposition is based on two assumptions validated by the existing literature. The first considers that future occurrences of disasters can be taken as globally equivalent to past ones. The second considers that future disaster impacts will depend on two main factors: vulnerability and resilience. Based on these hypotheses, our proposed approach is split into five phases: (i) gathering data on past disasters and analysing it; (ii) defining a relevant zoning of the studied area; (iii) defining the probability of occurrence of each scenario; (iv) determining the expected impact of future disasters as a function of resilience and vulnerability factors; (v) assessing the consequences of future disasters on HL infrastructures. The results seem to be globally robust for Peru and could be used efficiently for future developments in terms of HL quantitative-based decision-support systems.

Table 6. Overview of potential reduction of capacities depending on earthquake intensity and region sensitivity.

Although the proposal is a significant first step towards solving the problem of relevant and plausible scenarios in HL, several limitations remain, which we propose to study in future research. The quality of the forecast should be assessed more deeply to confirm that our results are representative. To do so, complementary experiments will be carried out to consolidate and validate the methodology. The deviation ratio thresholds we used to validate the model should also be studied more deeply. Future uses of this approach and its results can be imagined. One concrete example of application is already developed in (Vargas *et al.*, 2015) to design a robust network of disaster warehouses to respond to recurrent disasters in Peru.

REFERENCES

Aldunce, P., Beilin, R., Handmer, J., & Howden, M. (2014). Framing disaster resilience: The implications of the diverse conceptualisations of bouncing back. *Disaster Prevention and Management*, *23*(3), 252–270. doi:10.1108/DPM-07-2013-0130

Alinovi, L., Mane, E., & Romano, D. (2009). Measuring household resilience to food insecurity: application to Palestinian households. In R. Benedetti, M. Bee, G. Espa, & F. Piersimoni (Eds.), *Agricultural Survey Methods*. John Wiley & Sons, Ltd.

Balcik, B., Jahre, M., & Fabbe-Costes, N. (2015). How standards and modularity can improve disaster supply chain responsiveness. *Journal of Disaster Logistics and Supply Chain Management, 3*, 348-386.

Birkmann, J., Seng, D. C., & Setiadi, N. (2013). Enhancing early warning in the light of migration and environmental shocks. *Environmental Science & Policy*, *27*(1), 76–88. doi:10.1016/j.envsci.2012.04.002

Bosch, R. (2010). Objectivity and Plausibility in the Study of Organizations. *Journal of Management Inquiry*, *19*(4), 383–391. doi:10.1177/1056492610369936

Braman, L. M., van Aalst, M. K., Mason, S. J., Suarez, P., Ait-Chellouche, Y., & Tall, A. (2013). Climate forecasts in disaster management: Red Cross flood operations in West Africa, 2008. *Disasters*, *37*(1), 144–164. doi:10.1111/j.1467-7717.2012.01297.x PMID:23066755

Carter, M. R., Little, P. D., Mogues, T., & Negatu, W. (2004). Shocks, sensitivity and resilience: Tracking the economic impacts of environmental disaster on assets in Ethiopia and Honduras. In *BASIS Research Program on Poverty, Inequality and Development*. US Agency for International Development.

Charles, A., & Lauras, M. (2011). An enterprise modelling approach for better optimisation modelling: Application to the disaster relief chain coordination problem. *OR-Spektrum*, *33*(3), 815–841. doi:10.100700291-011-0255-2

Charles, A., Lauras, M., Van Wassenhove, L. N., & Dupont, L. (2016). Designing an efficient disaster supply network. *Journal of Operations Management*, *47*(1), 58–70. doi:10.1016/j.jom.2016.05.012

Comes, T. (2016). Cognitive biases in disaster sensemaking and decision-making lessons from field research. *2016 IEEE International Multi-Disciplinary Conference on Cognitive Methods in Situation Awareness and Decision Support (CogSIMA)*, 56-62. 10.1109/COGSIMA.2016.7497786

Comes, T., Wijngaards, N., & Van de Walle, B. (2015). Exploring the future: Runtime Scenario Selection for Complex and Time-Bound Decisions. *Technological Forecasting and Social Change*, *97*(1), 29–46. doi:10.1016/j.techfore.2014.03.009

Di Domenica, N., Mitra, G., Valente, P., & Birbilis, G. (2007). Stochastic programming and scenario generation within a simulation framework: An information systems perspective. *Decision Support Systems*, *42*(4), 2197–2218. doi:10.1016/j.dss.2006.06.013

Dieckhaus, D., Heigh, I., Gomez-Tagle Leonard, N., Jahre, M., & Navangul, K. A. (2011), Predicting the Unpredictable – Demand Forecasting in International Disaster Response. IFRC Global Logistics Service Annual Report.

Djalante, R., Holley, C., & Thomalla, F. (2011). Adaptive governance and managing resilience to natural hazards. *International Journal of Disaster Risk Science*, *2*(4), 1–14. doi:10.100713753-011-0015-6

Dupačová, J., Consigli, G., & Wallace, S. W. (2000). Scenarios for Multistage Stochastic Programs. *Annals of Operations Research*, *100*(1), 25–53. doi:10.1023/A:1019206915174

Ferris, E., Petz, D., & Stark, C. (2013). The year of recurring disasters: A review of natural disasters in 2012. The Brookings Institution – London School of Economics – Project on Internal Displacement.

Frigg, R., & Hartmann, S. (2012). Models in Science. The Stanford Encyclopedia of Philosophy, 23.

Galindo, G., & Batta, R. (2013). Review of recent developments in OR/MS research in Humanitarian Logistics. *European Journal of Operational Research*, *230*(2), 201–211. doi:10.1016/j.ejor.2013.01.039

Hair, J. F., Black, W. C., Babin, B. J., Anderson, R. E., & Tatham, R. L. (2006). *Multivariate data analysis* (Vol. 6). Pearson Prentice Hall.

Jahre, M., & Fabbe-Costes, N. (2015). How standards and modularity can improve disaster supply chain responsiveness: The case of emergency response units. *Journal of Disaster Logistics and Supply Chain Management*, *5*(3), 348–386.

Jolliffe, I. (2002). *Principal component analysis*. John Wiley & Sons, Ltd.

Karimi, I., & Hüllermeier, E. (2007). Risk assessment system of natural hazards: A new approach based on fuzzy probability. *Fuzzy Sets and Systems*, *158*(9), 987–999. doi:10.1016/j.fss.2006.12.013

Klibi, W., & Martel, A. (2012). Scenario-based supply chain network risk modelling. *European Journal of Operational Research, 223*(3), 644–658. doi:10.1016/j.ejor.2012.06.027

Kovács, G., & Spens, K. M. (2007). Disaster HL in disaster relief operations. *International Journal of Physical Distribution & Logistics Management, 37*(2), 99–114. doi:10.1108/09600030710734820

Laguna Salvadó, L., Lauras, M., & Comes, T. (2015). Towards More Relevant Research on Disaster Disaster Management Coordination. *Proceedings of the 12th Information Systems for Crisis Response And Management (ISCRAM) Conference.* http://idl.iscram.org

Laguna Salvadó, L., Lauras, M., & Comes, T. (2016). Towards a Monitoring System for American IFRC Logistics Network. *Proceedings of the 13th Information Systems for Crisis Response And Management (ISCRAM) Conference.* http://idl.iscram.org

Mendonca, D., Beroggi, G. E., Van Gent, D., & Wallace, W. A. (2006). Designing gaming simulations for the assessment of group decision support systems in emergency response. *Safety Science, 44*(6), 523–535. doi:10.1016/j.ssci.2005.12.006

Merz, M., Hiete, M., Comes, T., & Schultmann, F. (2013). A composite indicator model to assess natural disaster risks in industry on a spatial level. *Journal of Risk Research, 16*(9), 1077–1099. doi:10.1080/13669877.2012.737820

Ndille, R., & Belle, J. A. (2014). Managing the Limbe floods: Considerations for disaster risk reduction in Cameroon. *International Journal of Disaster Risk Science, 5*(2), 147–156. doi:10.100713753-014-0019-0

Oloruntoba, R., & Gray, R. (2006). Disaster aid: An agile supply chain? *Supply Chain Management, 11*(2), 115–120. doi:10.1108/13598540610652492

Peres, E. Q., Brito, I. Jr, Leiras, A., & Yoshizaki, H. (2012). Disaster logistics and disaster relief research: trends, applications, and future research directions. *Proceedings of the 4th International Conference on Information Systems, Logistics and Supply Chain*, 26-29.

Tatham, P., Oloruntoba, R., & Spens, K. (2012). Cyclone preparedness and response: An analysis of lessons identified using an adapted military planning framework. *Disasters, 36*(1), 54–82. doi:10.1111/j.1467-7717.2011.01249.x PMID:21702893

Tietje, O. (2005). Identification of a small reliable and efficient set of consistent scenarios. *European Journal of Operational Research, 162*(2), 418–432. doi:10.1016/j.ejor.2003.08.054

Tveiten, C. K., Albrechtsen, E., Wærø, I., & Wahl, A. M. (2012). Building resilience into emergency management. *Safety Science*, *50*(10), 1960–1966. doi:10.1016/j.ssci.2012.03.001

UNDP. (2004). *Reducing Disaster Risk: A Challenge for Development–A Global Report*. UN Press.

UNESCAP. (2008). *Building Community Resilience to Natural Disasters through Partnership: Sharing Experience and Expertise in the Region*. UN Press.

UNISDR. (2009). *Terminology on Disaster Risk Reduction*. UN Press.

Van de Walle, B., & Comes, T. (2015). On the nature of information management in complex and natural disasters. *Procedia Engineering*, *107*(1), 403–411. doi:10.1016/j.proeng.2015.06.098

van der Laan, E., van Dalen, J., Rohrmoser, M., & Simpson, R. (2016). Demand forecasting and order planning for disaster logistics: An empirical assessment. *Journal of Operations Management*, *45*(1), 114–122. doi:10.1016/j.jom.2016.05.004

Vargas, J., Lauras, M., Okongwu, U., & Dupont, L. (2015). A decision support system for robust disaster facility location. *Engineering Applications of Artificial Intelligence*, *46*(1), 326–335. doi:10.1016/j.engappai.2015.06.020

Vargas, J., Rojas, J., Inga, A., Mantilla, W., Añasco, H., Basurto, M. F., Campos, R., Sánchez, J., & Checa, P. I. (2016). Towards Reliable Recurrent Disaster Forecasting Methods: Peruvian Earthquake Case. *Proceedings of the 13th Information Systems for Crisis Response And Management (ISCRAM) Conference*. http://idl.iscram.org

Vitoriano, B., de Juan, J. M., & Ruan, D. (2013). *Decision aid models for disaster management and emergencies*. Springer Science & Business Media. doi:10.2991/978-94-91216-74-9

Weichselgartner, J. (2001). Disaster mitigation: The concept of vulnerability revisited. *Disaster Prevention and Management: An International Journal*, *10*(2), 85–95. doi:10.1108/09653560110388609

WGCEP. (2007). *The Uniform California Earthquake Rupture Forecast*. U.S. Geological Survey Open-File Report and California Geological Survey Special Report. https://pubs.usgs.gov/of/2007/1091/

Wisner, B., Blaikie, P., Cannon, T., & Davis, I. (2004). At risk. Natural people's vulnerability and disasters. Routledge.

Wright, G., Cairns, G., & Goodwin, P. (2009). Teaching scenario planning: Lessons from practice in academe and business. *European Journal of Operational Research, 194*(1), 323–335. doi:10.1016/j.ejor.2007.12.003

Xu, H., Zhang, K., Shen, J., & Li, Y. (2010). Storm surge simulation along the US East and Gulf Coasts using a multi-scale numerical model approach. *Ocean Dynamics, 60*(6), 1597–1619. doi:10.100710236-010-0321-3

Zhang, K., Li, Y., Liu, H., Xu, H., & Shen, J. (2013). Comparison of three methods for estimating the sea level rise effect on storm surge flooding. *Climatic Change, 118*(2), 487–500. doi:10.100710584-012-0645-8

Chapter 3
Demands and Sales Forecasting for Retailers by Analyzing Google Trends and Historical Data

Md Rokon Uddin
Department of Mechanical and Industrial Engineering, Ryerson University, Canada

Saman Hassanzadeh Amin
Department of Mechanical and Industrial Engineering, Ryerson University, Canada

Guoqing Zhang
https://orcid.org/0000-0003-0821-8787
Supply Chain and Logistics Optimization Research Center, University of Windsor, Canada

ABSTRACT

A supply chain includes several elements such as suppliers, manufacturers, retails, and customers. Forecasting the demands and sales is a challenging task in supply chain management (SCM). The main goal of this research is to create forecasting models for retailers by using artificial neural network (ANN) and to enable them to make accurate business decisions by visualizing future data. Two forecasting models are investigated in this research. One is a sales model that predicts future sales, and the second one is a demand model that predicts future demands. To achieve the mentioned goal, CNN-LSTM model is used for both sales and demand predictions. Based on the obtained results, this hybrid model can learn from very long range of historical data and can predict the future efficiently.

DOI: 10.4018/978-1-7998-3805-0.ch003

1. INTRODUCTION

Every moment, someone is buying something, and someone is selling something. The buyer has concerns about getting the product/service at his/her convenience, and the seller has concerns about fulfilling the demand of the buyer. In a supply chain, the seller needs to know about the market demand and sales information of the products, so he/she could measure a future demand of the products, and prepare inventory beforehand (Martins and Pato, 2019; Kamble et al., 2020).

Artificial Neural Network (ANN) helps supply chain managers to predict these values, and to investigate some topics such as optimization, forecasting, and decision support systems. In this study, ANN is used for forecasting future demands and sales of the stores of a grocery chain. To this aim, the historical sales dataset of the grocery chain and a demand dataset (captured from Google Trends) are utilized.

This book chapter is organized as follows. Section 2 is devoted to the literature review. The methodology is discussed in Section 3. In addition, the results and discussions are provided in Section 4. Finally, conclusions and potential future research are provided in Section 5.

2. LITERATURE REVIEW

Prediction of future demand and sales has been a very helpful tool for business decision-makers. Recently, ANN has gained significant attention in Supply Chain Management (SCM) because of its capability to predict future, to process large datasets, to handle very complex non-linear functions, and for its efficiency and robustness in prediction. ANN is helpful even if the data of the problem is partially present.

There are some researchers who have applied ANN to design their own prediction models to forecast demands and sales. Aburto and Weber (2007) developed an inventory management system for a supermarket and explained a hybrid intelligent model for forecasting demand in SCM. This hybrid model is a combination of autoregressive integrated moving average and neural network models. Yin et al. (2008) introduced an adaptive neural network model that had more accurate forecasting results than the traditional neural network. Amin-Naseri and Tabar (2008) applied a comparative study of various neural network models, and concluded that Recurrent Neural Network (RNN) model has the most precise forecasting results.

Google Trends and searches have been utilized in some investigations. Su (2008) analyzed the impact of the ease of online searches on consumers' online search intentions, and showed that there is a noticeable positive impact of cross-site and in-site searches on both priced and non-priced item searches. Ginsberg et al. (2009)

revealed that Google Trends was able to trace and predict the spread of influenza earlier than the Centers for Disease Control and Prevention. Choi and Varian (2009) claimed that Google Trends data can be utilized for predicting unemployment rate. They showed in their later research (Choi and Varian, 2012) that Google Trends has an important connection to car or house sales. Shimshoni et al. (2009) explained predictability of Google Trends data itself.

Goel et al. (2010) illustrated some restrictions of search data. They mentioned that search data is helpful in making predictions, but the predictability may not increase noticeably. Guzman (2011) utilized Google search data to predict inflation. Baker and Fradkin (2011) investigated how job search respond to extensions of unemployment payments using Google search data.

Kandananond (2012) compared two data mining methods including ANN and Support Vector Machine (SVM), and used these models to predict the demand of consumer products. They concluded that the SVM had more accurate results in term of Mean Absolute Percentage Error (MAPE) than the ANN. Jun et al. (2014) analyzed that Google Search provides an outstanding platform for observing consumers' activities of information seeking. It reflects the needs, demands, and interests of the customers. As a result, customer preferences can be predicted.

In a research, Kourentzesa et al. (2014) concluded that in around 73% cases, the artificial neural network models do better than the traditional forecasting methods. Liu (2015) used a neural network model and linear regression to make a forecasting analysis for the market demand of bikes. The Back Propagation (BP) neural network was selected as the learning algorithm. The number of hidden layers was one. The results showed that the prediction accuracy of BP-NN was better than the regression model. Kochak and Sharma (2015) developed Forward and Backward Propagation NN in MATLAB to foresee sales of fuel filter for next year based on the sales data of previous years.

Bhadouria and Jayant (2017) focused on a gear manufacturing company and developed three ANN models using MATLAB for forecasting the demand of different types of parts that the gear company manufactures. Wijnhoven and Plant (2017) analyzed about 500,000 social media posts for eleven car models, and used linear regression technique to forecast the car sales. They applied a time lag using the cross-correlation function of SPSS software.

Counter (2017) showed that Google has maintained 90% of the global search engine market share from 2010 to onward. Kaya and Turkyilmaz (2018) developed some demand forecasting methods which consider special intermittent demand features. Intermittent demand occurs randomly with changing values. Several periods have zero demand in their study.

The mentioned investigations have proved that when people buy something from stores, it creates sales data which can be analyzed through ANN to predict future sales of products or services accurately. Nowadays, people spend more time on the internet to search their desired products or services before buying them, and this data can be analyzed through ANN to predict future demands of those products or services. To predict future demands and sales accurately, an ANN model should be designed to remember as much historical data as possible. The speed of the model is an important factor. The ANN model also has to adopt new data continuously and predict based on the historical data and the new data. They involve supervised learning and time series forecasting methods.

3. METHODOLOGY

This section is devoted to artificial neural network, time series forecasting, supervised learning, and ANN models.

3.1. Artifical Neural Network (ANN)

ANN is a mathematical model which is on the basis of the idea of the neural function of human brain (Jain et al., 1996). The main elements of ANN are neurons which are highly interconnected with each other and capable of solving given problems all together. ANN has three main components including neurons, interconnectivity, and learning algorithms. ANN can have two or more neurons, and they learn based on the method of the learning algorithm. There are two types of learning: supervised and unsupervised learning. In supply chain management, ANN is used very widely to forecast data (Kochak and Sharma, 2015).

3.2. Time Series Forecasting

If machine learning datasets are transformable based on date or time, time plays an important role in the datasets. Datasets used in this study are transformable based on date (time series datasets). A time series dataset is different from a usual dataset. It adds a time dimension between the observations. Forecasting means creating a model to fit on historical data for predicting future observations. Because the future is totally unavailable, and predictions must be made from what happened in the past (Montgomery et al., 2015).

3.3. Supervised Learning

Most of the machine learning models use supervised learning methods. A supervised learning is about learning the mapping technique from input to output. The purpose of this learning is to adopt the mapping technique so well that when new data arrives, they can predict the output. Learning from time series data is a supervised learning. Learning can be achieved using past time steps as the input variables, in addition to the next time step as the output variable.

3.4. ANN Models

To choose the best ANN model for the selected datasets, four models including Multilayer Perceptron (MLP), Convolutional Neural Network (CNN), Long Short-Term Memory (LSTM), and CNN-LSTM are selected, and the sample datasets are fed to those models to observe the results.

MLP is a traditional ANN. As illustrated in Figure 1, it has an input layer to receive data and an output layer to make prediction about the input. Some hidden layers exist as the processing units of MLP (Skymind AI Wiki, 2019).

Figure 1. MLP architecture

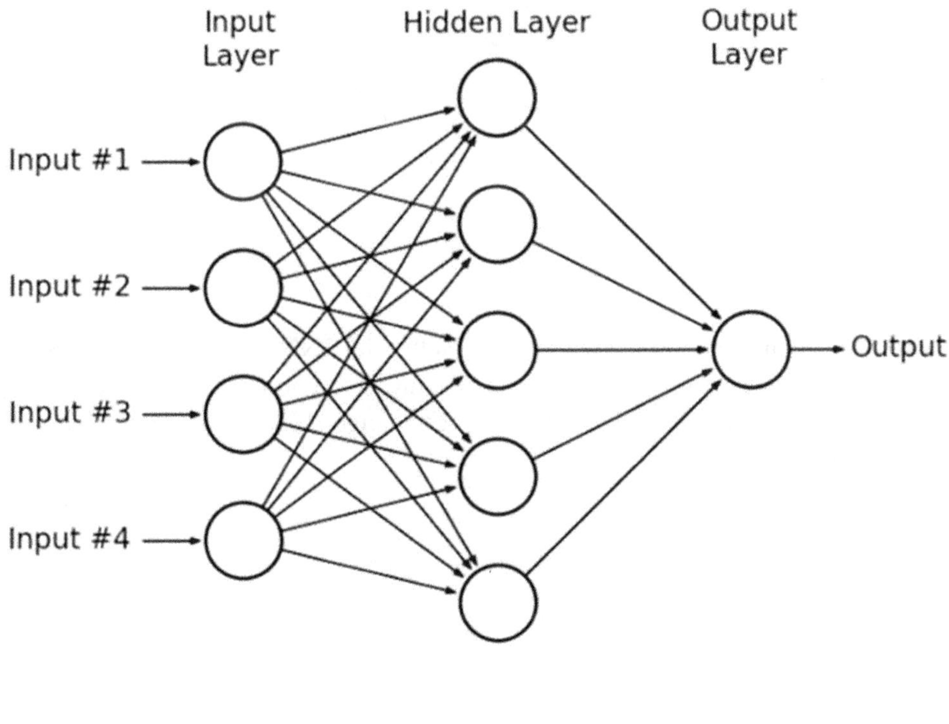

CNN is a regularized version of MLP, and can pull together more complex sequences or patterns using smaller and simpler sequences or patterns (Hirschkind et al., 2019). The CNN architecture is illustrated in Figure 2.

Figure 2. CNN architecture (Hirschkind et al., 2019)

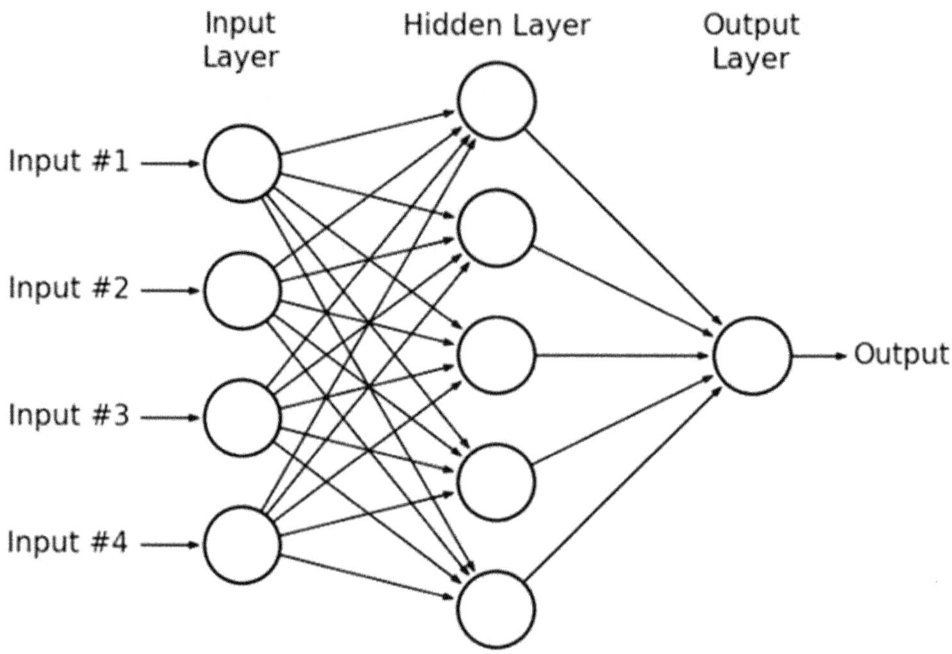

LSTM is an artificial Recurrent Neural Network (RNN) which is illustrated in Figure 3. It has feedback connections. As a result, it can process single data points as well as entire sequences of the data (StackExchange, 2018). It can learn patterns from long sequenced data.

Figure 3. LSTM architecture (StackExchange, 2018)

```
Train Error (RMSE): 0.10162008847270289
Test Error (RMSE): 0.11135429285840663
```

CNN and LSTM are used widely for time series forecasting. CNN-LSTM is a hybrid model of CNN and LSTM. The architecture is illustrated in Figure 4. The benefit of the hybrid model over other models is that it can predict the output efficiently because CNN-LSTM model supports very long input sequences which are read as subsequences by CNN model, and then patched together by LSTM model (Lin and Aberer, 2017). The CNN model interprets each subsequence, and LSTM model reconstructs the interpretations from the subsequences.

Figure 4. CNN-LSTM architecture (Sosa, 2018)

```
model_cnn_lstm = Sequential()
model_cnn_lstm.add(TimeDistributed(Conv1D(filters = 64, kernel_size = 1, activation = 'relu'),
                                   input_shape = (None, X_train_series_sub.shape[2], X_train_series_sub.shape[3])))
model_cnn_lstm.add(TimeDistributed(MaxPooling1D(pool_size=2)))
model_cnn_lstm.add(TimeDistributed(Flatten()))
model_cnn_lstm.add(LSTM(60, activation = 'relu'))
model_cnn_lstm.add(Dropout(0.1))
model_cnn_lstm.add(Dense(30, activation = 'relu'))
model_cnn_lstm.add(Dropout(0.1))
model_cnn_lstm.add(Dense(1))
model_cnn_lstm.compile(loss = 'mse', optimizer = 'adam')
model_cnn_lstm.summary()
```

Performance evaluation is done on these models for the sample datasets based on Mean Squared Error (MSE). The results are displayed in Figure 5. The graphs in Figure 5 show that the CNN-LSTM model has less MSEs, i.e., it's performing better than the other models. Considering these two facts (one is the capability of learning from long sequenced data, and the other one is lower MSE) a hybrid CNN-LSTM model is used in this research because the demand and sales datasets could have hundreds of years of data. Each sample is divided into two subsequences, and the CNN model is defined to anticipate two-time steps (with one feature) per subsequence. Then, entire CNN model is wrapped in layers of time distributed wrapper so that it can be applied on each subsequence of the sample data, and the results can be interpreted by LSTM model before making a prediction. This hybrid CNN-LSTM model uses Adam version of the stochastic gradient descent, and MSE as a loss function. The model gets updated on weekly basis to predict the next future data based on the time step.

4. RESULTS AND DISCUSSIONS

The data preparation process and the developed dashboard are described in this section.

Figure 5. Comparison between different ANN models

```
_________________________________________________________________
Layer (type)                 Output Shape              Param #
=================================================================
time_distributed_49 (TimeDis (None, None, 59, 64)      128
_________________________________________________________________
time_distributed_50 (TimeDis (None, None, 29, 64)      0
_________________________________________________________________
time_distributed_51 (TimeDis (None, None, 1856)        0
_________________________________________________________________
lstm_17 (LSTM)               (None, 60)                460080
_________________________________________________________________
dropout_33 (Dropout)         (None, 60)                0
_________________________________________________________________
dense_33 (Dense)             (None, 30)                1830
_________________________________________________________________
dropout_34 (Dropout)         (None, 30)                0
_________________________________________________________________
dense_34 (Dense)             (None, 1)                 31
=================================================================
Total params: 462,069
Trainable params: 462,069
Non-trainable params: 0
_________________________________________________________________
```

4.1. Data Preparation

In this book chapter, two data sources are used to forecast the demand and sales. They include Kaggle, 2019 and Google Trends, 2019.

Kaggle's dataset is named as Weekly Sales dataset, and Google Trends' dataset is named as Weekly Demand dataset. To fetch data from Google Trends, Python's library "pytrends" is used (Python Software Foundation, 2016). The sales dataset (sales data-set.csv) has weekly sales data (in dollars) of 45 stores and 99 items starting from February 5, 2010 to October 26, 2012. The dates after October 26, 2012 presented in the data or graph are considered as "Future dates", and the data are predicted data. Kaggle's dataset (sales data-set.csv) has many columns but only Store, Item, Date, and Weekly_Sales columns are taken for sales forecasting.

In the sales dataset, periodic weekly sales dates are Fridays. Google Trends can give weekly search interest of an item, but the dates are Sundays. To match with Google Trends data, the weekly sales dates are shifted 2 days to make them Sundays. Google Trends gives data about "Interest over time" of an item which has numbers from 0 to 100. A value of 100 represents high interest, 50 represents moderate interest, and 0 represents that there is not enough data to show for this item. For the ease of comparison, these values are scaled down by dividing by 10. As a result, a value of 10 represents high interest, 5 represents moderate interest, and 0 represents that there is not enough data to show for this item.

In this investigation, “Interest over time” is renamed as “Demand” for an item. There are two additional datasets which define item names and locations of the stores. Item names and store locations are required to get data from Google Trends. 99 items or product names are collected from Delish (Delish, 2018). For example, Item code 1 in sales dataset which has name “chicken drumstick” is used as the search term for Google Trends. Therefore, demand and sales can be compared for “chicken drumstick” and the location of the store is in Ontario. Weekly demand and sales datasets look like Figure 6.

Figure 6. Weekly sales dataset for “chicken drumstick”

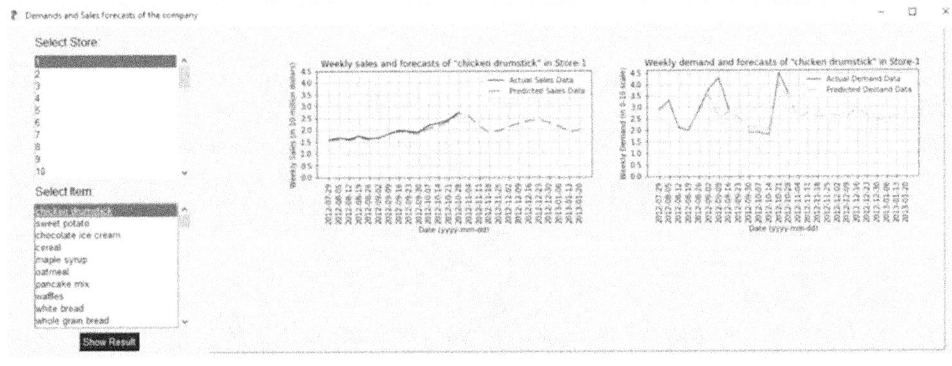

Figure 7 represents the weekly demand data for “chicken drumstick”. Figure 8 and Figure 9 illustrate the time series data for weekly sales and weekly demand. Figure 10 represents the performance of the ANN which is designed for this study in terms of RMSE. Lower RMSE means better accuracy in predicting the future values.

To achieve the mentioned objective, a CNN-LSTM hybrid artificial neural network is designed. The configuration and summary of the base neural network model are given in Figures 11 and 12.

To feed the network, the dataset is transformed into time series data in such a way that the model uses last 117 weekly sales data and the current time step of the dataset (7 days). So, it forecasts next weekly sales data, 12 weeks ahead. A Kernel size of 2 is defined, and a convolutional layer with 64 filter maps is utilized. Then, a max pooling layer and a dense layer are defined to interpret the input feature.

Figure 7. Weekly demand dataset for "chicken drumstick"

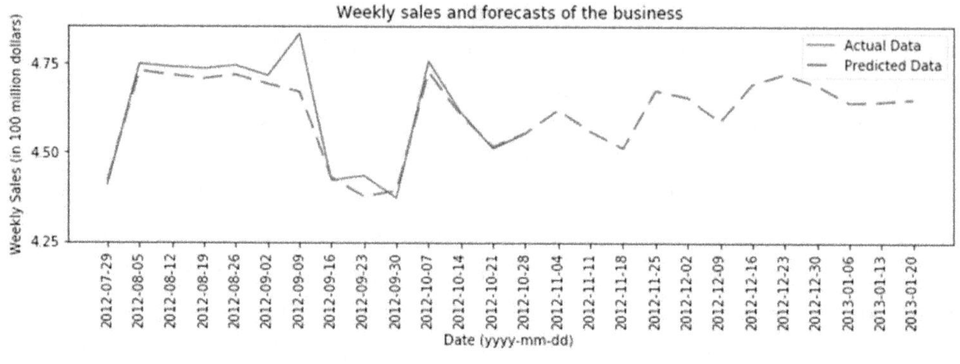

Figure 8. Time series data for weekly sales (in 10 million dollars)

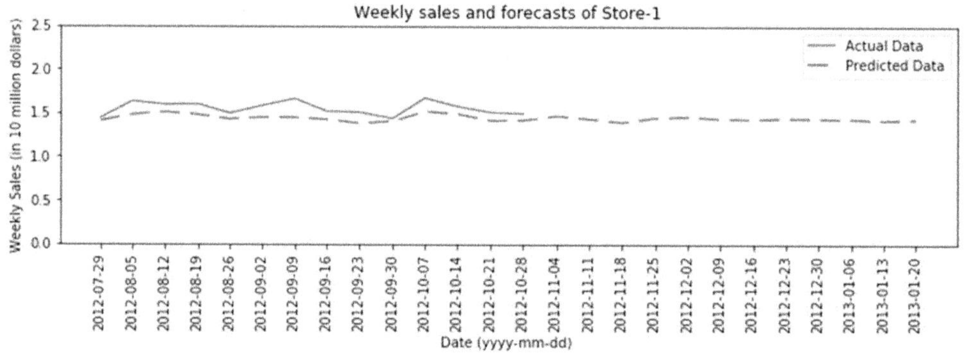

Figure 9. Time series data for weekly demand (in scale of 0 - 10)

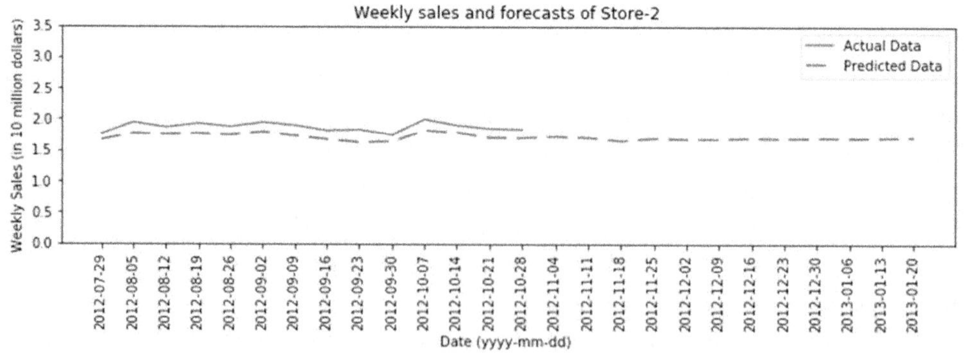

Figure 10. RMSE of the model for sample data

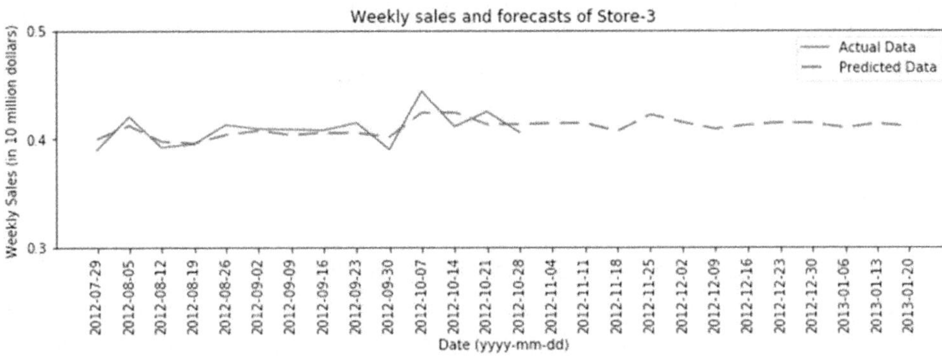

Figure 11. CNN-LSTM configuration

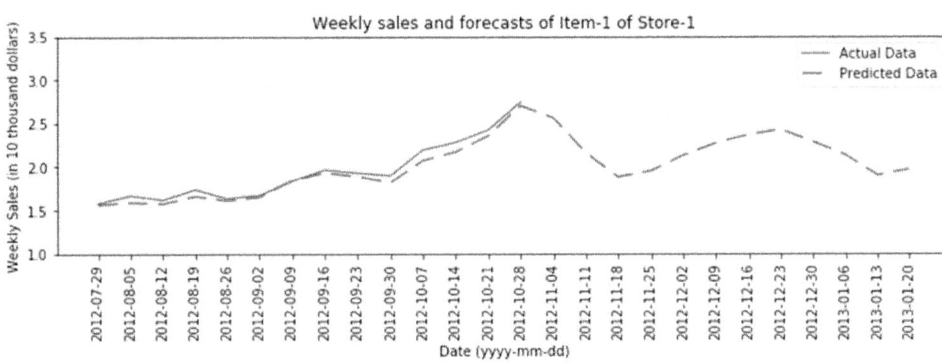

Figure 12. CNN-LSTM summary

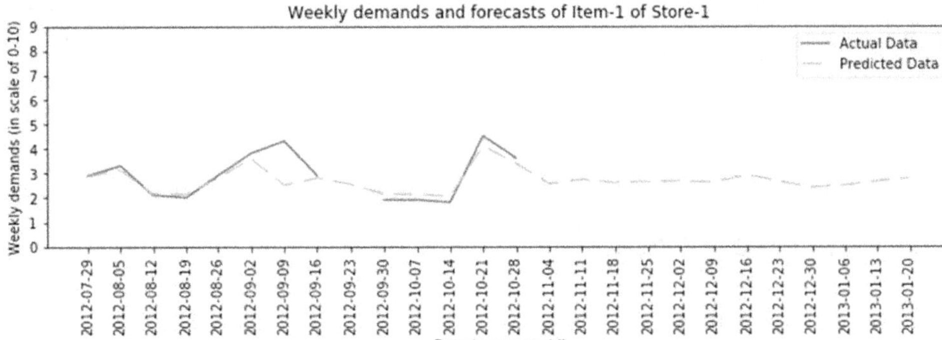

An output layer is also defined to predict a single value. This model has 60 neurons in the input layer, 30 in the hidden layer, and 1 in the output layer. Furthermore, 'relu' activation function is used. The model uses "adam" version of Stochastic Gradient Descent, and "mse" as a loss function. Zeros in the demands and sales data are presented as NaN, and are not plotted in the graph.

4.2. Dashboard

An interactive dashboard is created in Python to present the demand and sales data. The dashboard takes inputs from a user, and presents actual and predicted data of demand and sales. The user has to select the store number and item name to get the results in line charts. A sample dashboard is represented in Figure 13.

The predictions or forecasting are divided into three levels:

a) High level: It shows demand and sales forecasts of all stores.
b) Store level: It illustrates demand and sales forecasts of individual stores.
c) Item level: It demonstrates demand and sales forecasts of individual item of each store.

Figure 13. The Dashboard for demand and sales data

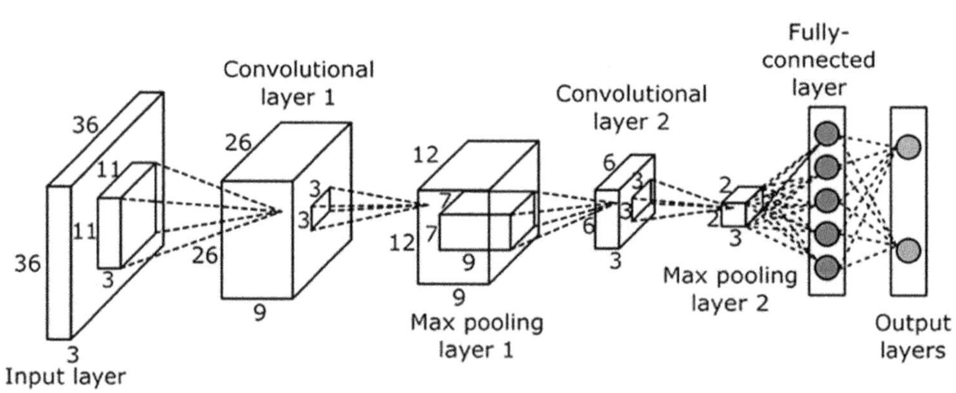

4.2.1. High Level Forecast

This level of forecasting represents a high-level picture of sales. The CNN-LSTM neural network predicts the total weekly sales of all stores. The data are written in Table 1. Figure 14 shows the actual and the predicted data based on the data of Table 1.

Table 1. Weekly actual sales data and forecasted data of the business (Weekly_Sales_x is the actual data and Weekly_Sales_y is the predicted data)

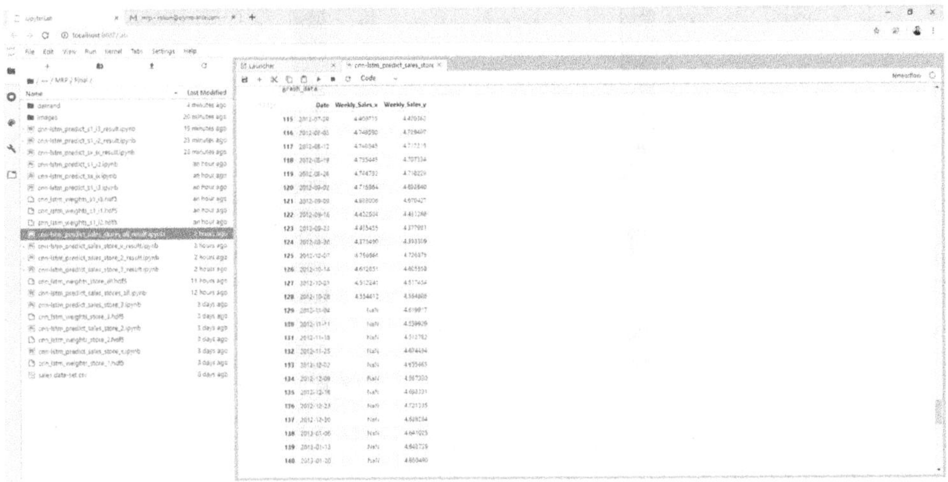

Figure 14. Weekly sales and forecasts of the business

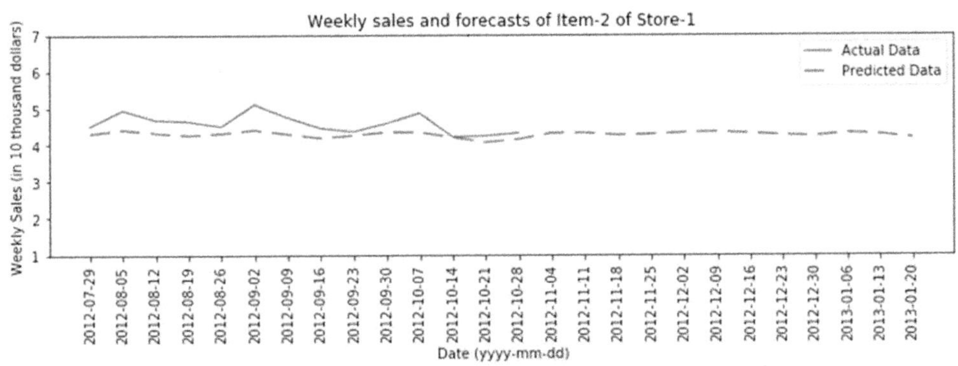

4.2.2. Store Level Forecast

In this level, the neural network considers the total weekly sales of individual stores and forecasts accordingly. Table 2 represents comparison between weekly actual sales data and forecasted data of the stores. Figures 15, 16, and 17 show the actual and predicted data of the stores based on the data of Table 2.

Table 2. Weekly actual sales data and forecasted data of stores (Weekly_Sales_x is actual data and Weekly_Sales_y is predicted data)

	Date	Weekly_Sales_x	Weekly_Sales_y
115	2012-07-29	1.439124	1.406558
116	2012-08-05	1.631136	1.478638
117	2012-08-12	1.592410	1.506962
118	2012-08-19	1.597868	1.476750
119	2012-08-26	1.494122	1.427504
120	2012-09-02	1.582083	1.448102
121	2012-09-09	1.661767	1.445305
122	2012-09-16	1.517429	1.424359
123	2012-09-23	1.506126	1.382246
124	2012-09-30	1.437059	1.403591
125	2012-10-07	1.670786	1.514501
126	2012-10-14	1.573073	1.488537
127	2012-10-21	1.508069	1.413779
128	2012-10-28	1.493660	1.415701
129	2012-11-04	NaN	1.466368
130	2012-11-11	NaN	1.430293

	Date	Weekly_Sales_x	Weekly_Sales_y
115	2012-07-29	1.757924	1.667461
116	2012-08-05	1.946105	1.766106
117	2012-08-12	1.866720	1.755983
118	2012-08-19	1.928016	1.765238
119	2012-08-26	1.876788	1.745841
120	2012-09-02	1.947083	1.792644
121	2012-09-09	1.898777	1.734485
122	2012-09-16	1.814807	1.674197
123	2012-09-23	1.829416	1.627486
124	2012-09-30	1.746471	1.640727
125	2012-10-07	1.998321	1.815602
126	2012-10-14	1.900745	1.787526
127	2012-10-21	1.847990	1.704801
128	2012-10-28	1.834458	1.700089
129	2012-11-04	NaN	1.722610
130	2012-11-11	NaN	1.703818

	Date	Weekly_Sales_x	Weekly_Sales_y
115	2012-07-29	0.389428	0.399419
116	2012-08-05	0.419990	0.411922
117	2012-08-12	0.391812	0.397283
118	2012-08-19	0.394919	0.395514
119	2012-08-26	0.412450	0.403361
120	2012-09-02	0.408839	0.407125
121	2012-09-09	0.408230	0.403411
122	2012-09-16	0.407589	0.405206
123	2012-09-23	0.414392	0.405137
124	2012-09-30	0.389813	0.401394
125	2012-10-07	0.443558	0.423605
126	2012-10-14	0.410804	0.423741
127	2012-10-21	0.424513	0.412982
128	2012-10-28	0.405433	0.412991
129	2012-11-04	NaN	0.413893
130	2012-11-11	NaN	0.414056

Figure 15. Weekly sales and forecasts of Store-1

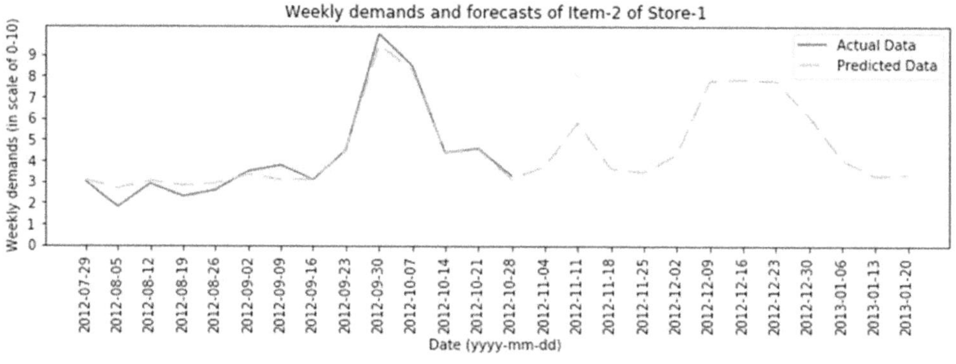

4.2.3. Item Level Forecast

This is the individual item level forecasting. The neural networks are designed to forecast individual item's weekly demands and sales. The data are provided in Table 3 and Table 4. The demand data is coming from Google Trends. Figures 18-23 show the actual and predicted data of the items based on the data of Tables 3 and 4.

Figure 16. Weekly sales and forecasts of Store-2

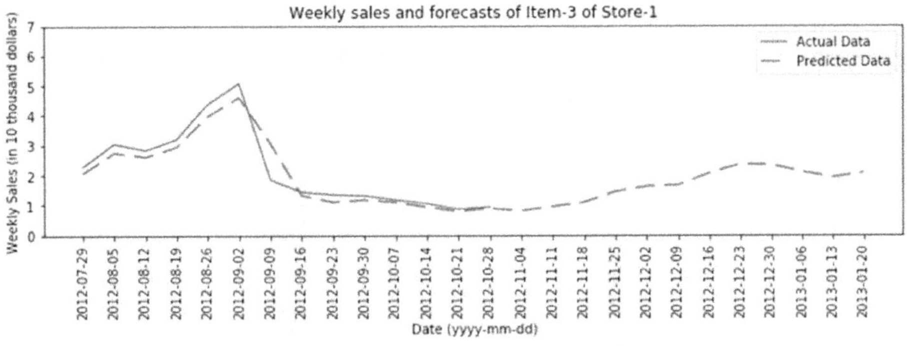

Figure 17. Weekly sales and forecasts of Store-3

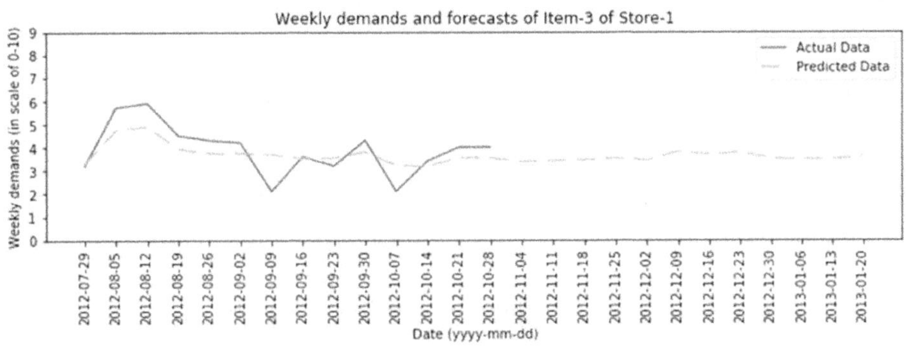

Table 3. Weekly actual sales data and forecasted data of items of Store-1 (Weekly_Sales_x is actual data and Weekly_Sales_y is predicted data)

	Date	Weekly_Sales_x	Weekly_Sales_y
115	2012-07-29	1.573118	1.558162
116	2012-08-05	1.662831	1.583403
117	2012-08-12	1.611992	1.568078
118	2012-08-19	1.733070	1.654775
119	2012-08-26	1.628640	1.603225
120	2012-09-02	1.668024	1.646587
121	2012-09-09	1.832237	1.839685
122	2012-09-16	1.961622	1.927592
123	2012-09-23	1.925150	1.883424
124	2012-09-30	1.894781	1.814188
125	2012-10-07	2.190447	2.068691
126	2012-10-14	2.276401	2.167207
127	2012-10-21	2.418527	2.350990
128	2012-10-28	2.739081	2.698830
129	2012-11-04	NaN	2.557346
130	2012-11-11	NaN	2.157326

	Date	Weekly_Sales_x	Weekly_Sales_y
115	2012-07-29	4.500822	4.297863
116	2012-08-05	4.942406	4.407407
117	2012-08-12	4.672991	4.317122
118	2012-08-19	4.635097	4.255374
119	2012-08-26	4.497252	4.306946
120	2012-09-02	5.099550	4.402359
121	2012-09-09	4.734450	4.283000
122	2012-09-16	4.449361	4.180377
123	2012-09-23	4.354107	4.249620
124	2012-09-30	4.578476	4.337623
125	2012-10-07	4.857708	4.330780
126	2012-10-14	4.211267	4.195915
127	2012-10-21	4.235472	4.059920
128	2012-10-28	4.313488	4.140064
129	2012-11-04	NaN	4.309576
130	2012-11-11	NaN	4.313106

	Date	Weekly_Sales_x	Weekly_Sales_y
115	2012-07-29	2.271670	2.051802
116	2012-08-05	3.033169	2.736810
117	2012-08-12	2.825730	2.601604
118	2012-08-19	3.190597	2.932225
119	2012-08-26	4.371278	3.956702
120	2012-09-02	5.070130	4.595080
121	2012-09-09	1.836851	3.046339
122	2012-09-16	1.428822	1.313815
123	2012-09-23	1.340363	1.093244
124	2012-09-30	1.308595	1.165990
125	2012-10-07	1.167698	1.088619
126	2012-10-14	1.048717	0.930800
127	2012-10-21	0.854887	0.785540
128	2012-10-28	0.935090	0.884650
129	2012-11-04	NaN	0.804076
130	2012-11-11	NaN	0.942208

Table 4. Weekly actual demands data and forecasted data of items of Store-1 (Weekly_Demand_x is actual data and Weekly_ Demand _y is predicted data)

	Date	Weekly_Demand_x	Weekly_Demand_y
115	2012-07-29	2.9	2.87
116	2012-08-05	3.3	3.12
117	2012-08-12	2.1	2.15
118	2012-08-19	2.0	2.14
119	2012-08-26	2.9	2.79
120	2012-09-02	3.8	3.58
121	2012-09-09	4.3	2.51
122	2012-09-16	2.9	2.80
123	2012-09-23	NaN	2.55
124	2012-09-30	1.9	2.13
125	2012-10-07	1.9	2.13
126	2012-10-14	1.8	2.05
127	2012-10-21	4.5	4.09
128	2012-10-28	3.6	3.39
129	2012-11-04	NaN	2.55
130	2012-11-11	NaN	2.73

	Date	Weekly_Demand_x	Weekly_Demand_y
115	2012-07-29	3.0	3.08
116	2012-08-05	1.8	2.69
117	2012-08-12	2.9	3.04
118	2012-08-19	2.3	2.82
119	2012-08-26	2.6	2.93
120	2012-09-02	3.5	3.33
121	2012-09-09	3.8	3.10
122	2012-09-16	3.1	3.10
123	2012-09-23	4.5	4.54
124	2012-09-30	10.0	9.47
125	2012-10-07	8.5	8.30
126	2012-10-14	4.4	4.39
127	2012-10-21	4.6	4.56
128	2012-10-28	3.3	3.12
129	2012-11-04	NaN	3.74
130	2012-11-11	NaN	5.80

	Date	Weekly_Demand_x	Weekly_Demand_y
115	2012-07-29	3.2	3.27
116	2012-08-05	5.7	4.73
117	2012-08-12	5.9	4.89
118	2012-08-19	4.5	3.93
119	2012-08-26	4.3	3.73
120	2012-09-02	4.2	3.74
121	2012-09-09	2.1	3.69
122	2012-09-16	3.6	3.51
123	2012-09-23	3.2	3.53
124	2012-09-30	4.3	3.80
125	2012-10-07	2.1	3.22
126	2012-10-14	3.4	3.18
127	2012-10-21	4.0	3.55
128	2012-10-28	4.0	3.54
129	2012-11-04	NaN	3.38
130	2012-11-11	NaN	3.41

Figure 18. Weekly sales and forecasts of Item-1 (chicken drumstick) of Store-1

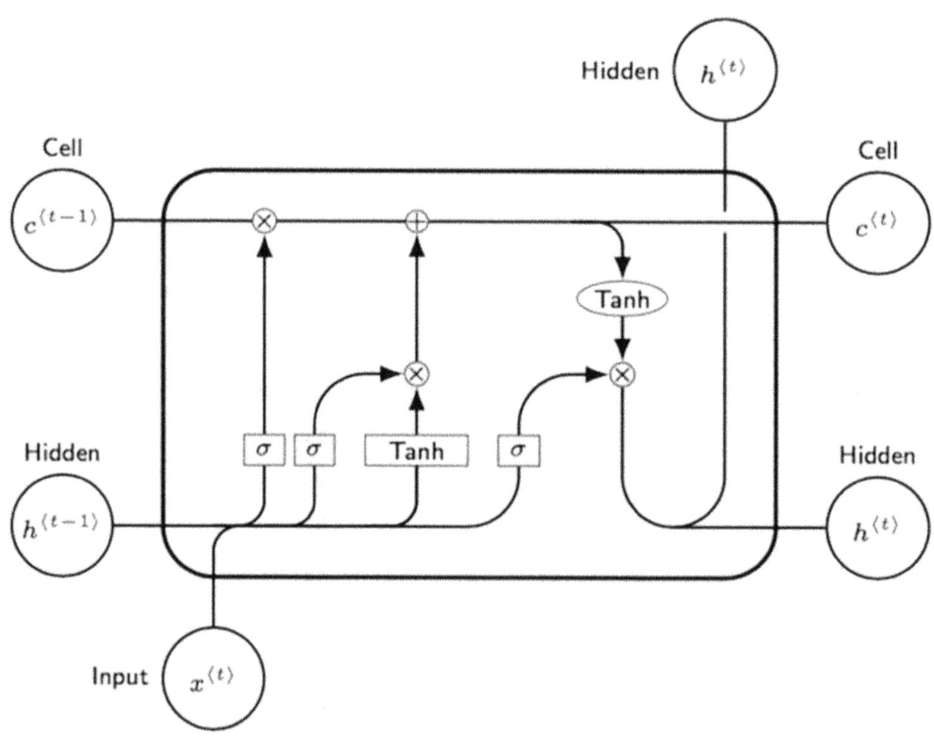

Figure 19. Weekly demands and forecasts of Item-1 (chicken drumstick) of Store-1

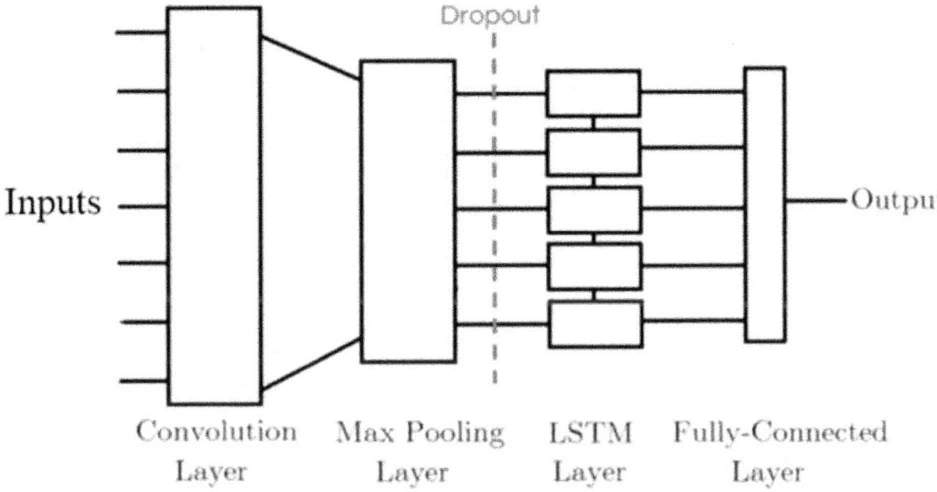

Figure 20. Weekly sales and forecasts of Item-2 (sweet potato) of Store-1

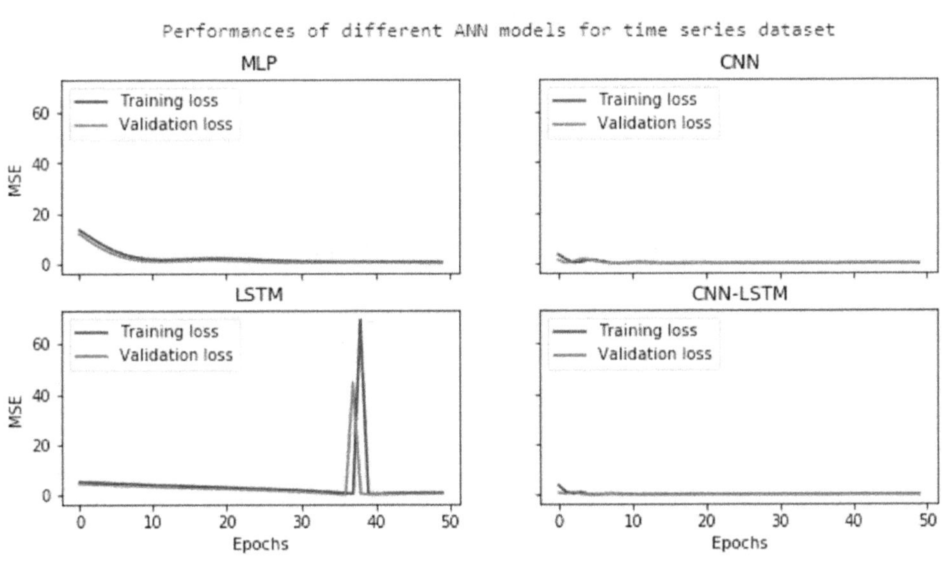

Figure 21. Weekly demands and forecasts of Item-2 (sweet potato) of Store-1

Store	Item	Date	Weekly_Sales
1	1	2010-02-07	24924.50
1	1	2010-02-14	46039.49
1	1	2010-02-21	41595.55
1	1	2010-02-28	19403.54
1	1	2010-03-07	21827.90

Figure 22. Weekly sales and forecasts of Item-3 (chocolate ice cream) of Store-1

Store	Item	Date	Weekly_Demand
1	1	2010-02-07	99
1	1	2010-02-14	54
1	1	2010-02-21	100
1	1	2010-02-28	0
1	1	2010-03-07	51

Figure 23. Weekly demands and forecasts of Item-3 (chocolate ice cream) of Store-1

Date(t-113)	Weekly_Sales(t-113)	...	Date(t-3)	Weekly_Sales(t-3)	Date(t-2)	Weekly_Sales(t-2)	Date(t-1)	Weekly_Sales(t-1)	Date(t)	Weekly_Sales(t)	Date(t+12)	Weekly_Sales(t+12)
2010-03-07	1.55	...	2012-04-15	1.62	2012-04-22	1.52	2012-04-29	1.47	2012-05-06	1.68	2012-07-29	1.44
2010-03-14	1.44	...	2012-04-22	1.52	2012-04-29	1.47	2012-05-06	1.68	2012-05-13	1.61	2012-08-05	1.63
2010-03-21	1.47	...	2012-04-29	1.47	2012-05-06	1.68	2012-05-13	1.61	2012-05-20	1.60	2012-08-12	1.59
2010-03-28	1.40	...	2012-05-06	1.68	2012-05-13	1.61	2012-05-20	1.60	2012-05-27	1.56	2012-08-19	1.60
2010-04-04	1.59	...	2012-05-13	1.61	2012-05-20	1.60	2012-05-27	1.56	2012-06-03	1.62	2012-08-26	1.49

5. CONCLUSION

In this research, advanced forecasting models have been applied. The forecasting models presented here can provide predictions about future demands and sales of products from very high level to individual item level, and they can keep learning on weekly basis. As a result, a retailer could get help to make his/her next business decision from the data.

The developed models are capable of learning long historical data sequences. Long sequences take longer time to learn. Therefore, a future improvement could be minimizing the learning time of the models. In this research, the demands and sales of the products have been presented through a dashboard. This dashboard generates the predictions in real-time, and can become a very powerful tool for the retailers. This is basically a query tool where retailers have to input some criteria to get the result. A future work could be adding more criteria so that the retailer can set those criteria and generate different types of results. This dashboard can become the tool from where retailers can get the picture of their business from different points of view.

ACKNOWLEDGMENT

This research has been supported by an NSERC Discovery grant. The authors would like to thank the editor and reviewers for the great comments that improved the quality of this book chapter. In addition, they would like to thank Dr. Ayse Bener who is the Program Director of the MSc program in Data Science and Analytics at Ryerson University. This research was completed as a part of this program.

REFERENCES

Aburto, L., & Weber, R. (2007). Improved supply chain management based on hybrid demand forecasts. *Applied Soft Computing*, *7*(1), 136–144. doi:10.1016/j.asoc.2005.06.001

Amin-Naseri, M. R., & Tabar, B. R. (2008, May). Neural network approach to lumpy demand forecasting for spare parts in process industries. In *2008 International Conference on Computer and Communication Engineering* (pp. 1378-1382). IEEE. 10.1109/ICCCE.2008.4580831

Baker, S., & Fradkin, A. (2011). What drives job search? Evidence from Google search data. *Discussion Papers*, 10-020.

Bhadouria, S., & Jayant, A. (2017). Development of ANN models for demand forecasting. *Am. J. Eng. Res*, *6*, 142–147.

Choi, H., & Varian, H. (2009). Predicting initial claims for unemployment benefits. *Google Inc*, 1-5.

Choi, H., & Varian, H. (2012). Predicting the present with Google Trends. *The Economic Record*, *88*, 2–9. doi:10.1111/j.1475-4932.2012.00809.x

Counter, S. (2017). Search engine market share worldwide. *StatCounter 1997–2017.*

Delish, E. (2018). *America's Most Delish*. https://www.delish.com/food/a23117553/america-most-delish-grocery-items-2018/

Ginsberg, J., Mohebbi, M. H., Patel, R. S., Brammer, L., Smolinski, M. S., & Brilliant, L. (2009). Detecting influenza epidemics using search engine query data. *Nature*, *457*(7232), 1012–1014. doi:10.1038/nature07634 PMID:19020500

Goel, S., Hofman, J. M., Lahaie, S., Pennock, D. M., & Watts, D. J. (2010). Predicting consumer behavior with Web search. *Proceedings of the National Academy of Sciences of the United States of America*, *107*(41), 17486–17490. doi:10.1073/pnas.1005962107 PMID:20876140

Google Trends. (2019). https://trends.google.com/trends

Guzman, G. (2011). Internet search behavior as an economic forecasting tool: The case of inflation expectations. *Journal of Economic and Social Measurement*, *36*(3), 119–167. doi:10.3233/JEM-2011-0342

Hirschkind, N., Mollick, S., Pari, J., & Khim, J. (2019). Convolutional Neural Network. *BRILLIANT*. https://brilliant.org/wiki/convolutional-neural-network/

Jain, A. K., Mao, J., & Mohiuddin, K. M. (1996). Artificial neural networks: A tutorial. *Computer*, *29*(3), 31–44. doi:10.1109/2.485891

Jun, S. P., Park, D. H., & Yeom, J. (2014). The possibility of using search traffic information to explore consumer product attitudes and forecast consumer preference. *Technological Forecasting and Social Change*, *86*, 237–253. doi:10.1016/j.techfore.2013.10.021

Kaggle. (2019). https://www.kaggle.com/manjeetsingh/retaildataset

Kamble, S. S., Gunasekaran, A., & Gawankar, S. A. (2020). Achieving sustainable performance in a data-driven agriculture supply chain: A review for research and applications. *International Journal of Production Economics*, *219*, 179–194. doi:10.1016/j.ijpe.2019.05.022

Kandananond, K. (2012). Consumer product demand forecasting based on artificial neural network and support vector machine. *World Academy of Science, Engineering and Technology*, *63*, 372–375.

Kaya, G. O., & Turkyilmaz, A. (2018). Intermittent demand forecasting using data mining techniques. *Applied Computer Science, 14*.

Kochak, A., & Sharma, S. (2015). Demand forecasting using neural network for supply chain management. *International Journal of Mechanical Engineering and Robotics Research, 4*(1), 96-104.

Kourentzes, N., Barrow, D. K., & Crone, S. F. (2014). Neural network ensemble operators for time series forecasting. *Expert Systems with Applications*, *41*(9), 4235–4244. doi:10.1016/j.eswa.2013.12.011

Lin, T., Guo, T., & Aberer, K. (2017). Hybrid Neural Networks Over Time Series For Trend Forecasting. *Proceedings of the Twenty-Sixth International Joint Conference on Artificial Intelligence*. 10.24963/ijcai.2017/316

Liu, H. (2015, April). Forecasting Model of Supply Chain Management Based on Neural Network. In *2015 International Conference on Automation, Mechanical Control and Computational Engineering*. Atlantis Press. 10.2991/amcce-15.2015.32

Martins, C. L., & Pato, M. V. (2019). Supply chain sustainability: A tertiary literature review. *Journal of Cleaner Production*, *225*, 995–1016. doi:10.1016/j.jclepro.2019.03.250

Montgomery, D. C., Jennings, C. L., & Kulahci, M. (2015). *Introduction to time series analysis and forecasting*. John Wiley & Sons.

Python Software Foundation. (2016). *Pytrends*. https://pypi.org/project/pytrends/1.1.3/

Shimshoni, Y., Efron, N., & Matias, Y. (2009). *On the predictability of search trends. Technical report*. Google.

Skymind, A. I. Wiki. (2019). *The Artificial Intelligence Wiki*. https://skymind.ai/wiki/

Sosa, P. M. (2018). *Twitter Sentiment Analysis using Combined LSTM-CNN Models*. http://konukoii.com/blog/2018/02/19/twitter-sentiment-analysis-using-combined-lstm-cnn-models/

StackExchange. (2018). *Structure of LSTM RNNs*. https://ai.stackexchange.com/questions/6961/structure-of-lstm-rnns

Su, B. C. (2008). Characteristics of consumer search on-line: How much do we search? *International Journal of Electronic Commerce*, *13*(1), 109–129. doi:10.2753/JEC1086-4415130104

Wijnhoven, F., & Plant, O. (2017). Sentiment Analysis and Google Trends Data for Predicting Car Sales. *Thirty Eighth International Conference on Information Systems.*

Yin, Y., Bu, X., & Yu, F. (2008, October). Adaptive neural network in logistics demand forecasting. In *2008 International Conference on Intelligent Computation Technology and Automation (ICICTA)* (Vol. 1, pp. 168-172). IEEE. 10.1109/ICICTA.2008.73

Chapter 4
A Cluster First-Route Second Solution Approach for the Multi-Period Home Healthcare Routing and Scheduling Problem

Mehmet Erdem
https://orcid.org/0000-0003-4396-2149
Ondokuz Mayıs University, Turkey

Serol Bulkan
https://orcid.org/0000-0002-4815-4389
Marmara University, Turkey

ABSTRACT

In the home healthcare routing and scheduling problem (HHCRSP), nurses are allocated to a variety of services demanded by clients during a planning horizon. The properties of this problem resemble vehicle routing and nurse scheduling. To propose an efficient solution, the authors consider various issues such as multi-depot, travelling time, time windows, synchronisation, the qualification levels, and other features of nurses and clients. In addition, the continuity of care and work overload should not be ignored in this perspective. First, the authors developed a model in which the continuity of care is redefined by considering connected (synchronous) jobs and the work overload is formulated considering nurse-to-patient staffing ratio. Second, a two-stage solution approach based on a cluster-assign algorithm and variable neighbourhood search (VNS) and variable neighbourhood descent (VND) algorithms are tested on a series of large-scale instances. Computational results present the relations and trade-offs among the aforementioned issues.

DOI: 10.4018/978-1-7998-3805-0.ch004

1 INTRODUCTION

Home healthcare (HHC) can be defined as a wide range of medical and non-medical care services that clients/elderly people receive in their homes. The HHC services cover activities such as checking a client's eating and drinking habit, blood pressure, body temperature, breathing, and following upon their prescription and treatments. The aim of these services is to aid clients by improving their living conditions with greater independence, increasing their level of well-being/welfare, receiving care at home instead of hospitals and healthcare institutions over extended periods of time (medicare.gov, 2016). Moreover, compared with the traditional hospital care, HHC services have been found to be cost-efficient in case of certain diseases (NAHC, 2010).

Today, the importance of HHC is even more increased with advancing age and growing populations worldwide. According to the United Nations' (UN) report released in 2010, those at the age of 65 and older comprise 11% of the worlds' population, and this group is expected to grow by 26% by 2050. Therefore, it is estimated that the number of elderly people will be 400 million and 1.5 billion in the developed and developing countries, respectively. Statistics show that in 21 European countries the proportion of the number of 60 year-olds and higher to the entire population has exceeded 20% according to the 2013 figures (Health, 2015; Mattke et al., 2010).

The importance of supply chain management is currently indisputable, but the importance of health supply chains has received attention recently (Nagurney A., 2012). Due to the high cost of human logistics and supply chain management and limited funding available, it is important that countries and organizations make the most of the limited resources (Vaillancourt, Tatham, Wu, & Haavisto, 2018) . It is estimated that more than 40% of the financial resources used by the humanitarian logistics operation is wasted (Day, Melnyk, Larson, Davis, & Whybark, 2012). Pan American Health Organization underlines two important issues humanitarian supply logistics (PAHO, 2001):

1. Supply chain management should be an integrated approach. The alignment across the business processes and their interdependence should not be ignored in this framework. 2. Employing human resources appropriately and identifying their availability, capabilities, and locations are crucial activities. Therefore, the planning/scheduling and preparedness are important not only for countries, but also for organizations.

In the USA, it was calculated that HHC workers drive 7.88 billion miles (more than 40 round-trips to the sun) and 718 million visits in 2013 alone. In 2006, the estimated number of miles driven for these services was 4.76 billion. This means

200% increase in the estimated number of miles driven (NAHC, 2015). These figures emphasize the importance of proposing tangible solutions for healthcare systems with minimum distance.

Generally speaking, HHC is a more convenient and effective way to make services available in clients' familiar environments with less costs in the long-term. However, designing schedules is difficult due to certain considerations such as preferences, policies, visiting time intervals, and travelling times. The scheduling of the HHC is still based upon ad hoc methods; hence, finding an optimum solution to meet the increasing demands as well as client/nurse satisfaction is a challenging task.

In this work, the authors address and solve the multi-period home healthcare routing and scheduling problem (HHCRSP). The contribution of this work is to propose a solution approach to be used for assigning nurses to clients while considering the continuity of care, work overload and their preferences. Besides, issues such as minimizing the total time (costs) (travelling time of nurses and waiting time) and overtime work, covering all the jobs as much as possible, and fulfilling those jobs at the clients' preferred starting time is also considered.

This work is organized as follows: in Section 2, a literature review on the multi-period HHCRSP is given. In Section 3, the definition of the problem and the mathematical model are described. The proposed solution approach is presented in Section 4. The results and computational comparisons are reported in Section 5. Finally, the article is concluded and future research is discussed in the last section.

2 LITERATURE REVIEW

The literature related to the HHC routing and scheduling problems has been reviewed in (Cissé et al., 2017; Fikar & Hirsch, 2017). These recently published works already provided taxonomic reviews about existing works, this section covers a summary of the most relevant publications. The existing literature is mainly classified in terms of the length of the planning horizon. The decisions of Operations Management (OM) can be divided into four levels according to the time horizon. These are strategic (1-5 years), tactical (6-12 months), operational (weeks-months), and detailed operational levels (hours-days) (Matta, Chahed, Sahin, & Dallery, 2014). In this work, the authors address the operational level of scheduling and routing problem. The publications dealing with this problem have three main differences, namely (1) particular objectives, (2) constraints, and (3) solution methodology. The objectives of the multi-term HHCRSP are summarized in Table 1. While the multi-term papers are introduced in the first column, the performance measures or objectives are represented in the others. If a paper covers one of these objectives, it is assigned a plus (+) symbol in the corresponding cells. Moreover, if a paper does

Table 1. Objectives of the multi-term HHCRSPs (Fikar & Hirsch, 2017)

Paper	T	C	D	WT	OT	BW	PR	NJ	NN	NU	SM	PRI	CC
Begur et al. (1997)	+	-	+	-	-	-	-	-	-	-	-	-	-
De Angelis (1998)	-	-	-	-	-	-	-	+	-	-	-	-	-
Hertz and Lahrichi (2009)	-	-	+	-	-	+	-	-	-	-	+	-	-
Bachouch et al. (2011)	-	-	+	-	-	-	-	-	-	-	-	-	-
Bennett and Erera (2011)	-	-	-	-	-	-	-	+	-	-	-	-	-
Barrera et al. (2012)	-	-	-	-	-	+	-	-	+	-	-	-	-
Gamst and Jensen (2012)	+	+	-	-	-	-	+	-	-	-	-	+	-
Nickel et al. (2012)	-	-	+	-	+	-	-	-	-	+	-	-	+
Shao et al. (2012)	-	+	-	-	+	-	-	-	-	-	-	-	-
Bennett-Milburn and Spicer (2013)	-	+	-	-	-	+	-	-	-	-	-	-	+
Cappanera and Scutellà (2013)	-	-	-	-	-	+	-	-	-	-	-	-	-
Bard, Shao, and Jarrah (2014)	-	+	-	-	+	-	-	-	-	-	-	-	-
Bard, Shao, Qi, et al. (2014)	-	+	-	-	+	-	-	-	-	-	-	-	-
Ramos et al. (2014)	+	-	-	-	-	-	-	-	-	-	-	-	-
Trautsamwieser and Hirsch (2014)	+	-	-	+	-	-	-	-	-	-	-	-	-
Cappanera and Scutellà (2015)	-	-	-	-	-	+	-	-	-	-	-	-	-
Maya Duque et al. (2015)	-	-	+	-	-	-	+	-	-	-	-	-	-
Wirnitzer et al. (2016)	-	-	-	-	-	-	-	+	-	-	-	-	+
Yalçındağ et al. (2016)	-	+	-	-	-	+	-	-	-	-	-	-	-
The proposed study	+	-	+	+	+	+	+	-	+	+	-	-	+

Time:T, Cost:C, Distance:D, Waiting:WT, Overtime work:OT, Balance of the workload:BW, Patient-Staff preferences:PR, Number of admitted patients (or jobs):NJ, Number of nurses:NN, Uncovered visits:NU, Skill matching:SM, Priority:PRI, Continuity of care:CC

not involve an objective/a constraint, a dash (-) symbol assigns. The meanings of the abbreviations in the tables are given under the tables.

Generally, the HHCRSP is modelled based on the VRP (Bard, Shao, & Jarrah, 2014; Begur, Miller, & Weaver, 1997; Nickel, Schröder, & Steeg, 2012; Ramos, Lizarazo, Rubiano, & Araújo, 2014; Trautsamwieser & Hirsch, 2014); hence, travelling time and related costs are most frequently used as basic criteria. In addition, the issues such as overtime work (Bard, Shao, & Jarrah, 2014; Bard, Shao, Qi, & Jarrah, 2014; Nickel et al., 2012; Shao, Bard, & Jarrah, 2012), workload balance (Barrera, Velasco, & Amaya, 2012; Bennett-Milburn & Spicer, 2013; Cappanera & Scutellà, 2013, 2015), the continuity of care (Bennett-Milburn & Spicer, 2013; Nickel et al., 2012; Wirnitzer, Heckmann, Meyer, & Nickel, 2016), and unscheduled visits (Nickel et al., 2012) are also examined in various works. The minimization of overtime works is considered as an important objective in some studies (e.g. (Bard, Shao, & Jarrah, 2014; Bard, Shao, Qi, et al., 2014; Nickel et al., 2012; Shao et al.,

2012)). Decreasing the overtime work, which is considered as a cost component, is as important factor as workload balance. However, none of the works consider the nurse-to-patient staffing ratio of 1:8. This ratio indicates a risk level and it does not mean a recommended minimum ratio. When the assigned number of patients to a nurse exceeds this level, the patients may be at the risk of harm. Therefore, this ratio is defined as a term 'over workload' and integrated in the proposed multi-period model for a quality indicator of the solution.

Many works (Bachouch, Guinet, & Hajri-Gabouj, 2011; Bennett-Milburn & Spicer, 2013; Nickel et al., 2012; Wirnitzer et al., 2016) deal with the continuity of care which can be defined as a few nurses visit same client during the planning horizon. This formulation can be misleading, given the fact that some of the jobs are connected (synchronous) jobs. On the other hand, our newly developed constraint for the continuity of care does not ignore these jobs.

Similarly, Table 2 presents the constraints of the multi-term HHCRSP. The majority of model covers time windows, working regulations, and skill matching as constraints. Although the continuity of care is considered as an objective, this term is also employed as hard and soft constraints in many of the publications (Bachouch et al., 2011; Cappanera & Scutellà, 2015; Maya Duque, Castro, Sörensen, & Goos, 2015; Yalçındağ et al., 2016). Time windows can also be defined as hard (Bard, Shao, & Jarrah, 2014) or soft (Nickel et al., 2012; Trautsamwieser & Hirsch, 2014) constraint. In the first case (hard time windows), nurses must visit clients within the desired time windows. In the second case (soft time windows), the deviations from the time windows are penalized.

The issues such as connected jobs or temporal precedence has received little attention in the multi-period problems. In order to perform a synchronous job (e.g. lifting a heavy client), more than one nurse should visit the same client at the same time. It is reported that connected jobs or temporal precedence constitute between 10% and 30% of all healthcare services (Fikar & Hirsch, 2017).

In order to solve the multi-period HHCRSP, a series of exact, heuristic/ metaheuristic, and hybrid approaches have been proposed. Exact algorithms can be dealt with only in small instances. The multi-period HHCRSP is NP-hard (Rasmussen et al., 2012) and cannot be solved in polynomial time; therefore, the authors developed a metaheuristic approach based on the VNS and VNS algorithms to solve large-scale instances.

Table 2. Constraints of the multi-term HHCRSPs (Fikar & Hirsch, 2017)

Paper	TW	SM	PR	PE	TR	S	WT	B	U	CC
Begur et al. (1997)	+	+	-	+	+	-	-	-	-	-
De Angelis (1998)	-	-	-	-	-	-	-	-	+	-
Hertz and Lahrichi (2009)	-	+	-	-	-	-	-	-	-	-
Bachouch et al. (2011)	+	+	-	-	+	+	+	+	-	+
Bennett and Erera (2011)	+	-	-	-	-	-	+	-	+	-
Barrera et al. (2012)	+	-	-	-	-	-	-	-	-	-
Gamst and Jensen (2012)	+	+	-	+	-	-	-	-	-	-
Nickel et al. (2012)	+	+	-	-	-	-	+	-	-	-
Shao et al. (2012)	+	+	-	-	+	-	-	+	-	-
Bennett-Milburn and Spicer (2013)	-	-	-	-	-	-	+	-	-	-
Cappanera and Scutellà (2013)	-	+	-	-	-	-	+	-	-	-
Bard, Shao, and Jarrah (2014)	+	+	+	-	-	-	+	+	-	-
Bard, Shao, Qi, et al. (2014)	+	+	+	-	-	-	+	+	-	-
Ramos et al. (2014)	-	-	+	+	-	-	-	-	-	-
Trautsamwieser and Hirsch (2014)	+	+	-	-	-	-	+	+	-	-
Cappanera and Scutellà (2015)	+	+	-	-	-	-	+	-	-	+
Maya Duque et al. (2015)	+	+	+	-	-	-	+	-	-	+
Wirnitzer et al. (2016)	-	+	-	-	-	-	+	+	-	-
Yalçındağ et al. (2016)	-	+	-	-	-	-	+	-	-	+
The proposed study	+	+	+	-	-	+	+	-	-	+

Time windows:TW, Skill matching:SM, Preferences:PR, Periodicity:PE, Time relation:TR, Synchronization:S, Working Time Regulations:WT, Breaks:B, Uncertainty:U, Continuity of care:CC

3 THE MULTI-PERIOD HOME HEALTH CARE ROUTING AND SCHEDULING PROBLEM

The Home Healthcare Routing and Scheduling Problem (HHCRSP) is a combination of two NP hard problems: vehicles routing problem with time windows (VRPTW) and nurse rostering problem (NRP). The goal of HHC services is to increase the living conditions of clients with greater independence, to decrease the effects of the diseases, to receive care at home instead of hospitals and healthcare institutions. The HHCRSP considers the assignment, routing, and scheduling for a set of clients scattered in different locations. The difference between the single-period and multi-period HHCRSP is that not all the healthcare demands emerge in one-period. Therefore, in the multi-period HHCRSP clients demand a set of different types of services at different times of planning horizon. Moreover, a varied range of challenging factors such as the assignment of heterogeneous nurses, the continuity of care, qualification levels and the features of nurses and clients should be considered.

The set of the days is denoted by *G*, which also represents a planning horizon. The set of the nurses and clients are denoted by *N* and *C*, respectively. Each client can be visited more than once each day. Hence, the set of jobs is shown by *J*. Moreover, in order to achieve a job, the synchronisation may be necessary. For this reason, a set of synchronized jobs (*P*) is also defined. Each nurse starts and ends her/his route from her/his own home location. Hence, the location of home is represented by two artificial jobs $\{h_n, h'_n\}$, where h_n corresponds to start respectively, ending home at the location of nurse *n*. For each nurse *n*, the set of all possible jobs is defined as $JA_n = J \cup \{h_n, h'_n\}$. Each job *i* has a time window, a desired starting time, and a duration which are represented by $[a'_i, b'_i]$, $t'_{ig} \in [a'_i, b'_i]$, and d_{ig}. The working time interval is defined by $[a_n, b_n]$, which is the same for the artificial jobs. Nurse *n* cannot start before a_n and should achieve the assigned job(s) before b_n. The generation of different types of shifts is ignored to generalize the problem. In this way, the contract specific properties are neglected. Nurse *n* can only work overtime if s/he starts before b_n; otherwise, nurse *n* is not allowed to work overtime. There is no duration and desired starting time for the artificial jobs. Each client can request a wide range of healthcare services such as applying medical treatments, checking blood pressure, cleaning clients' home, etc. These daily requests of a client are defined as jobs. On the other hand, a job which is demanded by a client occurs many times in the planning horizon, therefore achieving each job is defined as a task. When a client demands a set of jobs which also generate several tasks (Nickel et al., 2012). The parameter r_{ig} represents service requests. r_{ig}=1 if a job *i* is required on day *g*; otherwise, zero.

Each nurse is allowed to use a predetermined mode. The travelling time between two jobs (*i* and *j*) depends on the transportation modes. Parameter s_{ijn} states the travelling time from job *i* to *j* for nurse *n*. Moreover, the travelling time from/to any of the artificial jobs is set to be zero. The parameter p_{cjg} is defined for the synchronous jobs requested by client *c*. p_{cjg}=1 if a client *c* demands a synchronous job *j* on day *g*; otherwise, p_{cjg}=0.

The time cost (c_{ijng}) consists of the travelling time, the duration of job *i* on day *g* (d_{ig}), and also the waiting time (e_{ing}) of nurse *n* if s/he arrives before ja_i on day *g*. The arriving time at job *i* by nurse *n* on day *g* is represented by v_{ing}. The scheduling variable t_{ing} is defined as the starting time of the job *i* by nurse *n* on day *g*, and t_{ng} is the nurse *n*'s completion time of the last assigned job on day *g*. o_{ng} is the overtime work by nurse *n* on day *g*.

The continuity of care, can be defined as a few nurses visit one client (Nickel et al., 2012), is a crucial component of planning that prevents of breakdowns in healthcare, increases customer satisfaction, creates a friendly environment and develops a personal relationship. Therefore, the authors have redefined the term 'continuity of care' as the difference between the total number of different nurses that care for the same clients and the number of synchronized jobs demanded by clients during the planning horizon. For the calculation of the continuity of care, the authors also subtract one which means if a client is cared for by the same nurse, then the continuity of care gets zero for this client. The number of synchronized jobs throughout the planning horizon and the continuity of care for a client c are defined by μ_c and δ_c, respectively. As mentioned earlier, some of the jobs are required the presence of more than one nurse, hence each of the synchronous job is involved in the route/roster of two nurses. The new redefinition of continuity of care is included in the proposed model. Hence, our newly developed constraint considers the number of nurses treating connected jobs (here synchronized jobs) and prevent duplication in contrast to (Bachouch et al., 2011). Suppose that a client requests a synchronous job every day (everyday visit). According to the general formulation in the literature, a total of 14 nurses will visit this client (where different nurses are allocated in each time). Considering that a synchronous job requires two different nurses, this request of 7 visits (or tasks) is incorrectly calculated as 14 visits (or tasks) in terms of the same client. It is obvious that this incorrect calculation leads to increase in the continuity of care.

For the safety and quality of healthcare, the nurse-to-patient staffing ratio is suggested not to exceed that of 1:8 (Aiken, Clarke, Sloane, Sochalski, & Silber, 2002) for hospitals. In our case, the authors convert the nurse-to-patient staffing ratio into the nurse-to-job ratio and take into account that this ratio does not exceed 1:8 for the HHC system. In our study, the work overload is calculated in terms of the number of assigned jobs. Therefore, it is considered that exceeding the rate of nurse-to-job ratio leads to the status of work overload. If the total assigned number of jobs to a nurse is more than eight in a working day, it means that the work overload occurs and the quality level of HHC decreases. The number of working days and work overload for nurse n are computed by α_n and β_n, respectively.

Hierarchical qualification levels are defined for the nurses and jobs from one to five. A nurse can achieve a job if s/he has an equal or higher level. q_n and q'_i represent the qualifications of the nurses and jobs, respectively. Similarly, the features of nurses (f_n) and clients (f'_i), such as gender, smoking habits, pet (cat and dog) ownership/allergy, are considered and incompatibility is not allowed. For instance, a female client (c_i) representing her characteristics with a vector (0,1,0,0,0) may disapprove to be treated by a male caretaker (n_n) (0,1,0,0,0); hence, a female nurse n_m (1,0,0,0,0) must be assigned to the clients.

In the following mathematical model, the authors denote x_{ijng} as the binary routing variable that equals 1 if nurse n travels through job j after handling job i on day g, and otherwise 0. The binary coverage variable is denoted u_{ig} that is 1 if job i on day g is uncovered, and otherwise zero. Similarly, the binary coverage variable u'_{ijg} is introduced for the synchronized jobs. The binary decision variable (y_{cng}) is defined for the calculation of continuity of care. y_{cng} is 1 if nurse n visits customer c on day g; otherwise 0. The multi-period formulation is extended from the single-period formulation work of (Bredström & Rönnqvist, 2008; Rasmussen et al., 2012) The extended multi-period formulation also considers the issues such as the features of clients and nurses, overtime work, the continuity of care, work overload, and the desired starting time of jobs. The HHCRSP can be modelled as follows:

$$Min.\ w_1\left(\gamma_1\sum_{n\in N}\sum_{i\in JA_n}\sum_{j\in JA_n}\sum_{g\in G}c_{ijng}x_{ijng}\right)+w_2\left(\gamma_2\sum_{i\in J}\sum_{g\in G}z_{ig}\right)+w_3\left(\gamma_3\sum_{i\in J}\sum_{g\in G}u_{ig}\right)$$
$$+w_4\left(\gamma_4\sum_{n\in N}\sum_{g\in G}o_{ng}\right)+w_5\left(\gamma_5\sum_{n\in N}\beta_n\right)+w_6\left(\gamma_6\sum_{c\in C}\delta_c\right) \tag{1}$$

$$st.\ \sum_{n\in N}\sum_{j\in JA_n}x_{ijng}+u_{ig}=r_{ig} \qquad \forall i\in J,\ \forall g\in G \tag{2}$$

$$u_{ig}+u_{jg}=2u'_{ijg} \qquad \forall (c,i)\text{ and }(c,j)\in P,\ \forall g\in G \tag{3}$$

$$\sum_{j\in JA_n}x_{ijng}q'_i\le q_n \qquad \forall n\in N,\ \forall i\in J,\ \forall g\in G \tag{4}$$

$$\sum_{j\in JA_n}x_{ijng}\le y_{cng} \qquad \forall n\in N,\ \forall i\in JA_n,\ \forall g\in G,\ \forall c\in C \tag{5}$$

$$\mu_c=\sum_{g\in G}\sum_{j\in J}p_{cjg} \qquad \forall c\in C \tag{6}$$

$$\delta_c = \sum_{n \in N} \sum_{g \in G} y_{cng} - \mu_c - 1 \qquad \forall c \in C \tag{7}$$

$$\sum_{j \in JA_n} x_{h_n jng} = 1 \qquad \forall n \in N,\ \forall g \in G \tag{8}$$

$$\sum_{i \in JA_n} x_{ih'_n ng} = 1 \qquad \forall n \in N,\ \forall g \in G \tag{9}$$

$$\sum_{i \in JA_n} x_{ikng} = \sum_{j \in JA_n} x_{kjng} \qquad \forall n \in N,\ \forall k \in J,\ \forall g \in G \tag{10}$$

$$a'_i \sum_{j \in JA_n} x_{ijng} \le t_{ing} \le b'_i \sum_{j \in JA_n} x_{ijng} \qquad \forall n \in N,\ \forall i \in J \cup \{h'_n\},\ \forall g \in G \tag{11}$$

$$a_n \le t_{ing} \le b_n \qquad \forall n \in N,\ \forall i \in J,\ \forall g \in G \tag{12}$$

$$t_{ing} + s_{ijn} x_{ijng} + d_{ig} x_{ijng} \le t_{jng} + b'_i (1 - x_{ijng}) \qquad \forall n \in N,\ \forall i, j \in JA_n, \forall g \in G \tag{13}$$

$$\sum_{n \in N} t_{ing} = \sum_{n \in N} t_{jng} \qquad \forall (c,i) \text{ and } (c,j) \in P,\ \forall g \in G \tag{14}$$

$$\sum_{l \in JA_n} x_{ling} - \sum_{l \in JA_n} x_{ljng} \le 1 \qquad \forall n \in N,\ \forall (c,i) \text{ and } (c,j) \in P,\ \forall g \in G \tag{15}$$

$$o_{ng} \ge (t_{ng} - b_n) \qquad \forall n \in N,\ \forall g \in G \tag{16}$$

$$\sum_{j \in JA_n} x_{ijng} \left(f_n + f'_i \right) \le \mathbf{1} \qquad \forall n \in N,\ \forall i \in J,\ \forall g \in G \tag{17}$$

$$\left(\sum_{n\in N} t_{ing} - t'_{ig}\right) \le z_{ig} \qquad \forall i \in JA_n,\ \forall g \in G \qquad (18)$$

$$-\left(\sum_{n\in N} t_{ing} - t'_{ig}\right) \le z_{ig} \qquad \forall i \in JA_n,\ \forall g \in G \qquad (19)$$

$$\alpha_n = \sum_{g\in G} y_{cng} \qquad \forall n \in N,\ \forall c \in C \qquad (20)$$

$$\beta_n = \left(\sum_{i\in J}\sum_{g\in G} x_{ijng} - 8\alpha_n\right) \qquad \forall n \in N \qquad (21)$$

$$c_{ijng} = d_{ig} + s_{ijn} + e_{ing} \qquad \forall n \in N,\ \forall i,j \in J,\ \forall g \in G \qquad (22)$$

$$v_{ing} = t_{kng} + d_{kg} + s_{ink} \qquad \forall n \in N,\ \forall i \in J,\ \forall k \in J \cup \{h'_n\},\ \forall g \in G \qquad (23)$$

$$e_{ing} \ge t_{ing} - v_{ing} \qquad \forall n \in N,\ \forall i \in J,\ \forall g \in G \qquad (24)$$

$$o_{ng} \ge 0 \qquad \forall n \in N, \forall g \in G \qquad (25)$$

$$\beta_n \ge 0 \qquad \forall n \in N \qquad (26)$$

$$e_{ing} \ge 0 \qquad \forall n \in N,\ \forall i \in J,\ \forall g \in G \qquad (27)$$

$$x_{ijng} \in \{0,1\} \qquad \forall n \in N,\ \forall\, i,j \in JA_n,\ \forall g \in G \qquad (28)$$

$$u_{ig} \in \{0,1\} \qquad \forall i \in J,\ \forall g \in G \qquad (29)$$

$$y_{cng} \in \{0,1\} \qquad \forall c \in C,\ \forall n \in N,\ \forall g \in G \tag{30}$$

$$u'_{ijg} \in \{0,1\} \qquad \forall (c,i) \text{ and } (c,j) \in P,\ \forall g \in G \tag{31}$$

$$t_{ng}, t_{ing} \in \mathbb{N} \qquad \forall i \in JA_n,\ \forall n \in N,\ \forall g \in G \tag{32}$$

$$z_{ig} \in \mathbb{R} \qquad \forall i \in JA_n,\ \forall g \in G \tag{33}$$

The objective function (1) aims at minimizing the total time (costs), deviation from the desired starting time, uncovered visits, overtime work, work overload and continuity of care. The authors use scalarization parameters for the terms of the multi-objective function so that bring the objective values into the same scale. This is accomplished by setting $\gamma_1 = \gamma_2 = 1$, $\gamma_3 = T$, $\gamma_4 = C/2$, $\gamma_5 = C$, and $\gamma_6 = C/20$, in which T and C are the number of tasks and clients, respectively (parameters are in time units). The terms of the objective function are equally weighted ($w_k = 1/6$, $k = 1,2,\ldots,6$). Constraints (2) guarantee that each job is either covered or uncovered. Similar to (2), constraints (3) satisfy the synchronized jobs performed or not performed. Constraints (4) ensure that each nurse is allocated to care a job if her/his qualification level is equal or higher. Constraints (5)-(7) are introduced to compute the continuity of care. The number of different nurses treating client c is computed by (5) and, similarly the number of connected jobs is calculated by (6). The redefined continuity of care is formulated by introducing constraints in (7). Moreover, these newly developed constraints prevent double calculation of the number of nurses treating synchronous jobs. Constraints (8)-(9) ensure that home location is the starting and ending point of route for each nurse. Constraints (10) guarantee the flow conservation. In order to ensure that all jobs are performed within their pre-determined time windows and that nurses are only allocated tasks within their working time windows, constraints (11) and (12) are added to the model. The travelling times between two locations are considered via (13). Constraints (14)-(15) are employed for the synchronization. The overtime work is computed via constraints (16). The features of clients and nurses are taken into consideration based on constraints (17). The deviation from the desired starting time of the jobs which expresses a piecewise linear function is calculated by constraints (18)-(19). The total number of working days for each nurse is computed by constraints (20). Constraints (21) determine the work overload of nurses. For each nurse the work overload calculated as the difference between the total number of performed jobs (during the planning horizon) and the multiplication of α_n (the number of working days) and 8 (the nurse-to-job ratio). The total time (costs), the arriving time of nurses, and the waiting time of nurses are calculated by (22)-(24). (25)-(27) are non-negativity constraints. The domains of the decision variables are set by constraints (28)-(33).

4 SOLUTION APPROACH

To solve the multi-period HHCRSP, the authors introduce a two-stage solution approach. Each stage of this approach is summarized in Figure 1. In the first stage, a cluster-assign algorithm is employed for decreasing the dimension of the problem. This algorithm does not yield deterministic solutions. In the next stage, the authors generate the initial solution by using one of the three different construction algorithms (CAs), and then, the authors improve the obtained solution by means of either VNS or VND heuristic. In the literature, generally, employs simple and basic local search operators; whereas our proposed neighbourhood structures are used for not only search, but also to utilize the idle components (nurses) of the solutions. On the other hand, ours do not ignore free nurses and nurses who are allocated only one job on a daily basis. Hence, our proposed neighbourhood structures increase the utilization of human resources. And, this approach is free from parameter tuning. In the following, each stage of the proposed approach is described.

Figure 1. Solution approach for the multi-period HHCRSP

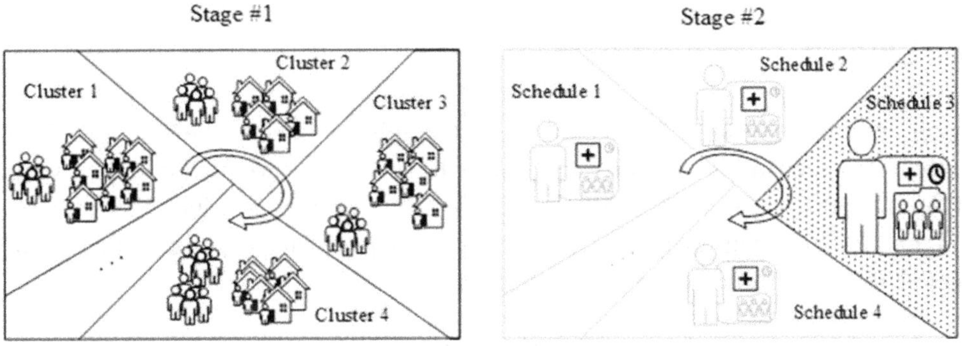

4.1 Stage 1

Before the improvement of the solution, the cluster-assign algorithm is employed to reduce the complexity of the problem. This algorithm starts with forming clusters by using a two-step clustering (TSC) algorithm (Chiu, Fang, Chen, Wang, & Jeris, 2001) as pre-clustering and clustering steps. In the initial step of the algorithm, the data is analysed and then a decision is made based on the distance as a criterion; whether, that is a case is to be added to obtained clusters, or a new cluster is to be constructed. By constructing the cluster feature tree, each pre-cluster is identified. The pre-clusters are the input of the next (clustering) step. The hierarchical clustering algorithm scans each of the pre-clusters by using a bottom-up strategy and combines the two closest ones together. The TSC algorithm has the opportunity to yield the number of clusters automatically. This is achieved in the second step, where the Bayesian information criterion (BIC) for each cluster is minimized and the distance measure is maximized (Chiu et al., 2001).

The TSC algorithm is used for constructing the clusters (nurse and client) automatically based on the location as represented by latitude and longitude. Afterwards, if the number of clusters for the nurse and the client is different, the maximum number of clusters is re-constructed according to the minimum number of clusters by using the TSC algorithm. After obtaining an equal size of clusters for the nurse and the client, the second step begins with the assignment. For the appropriateness of the assignment, the working time windows and the desired starting time of the jobs should be both applicable and convenient. Moreover, while time convenience is considered, the construction of cluster pairs is also formed by the travelling (time) between them. Consequently, the cluster pairs are formed with respect to location and time.

4.2 Stage 2

After obtaining the pair of clusters, the next step is to generate the solutions. The authors first construct solutions and, then, these are improved using either VNS or VND heuristic. The VNS has a local search procedure, in which the order of neighbourhoods changes dynamically based on the performance, on the other hand, the VND has a deterministic order procedure.

4.2.1 Variable Neighbourhood Search (VNS)

VNS is a metaheuristic approach proposed by Mladenovic and Hansen (1997) about two decades ago, and proposes a principle that depends upon the change of neighbourhood systematically so as to search for a local optimum. Moreover, it also avoids being trapped in local minima. Initially, it was designed for the approximate calculation of optimization problems. Applications can be found in a variety of fields such as clustering, artificial intelligence, biology, reliability, etc. (Pierre Hansen, Mladenović, Brimberg, & Pérez, 2010). Moreover, the VNS algorithm is also successfully applied to the fields of scheduling and routing (Bräysy & Gendreau, 2005). In contrast to other metaheuristics, VNS proposes simplicity and uses fewer parameters. In the proposed VNS algorithm, the neighbourhoods are reordered dynamically (Prandtstetter, Raidl, & Misar, 2009) in the local search process. If a neighbourhood shows a higher improvement on the objective function, then the order of the neighbourhoods is modified according to such performance. In the proposed VNS algorithm, our local search structure covers a series of neighbourhoods that provide higher capabilities and also shaking is accomplished by two operators. On the other hand, in the VND algorithm the neighbourhoods are changed only deterministically and the VND does not cover a shaking procedure.

4.2.2 Initial Solution

Stage 2 starts with one of the three construction algorithms (CAs), which are deterministic (CA1), random (CA2), and hybrid (CA3, deterministic-random). CA1 considers the idle smallest indexed nurse and assigns the unscheduled smallest indexed job if the set of constraints is satisfied. In CA1, the assignments of nurse-job are determined deterministically; whereas, in CA2 the assignments are decided randomly. That is, CA2 tries to assign randomly-selected jobs to randomly-selected nurses. Finally, initial schedules are generated by CA3, in which randomly chosen jobs are allocated to the idle smallest indexed nurse. At the end of running the CAs, some requested jobs remain uncovered. In this way, all CAs yield a more relaxed solution compared to the algorithms that start with the exact solution.

4.2.3 Neighbourhood Structures

The neighbourhood structures, which are illustrated in Figure 2, group into three categories: cross, vertical, and horizontal. Here circular and square nodes correspond to nurse and job, respectively. Dashed arcs indicate available movements for each strategy. Each of these has three sub-strategies. The cross neighbourhood structures (Figure 2 a-c) focus on the idle nurses (Strategy 2), unscheduled jobs (Strategy 3), and the nurses who are allocated to only one job within the generated schedule (Strategy 4). If the uncovered job list is not empty, then Strategy 3 selects one of the uncovered jobs and tries to allocate this job to a nurse. Strategy 2 tries to swap working and idle nurses for the improvement of the objective. Strategy 4 focuses on the one-job routes for destruction if there is an improvement. The element of the one-job route is then assigned to another working nurse. By means of this group, the authors increase the utility of human resource. The vertical neighbourhood structures (Figure 2 d-f) contain an exchange strategy for nurses (Strategy 1) and jobs (Strategy 5), and an insertion strategy for a job (Strategy 6). Strategy 1 deals with the swapping two working nurses, here all the assigned jobs are replaced. Strategy 5 is proposed to swap two jobs. Strategy 6 chooses one of the assigned jobs and allocates this job to a different working nurse.

Figure 2. Neighbourhood structures

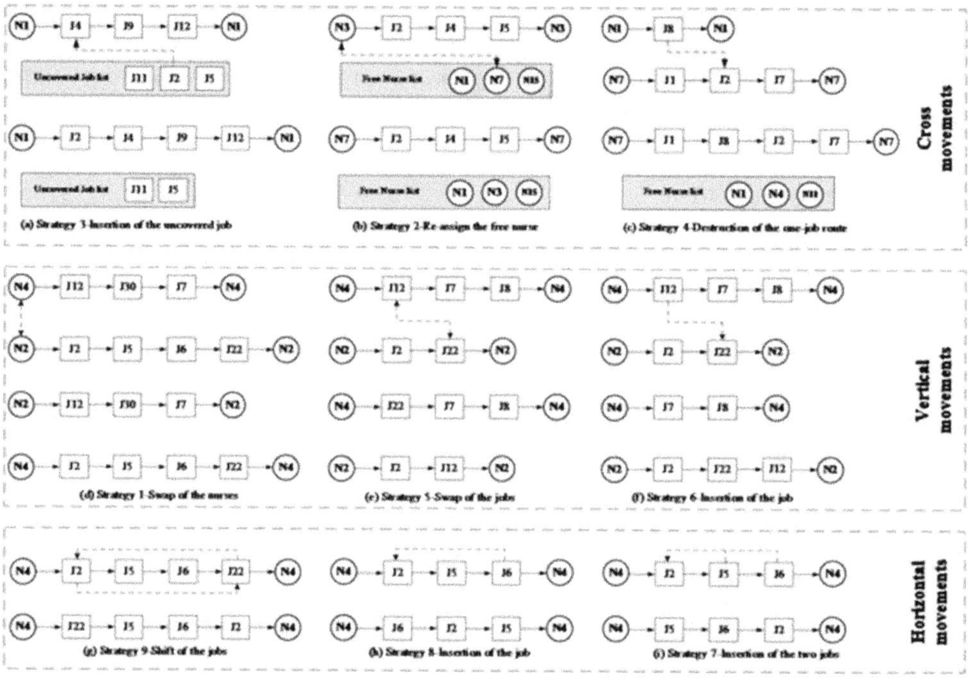

The last neighbourhood structures consist of horizontal movements (Figure 2 g-i). Two insertion strategies (Strategies 7-8) and a shift strategy (Strategy 9) are employed for finding the appropriate order of the assigned jobs to nurses. All of the aforementioned improvement strategies select job(s) or nurse(s) at random. In the second stage, the authors use the VNS algorithm with a dynamic reordering mechanism (with nine neighbourhoods) and also the VND algorithm with nine neighbourhoods for the problem. In addition, the VNS algorithm has also a shaking procedure, where Strategies 1 and 3 are used. If there is no improvement, a shaking procedure starts with Strategy 1, then Strategy 3 continues to cover the uncovered jobs.

The order of strategies in the local search is arranged considering the performance of the algorithm.

5 COMPUTATIONAL EXPERIMENTS

In order to test the proposed approach, the authors used the publicly available instances provided by the authors of (Erdem & Bulkan, 2017; Hiermann et al., 2015a) as single-period work. The set of instances is extended to a weekly planning horizon problem. The authors generated 12 of small-scale (up to 7 days, 5 nurses, 5 clients, 11 jobs, 51 tasks) and 45 large-scale instances (up to 7 days, 1580 nurses, 1561 clients, 2709 jobs, 11112 tasks) from these to maintain the same ratio of given features. For each instance, the number of instances (I), nurses (N), clients (C), jobs (J), and tasks (T) are given. Here, T means the number of tasks which equals to total service requests. Furthermore, S refers to the name of the small-scale instances. The clients and nurses are equally distributed in an area of 400 km^2. For each instance the 5% jobs are added to the synchronization. The distance between two nodes is defined as a time unit for different modes of transportation (personal car and public transportation); similarly, each instance has a variety of working time windows and pre-determined time windows for the jobs. A time unit corresponds to 5 minutes. On the other hand, during the planning horizon the service time, otherwise, refers to as 'the duration of jobs', the preferred starting time of the job, and the frequency of jobs are generated randomly. The durations are uniformly distributed in [1, 30], which also equals to [5, 150] minutes range, each job i has a uniformly distributed preferred starting time in its specified time window $[a_i', b_i']$. The time window and duration of each job are fixed and dependent of a day; however, the preferred starting time of each job is independent of a day. The healthcare service frequency is formed by considering the four types of client schemes, which are everyday visit, twice-a-week visit, and every-other-day visit, and once-a-week visit, and are generated randomly while keeping the ratio of 40%, 20%, 20%, and 20%, respectively. Our proposed algorithm was run ten times for each (small-scale and large-scale) instance with a limit of 30,000 iterations. All tests were run on an i7-5500U 2.4GHz with 8GB memory. A limit of 2 hours was set for Cplex.

5.1 Results for the Small-scale Instances

The authors first compare our solution approach with the exact method for a series of small-scale instances. Here, the cluster-assign algorithm did not work because of the small size of the instances. Hence, the authors could analyse the performance of Stage 2 of the proposed approach. The objective functions of VNS and VND algorithms with different CAs and Cplex are reported in Table 3. All the neighbourhood structures were used in the local search procedure and Strategies 1 and 3 were employed in the shaking. The first column, in this table, corresponds to the name of the small instances (S). The second column presents the results of Cplex and between the third and eighth columns represent the solutions of the VNS and VNS with different initializations. The optimal solutions are marked in italic and the best obtained solutions in bold. Except small instance 4, our algorithm was able to find the best or optimal solution. The authors could not find optimal solutions for some of the small-scale instances (S5 and S7-S12), but our approach made improvements. Lower bound (LB) and percentage gaps (shown in columns 9-15) are also reported in Table 3. The percentage gap is computed as the difference between Cplex solution and any solution obtained from the VNS and VND algorithms. According to the percentage gap, our solution approach deviated between 0.13 and 11.93, which is high and can be considered as less efficient.

Table 3. Comparison results and percentage gap for the small-scale instances*

I	Cplex	VNS			VND			LB gap %	VNS			VND		
		CA1	CA2	CA3	CA1	CA2	CA3		CA1 %	CA2 %	CA3 %	CA1 %	CA2 %	CA3 %
S1	***122.08***	129.05	**122.08**	129.27	**122.08**	131.52	126.93	-	5.7	0.0	5.9	0.0	7.7	4.0
S2	***178.13***	182.25	181.13	192.85	183.52	**178.13**	209.45	-	2.3	1.7	8.3	3.0	0.0	17.6
S3	***194.37***	**194.37**	194.85	208.72	197.07	**194.37**	207.85	-	0.0	0.2	7.4	1.4	0.0	6.9
S4	***174.73***	228.47	196.23	235.23	223.93	182.03	239.27	-	30.8	12.3	34.6	28.2	4.2	36.9
S5	275.00	264.18	280.70	271.15	**262.65**	269.22	349.18	6.06	-3.9	2.1	-1.4	-4.5	-2.1	27.0
S6	***198.80***	199.15	212.43	219.75	223.87	**198.80**	216.15	-	0.2	6.9	10.5	12.6	0.0	8.7
S7	321.58	292.92	295.75	300.83	320.08	**291.58**	322.88	12.65	-8.9	-8.0	-6.5	-0.5	-9.3	0.4
S8	329.58	331.25	**314.08**	355.67	318.25	349.08	359.75	6.42	0.5	-4.7	7.9	-3.4	5.9	9.2
S9	283.87	280.03	274.25	292.63	**272.38**	290.43	322.02	9.58	-1.4	-3.4	3.1	-4.0	2.3	13.4
S10	406.83	460.42	**403.90**	444.15	466.40	422.67	442.02	9.61	13.2	-0.7	9.2	14.6	3.9	8.6
S11	487.30	521.43	**467.05**	519.23	503.07	477.55	512.12	9.21	7.0	-4.2	6.6	3.2	-2.0	5.1
S12	340.40	354.40	**338.33**	371.20	404.53	339.13	358.63	11.57	4.1	-0.6	9.0	18.8	-0.4	5.4
Avg.	276.05	286.50	273.40	295.05	291.48	277.05	305.52	5.43	4.13	0.13	7.88	5.78	0.85	11.93

Note: I:Instance, S: the name of small-scale instances, CA: Construction algorithm.* indicates the average computational results of ten runs (for VNS and VND).

5.2 Results for the Large-scale Instances

Second, the authors investigate the efficiency of Stage 1 at randomly-selected instance 13. The results are shown in Figures 3 and 4. In Figure 3, the objective function value is given on the left vertical axis, the runtime is given on the right vertical axis and the solution with different number cluster set is shown on the horizontal axis. While the black straight line, the black dashed line, and the black double line correspond to the VNS algorithm starting with different CAs, the grey straight line, the grey dashed line, and the grey double line refer to the VND algorithm starting with different CAs. Similarly, the black and grey columns represent the runtime, the VNS and VND, respectively. In Figure 4, the number of working nurses is given on the right vertical axis and the continuity of care is shown on the left vertical axis. The black and grey columns represent the number of working nurses, the VNS and VND, respectively. The results of continuity of care are shown by the lines. In both of these figures, as the number of clusters increases, the improvement is clearly observed. Broadly speaking, clustering has a positive effect on the continuity of care; on the other hand, minimizing the number of working nurses does not mean the continuity of care will be improved. Similar results are also obtained for different sizes of instances.

For the evaluation of performance, the authors compare the VNS algorithm in which the neighbourhoods are reordered dynamically based on the VND algorithm with nine neighbourhoods. For this purpose, the authors select different sizes of three instances randomly. The detailed average results of these instances are illustrated in Table 4. The terms that the authors use for performance evaluation are shown in these tables (with different constructions) the VNS and VND algorithms. There is

Figure 3. The efficiency of Algorithm on the objective and the runtime (for Instance 13)

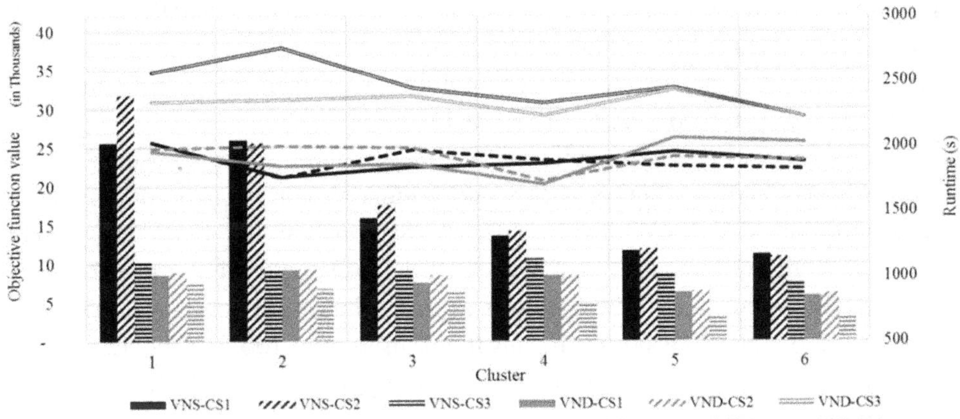

Figure 4. The efficiency of Algorithm on the number of working nurses and the continuity of care (for Instance 13)

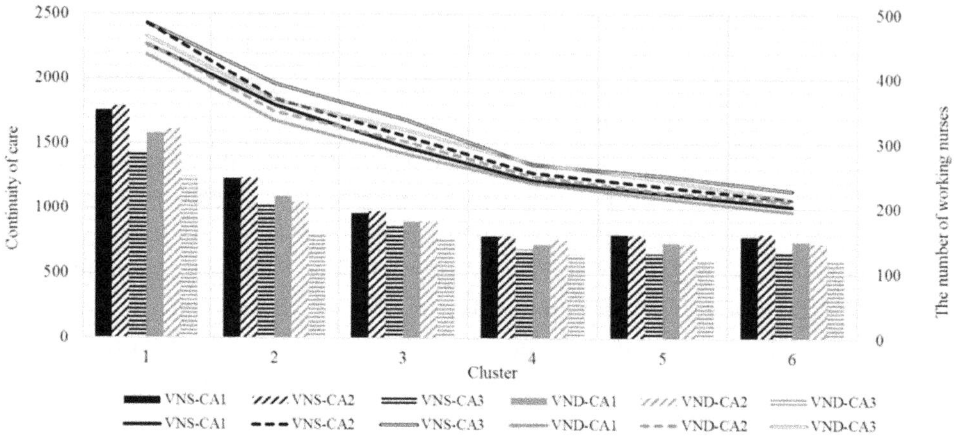

no uncovered job in these solutions, that is all jobs are allocated to the appropriate nurses. Therefore, the number of uncovered jobs is not included in these tables. The total time (cost) is the summation of the travelling time, duration and waiting time. The total calculation for the overtime work, the deviation from starting time, the continuity of care, and the work overload are also presented in these tables. In addition, the objective function of each instance is summarized with the number of free and working nurses, clients, jobs, tasks (the number of visits during a week), working days and clusters. Instance 1 consists of 250 nurses and 260 clients who request 393 jobs. In Stage 1, cluster-assign algorithm divides this sample into 4 clusters. In Stage 2, the VND-CA3 uses average 68.0 nurses and performs 1551 tasks. 182.0 nurses do not work, and, hence, this number is defined as free nurses. When Tables 4 is examined further, the VND algorithm outperforms the VNS algorithm. The VND algorithm yields a slightly better performance according to the continuity of care, and consumes less human resource. It is obvious that the employment of minimum number of nurses means also a minimum number of working days and does not imply that the continuity of care is improved.

The question of whether the applied algorithms send more overqualified nurses is also investigated. The distribution of the working nurses according to the qualification level is summarized in Table 5 for Instances 17 and 36. Instance 17 comprises 549 nurses with 5 different qualification levels. Of the 549 nurses, 422 are at the third level of qualification. The VND algorithm initialized with CS3 employed only 149 nurses from 549 nurses, besides it means that it used only 100.4 of the 422 nurses with a third-level qualification. Without considering the VNS and VND heuristics,

Table 4. Comparison results for Instances 1, 17 and 36*

	VNS			VND		
	CA1	**CA2**	**CA3**	**CA1**	**CA2**	**CA3**
Instance 1						
Total time cost	29203.4	29676	28963.6	29461.8	29574.4	**29312.8**
Total deviation from preferred time	6458.4	6410.2	6901.8	6395.6	6504.2	**6921.6**
Total overtime work	44.8	29.4	64.4	13.8	11.2	**31.4**
Total continuity of care	305	325.8	330.4	293.6	310.8	**319.4**
Total work overload	38.8	11.4	37.1	17.7	20.9	**33.0**
Number of nurses	250.0	250.0	250.0	250.0	250.0	**250.0**
Number of free nurses	161.0	164.2	174.8	170.4	167.2	**182.0**
Number of working nurses	89.0	85.8	75.2	79.6	82.8	**68.0**
Number of working days	368.6	340.6	312.2	354.8	340.2	**303.2**
Number of customers	260.0	260.0	260.0	260.0	260.0	**260.0**
Number of jobs	393.0	393.0	393.0	393.0	393.0	**393.0**
Number of tasks	1551.0	1551.0	1551.0	1551.0	1551.0	**1551.0**
Number of clusters	4.0	4.0	4.0	4.0	4.0	**4.0**
Runtime (s)	852.8	877.0	651.3	688.8	808.3	**623.3**
Objective Function	9256.47	7851.27	9696.43	**7678.37**	7834.83	**8841.43**
Instance 17						
Total time cost	63703.2	63856.0	63373.8	63694.8	63905.4	**63150.8**
Total deviation from preferred time	14892.2	15067.4	16246.0	14689.8	14415.8	**15739.8**
Total overtime work	57.6	55.4	91.2	33.0	34.8	**101.6**
Total continuity of care	1144.0	1204.6	1270.4	1128	1162.8	**1232.8**
Total work overload	47.6	35.4	71.4	53.1	10.3	**83.9**
Number of nurses	549.0	549.0	549.0	549.0	549.0	**549.0**
Number of free nurses	349.4	350.8	392.4	360.4	363.8	**400.0**
Number of working nurses	199.6	198.2	156.6	188.6	185.2	**149.0**
Number of working days	774.2	752.6	643.0	759.8	746.8	**628.0**
Number of customers	450.0	450.0	450.0	450.0	450.0	**450.0**
Number of jobs	858.0	858.0	858.0	858.0	858.0	**858.0**
Number of tasks	3437.0	3437.0	3437.0	3437.0	3437.0	**3437.0**
Number of clusters	4.0	4.0	4.0	4.0	4.0	**4.0**
Runtime (s)	1335.4	1433.5	1215.7	914.1	1003.6	**769.9**
Objective Function	23119.23	22403.65	26808.97	22514.10	**19491.53**	**27873.93**

continues on following page

Table 4. Continued

	VNS			VND		
	CA1	CA2	CA3	CA1	CA2	CA3
Instance 36						
Total time cost	116474.5	117620.8	116205.7	117250.3	117830.7	**116310.7**
Total deviation from preferred time	26003.8	25525.3	29518.0	25716.3	24832.0	**30764.7**
Total overtime work	110.0	183.0	213.0	104.7	73.3	**521.0**
Total continuity of care	3450.8	3620.3	3771.3	3364.3	3559.0	**3736.7**
Total work overload	14.8	14.6	77.9	33.6	12.4	**116.5**
Number of nurses	991.0	991.0	991.0	991.0	991.0	**991.0**
Number of free nurses	426.8	427.8	571.7	457.7	442.3	**589.3**
Number of working nurses	564.2	563.2	419.3	533.3	548.7	**401.7**
Number of working days	1830.0	1792.3	1370.7	1746.3	1719.7	**1316.0**
Number of customers	863.0	863.0	863.0	863.0	863.0	**863.0**
Number of jobs	1546.0	1546.0	1546.0	1546.0	1546.0	**1546.0**
Number of tasks	6378.0	6378.0	6378.0	6377.7	6377.7	**6377.7**
Number of clusters	3.0	3.0	3.0	3.0	3.0	**3.0**
Runtime (s)	2564.2	2770.1	2199.6	1781.8	1819.3	**1437.7**
Objective Function	58602.95	65154.383	77932.083	60385.15	**56427.28**	**105610.83**

Note: CA: Construction algorithm, * indicates the average computational results of ten runs.

our CAs do not allocate more-qualified nurses to the lower jobs in spite of the fact that they reduce the number of nurses from each level of qualification.

Owing to the fact that the VND algorithm yields a minimum objective function and runs fast on seven randomly-selected instances, the rest of the instances will be solved by applying it. The average results of the large-scale instance set are summarized in Table 6. The objective function value and the number of working nurses are summarized according to the different CAs. Consisting of 250 nurses, 260 clients, and 393 jobs, Instance 1 was calculated 7678.37 with the starting of CA1, and with this solution 79.6 nurses were employed. The continuity of care was computed as 293.6. The results in Table 6 show that the VND with CA3 is capable of allocating a minimum number of nurses to cover all the jobs. Generally, the solutions initialized with CA1 and CA2 have a similar performance in terms of objective function value.

Table 5. The distribution of working nurses for Instances 17 and 36*

Qualification levels		1	2	3	4	5	Total
Instance 17							
Number of nurses		**4**	**24**	**422**	**41**	**58**	**549**
The VNS	CA1	0.0	0.4	148.2	18.4	32.6	199.6
	CA2	0.0	0.2	145.0	18.0	35.0	198.2
	CA3	0.0	0.4	109.4	17.4	29.4	156.6
The VND	CA1	0.0	0.6	136.4	18.0	33.6	188.6
	CA2	0.0	1.0	134.0	19.4	30.8	185.2
	CA3	0.0	0.4	100.4	17.0	31.2	149.0
Instance 36							
Number of nurses		**10**	**48**	**768**	**79**	**86**	**991**
The VNS	CA1	0.0	6.0	436.0	62.3	60.0	564.3
	CA2	0.0	5.0	428.3	64.3	65.7	563.3
	CA3	0.0	7.3	312.0	50.3	49.7	419.3
The VND	CA1	0.0	4.3	411.3	61.7	56.0	533.3
	CA2	0.0	5.0	421.0	62.7	60.0	548.7
	CA3	0.0	6.3	296.7	48.7	50.0	401.7

Note: CA: Construction algorithm, * indicates the average computational results of ten runs.

Table 6. Computational results for all instances*

I	Objective Function			Number of working nurses			Total continuity of care		
	CA1	CA2	CA3	CA1	CA2	CA3	CA1	CA2	CA3
1	**7678.37**	7834.83	8841.43	79.6	82.8	68.0	293.6	310.8	319.4
2	7787.20	9535.02	**7784.67**	78.4	76.8	64.2	314.2	339.4	319.8
3	7875.17	**7568.98**	8686.85	79.0	80.7	66.6	303.6	330.6	335.4
4	**6538.85**	6665.77	7228.67	72.6	73.9	57.7	257.6	295.6	299.0
5	7060.08	**6049.23**	6766.93	75.4	75.7	58.7	249.6	285.0	270.7
6	7775.65	**6866.95**	7893.52	66.1	71.2	54.6	269.4	272.4	291.2
7	8204.80	**7347.42**	8489.60	75.8	78.8	59.2	388.4	394.2	430.6
8	**7340.35**	7426.67	8229.00	70.6	72.5	61.6	356.2	372.4	430.0
9	**7476.55**	7704.85	8618.22	81.8	74.3	69.4	333.8	333.8	351.6
10	**7840.02**	8263.82	10239.07	77.7	79.8	59.6	313.7	343.0	350.4
11	8240.60	**7737.23**	9294.55	62.2	76.9	62.8	365.0	376.4	405.2
12	**6844.48**	7709.15	10083.53	77.1	81.5	50.9	373.4	376.0	418.0
13	**21537.10**	22949.10	29342.50	145.4	152.6	129.8	1029.0	1081.4	1182.2

continues on following page

Table 6. Continued

I	Objective Function			Number of working nurses			Total continuity of care		
	CA1	CA2	CA3	CA1	CA2	CA3	CA1	CA2	CA3
14	**15130.23**	15626.43	20616.13	196.6	180.4	133.6	1077.6	1078.6	1130.2
15	**20229.52**	20447.82	24479.48	155.0	153.6	132.0	1012.0	1005.0	1070.8
16	19148.57	**16714.03**	26008.72	159.2	166.2	133.6	1022.0	1025.6	1172.0
17	22514.10	**19491.53**	27873.93	188.6	185.2	149.0	1128.0	1162.8	1232.8
18	21216.08	**20362.85**	29874.42	183.8	182.6	150.7	1120.2	1150.0	1221.4
19	**19193.02**	21463.82	24718.50	183.4	176.9	142.6	1044.4	1114.6	1214.6
20	**14737.05**	15081.68	21049.90	155.4	159.0	121.2	852.6	873.2	963.0
21	**17380.27**	19129.25	20877.12	178.0	182.3	133.9	1039.8	1102.2	1161.0
22	18608.77	**18170.23**	23455.92	161.4	172.2	128.9	877.6	974.4	1033.6
23	**18843.87**	19242.48	25028.77	159.4	160.2	132.0	1038.4	1043.0	1151.0
24	19468.10	**19180.87**	27993.32	167.7	161.6	140.0	1038.0	1067.2	1172.2
25	**18412.98**	19174.57	26446.85	156.2	151.0	128.7	866.0	906.4	968.0
26	18692.02	**18574.62**	28069.58	165.0	167.2	126.3	1025.4	1103.8	1217.0
27	19259.52	**18843.43**	27781.50	166.0	171.7	138.1	1054.8	1112.2	1218.0
28	**17507.27**	18214.78	28354.02	151.6	159.8	128.6	931.4	969.4	1082.2
29	57688.33	**52817.68**	79314.65	436.9	450.3	331.8	2862.3	3021.8	3269.7
30	55987.73	**52876.40**	102136.10	458.7	439.1	345.2	2886.7	3036.7	3219.3
31	56967.38	**54755.63**	89345.12	501.4	492.7	395.0	2863.3	2998.0	3121.0
32	49245.75	**43982.80**	84632.08	490.3	482.5	347.7	2912.7	3048.3	3157.3
33	**45815.63**	47109.65	75729.88	389.3	365.9	277.0	2054.0	2204.7	2394.7
34	**49546.42**	57602.03	95791.17	641.0	639.7	438.3	3286.7	3586.7	3634.0
35	62780.15	**53106.37**	107479.62	418.7	412.7	324.1	2989.7	3068.7	3332.7
36	60385.15	**56427.28**	105610.83	533.3	548.7	401.7	3364.3	3559.0	3736.7
37	57430.82	**50293.77**	98665.35	403.7	403.5	307.5	2876.7	2957.0	3237.3
38	57886.97	**56427.20**	113878.87	428.7	440.1	317.7	3107.0	3189.0	3391.7
39	**54300.93**	55783.83	98315.85	462.3	476.7	332.3	3042.7	3164.7	3370.7
40	53564.58	**47630.07**	109605.98	456.7	468.5	325.5	2942.0	3033.7	3261.3
41	**108582.82**	112725.53	242168.42	878.3	867.1	636.8	5258.7	5664.0	5962.7
42	**102836.55**	118769.67	192215.28	857.4	873.0	617.7	5298.4	5593.4	5768.7
43	110611.80	**108687.20**	241127.02	825.3	824.0	588.6	5073.3	5430.0	5650.7
44	**122481.02**	140489.63	209278.03	913.9	915.9	656.7	5532.7	5910.7	6096.0
45	**158450.63**	159236.98	362040.62	956.0	971.0	730.4	6324.0	6614.3	6868.3

Note: I:Instance, CA: Construction algorithm, * indicates the average computational results of ten runs.

6 CONCLUSION

In this work, the authors have considered a multi-period scheduling and routing problem for the HHC services in which different objectives, e.g. the continuity of care, the number of working nurses, work overload, and overtime work have been taken into account. In the proposed mathematical model, the authors redefined the term 'continuity of care' by considering connected (synchronous) jobs. Similarly, considering nurse to patient staffing ratio the work overload of nurses is defined. To solve the multi-period HHCSRP, first a cluster-assign algorithm is used for dividing the large-scale instances into feasible sub-problems; second, by using any of the three different CAs, the authors generate solution from the obtained pair of clusters, and the VNS and VND algorithms are employed to improve these with nine different neighbourhood structures.

In Stage 1, the introduced algorithm provides improvements in the objectives; moreover, as the number of clusters increases, the continuity of care decreases/improves. However, the minimum continuity of care, which is calculated by a quantity-based definition, does not mean that the number of workers is minimized. To achieve a better continuity of care, the number of clusters and nurses must be chosen appropriately. The allocation of the minimum number of workers to clients leads to a decrease in the total time cost, while resulting in an increasing work overload and overtime work. In this work, it has been observed that reducing the number of nurses can reduce costs and provide flexible arrangements.

In future works, the nurses working below the average workload can be weighted by the qualification level of the assigned jobs which can be integrated in the model for a more balanced solution. The working time regulations such as the maximum weekly working hours, weekly and daily rests, breaks and night works can be integrated in the model.

REFERENCES

Aiken, L., Clarke, S., Sloane, D., Sochalski, J., & Silber, J. (2002). Hospital nurse staffing and patient mortality, nurse burnout, and job dissatisfaction. *Journal of the American Medical Association, 288*(16), 1987–1993. doi:10.1001/jama.288.16.1987 PMID:12387650

Bachouch, R. B., Guinet, A., & Hajri-Gabouj, S. (2011). A Decision-Making Tool for Home Health Care Nurses' Planning. *Supply Chain Forum: An International Journal, 12*(1), 14-20. doi:10.1080/16258312.2011.11517250

Bard, J. F., Shao, Y., & Jarrah, A. I. (2014). A sequential GRASP for the therapist routing and scheduling problem. *Journal of Scheduling*, *17*(2), 109–133. doi:10.100710951-013-0345-x

Bard, J. F., Shao, Y., Qi, X., & Jarrah, A. I. (2014). The traveling therapist scheduling problem. *IIE Transactions*, *46*(7), 683–706. doi:10.1080/0740817X.2013.851434

Barrera, D., Velasco, N., & Amaya, C. A. (2012). A network-based approach to the multi-activity combined timetabling and crew scheduling problem: Workforce scheduling for public health policy implementation. *Computers & Industrial Engineering*, *63*(4), 802–812. doi:10.1016/j.cie.2012.05.002

Begur, S. V., Miller, D. M., & Weaver, J. R. (1997). An Integrated Spatial DSS for Scheduling and Routing Home-Health-Care Nurses. *Interfaces*, *27*(4), 35–48. doi:10.1287/inte.27.4.35

Bennett, A. R., & Erera, A. L. (2011). Dynamic periodic fixed appointment scheduling for home health. *IIE Transactions on Healthcare Systems Engineering*, *1*(1), 6–19. doi:10.1080/19488300.2010.549818

Bennett-Milburn, A., & Spicer, J. (2013). Multi-objective home health nurse routing with remote monitoring devices. *Int J Plan Sched*, *1*(4), 242–263. doi:10.1504/IJPS.2013.059677

Bräysy, O., & Gendreau, M. (2005). Vehicle Routing Problem with Time Windows, Part II: Metaheuristics. *Transportation Science*, *39*(1), 119–139. doi:10.1287/trsc.1030.0057

Bredström, D., & Rönnqvist, M. (2008). Combined vehicle routing and scheduling with temporal precedence and synchronization constraints. *European Journal of Operational Research*, *191*(1), 19–31. doi:10.1016/j.ejor.2007.07.033

Cappanera, P., & Scutellà, M. G. (2013). Home Care optimization: Impact of pattern generation policies on scheduling and routing decisions. *Electronic Notes in Discrete Mathematics*, *41*, 53–60. doi:10.1016/j.endm.2013.05.075

Cappanera, P., & Scutellà, M. G. (2015). Joint Assignment, Scheduling, and Routing Models to Home Care Optimization: A Pattern-Based Approach. *Transportation Science*, *49*(4), 830–852. doi:10.1287/trsc.2014.0548

Chiu, T., Fang, D., Chen, J., Wang, Y., & Jeris, C. (2001). A robust and scalable clustering algorithm for mixed type attributes in large database environment. *Proceedings of the seventh ACM SIGKDD international conference on Knowledge discovery and data mining*. 10.1145/502512.502549

Cissé, M., Yalçındağ, S., Kergosien, Y., Şahin, E., Lenté, C., & Matta, A. (2017). OR problems related to Home Health Care: A review of relevant routing and scheduling problems. *Operations Research for Health Care, 13-14*, 1–22. Advance online publication. doi:10.1016/j.orhc.2017.06.001

Day, J. M., Melnyk, S. A., Larson, P. D., Davis, E. W., & Whybark, D. C. (2012). Humanitarian and Disaster Relief Supply Chains: A Matter of Life and Death. *The Journal of Supply Chain Management, 48*(2), 21–36. doi:10.1111/j.1745-493X.2012.03267.x

Erdem, M., & Bulkan, S. (2017). A Two-Stage Solution Approach for the Large-Scale Home Healthcare Routeing and Scheduling Problem. *South African Journal of Industrial Engineering, 28*(4), 133-149.

Fikar, C., & Hirsch, P. (2017). Home health care routing and scheduling: A review. *Computers & Operations Research, 77*, 86–95. doi:10.1016/j.cor.2016.07.019

Gamst, M., & Jensen, T. S. (2012). A branch-and-price algorithm for the long-term home care scheduling problem. In D. Klatte, H.-J. Lüthi, & K. Schmedders (Eds.), *Operations Research Proceedings 2011: Selected Papers of the International Conference on Operations Research (OR 2011)* (pp. 483-488). Berlin: Springer Berlin Heidelberg. 10.1007/978-3-642-29210-1_77

Hansen, P., & Mladenovic, N. (2002). Developments of Variable Neighborhood Search. In C. C. Ribeiro & P. Hansen (Eds.), *Essays and Surveys in Metaheuristics* (1st ed., pp. 415–439). doi:10.1007/978-1-4615-1507-4_19

Hansen, P., Mladenović, N., Brimberg, J., & Pérez, J. A. M. (2010). Variable Neighborhood Search. In M. Gendreau & J.-Y. Potvin (Eds.), *Handbook of Metaheuristics* (pp. 61–86). Springer US. doi:10.1007/978-1-4419-1665-5_3

Health, M. o. (2015). *Ministry of Health* (960). Ankara: Türkiye Sağlıklı Yaşlanma Eylem Planı ve Uygulama Programı 2015-2020. Retrieved from http://sbu.saglik.gov.tr/Ekutuphane/Yayin/508

Hertz, A., & Lahrichi, N. (2009). A patient assignment algorithm for home care services. *The Journal of the Operational Research Society, 60*(4), 481–495. doi:10.1057/palgrave.jors.2602574

Hiermann, G., Prandtstetter, M., Rendl, A., Puchinger, J., & Raidl, G. (2015a). Metaheuristics for solving a multimodal home-healthcare scheduling problem. *Central European Journal of Operations Research, 23*(1), 89–113. doi:10.100710100-013-0305-8

Hiermann, G., Prandtstetter, M., Rendl, A., Puchinger, J., & Raidl, G. R. (2015b). *Appendix of: Metaheuristics for Solving a Multimodal Home-Healthcare Scheduling Problem.* Retrieved from https://www.ac.tuwien.ac.at/research/problem-instances/

Matta, A., Chahed, S., Sahin, E., & Dallery, Y. (2014). Modelling home care organisations from an operations management perspective. *Flexible Services and Manufacturing Journal, 26*(3), 295–319. doi:10.100710696-012-9157-0

Mattke, S., Klautzer, L., Mengistu, T., Garnett, J., Hu, J., & Wu, H. (2010). *Health and Well-Being in the Home: A Global Analysis of Needs, Expectations, and Priorities for Home Health Care Technology*. https://www.rand.org/pubs/occasional_papers/OP323.html

Maya Duque, P. A., Castro, M., Sörensen, K., & Goos, P. (2015). Home care service planning. The case of Landelijke Thuiszorg. *European Journal of Operational Research, 243*(1), 292–301. doi:10.1016/j.ejor.2014.11.008

medicare.gov. (2016). *What's home health care?* Retrieved from https://www.medicare.gov/what-medicare-covers/home-health-care/home-health-care-what-is-it-what-to-expect.html

Mladenovic, N., & Hansen, P. (1997). Variable neighborhood search. *Computers & Operations Research, 24*(11), 1097–1100. doi:10.1016/S0305-0548(97)00031-2

Nagurney, A. Y. M., & Qiang, Q. (2012). *Multiproduct Humanitarian Healthcare Supply Chains: A Network Modeling and Computational Framework.* Paper presented at the the 23rd Annual POMS Conference, Chicago, IL. 10.2139srn.1636294

NAHC. (2010). *Basic Statistics About Home Care*. Retrieved from www.nahc.org/assets/1/7/10hc_stats.pdf

NAHC. (2015). *Foundation for Hospice and Homecare and NAHC Hold Press Conference on Miles Traveled Each Year By Home Care Nurses*. Retrieved from http://www.nahc.org/NAHCReport/nr151215_1/

Nickel, S., Schröder, M., & Steeg, J. (2012). Mid-term and short-term planning support for home health care services. *European Journal of Operational Research, 219*(3), 574–587. doi:10.1016/j.ejor.2011.10.042

PAHO. (2001). *Humanitarian Supply Management and Logistics in the Health Sector, Pan American Health Organization*. PAHO.

Prandtstetter, M., Raidl, G. R., & Misar, T. (2009). A Hybrid Algorithm for Computing Tours in a Spare Parts Warehouse. In C. Cotta & P. Cowling (Eds.), *Evolutionary Computation in Combinatorial Optimization: 9th European Conference, EvoCOP 2009* (pp. 25-36). Berlin: Springer Berlin Heidelberg. 10.1007/978-3-642-01009-5_3

Ramos, A. F. T., Lizarazo, E. H. A., Rubiano, L. S. R., & Araújo, C. L. Q. (2014). *Mathematical Model for the Home Health Care routing and scheduling problem with multiple treatment and time windows.* Paper presented at the Mathematical Methods in Science and Engineering, Athens, Greece.

Rasmussen, M. S., Justesen, T., Dohn, A., & Larsen, J. (2012). The Home Care Crew Scheduling Problem: Preference-based visit clustering and temporal dependencies. *European Journal of Operational Research, 219*(3), 598–610. doi:10.1016/j.ejor.2011.10.048

Shao, Y., Bard, J. F., & Jarrah, A. I. (2012). The therapist routing and scheduling problem. *IIE Transactions, 44*(10), 868–893. doi:10.1080/0740817X.2012.665202

Trautsamwieser, A., & Hirsch, P. (2014). A Branch-Price-and-Cut approach for solving the medium-term home health care planning problem. *Networks, 64*(3), 143–159. doi:10.1002/net.21566

Vaillancourt, A., Tatham, P., Wu, Y., & Haavisto, I. (2018). Humanitarian health project supply chain costs. *Supply Chain Forum: An International Journal, 19*(1), 70-80. doi:10.1080/16258312.2017.1394775

WHO. (2013). *A Universal Truth: No Health Without a Workforce*. Retrieved from https://www.who.int/workforcealliance/knowledge/resources/hrhreport2013/en/

Wirnitzer, J., Heckmann, I., Meyer, A., & Nickel, S. (2016). Patient-based nurse rostering in home care. *Operations Research for Health Care, 8*, 91–102. doi:10.1016/j.orhc.2015.08.005

Yalçındağ, S., Cappanera, P., Grazia Scutellà, M., Şahin, E., & Matta, A. (2016). Pattern-based decompositions for human resource planning in home health care services. *Computers & Operations Research, 73*, 12–26. doi:10.1016/j.cor.2016.02.011

Chapter 5
Demand Forecasting in Supply Chain Management Using Different Deep Learning Methods

Asma Husna
Department of Mechanical and Industrial Engineering, Ryerson University, Canada

Saman Hassanzadeh Amin
Department of Mechanical and Industrial Engineering, Ryerson University, Canada

Bharat Shah
Ted Rogers School of Management, Ryerson University, Canada

ABSTRACT

Supply chain management (SCM) is a fast growing and largely studied field of research. Forecasting of the required materials and parts is an important task in companies and can have a significant impact on the total cost. To have a reliable forecast, some advanced methods such as deep learning techniques are helpful. The main goal of this chapter is to forecast the unit sales of thousands of items sold at different chain stores located in Ecuador with holistic techniques. Three deep learning approaches including artificial neural network (ANN), convolutional neural network (CNN), and long short-term memory (LSTM) are adopted here for predictions from the Corporación Favorita grocery sales forecasting dataset collected from Kaggle website. Finally, the performances of the applied models are evaluated and compared. The results show that LSTM network tends to outperform the other two approaches in terms of performance. All experiments are conducted using Python's deep learning library and Keras and Tensorflow packages.

DOI: 10.4018/978-1-7998-3805-0.ch005

1. INTRODUCTION

Supply Chain Management (SCM) is a very fast-growing and largely studied field of research that is gaining popularity and importance (Meherishi et al., 2019). According to Mentzer et al., (2001), a supply chain is a collection of some elements that are connected by flows of products, information, and/or services. Most organizations focus on cost optimization and maintaining ideal inventory levels to keep consumer's satisfaction particularly in SCM of fresh products. Accurate demand forecasts enable industries to predict demand and maintain the right amount of inventory.

Machine Learning (ML) is a subset of Artificial Intelligence (AI). It enables machines for learning from the past data, experiences, and patterns to have correct forecast. Generally, ML means extracting knowledge about future behaviour from the older data. ML approaches mostly fall into three broad categories depending on the nature of the learning system including Supervised, Unsupervised, and Reinforcement Learning (RL). During a supervised learning, a large amount of labelled input data and desired output are provided for learning in the algorithms. In contrast, an unsupervised learning system uses only "unlabelled" input data for learning. Generally, unsupervised algorithms work with raw data for finding hidden patterns and achieve the best result. Reinforcement Learning (RL) is another subcategory of machine learning. RL interacts with a dynamic environment and utilizes trial and error technique to obtain a human-level performance. Besides of the three-fold categorisation, there is another classification which is called semi-supervised learning. In these algorithms usually small amounts of labelled data and large unlabelled data are utilized together.

Deep Learning is a subfield of ML where algorithms are inspired by the human brain to solve complex problems, learn from large amounts of very diverse, unstructured and inter-connected data sets. These algorithmic approaches have various layers (deep) to enable learning. Deep architectures can be supervised or unsupervised. This biologically-inspired programming paradigm currently provides the best solutions to many real-life problems such as image and video processing, speech recognition, text analysis, natural language processing, and different types of classifiers. Deep learning techniques are novel and useful methods for obtaining accurate forecasts in SCM. However, diverse deep learning techniques perform differently on different types of problems, and some techniques perform better than the others.

In this study, the main aim is to predict the unit sales of thousands of items sold at different chain stores in Ecuador to avoid overstocking, minimize understocking, reduce waste and loss, and increase customer's satisfaction. In this case, good predictions are highly desirable to increase efficiency and determine the prices of products for customers. In this investigation, Corporación Favorita Grocery Sales Forecasting dataset is collected from Kaggle website for forecasting the product sales accurately. Three diverse deep learning methods including Artificial Neural Network (ANN), Convolutional Neural Network (CNN), and Long Short Term Memory (LSTM) are used to build and train the predictive models. In these models, different parameters and weights are used to forecast the unit sales. In this work, some open-source data science tools and Python and packages are used. Furthermore, Mean Squared Error (MSE) and Root Mean Squared Error (RMSE) are adopted as the two indicators for evaluating and comparing the models. The results show that LSTM performs better than ANN and CNN for forecasting the sales units in this case.

This book chapter is structured as follows. Section 2 includes a literature review about some approaches related to this field. Section 3 describes the exploratory analysis of the data, and Section 4 focuses on the systems and the experiment. The obtained results from the experiment are included in Section 5. Finally, conclusions and future research are provided in Section 6. Figure 1(a) represents artificial intelligence, machine learning, and deep learning together. In addition, Figure 1(b) shows the categories of machine learning.

Figure 1. (a) Artificial Intelligence versus Machine Learning versus Deep Learning, (b) the categories of Machine Learning

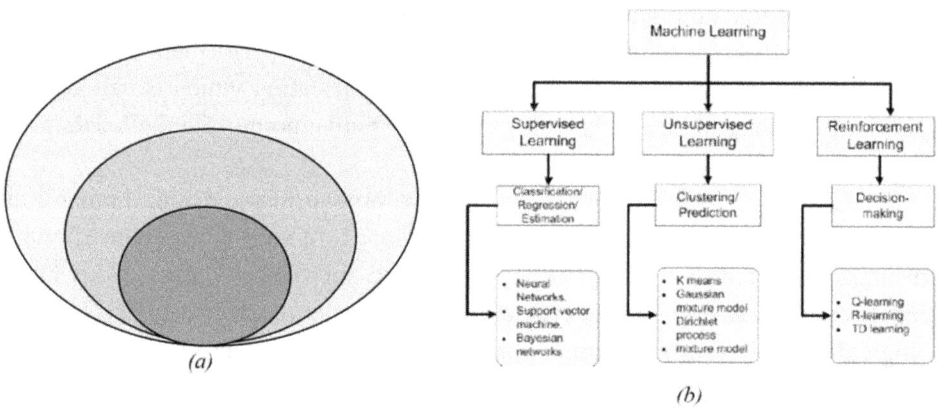

2. LITERATURE REVIEW

Machine and deep learning techniques play important roles in forecasting demands in SCM and logistics fields. This section contains the earlier studies related to this research and an overview of the related articles.

The investigations done by Kohonen (1990), Leung (1995), Kaylani et al. (2010), and Chang et al. (2011) have shown that ANNs have been potentially suitable, very effective, and significantly better for all supply chain forecasting activities. Al-Saba and El-Amin (1999) used ANN for forecasting the annual peak demand for electricity. Chao-ting et al. (2000) used recurrent neural networks for demand forecasting of inventory management to reduce uncertainty and summarized the applications of neural networks in SCM including optimization, prediction modeling, decision support processes, simulation modelling, and management systems. Zhikai and Ge (2002) combined data mining and knowledge discovery, and developed some neural networks forecasting models to investigate the impact of supply chain performance. Choy et al. (2003) showed the importance of selecting proper techniques for forecasting in SCM. Beccali et al. (2004) used an integrated solution of supervised and unsupervised neural networks for the electric energy short or long-term demand forecasting of a residential area. Pai and Lin (2005), and Campbell and Ying (2011) addressed some limitations using a simple neural network, and used combined hybrid models to compare the performances.

Aburto and Weber (2007) developed an integrated intelligent system for demand forecasting which has been combined with neural networks and autoregressive integrated moving average models. They presented an inventory management system for a Chilean supermarket. The results showed improvements in forecasting accuracy including fewer sales failures and lower inventory levels than Chilean supermarket's previous solution. Moreover, the authors proposed a replenishment system.

Kochak and Sharma (2015) presented a new investigation using ANN algorithms (Forward and Backward Propagation NN), and observed the influence and performance of product demand forecasting. In addition, they identified the best training method to predict the next year's consumption. To train the models, the monthly sales data of a fuel filter distributor between 2011 and 2013 have been used as inputs and outputs. They considered the base year data of 2011 in 12th month and 2012 data in 12th month to predict 2012 and 2013 as target data and to calculate the forecasting error and forecasting data of 2014. Their results indicated that the train Levenberg-Marquardt method performed better and was more reliable than the other used methods. They utilized MATLAB 7.0 for simulation. Gaur et al. (2015) introduced a close comparison between Nearest Neighbor method and Bayesian Networks using the confusion matrix as a performance metric. A dataset from Walmart including 1,200 tuples and 35 attributes have been used in this investigation. The authors concluded that the Bayesian Networks technique performed better than K-neighbors in detecting relations in the dataset for demand prediction in the supply chain.

Bousqaoui et al. (2017) examined multiple algorithms of machine learning, and explored their applications for various supply chain processes. Their research started with collecting data from ScienceDirect database using some keywords such as linear regression, machine learning, and deep learning. They selected 42 papers that have been published after 2010. In their paper, Support Vector Machines, Gamma Classifier models, Decision Trees, K-means Algorithms, Random Forests, Linear Regression, Hyperbox Classifier, and Neural Network techniques and the related papers have been examined. Their analysis showed that the most used technique was Neural Network followed by Support Vector Machines and Linear Regression.

There are some limitations in accurate demand forecasting. For instance, it requires a large amount of data to guarantee a correct prediction. In addition, non-linear patterns are difficult to capture, and the estimation of the model parameters can be biased by the outliers. Neural Networks are widely used in demand forecasting because they overcome many of these limitations. Huang and Hou (2017) proposed an ANN model combined with Genetic Algorithm (GA) for demand forecasting in the tourism industry. The GA was used to determine the hidden nodes of a feedforward neural network. The results showed that a reliable prediction has been obtained in that case study.

Three ANN models have been developed for forecasting the demand of different types of parts produced by a gear manufacturing company by Bhadouria and Jayant (2017). They provided a comparative analysis of different ANN models and various traditional forecasting methods like moving average, exponential smoothing, and weighted moving average method based on the obtained results of applying forecasting models. MATLAB 16 and various backpropagation algorithms available in MATLAB ANN toolbox were used for neural network implementation. Their results illustrated that the ANN model with TANSIGMOID transfer function is far better and more accurate than ANN model with LOGSIGMOID and LINEAR and transfer function in terms of Mean Absolute Deviation (MAD), MAPE, and MSE. Kaya and Turkyilmaz (2018) proposed Ad hoc intermittent methods for forecasting demand which considered special intermittent demand features using ANNs, decision tree methods, and support vector regressions. They utilized R programming in this investigation. Based on their study, the Support Vector Machine was the best method among the others in terms of performance.

The closest approach to this book chapter has been proposed by Mupparaju et al., (2008) where they built Factorization Machines, Gradient Boosting, and three variations of Deep Neural Networks (DNN) predictive models to predict demand of grocery items applying Python's deep learning library. In addition, they investigated the impact of categorical embedding layers and sequence-to-sequence type architecture on the forecasted demand. In general, their best neural network model is a final neural network model (NN3) with embedding layers and seq2seq meta, and that model also runs in an acceptable amount of time. Our methods and datasets are different from the mentioned paper.

3. EXPLORATORY ANALYSIS

In this research, the Corporación Favorita Grocery Sales Forecasting dataset for accurately forecasting product sales is collected from Kaggle website (Corporación Favorita Grocery Sales Forecasting, 2019). The data contain the unit sales for thousands of items sold at different Favorita stores located in Ecuador. The data files include test.csv, train.csv, stores.csv, items.csv, transaction.csv, oil.csv, and holidays_events.csv.

The important columns between each data table include (train.csv, Variable:Id, Type:Integer, Description:Identifier defined at the date-store-item-promotion level), (train.csv, Variable:Unit_Sales, Type:Numeric, Description:Sales defined at the date-store-item-promotion level), (transaction.csv, Variable:Date, Type:Date, Description:Date of transaction for an item), (stores.csv, Variable:Store_Nbr, Type:Integer, Description:Store identifier), (items.csv, Variable:Item_Nbr, Type:Integer, Description: Item identifier), (train.csv, Variable:Onpromotion, Type:Boolean, Description:Whether the item is on promotion), (stores.csv, Variable:City, Type:Text, Description:City in which store is located), (stores.csv, Variable:State, Type:Text, Description - State in which store is located), (holidays_events.csv, Variable:Type, Type:Text, Description:internal store categorization), (stores.csv, Variable:Cluster, Type:Integer, Description:internal store clustering), (items.csv, Variable:Family, Type:Text, Description:The family of item), (items.csv, Variable:Class, Type:Text, Description:Class of items), (items.csv, Variable:Perishable, Type:Boolean, Description:Whether the item is perishable). Figure 2 represents the Entity Relationship Diagram (ERD) of the data which is helpful to see the relations at a glance.

3.1. Train and Test

The primary dataset train.csv contains 125 million observations which are the most basic sales data from January 1, 2013 to August 15, 2017. The training data file contains 125,497,040 rows and 6 columns (i.e., row id, date, store number, item number, unit sales, and onpromotion).

Unit sales columns values can be integer or float number, where -1 represents a returned item. The onpromotion column represents whether a particular item is on promotion or not on promotion for a specified date and store_nbr. Since the training set is so large, only 23,808,261 rows among 125,497,040 rows of training.csv file from January 1, 2017 to August 15, 2017 are used for data exploratory analysis and experiment.

Figure 2. Entity Relationship Diagram (ERD)

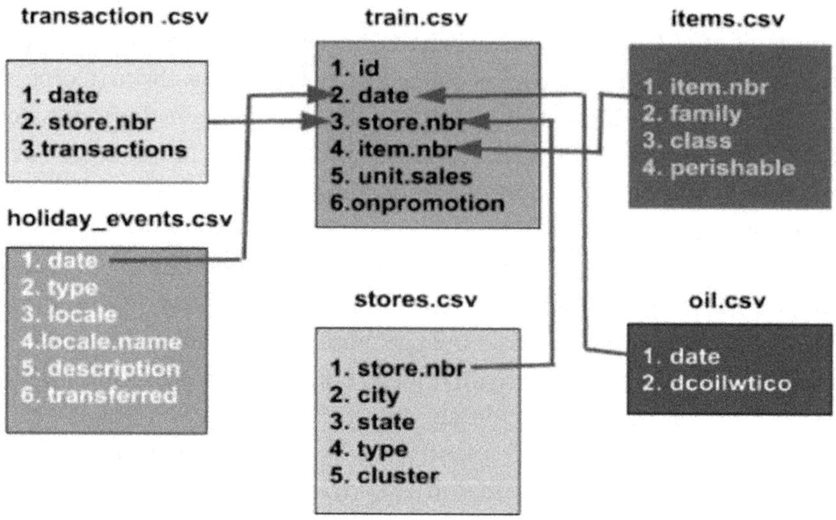

The test.csv file structure is similar to the train dataset; however, the only difference is the lack of unit sales column. The test data is related to July 16 to July 31, 2017 which contains 3,370,464 rows and 5 columns. Figure 3 and Figure 4 show the data structure of train.csv and test.csv data files, respectively.

The columns of training and test are checked for any null or missing values (see Figure 5). Figure 5(a) shows that approximately 17% of the train dataset "onpromotion" variables are missing and shows the NaN values. However, the training dataset of 2017 used in this work has no missing data which is shown in Figure 5(b). In Figure 5(c), it is clear that the test dataset has no missing value.

Figure 3. Data types and columns of train.csv

	id	date	store_nbr	item_nbr	unit_sales	onpromotion
0	0	2013-01-01	25	103665	7.0	NaN
1	1	2013-01-01	25	105574	1.0	NaN
2	2	2013-01-01	25	105575	2.0	NaN
3	3	2013-01-01	25	108079	1.0	NaN
4	4	2013-01-01	25	108701	1.0	NaN

Figure 4. Data types and columns of test.csv

	id	date	store_nbr	item_nbr	onpromotion
0	125497040	2017-08-16	1	96995	False
1	125497041	2017-08-16	1	99197	False
2	125497042	2017-08-16	1	103501	False
3	125497043	2017-08-16	1	103520	False
4	125497044	2017-08-16	1	103665	False

Figure 5. (a) Full training data, (b) 1 January - 15 August 2017, (c) Null values test

```
Training Data
id False
date False
store_nbr False
item_nbr False
unit_sales False
onpromotion True
```

(a)

```
Training Data
id False
date False
store_nbr False
item_nbr False
unit_sales False
onpromotion False
```

(b)

```
Test Data
id False
date False
store_nbr False
item_nbr False
onpromotion False
```

(c)

Figure 6 includes two parts. Figure 6(a) shows how the train observations are distributed by month. The chart is almost uniformly distributed by months of 2017. The maximum observations are in May and July, and the minimum observations are in August. Figure 6(b) represents the train observations distributed by day which is also almost uniformly distributed. The test observations are distributed by year, month, and day in Figure 7.

3.2. Items

In items.csv, there are not too many attributes. The attributes include item id, family, class, and whether the specific item is perishable or not. The "item_nbr" attribute is unique which indicates specific grocery items. Figure 8(a) shows the data structure of items.csv data, and that items file contains 4,100 rows and 4 columns. There is no missing value in the data which is shown in Figure 8(b). In the training dataset, 4,018 unique variety of items are available during 2017 and in the test dataset, the different types of items are 3,901. After joining the items.csv with the training.csv data, the data structure is visualized in Figure 9.

Figure 6. (a) Train data distribution by month, (b) Train data distribution by day

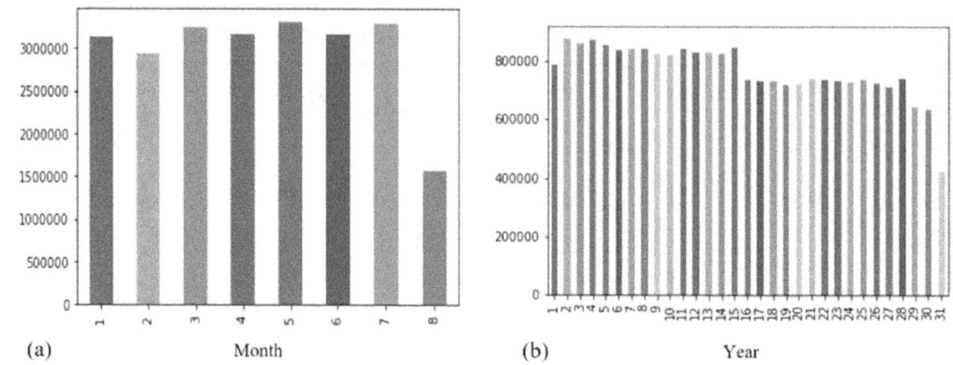

Figure 7. (a). The data distribution by year, (b). The data distribution by month, (c) The data distribution by day

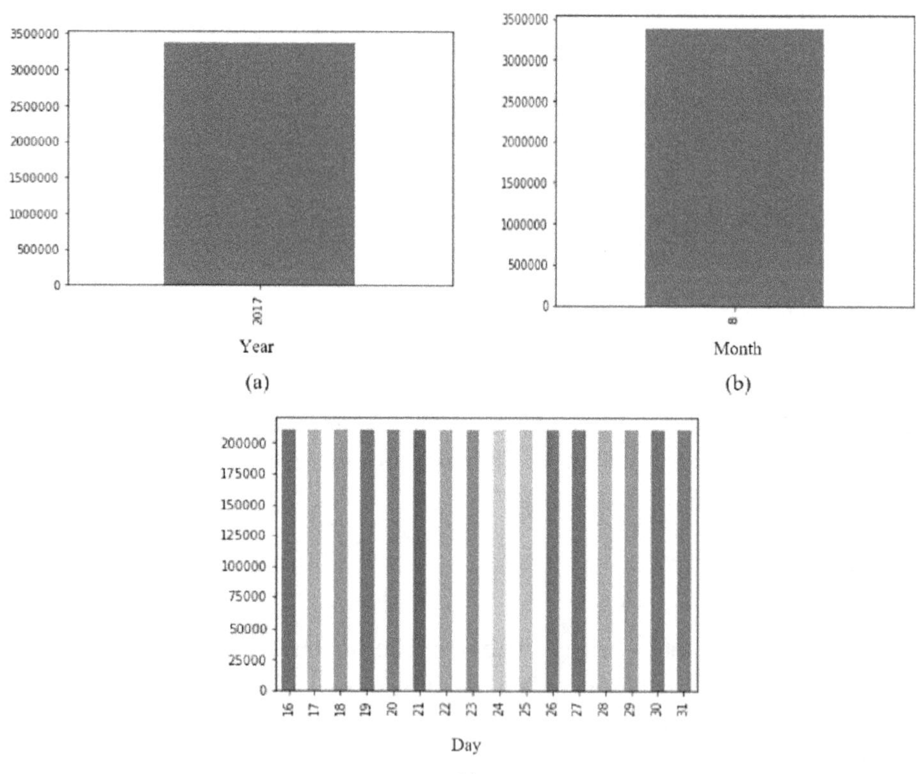

Figure 8. (a). Data types and columns of items.csv, (b) Items data null values

	item_nbr	family	class	perishable
0	96995	GROCERY I	1093	0
1	99197	GROCERY I	1067	0
2	103501	CLEANING	3008	0
3	103520	GROCERY I	1028	0
4	103665	BREAD/BAKERY	2712	1

(a)

```
Items Data
item_nbr False
family False
class False
perishable False
```

(b)

Figure 9. Data types and columns after joining the items.csv with the training.csv data

	id	date	store_nbr	item_nbr	unit_sales	onpromotion	family	class	perishable
23808256	125471184	2017-08-15	43	2123839	2.0	False	BEVERAGES	1122	0
23808257	125476599	2017-08-15	45	2123839	1.0	False	BEVERAGES	1122	0
23808258	125484285	2017-08-15	48	2123839	1.0	False	BEVERAGES	1122	0
23808259	125489307	2017-08-15	50	2123839	1.0	False	BEVERAGES	1122	0
23808260	125309124	2017-08-14	8	2011451	1.0	False	GROCERY I	1063	0

The available different item families can be visualized in Figure 10. In addition, the top and the bottom 15 sold item families are shown in Figure 11(a) and Figure 11(b), respectively. The top sold product family is "GROCERY I", and the bottom one is "BOOKS".

After joining the items.csv with the training.csv data, the top and the bottom 15 sold items across all stores are shown in Figure 12(a) and Figure 12(b), respectively. The percentages of top and bottom 15 sold items family are visualized respectively in Figure 13(a) and Figure 13(b).

3.3. Stores

From Figure 14, it is found that the stores.csv data file contains 54 rows and 5 columns. There are 54 stores which are presented using a unique attribute "store_nbr" and "cluster" attribute indicating the store groups. There is no missing value in the data.

There are five types of stores. Figure 15 and Figure 16 show the store types distributed across different cities and the store types distributed across different states, respectively. Two cities (Guayaquil and Quito) have all the variety of store types as well as the largest counts of store_nbrs attributed in those two cities. Figure 17 shows the relationships between the store types and the clusters. The store type "D" contains a mix of the clusters, whereas only type "E" has a single cluster of Clusters 10.

Figure 10. Different item families

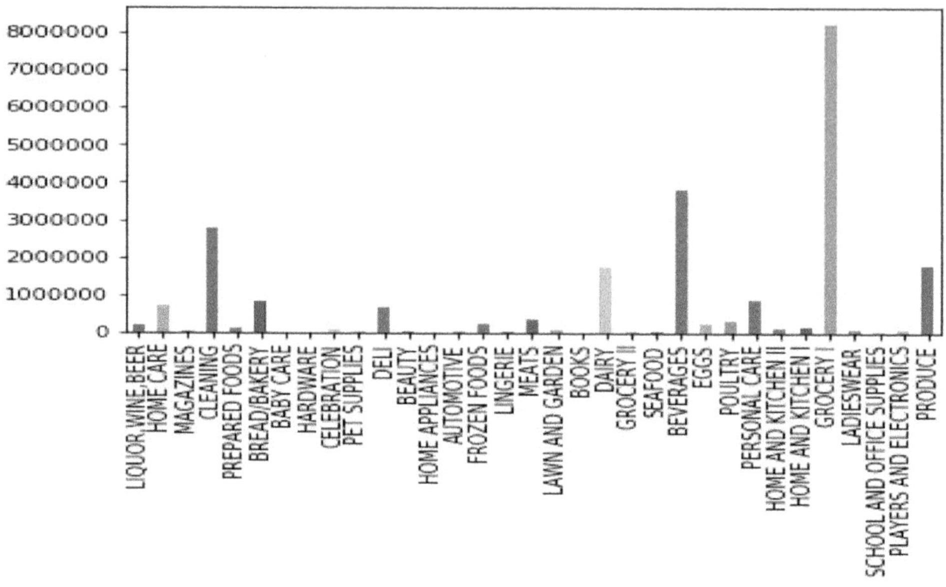

Figure 11. (a) Top 15 item families sold, (b) Bottom 15 item families sold

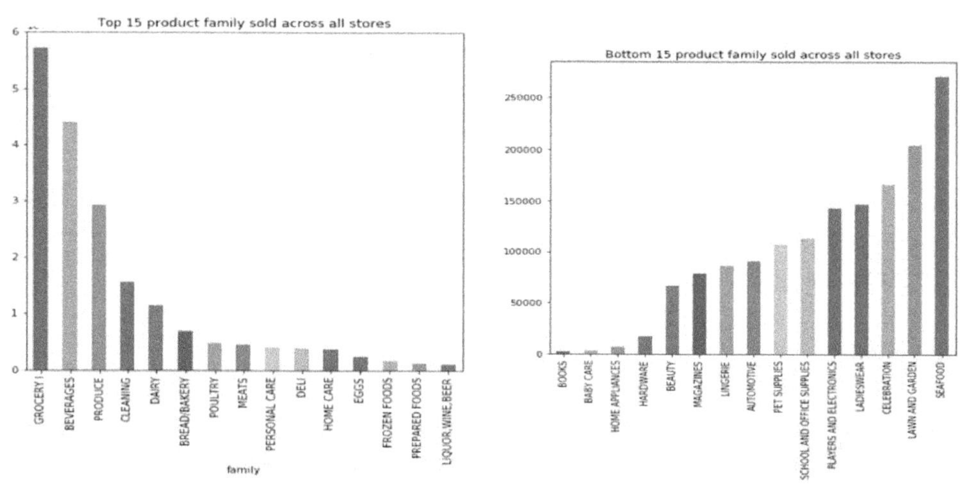

(a) (b)

Figure 12. (a) Top 15 sold items, (b) Bottom 15 sold items

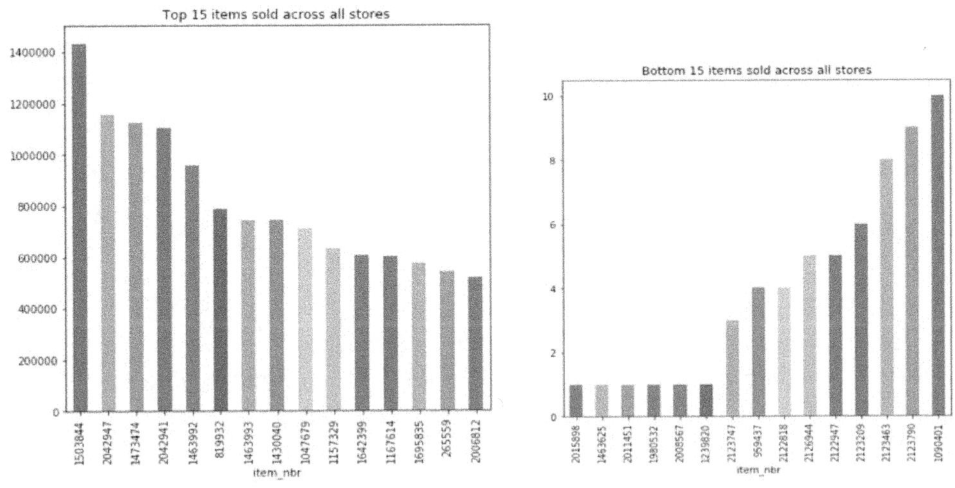

(a) (b)

Figure 13. (a) Sold top 15 item family's ratio, (b) Sold bottom 15 item family's ratio

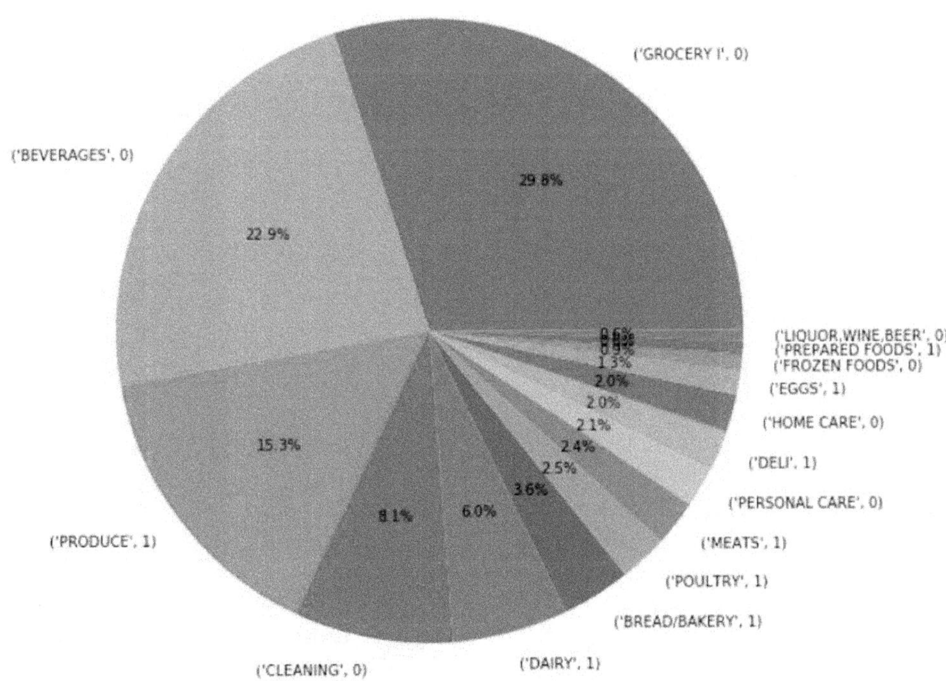

Figure 14. Datatypes and columns of items.csv

	store_nbr	city	state	type	cluster
0	1	Quito	Pichincha	D	13
1	2	Quito	Pichincha	D	13
2	3	Quito	Pichincha	D	8
3	4	Quito	Pichincha	D	9
4	5	Santo Domingo	Santo Domingo de los Tsachilas	D	4

Figure 15. Number of stores and types distributed across different cities

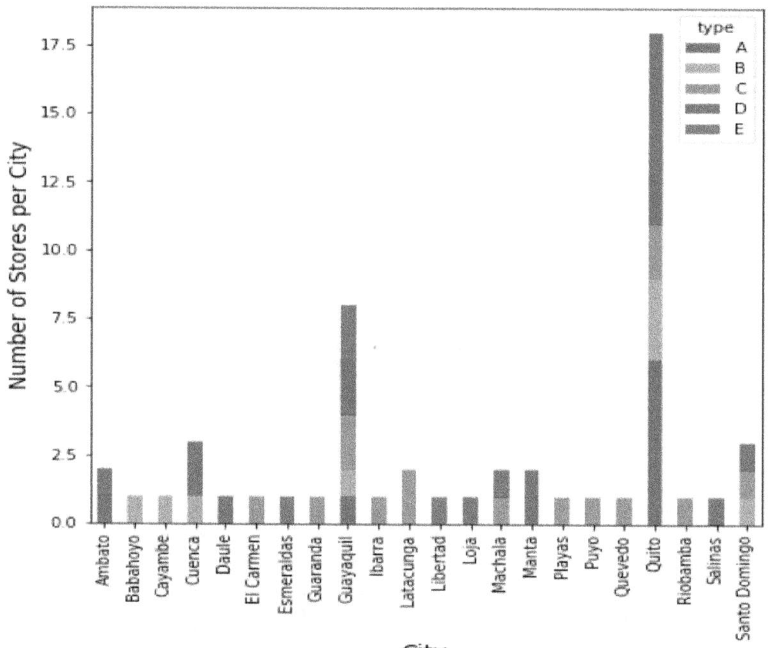

3.4. Holiday Events

The "holiday_events.csv" file contains the data of the national, regional, and local levels of Ecuador, where the "transferred" column is important. Figure 18 shows the data structure of items.csv file. No missing value is available in the data shown in Figure 19. In Figure 20 and Figure 21, we see that the most of the types of holidays are actually "holiday" followed by "Additional" and "Event". In addition, there are very few "regional" events, and most of the events are not transferred.

Figure 16. Number of stores and types distributed across different states

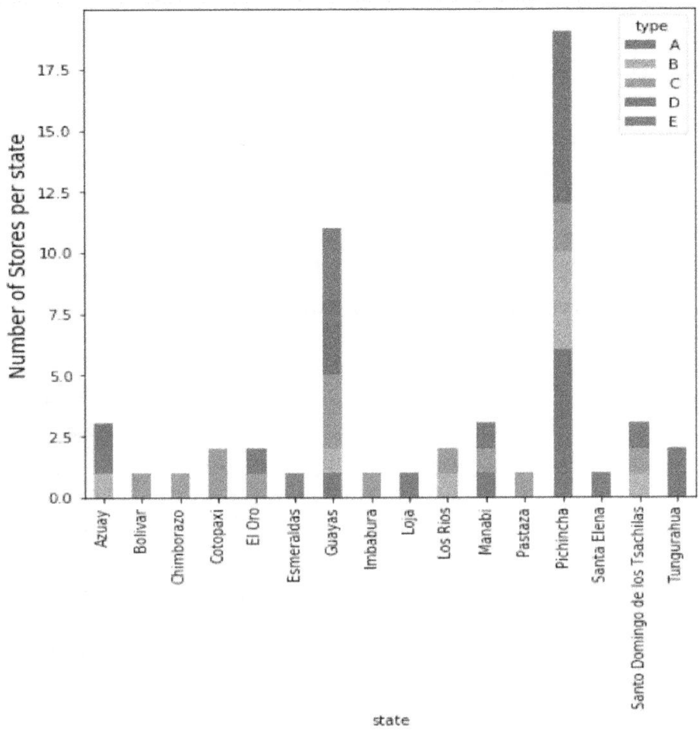

Figure 18. Data types and columns of holiday_events.csv

	date	type	locale	locale_name	description	transferred
0	2012-03-02	Holiday	Local	Manta	Fundacion de Manta	False
1	2012-04-01	Holiday	Regional	Cotopaxi	Provincializacion de Cotopaxi	False
2	2012-04-12	Holiday	Local	Cuenca	Fundacion de Cuenca	False
3	2012-04-14	Holiday	Local	Libertad	Cantonizacion de Libertad	False
4	2012-04-21	Holiday	Local	Riobamba	Cantonizacion de Riobamba	False

3.5. Oil

Figure 22(a) and Figure 22(b) show the data structure and the missing values of oil. csv data file. In addition, Figure 23 displays the change of oil in price over time, which seems that the oil price has a decreasing trend from January 2013 to July 2017. In the middle of 2014, there was a drastic drop in the price of oil.

Figure 19. Missing value of holiday_ events.csv

```
holidays_events Data
date False
type False
locale False
locale_name False
description False
transferred False
```

Figure 20. Subplot of type, locate, and transferred

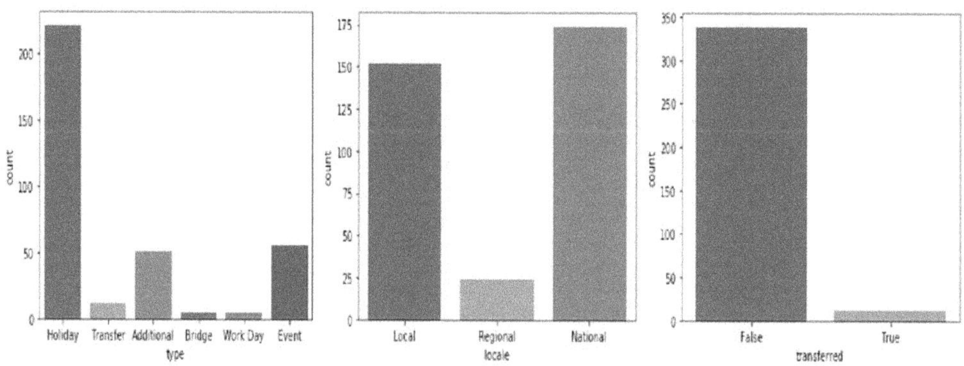

3.6. Transactions

In the transaction.csv file, there are 83,488 observations and three columns (i.e., date, store number, and the number of transactions). Figure 24(a) shows the data structure of the data file. No missing value is available in the data which is shown in Figure 24(b).

The transaction data are only available for the training set which counts the number of transactions in each store in each business day. Figure 25 represents the transactions data distributed by year, month, and day. Figure 25(a) shows that the observations are from 2013 to 2017 with the increasing observations except for 2017. It is noticeable that partial data is available for 2017, from January to August. Figure 25(b) illustrates that the transactions are mostly related to January to August rather than the other months of the year which are cooler months. Figure 25(c) displays that the transactions data are distributed by day, which is almost uniformly distributed. The distribution of the observations is low at the 1st and 25th days of the month due to the New Year and Christmas times. Furthermore, 31st days of the month observations are minimum because some months have 31 days.

Figure 21. Holiday_events count based on the location

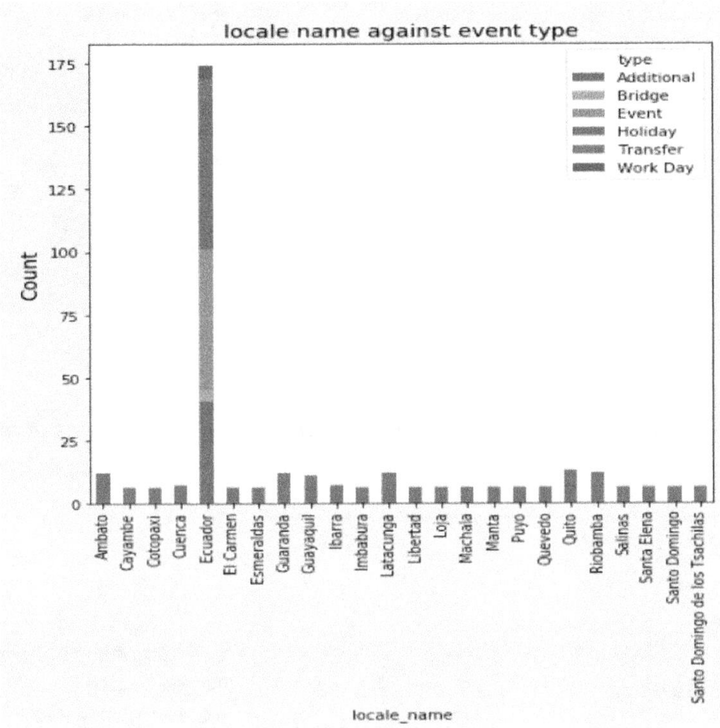

Figure 22. (a) Data types and columns of oil.csv, (b) Null values of oil.csv

	date	dcoilwtico
0	2013-01-01	NaN
1	2013-01-02	93.14
2	2013-01-03	92.97
3	2013-01-04	93.12
4	2013-01-07	93.20

(a)

```
Oil Data
date False
dcoilwtico True
```

(b)

Figure 23. The change of oil price over time

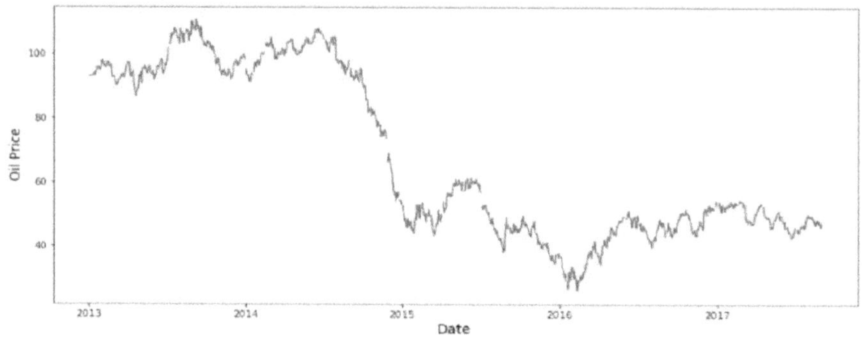

Figure 24. (a) Data types and columns of transaction, (b) Null values of transaction

	date	store_nbr	transactions
0	2013-01-01	25	770
1	2013-01-02	1	2111
2	2013-01-02	2	2358
3	2013-01-02	3	3487
4	2013-01-02	4	1922

(a)

```
transactions Data
date False
store_nbr False
transactions False
```

(b)

Figure 25. (a) Transactions distribution by year, (b) Transactions distribution by month, (c) Transactions distribution by day

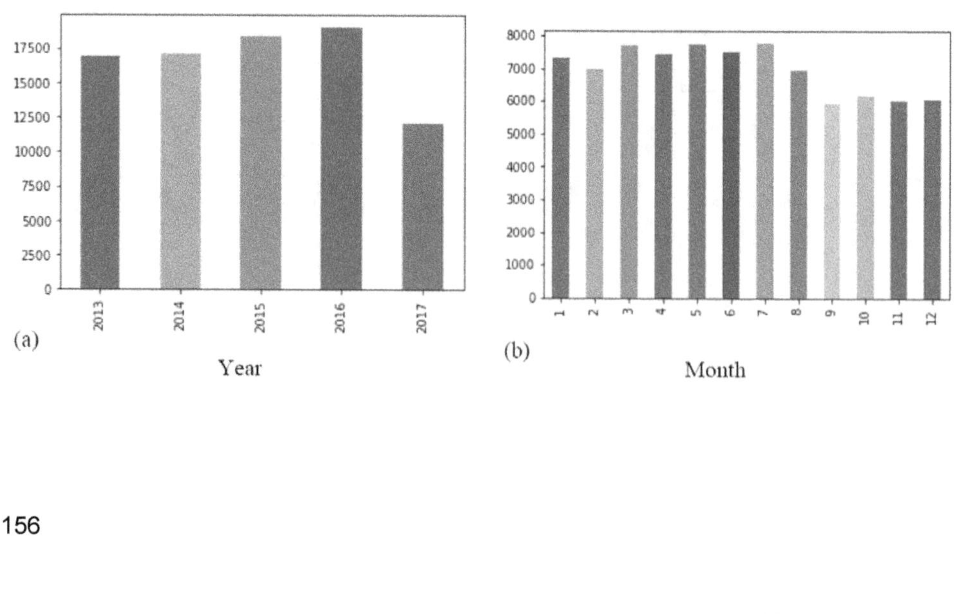

4. METHODOLOGY AND EXPERIMENT

The main aim of this research is to forecast the unit sales of thousands of items sold at different chain stores located in Ecuador to avoid overstocking, minimize understocking, reduce waste and loss, and increase customer satisfaction. In this research, good predictions are highly desirable because the chain stores can increase their efficiency and determine the prices of products for customers accurately. The training data is provided where stores, items, and dates information are given including the promoted items and unit sales. Some supplementary information is provided to avoid complexity and enhance the forecasting process.

In this study, the explored forecasting models are Artificial Neural Network (ANN), Convolutional Neural Network (CNN), and Long Short Term Memory Neural Network (LSTM). Besides, dropout layer is used for ANN and LSTM to increase the effectiveness and the speed of learning. In this research, a comparative study is performed on the performances of the models based on predictive accuracy, runtime, scalability, and ease of use. The methodology of this experiment is outlined in Figure 26.

Figure 26. The workflow of the experiment

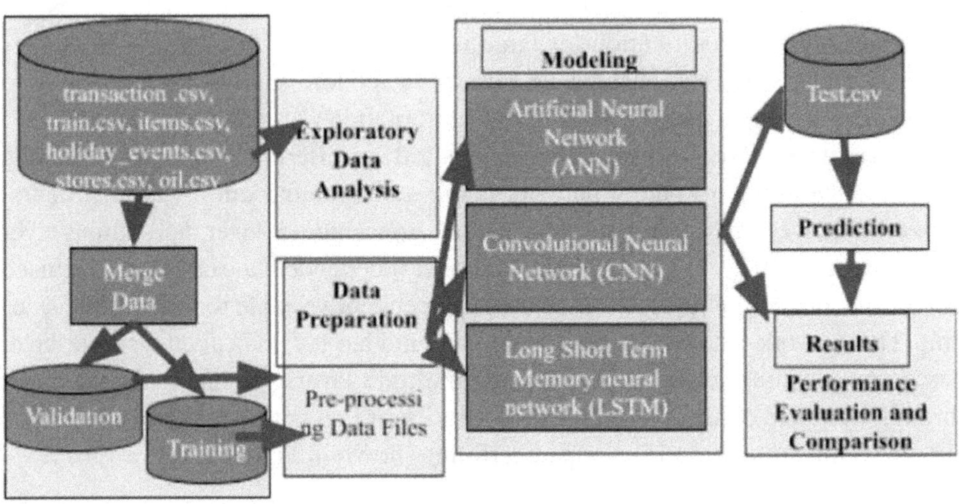

4.1. Preliminaries

This research is started by understanding the business's features of real-life problems such as "Oil Price", and "Holidays". The external factors affect the demand of products particularly the perishable goods. The data files of this investigation are pre-processed (e.g., the null values of promotion, holidays, and oil data files are taken care of). The exploratory data analysis has been performed on the data as was described in the previous section. The following subsections provide backgrounds on ANN, LSTM, and CNN.

4.1.1. Artificial Neural Network (ANN)

ANNs are information processing structures that simulate the behavior of the human's brain (Martín and Sanz Molina, 2006). An artificial neural network is a highly connected array of neurons (Park et al., 1991). ANN usually is a network combined of a large number of massively interconnected neurons (simple processors) with each other in an organized fashion by defining weights, and which can operate in parallel and learn from previous examples (Specht, 1991). Simple processors called neurons process input information and convert inputs into reliable outputs (Zhang, 2004). In this research, ANN is proposed for predicting unit sales, as this approach has several advantages for predictive analytics. This technique produces a better and more reliable classification for large volumes of data. In addition, it handles complex underlying relationships, and it is very reliable and not very sensitive to the outliers. Besides, it is very strong for interpolation (Kumar et al., 1995).

Different neural networks have been proposed for different applications. Among them, the feed-forward neural network is the most popular one. A typical neural network involves three layers including input layer, hidden layer, and output layer (Sharma et al., 2013). The input layer comprises independent variables that are used to generate the output layer. It consists of a dependent variable to forecast the sales unit. The network which does not contain any hidden layer is called a single-layer perceptron. Neural networks that include multiple layers for interacting neurons through weighted connections are called Multilayer Perceptron (MLP) networks. A simple architecture of multilayer perceptron is shown in Figure 27.

4.1.2. Convolutional Neural Network (CNN)

CNN is a special kind of deep learning method which has been used for processing highly correlated data with a grid topology (LeCun and Bengio, 1995). CNN is effective for dealing with high-dimensional data, and has been successfully applied for the visual image classification, video and text categorization (Bengio et al.,

Figure 27. A simple architecture of Multilayer Perceptron (MLP) (Madan, 2017)

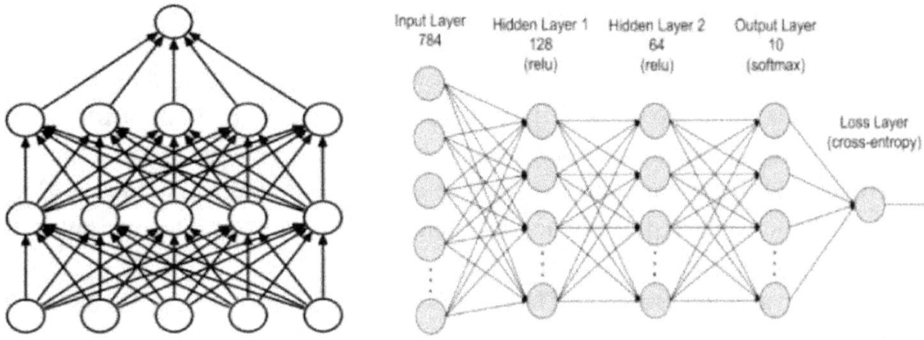

2017). A convolutional neural network architecture has an input, an output, and multiple hidden layers. The hidden layers classically have a series of convolution layers composed by a set of neurons completely independent in a single layer and fully connected to all neurons in the previous layer. The Convo (Convo + RELU) layer is a feature extractor layer where ReLU activation is a popular activation function to make all negative value to zero, followed by additional hidden layers such as pooling layer, fully connected (FC) layer, softmax or logistic layer, and output layer. Figure 28 shows the CNN architecture (Morabito et al., 2019). A pooling technique is applied to get another version of smaller input than the original size. A new convolutional layer followed by pooling layer steps can be repeated as many times as needed depending on the problem. Finally, when the layers become small enough, the process is completed.

Figure 28. CNN architecture (Morabito et al., 2019)

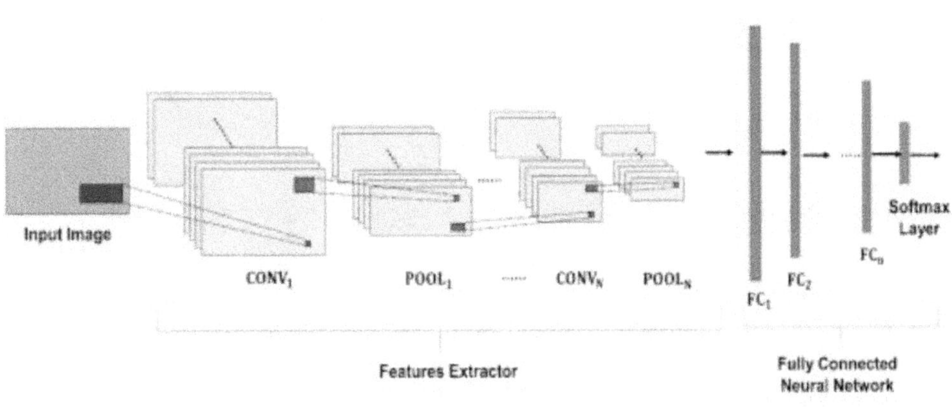

4.1.3. Long Short Term Memory Neural Network (LSTM)

The Long Short Term Memory Neural Network (LSTM) is similar to the Recurrent Neural Network (RNN) which was developed by Hochreiter and Schmidhuber (1997). RNN structure is similar to the Multilayer Perceptron (MLP), but the main difference is that RNN considers feedback connections to reflect the previous states output and the current input to generate the output. The main advantage of LSTM over RNN is to avoid the long-term dependency problem and remove/add information to the units' state over longer periods of time.

The detailed architecture of LSTM is shown in Figure 29. The key idea of LSTM is to regulate the flow of information using different internal mechanisms called gates (e.g., input, forget, and output gates). These gates can carry relevant information throughout the process. They can learn and decide which data in a sequence chain is important to keep or throw away during the training process. Based on Figure 29, the state of each LSTM's cell (ct-1) passes through the LSTM module to generate a state for the next step (ct).

Figure 29. The detailed architecture of LSTM (Jiang et al., 2018)

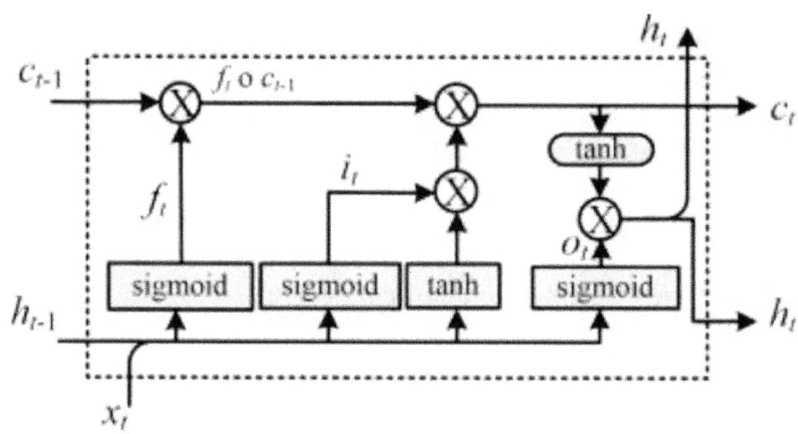

4.2. Experiment

In this study, we try to keep the algorithm as simple as possible to obtain maximum reproducibility. The multilayer perceptron architecture is utilized which is a fully connected network with two layers. Furthermore, to increase the effectiveness and stability and learning, dropping out units (hidden and visible) are used in the neural network. Because of this process, each hidden layer of the neural network can learn by itself independently from the other layers. The characteristics of the developed neural network are as follow:

- Model type is Sequential.
- Hidden layers have 64 neurons and the other one has 16 with the same activation function - "relu".
- The output layer has 1 neuron for prediction.
- Using "Adam" as the optimizer to change the weights and biases, and MSE as the loss metric.
- Fitting the model with 100 epochs with a batch size of 25.
- Finalizing the model parameters and prediction based on the test data.

The implemented CNN model is a sequential one. The features of this model are as follow:

- Model type is Sequential.
- Adding convolution layer (1-dimensional matrices).
- 64 number of nodes in the first layer.
- The activation function is ReLU or Rectified Linear Activation.
- Three parameters to compile CNN model: optimizer, loss, and metrics.
- The optimizer that adjusts the learning rate throughout training is "Adam".
- Training the model 'fit()' function parameters: training data, target data, validation data, verbose = 2.
- The number of epochs is 5.
- Predicting the test data.

To increase the effectiveness, stability, and learning, dropping out units (hidden and visible) are used for the LSTM model. The LSTM model has the following characteristics:

- Model type is Sequential.
- Adding the LSTM layer with 32 numbers of neurons.
- Adding a dropout layer for preventing data overfitting.
- Adding a dense layer, i.e., the output layer with 1 neuron to predict.
- Using compiler - "Adam" as the optimizer and MSE as the loss metric.
- Fitting the model to run on 5 epochs with a batch size of 512.
- Importing the test data and predicting.

4.3. Experimental Design

The implementation of the models is done on the Corporación Favorita Grocery Sales Forecasting dataset using Tensorflow in Python. The primary dataset (train.

csv) contains 125 million observations which are the most basic sales data from January 1, 2013 to August 15, 2017. Among 125,497,040 rows and 6 columns of the training.csv file, 23,808,261 rows are used for this research. The train file is divided to train.csv and validation.csv files, where the validation data contain January 2017 data. The test.csv file has 3,370,464 rows and 5 columns to predict unit sales. The holiday.csv null values are replaced with "no holiday" and promotion.csv, oil.csv. files null values are replaced with 0. All data files are merged with train.csv to build models and test the unit sales.

5. RESULTS AND DISCUSSION

The sales units of the Corporación Favorita Grocery Sales Forecasting dataset are produced using three different deep learning methods including Artificial Neural Network (ANN), Convolutional Neural Network (CNN), and Long Short Term Memory (LSTM) neural network using all data between 01/01/2017 and 08/15/2017. The similarities between all models are feed-forward networks, and the difference between them is related to their structures. Figures 30, 31, and 32 show the comparison of these models.

Figure 30. NN model summary

```
_________________________________________________________________
Layer (type)                 Output Shape              Param #
=================================================================
dense_30 (Dense)             (None, 64)                256
_________________________________________________________________
dropout_17 (Dropout)         (None, 64)                0
_________________________________________________________________
dense_31 (Dense)             (None, 16)                1040
_________________________________________________________________
dropout_18 (Dropout)         (None, 16)                0
_________________________________________________________________
dense_32 (Dense)             (None, 1)                 17
=================================================================
Total params: 1,313
Trainable params: 1,313
Non-trainable params: 0
_________________________________________________________________
```

Figure 31. CNN model summary

```
_________________________________________________________________
Layer (type)                 Output Shape              Param #
=================================================================
conv1d_5 (Conv1D)            (None, 1, 64)             256
_________________________________________________________________
max_pooling1d_2 (MaxPooling1 (None, 1, 64)             0
_________________________________________________________________
flatten_4 (Flatten)          (None, 64)                0
_________________________________________________________________
dense_4 (Dense)              (None, 50)                3250
_________________________________________________________________
dense_5 (Dense)              (None, 1)                 51
=================================================================
Total params: 3,557
Trainable params: 3,557
Non-trainable params: 0
_________________________________________________________________
```

Figure 32. LSTM model summary

```
_________________________________________________________________
Layer (type)                 Output Shape              Param #
=================================================================
lstm_1 (LSTM)                (None, 32)                4608
_________________________________________________________________
dropout_19 (Dropout)         (None, 32)                0
_________________________________________________________________
dense_33 (Dense)             (None, 32)                1056
_________________________________________________________________
dropout_20 (Dropout)         (None, 32)                0
_________________________________________________________________
dense_34 (Dense)             (None, 1)                 33
=================================================================
Total params: 5,697
Trainable params: 5,697
Non-trainable params: 0
_________________________________________________________________
```

Mean Squared Error (MSE) is adopted as an indicator for evaluating the models. It measures the average of the squares of errors. MSE is calculated based on Equation (1) where n is the vector of predictions generated from a sample of n data points, and Y is the vector of observed values of the variable being predicted (Wackerly et al., 2014).

$$MSE = \frac{1}{n}\sum_{i=1}^{n}(Y_i - \hat{Y}_i)^2 \quad (1)$$

In this research, Root Mean Squared Error (RMSE) also is utilized as an indicator for evaluating the models. Equation (2) shows the formula. The variables are observed over T times. $\hat{y}_t$ is the prediction value for time t. In addition, y_t is the variable (Hyndman and Koehler, 2006).

$$RMSE = \sqrt{\frac{\sum_{t=1}^{T}(\hat{y}_t - y_t)^2}{T}} \quad (2)$$

The models are built using different parameters and diverse weights. For instance, for the neural network, the MSE for Step 75/100 is 144.02 which is the lowest value. Again, for CNN and LSTM, the lowest MSEs are 175.20 and 75.22, respectively. Table 1 and Table 2 represent the comparison summary of the results of different forecasting models in terms of MSE and RMSE, respectively. Figure 33 and Figure 34 show that the LSTM performs better than the other two models for forecasting the sales units.

Table 2. The comparison of RMSE values

Approach	Training RMSE		Validation RMSE	
Artificial Neural Networks (ANN)	Step: 0 / 100	4.10	Step: 0 / 100	4.10
	Step: 25 / 100	4.11	Step: 25 / 100	4.11
	Step: 50 / 100	4.08	Step: 50 / 100	4.08
	Step: 75 / 100	**4.07**	**Step: 75 / 100**	**4.07**
Convolutional Neural Network (CNN)	Epoch 1/5	4.498	Epoch 1/5	3.980
	Epoch 2/5	4.115	Epoch 2/5	4.603
	Epoch 3/5	4.261	Epoch 3/5	4.268
	Epoch 4/5	4.147	Epoch 4/5	4.040
	Epoch 5/5	**3.963**	**Epoch 5/5**	**4.363**
Long Short-Term Memory Neural Network (LSTM)	**Step4-Epoch 4/5**	**3.00**	**Step4-Epoch 4/5**	**2.78**
	Step5-Epoch 3/5	3.05	Step5-Epoch 3/5	2.98
	Step7-Epoch 1/5	3.01	Step7-Epoch 1/5	3.11
	Step12-Epoch 3/5	3.08	Step12-Epoch 3/5	2.78
	Step16-Epoch 4/5	4.33	Step16-Epoch 4/5	4.03

Figure 33. Comparison summary of different forecasting models in terms of MSE

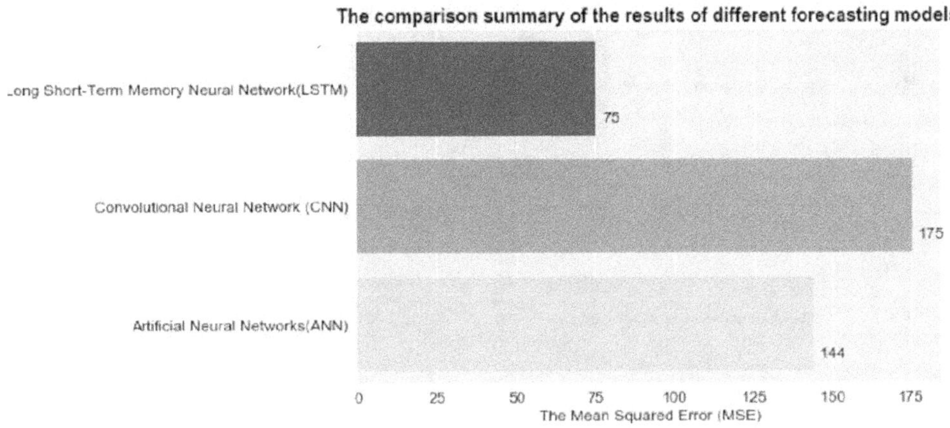

Table 1. The comparison of MSE values

Approach	Training MSE		Validation MSE	
Artificial Neural Networks (ANN)	Step: 0 / 100	148.65	Step: 0 / 100	148.65
	Step: 25 / 100	158.57	Step: 25 / 100	158.57
	Step: 50 / 100	149.17	Step: 50 / 100	149.17
	Step: 75 / 100	**144.02**	Step: 75 / 100	**144.02**
Convolutional Neural Network (CNN)	Epoch 1/5	192.69	Epoch 1/5	233.71
	Epoch 2/5	178.64	Epoch 2/5	241.89
	Epoch 3/5	179.52	**Epoch 3/5**	**215.98**
	Epoch 4/5	175.20	Epoch 4/5	217.25
	Epoch 5/5	172.93	Epoch 5/5	230.60
Long Short-Term Memory Neural Network (LSTM)	**Step4-Epoch 5/5**	**75.2203**	**Step4-Epoch 5/5**	**74.49**
	Step5-Epoch 3/5	88.7221	Step5-Epoch 3/5	87.85
	Step7-Epoch 4/5	279.7268	Step7-Epoch 4/5	279.30
	Step12-Epoch 3/5	170.3472	Step12-Epoch 3/5	169.83
	Step16-Epoch 4/5	458.8012	Step16-Epoch 4/5	463.09

Figure 34. Comparison summary of different forecasting models in terms of RMSE

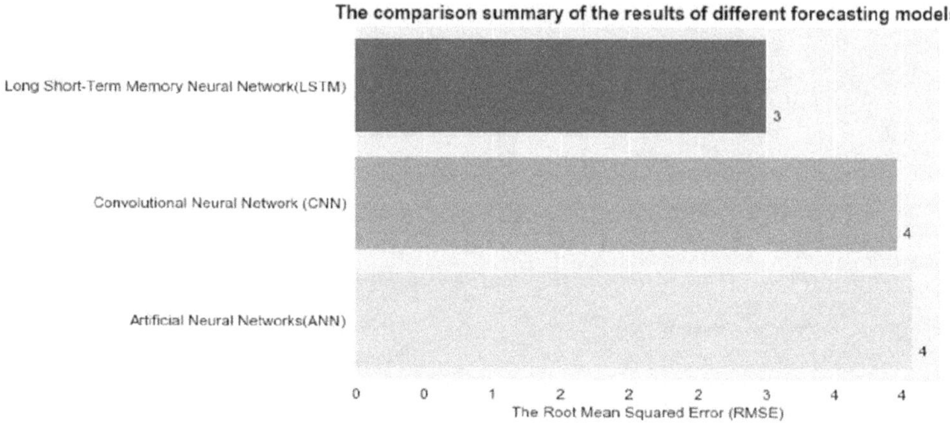

6. CONCLUSIONS AND FUTURE RESEARCH

In this research, forecasting the unit sales of thousands of items sold at diverse chain stores located in Ecuador has been investigated using advanced techniques. Three deep learning approaches including Artificial Neural Network (ANN), Convolutional Neural Network (CNN), and Long Short Term Memory (LSTM) have been adopted for reliable and good predictions from the Corporación Favorita Grocery Sales Forecasting dataset collected from Kaggle website. Then, the performances of these methods have been evaluated and compared.

Real data have been utilized in this research. The results show that LSTM has the best performance among the three techniques. In this case, the Mean Squared Error (MSE) is 75.22 for training. For CNN and ANN, the lowest MSE of training is 175.20 and 144.02, respectively.

The key challenge of this research is the resource (memory) limitation of the processor. As the train.csv file is so big, the data processing took a long time to obtain the results. Another challenge is receiving errors in some cases. An important future research direction is exploring more neural network techniques on the same dataset in addition to adding more feature extraction techniques for improvement of the model, and to get more accurate results. Furthermore, it would be interesting to investigate different deep learning techniques on more complex datasets to see there is any improvement in the results.

ACKNOWLEDGMENT

This research has been supported by an NSERC Discovery grant. The authors would like to thank the editor and reviewers for the great comments that improved the quality of this book chapter. In addition, they would like to thank Dr. Ayse Bener who is the Program Director of the MSc program in Data Science and Analytics at Ryerson University. This research was completed as a part of this program.

REFERENCES

Aburto, L., & Weber, R. (2007). Improved supply chain management based on hybrid demand forecasts. *Applied Soft Computing*, *7*(1), 136–144. doi:10.1016/j.asoc.2005.06.001

Al-Saba, T., & El-Amin, I. (1999). Artificial neural networks as applied to long-term demand forecasting. *Artificial Intelligence in Engineering*, *13*(2), 189–197. doi:10.1016/S0954-1810(98)00018-1

Beccali, M., Cellura, M., Brano, V. L., & Marvuglia, A. (2004). Forecasting daily urban electric load profiles using artificial neural networks. *Energy Conversion and Management*, *45*(18-19), 2879–2900. doi:10.1016/j.enconman.2004.01.006

Bengio, Y., Goodfellow, I., & Courville, A. (2017). *Deep learning* (Vol. 1). MIT Press.

Bhadouria, S., & Jayant, A. (2017). Development of ANN models for demand forecasting. *Am. J. Eng. Res*, *6*, 142–147.

Bousqaoui, H., Achchab, S., & Tikito, K. (2017). Machine learning applications in supply chains: An emphasis on neural network applications. In *2017 3rd International Conference of Cloud Computing Technologies and Applications (CloudTech)* (pp. 1-7). IEEE.

Campbell, C., & Ying, Y. (2011). Learning with support vector machines. *Synthesis Lectures on Artificial Intelligence and Machine Learning, 5*(1), 1-95.

Chang, P. C., Fan, C. Y., & Lin, J. J. (2011). Monthly electricity demand forecasting based on a weighted evolving fuzzy neural network approach. *International Journal of Electrical Power & Energy Systems*, *33*(1), 17–27. doi:10.1016/j.ijepes.2010.08.008

Chao-ting, X. U. A. N., Pei-qing, H., & Dong, L. (2000). Applications of Neural Network Technology in Supply Chain Management. *Industrial Engineering and Management, 3*.

Choy, K. L., Lee, W. B., & Lo, V. (2003). Design of an intelligent supplier relationship management system: A hybrid case based neural network approach. *Expert Systems with Applications*, *24*(2), 225–237. doi:10.1016/S0957-4174(02)00151-3

Corporación Favorita Grocery Sales Forecasting. (2019). https://www.kaggle.com/c/favorita-grocery-sales-forecasting/data

Gaur, M., Goel, S., & Jain, E. (2015, March). Comparison between Nearest Neighbours and Bayesian Network for demand forecasting in supply chain management. In *2015 2nd International Conference on Computing for Sustainable Global Development (INDIACom)* (pp. 1433-1436). IEEE.

Hochreiter, S., & Schmidhuber, J. (1997). Long short-term memory. *Neural Computation*, *9*(8), 1735–1780. doi:10.1162/neco.1997.9.8.1735 PMID:9377276

Huang, H. C., & Hou, C. I. (2017). Tourism Demand Forecasting Model Using Neural Network. *International. J. Comput. Sci. Inf. Technol*, *9*, 19–29.

Hyndman, R. J., & Koehler, A. B. (2006). Another look at measures of forecast accuracy. *International Journal of Forecasting*, *22*(4), 679–688. doi:10.1016/j.ijforecast.2006.03.001

Jiang, L., & Hu, G. (2018, November). Day-ahead price forecasting for electricity market using long-short term memory recurrent neural network. In *2018 15th International Conference on Control, Automation, Robotics and Vision (ICARCV)* (pp. 949-954). IEEE. 10.1109/ICARCV.2018.8581235

Kaya, G. O., & Turkyilmaz, A. (2018). Intermittent demand forecasting using data mining techniques. *Applied Computer Science, 14*.

Kaylani, A., Georgiopoulos, M., Mollaghasemi, M., Anagnostopoulos, G. C., Sentelle, C., & Zhong, M. (2010). An adaptive multiobjective approach to evolving ART architectures. *IEEE Transactions on Neural Networks*, *21*(4), 529–550. doi:10.1109/TNN.2009.2037813 PMID:20172827

Kochak, A., & Sharma, S. (2015). Demand forecasting using neural network for supply chain management. *International Journal of Mechanical Engineering and Robotics Research, 4*(1), 96-104.

Kohonen, T. (1990). The self-organizing map. *Proceedings of the IEEE*, *78*(9), 1464–1480. doi:10.1109/5.58325

Kumar, A., Rao, V. R., & Soni, H. (1995). An empirical comparison of neural network and logistic regression models. *Marketing Letters*, *6*(4), 251–263. doi:10.1007/BF00996189

LeCun, Y., & Bengio, Y. (1995). Convolutional networks for images, speech, and time series. The Handbook of Brain Theory and Neural Networks, 3361(10), 1995.

Leung, H. C. (1995, June). Neural networks in supply chain management. In *Proceedings for Operating Research and the Management Sciences* (pp. 347–352). IEEE. doi:10.1109/IEMC.1995.524607

Madan, V. (2017). *Introducing Gluon — An Easy-to-Use Programming Interface for Flexible Deep Learning*. https://aws.amazon.com/blogs/machine-learning/introducing-gluon-an-easy-to-use-programming-interface-for-flexible-deep-learning/

Martín del Bío, B., & Sanz Molina, A. (2006). *Neural networks and fuzzy systems*. Editorial RA-MA.

Meherishi, L., Narayana, S. A., & Ranjani, K. S. (2019). Sustainable packaging for supply chain management in the circular economy: A review. *Journal of Cleaner Production*, *237*, 117582. doi:10.1016/j.jclepro.2019.07.057

Mentzer, J. T., DeWitt, W., Keebler, J. S., Min, S., Nix, N. W., Smith, C. D., & Zacharia, Z. G. (2001). Defining supply chain management. *Journal of Business Logistics*, *22*(2), 1–25. doi:10.1002/j.2158-1592.2001.tb00001.x

Morabito, F. C., Campolo, M., Ieracitano, C., & Mammone, N. (2019). Deep Learning Approaches to Electrophysiological Multivariate Time-Series Analysis. In *Artificial Intelligence in the Age of Neural Networks and Brain Computing* (pp. 219–243). Academic Press.

Mupparaju, K., Soni, A., Gujela, P., & Lanham, M. A. (2008). *A Comparative Study of Machine Learning Frameworks for Demand Forecasting*. Academic Press.

Pai, P. F., & Lin, C. S. (2005). A hybrid ARIMA and support vector machines model in stock price forecasting. *Omega*, *33*(6), 497–505. doi:10.1016/j.omega.2004.07.024

Park, D. C., El-Sharkawi, M. A., Marks, R. J., Atlas, L. E., & Damborg, M. J. (1991). Electric load forecasting using an artificial neural network. *IEEE Transactions on Power Systems*, *6*(2), 442–449. doi:10.1109/59.76685

Sharma, A., Panigrahi, D., & Kumar, P. (2013). *A neural network based approach for predicting customer churn in cellular network services*. arXiv preprint arXiv:1309.3945

Specht, D. F. (1991). A general regression neural network. *IEEE Transactions on Neural Networks*, *2*(6), 568–576. doi:10.1109/72.97934 PMID:18282872

Sultan, K., Ali, H., & Zhang, Z. (2018). Big data perspective and challenges in next generation networks. *Future Internet, 10*(7), 56. doi:10.3390/fi10070056

Wackerly, D., Mendenhall, W., & Scheaffer, R. L. (2014). *Mathematical statistics with applications*. Cengage Learning.

Zhang, G. P. (2004). Business forecasting with artificial neural networks: An overview. In *Neural networks in business forecasting* (pp. 1–22). IGI Global. doi:10.4018/978-1-59140-176-6.ch001

Zhikai, H. Y. L. F. S., & Ge, Z. (2002). Neural Networks Technology for Inventory Management. *Computer Engineering and Applications, 15*.

Chapter 6
Logistics Providers in Syria Humanitarian Operations

Jomana Mahfod
University of Le Havre Normandie, France

Bashar Khoury
https://orcid.org/0000-0002-5912-0619
Selinus University of Sciences and Literature, Syria

Beatrice Canel-Depitre
University of Le Havre Normandie, France

Atour Taghipour
Normandy University, France

ABSTRACT

Logistics providers have become an important element in completing humanitarian relief work in countries experiencing armed conflict. Delivery aid assistances need to build logistics capacity and critical supply chain functions that help to meet the unconfirmed requirements of beneficiaries at right place, on right date, and with right fees. To reach the research goal, the authors will determine the weights of customer requirements (CRs) using the DEMATEL method, which considers the influences of inconformity and the causal relationship between CRs. This chapter employs quality function deployment (QFD) to integrate the voice of CRs and supplier criteria TRs using house of quality charts. This chapter focuses on case of humanitarian organizations collaborate with logistics service providers (LSPs) to maintain and enhance their performance by identify the crucial factors that effect on LSPs selection and their specified from the perspective of humanitarian relief organizations activated in Syrian humanitarian operation.

DOI: 10.4018/978-1-7998-3805-0.ch006

INTRODUCTION

Since the 1950s, the number and magnitude of disasters have grown exponentially, the number of affected people has grown in proportion (about 300 million persons per annum on the average since the 1990s) and the annual damage costs have risen to about 0.17 per cent of the world GDP (Guha-Sapir, Hoyois, & Below,2014). The increasing number of disasters and complex humanitarian emergencies put pressure on humanitarian aid agencies to deliver humanitarian aids in an appropriate and cost-effective way (Kovacz and Spens, 2007). Although, faster deliveries can substantially reduce suffering of beneficiaries in need (Perez-Rodrıguez and Holguın-Veras, 2016), but disasters create a massive demand for relief aids that include food, medicines, shelter, water and other resources without prediction and expectation which leading to limited preparation for mitigating the same.

In this respect, various humanitarian organizations collaborate with logistics service providers (LSPs) to maintain and enhance their performance. Nevertheless, there is little knowledge which describes what are the important factors for selecting LSPs. The question remains: how can HOs select the most appropriate LSP for humanitarian operation? Despite its practical significance, no explicit effort has been done to identify the criteria/factors in prioritizing and selecting LSPs for humanitarian relief. Therefore, there is an urgent need for an integrated approach to review the selection indicators of LSPs in the humanitarian sector because of the LSPs' roles in humanitarian relief has now gained much attention from practitioners, as well as from the academic community (Vega and Roussat 2015).

In despite that, there is lack of research in terms of LSPs selection approach; originally developed for commercial activities; which can be applicable in the context of humanitarian operations (Holguín-Veras et al. 2012; Swansson and Smith 2013). This study aims to identify the crucial factors that effect on LSPs selection and their priorities from the perspective of humanitarian relief organizations and to explore how these were implemented and practiced (Roh, Jang, 2018).

In fact, selecting LSPs can be challenging for relief organizations due to the complexities and uncertainties in humanitarian supply chains (Balcik et al., 2010). The problem of specific selection is a multi-criteria decision-making problem involving both qualitative and quantitative performance measures. Some researchers (e.g., Abidi et al. 2015; Kabra and Ramesh 2015) have applied Analytic Hierarchical Process (AHP) based MCDM method to selection-related humanitarian issues and assumed the used criteria to be independent. In the real world, however, the selection criteria are seldom independent, but always have some sort of interrelationships among themselves with cause and effect relationships (Ramkumar et al. 2016; Sharma et al. 2017). Usually, several conflicting criteria make the supplier selection problem a complex problem. It is often desirable to make a compromise among the conflicting criteria. Singh (2016) because of LSPs selection decisions conflict with one another. For instance, the low price of purchased materials from a certain supplier can be offset by the supplier's loose quality standards or chronic financial instability. On the other hand, the availability of more advanced technology from a supplier can be undermined by the sourcing supplier's high purchasing costs and excessive tariffs. It is obvious that effective supplier selection must deal with a host of quantitative and qualitative factors that conflict with one another. Hokey Min (1994) despite the scale and importance of integrated functions "supplier selecting, procurement, demand forecasting and order planning" in humanitarian supply chains, there are few studies that address procurement issues and decisions in the relief literature. Humanitarian organizations use similar criteria in evaluating and selecting suppliers to agreements; particularly, quality, price, and supplier's ability to meet lead time and demand fulfillment requirements are important factors (Logistics Cluster, 2011) Furthermore, there is a rich literature that addresses supply contracts and supplier selection problems in the commercial context, these topics have not received much attention in humanitarian logistics, in despite that, considering the supplier selection criteria that are important for relief organizations (Balcik,Ak,2013 ; Hu,Dong,2019)

This is due to the complexities and uncertainties of demands associated with disasters and a lack of supporting resources. This paper will contribute in theme of book by depth discussions about suppliers-selection problem that link directly with demand & order functions, consequently, provide insights and support executives concerned with humanitarian supply chain.

BACKGROUND

Today 80 per cent of humanitarian funding goes to conflict-driven disasters (GHA, 2017). At the same time, only a small fraction of humanitarian logistics research explicitly addresses man-made disasters and conflicts (Kunz and Reiner, 2012). A quick review of many papers in terms of humanitarian logistics illustrate surprisingly included no single study focusing on Syrian humanitarian operations. Maybe not surprisingly, because there are only few empirically grounded studies on conflicts since field studies would expose researchers and partnering organizations to risks (Lukosch, Comes, 2019).

Syria has suffered from worst human-disaster caused by civil conflicts since 2012. Due to World Food Programme, Situation Report #12 in December 2016. There are 3.5 million people require humanitarian assistance, 9 million people need of food assistance, and 6.3 million people displaced inside Syria. These huge figures led activated humanitarian organizations in Syria (UN agencies & INGOs) to purchase large amounts of demands present in variety of relief supplies (such as water, food, and tents…etc.).

Simultaneously, there was a growing interest by humanitarian organizations in outsourcing and offering logistics services in the humanitarian supply chain as a tool to attain competitive advantage (WFP, 2019; logistics cluster, 2015; Oloruntoba and Gray, 2009; Vandermerwe and Rada, 1988). Therefore, Logistics Service Providers (LSPs) have played lately an important role in humanitarian affairs, supporting NGOs and governments in responding to great disasters. Furthermore, new trends in logistics outsourcing are emerging in several international organizations including the World Food Programme (WFP) and the International Federation of Red Cross and Red Crescent Societies (IFRC) performed as Logistics Service Providers LSPs.(Roh & Jang 2018) WFP delivers and distributes relief supplies from other humanitarian organizations and the United Nations Humanitarian Relief Depot (UNHRD) or IFRC has set up distribution centers or warehouse hubs for humanitarian organizations by choosing strategically important locations (Heaslip, 2013). Currently, major logistics enterprises in the transport and commercial sector are working worldwide as Logistics Service Providers (LSPs) for HOs such as DHL, Agility, A. Moller Maersk, UPS and TNT which are being now as trademarks and leaders in humanitarian logistics and transportation field (Cozzolino, 2012).

This review of related literature presents many key facts such as the management of the supply chain in disaster relief operations is considered an essential element in the resolution of a crisis since the tsunami in South East Asia on December 26th, 2004 and Hurricane Katrina in August 2005. (Boltürk et al.,2016) The specific study illustrated the significant increasing in frequencies of publications on HL since 2004 up to 2016 because of researchers have been focused on HL especially after the mentioned humanitarian disasters, which caused the deaths of many people. (Boltürk et al., 2016 ; Laguna et al., 2015; Leiras et al., 2014). In beginning, we reviewed the official literatures of HOs activated in Syria, which illustrated the important role of suppliers within Syrian humanitarian logistics. Herein some of citations. “In line with our organizational beliefs and values, we only work with suppliers who share our commitment to ethical purchasing. We also seek to work with suppliers who have the least negative impact on climate change and the environment. Prospective suppliers should first read our Ethical and Environmental Policy.” (OXFAM, 2019) “Owing to the complex nature of WFP’s supply chain and difficult remote working environments, the organization depends on reliable and reputable suppliers. Even in the depth of crisis, we turn to local suppliers, thereby supporting local economies. Due the scope of WFP work, timing is essential in WFP contracts. Suppliers are expected to adhere strictly to delivery times stipulated in the contract.” (WFP, 2019) “UNICEF is interested in diversifying its supplier base and in finding new suppliers that can provide quality goods at competitive prices. By searching in the on-line

UNICEF Supply Catalogue, companies can determine if they can supply products that either exactly match or are similar to the products we procure." (UNICEF, 2019).

Reviewing of relevant literatures demonstrated that there are a few studies that present models for supplier selection decisions in the relief literature. Unlike in humanitarian relief, there is a rich literature that addresses procurement decisions; like suppliers' selection-decisions; in business supply chains. (Balcik and Ak, 2013) which has been widely studied in commercial supply chains by extensive literature exists to address this kind of decision. In fact, the most relevant research is the work of (Balcik and Ak, 2013), where a supplier selection problem for establishing framework agreements with a quantity flexibility contract was studied. They proposed a stochastic programming model that selects framework suppliers to minimize expected procurement and agreement costs while satisfying service requirements. However, the major limitation of their work is that they pre-assumed a fixed proportion (i.e., 60%) of the total demand that is satisfied by these cooperated suppliers, but do not consider the remaining demand (Hu and Dong, 2019). Another significant study is (Blecken, 2009) who made surveys in order to capture the state of SCM in the context of HL and illustrated that is humanitarian organizations neither adequately measure the performance of their suppliers or the associated logistics activities, nor do they have the capability to do so. Therefore, he investigated the tasks and responsibilities of humanitarian organizations and their supply chain partners when designing, planning, and implementing supply chain processes for humanitarian operations. He systematically presents the tasks of logistics service providers in the context of humanitarian operations (included the tasks of logistics service providers). A reference task model is developed which can be used by humanitarian organizations as a tool for process modelling and design in the areas of logistics and supply chain management. A number of supply chain processes (included suppliers' selection-process) illustrate the flexible application of the reference task model. This study was considering as key reference because of the author is working as academic and practitioner in terms of humanitarian supply chain process and he has worked on large UN project with thesis "Sustainable Procurement and the United Nations". Riloha (2013) in despite of that, there are many changes happened to humanitarian logistics operations since issue date of study.

Once of recently studies "Supplier selection and pre-positioning strategy in humanitarian relief" highlighted on one complication of the supplier selection decision which is the multi-criteria aspect. The specific research reviewed the previous work about supplier selection in business supply chains can provide directions for our work in this paper because relief agencies use similar criteria to evaluate and select cooperated suppliers, and these criteria include price, quality, suppliers' capability, lead time, quantity discount, transportation cost, carbon emission tax, currency exchange rate, price discount, delivery time, and service level. The same study assume that suppliers provide price discounts based on order quantity and required lead time, and these discounts will affect the selection of cooperated suppliers. Moreover, suppliers usually keep stock of relief items for satisfying regular business demands in practice and we assume that the relief agency can use this inventory for disaster response. Therefore, supplier physical inventory is also integrated into supplier selection criteria, and to the best of our knowledge, it is the first time to be considered for using in humanitarian relief.

Nevertheless, studies on humanitarian logistics have hardly been conducted on the key indicators of Logistics Service Providers (LSPs) selection and their relative importance. Balcik and Ak (2013) and Hu and Dong (2019) few previous studies conducted around one topic which is Logistics Service Providers (LSPs) such as (Vga and Roussat, 2015) investigated the role of logistics service providers in humanitarian relief. Also, (Saksrisathaporn et al., 2015) illustrated that many humanitarian agencies are trying to build or adopt the existing support tools of Logistics Service Providers (LSPs) selection, but most existing tools are mostly limited to information provision and do not support the decision-maker to achieve an appropriate decision. In despite of that, multi-criteria decision making (MCDM) methods have been used for disaster relief operations in recent years (e.g., Sharma et al. 2017; Trivedi and Singh 2017).

Our study reviewed related to the literatures that pertain to suppliers' selection-criteria and appropriate suppliers' attributes in respective of activated humanitarian organizations' needs generally. To best our knowledge about ideal attributes of logistics suppliers worldwide, we reviewed studies since 1966 until 2016 that investigated generally about suppliers' selection-criteria and especially for humanitarian organizations (e.g., Pazirandeh 2011 ; Aissaoui et al. 2007 ; Shahadat 2003 ; Weber et al., 1991; Dickson, 1966).

In result, review studies illustrated that supplier selection is a complex process involving several criteria such as procurement cost, material quality, delivery lead time, reliability of the supplier, these criteria can be defined variously as HOs take into account numerous conflicting factors (Singh, 2016).

Furthermore, most of the prior analytical studies considered only a limited number of attributes such as price, quality, delivery and service. Past empirical studies, however, reported that more than ten different attributes existed affecting the supplier selection decision. In addition, all but AHP and MOP overlooked the multiple objective nature of supplier selection problems, thereby failing to analyze the important trade-offs among conflicting factors. (Min, 1994). For examples, (Dickson, 1966) identified 23 criteria in his study of various supplier selection problems. He reported that quality, delivery, and performance history are the three most important criteria. Similarly, (Weber et al., 1991) in a review of 74 articles obtained similar results pertaining to the multi-criteria nature of supplier selection problem.

The literature shows a variety of methodologies and approaches used for the supplier selection problem. Traditionally, linear weighting models, total cost approach, multiple attribute utility theory, and total cost ownership are used for supplier selection. None of these approaches have received significant support in literature or in practice for their limitation to address the issues of real supplier selection environment. In the last one decade, researchers focused on optimization techniques, multi-objective programming, analytic hierarchy process, data envelopment analysis, artificial intelligence, and hybrid approaches (Singh, 2016).

Eventually, we summarized our review results within below table included specific references that focused on each specific sub-criterion underlying the main criterion.

The aim of this study is to select LSPs for humanitarian organizations through establishes the weights of customer requirements (CRs) using the DEMATEL method, which considers the influences of inconformity and the causal relationship between CRs. This paper employs quality function deployment (QFD) to integrate the voice of CRs and supplier criteria TRs using "HOQ" charts. Finally, to rank the supplier and choose the best LSP and mechanisms to select the best choices and alternatives, we apply the ELECTRE method. Through a case study of humanitarian organizations in Syria.

Table 1. The criteria and sub-criteria of supplier selection in the literature review

The criteria and sub-criteria of supplier selection		
Criteria	**Sub-criteria**	**Authors**
Performance of supplier	Quality	Vega and Roussat (2015), Burcu Balcik and Deniz Ak (2013), Singh (2016), Bansal & Kumar (2013), Bhatti et al. (2010), Chen and Wu (2011), Cirpin and Kabadayi (2015), Erkyaman et al. (2012), Govindan et al. (2012), Li et al. (2012), Hwang et al. (2016), Wong (2010), Roh & Jang (2018)
	Delivery	Jharkharia & Shankar (2007), Singh (2016), Bansal & Kumar (2013), Bhatti et al. (2010), Chen & Wu (2011), Cirpin & Kabadayi (2015), Erkyaman et al. (2012), Govindan et al. (2012), Hwang et al. (2016), Rajesh et al. (2011), Wong (2010), Vijayvargiya & Dey (2010), Roh & Jang (2018)
	Service	Fedrick (2011), Howden (2009), Pehief & Breal (2005), Wassenhove (2006), Kovacs (2007), Adam (2013), Jamison (2012), Drabek (2003), Graroveher (1973), Burt (1992), Podoln (1997), Wilna (2011), Pettit & Beresford (2005), Power et al. (2001), Kopele & Tuominen (1996), Wong (2005), De Brito et al (2007), Roh (2013), Masoud (2012), Henning (2014), Crumbly & Carter (2015), Gaurav & Ramesh (2015), Yadev & Barve (2015), Singh (2016), Bansal & Kumar (2013), Bhatti et al. (2010), Chen & Wu (2011), Cirpin & Kabadayi (2015), Erkyaman et al. (2012), Wong (2010), Govindan et al. (2012), Hwang et al. (2016), Li et al. (2012), Vijayvargiya & Dey (2010), Roh & Jang (2018)

continues on following page

Table 1. Continued

The criteria and sub-criteria of supplier selection		
Criteria	**Sub-criteria**	**Authors**
Technical & Capability	Technical & Capability	Humanitarian supply management and logistics in the health sector (2001), Alkhatib et al. (2015), Kovács et al. (2012), Balcik and Ak (2013), Singh (2016), Roh & Jang (2018), Bansal & Kumar (2013), Bhatti et al. (2010), Cirpin & Kabadayi (2015), Erkyaman et al. (2012), Chen & Wu (2011), Govindan et al. (2012), Li et al. (2012), Rajesh et al. (2011), Soh (2010), Wong (2010), Hwang et al. (2016)
	Structure	Singh (2016), Bansal & Kumar (2013), Hwang et al. (2016), Li et al. (2012), Soh (2010), Roh & Jang (2018)
	Culture	Kim S. et al. (2018), Vega & Roussat (2015), Bai & Sarkis (2010), Singh (2016), Hwang et al. (2016), Li et al. (2012), Percin (2009), Roh & Jang (2018)
Finance Status	Finance	Vega & Roussat (2015), Singh (2016), Govindan et al. (2012), Li et al. (2012), Rajesh et al. (2011), Soh (2010), Wong (2010), Roh & Jang (2018)
	Business Excellence	Jharkharia & Shankar (2007), Singh (2016), Bansal & Kumar (2013), Cirpin & Kabadayi (2015), Erkyaman et al. (2012), Govindan et al. (2012), Hwang et al. (2016), Li et al. (2012), Percin (2009), Soh (2010), Wong (2010), Roh & Jang (2018)
Supplier Quality System	Reliability	Humanitarian Supply Management and Logistics in the Health Sector (2001), Howden (2009), Chomillfen (2009), Wassenhove (2003), Coyne (2006), Roh (2013), Henning (2014), Jorge (2015), Gaurav and Ramesh (2015), Gaurav and Ramesh (2015), Hammervoll (2011), Power et al. (2001), Kopele and Tuominen (1996), Wong (2005), De Brito et al (2007), Ahmadi (2015), Singh (2016), Roh & Jang (2018), Bansal & Kumar (2013), Hwang et al. (2016), Govindan et al. (2012)
	Supplier's Profile	Bai and Sarkis (2010), Bai and Sarkis (2010), Howden (2009), Beaman & Balh (2006), Kovacs and Spen (2009), Apte (2009), Tatham & Spen (2011), Henning (2014), Jorge (2015), Ahmadi (2015), Gaurav and Ramesh (2015), Holguin Van (2007), Gaurav et al (2015), Jamison (2012), Tomasini & Wasssenhove (2009), Handeld et al (1999), Singh (2016), Bansal & Kumar (2013), Bhatti et al. (2010), Chen & Wu (2011), Cirpin & Kabadayi (2015), Erkyaman et al. (2012), Govindan et al. (2012), Hwang et al. (2016), Li et al. (2012), Wong (2010), Roh & Jang (2018)
	Risk Factor	Kovács and Spens (2007), UWDP (2004), Lock & Wu (2007), Gaurav et al (2015), Yadev & Barve (2015), Singh (2016), Percin (2009), Roh & Jang (2018)
	Stability	Singh (2016), Govindan et al. (2012), Roh & Jang (2018)
	Flexibility	Humanitarian Supply Management and Logistics in the Health Sector (2001), Jahre et al. (2009), Knight (1921), Salmora & Apte (2010), Hark (2010), Kavac (2009), Power et al. (2001), Kopele and Tuominen (1996), Wong (2005), De Brito et al (2007), Singh (2016), Erkyaman et al. (2012), Govindan et al. (2012), Hwang et al. (2016), Li et al. (2012), Roh & Jang (2018)
	Responsibility	Singh (2016), Roh & Jang (2018)
	Responsiveness	Howden (2009), Crumbly & Carter (2015), Gaurav & Ramesh (2015), Singh (2016), Roh & Jang (2018)

continues on following page

Table 1. Continued

The criteria and sub-criteria of supplier selection		
Criteria	**Sub-criteria**	**Authors**
Cost	Cost	Jharkharia &Shankar (2007), Alkhatib et al. (2015), Balcik & Deniz Ak (2013), Fedrick (2011), Adam (2013), Melnyk el al (2010), Power et al. (2001), Kopele &Tuominen (1996), Wong (2005), De Brito et al (2007), Roh (2013), Masoud (2012), Henning (2014), Ahmadi (2015), Yadev & Barve (2015), Singh (2016), Bansal & Kumar (2013), Chen &Wu (2011), Cirpin & Kabadayi (2015), Erkyaman et al. (2012), Govindan et al. (2012), Hwang et al. (2016), Rajesh et al. (2011), Vijayvargiya & Dey (2010), Roh & Jang (2018)
Environment	Geographic	Zhang et al (2011), Humanitarian Supply Management and Logistics in the Health Sector (2001), Balcik & Ak (2013), Singh (2016), Bansal & Kumar (2013), Govindan et al. (2012), Wong (2010), Roh & Jang (2018)
	Environment	Fedrick (2011), Wu & Down (1995), Wassenhove (2006), Jamisun (2012), Barrett et al. (2007), Gilbert (2008), Irish Aid (2009), OCHA & UNEP (2007), UNEP (2008), Kohn & Huge Brodin (2008), Gustavsson (2003), Jahre & Heigh (2008), Oloruntuba & Gray (2006), Gaurav & Ramesh (2015), Singh (2016), Bansal & Kumar (2013), Govindan et al. (2012), Roh & Jang (2018)
	Green Image	Singh (2016), Bansal & Kumar (2013), Roh & Jang (2018)

Source: Author's Calculation (2020)

This study depended on numerical rating scale (NRS) method as well-accepted and smooth method in field of logistics service, we designed two questionnaires; depending on specific criteria that extracted from review of literatures; first one designed to measure weight of each criterion against other criteria in respective of HOs within Syria, for example, costs against suppliers' performance and others…etc. Second, one designed to estimate ranking of each supplier against other suppliers in terms of attributes such as quality management, supplier's performance, capabilities, etc. The aim is that implementing the DEMATEL method to identify CRs to obtain the degree of the direct affect between each pair of this elements. These degree scores are always acquired by expert survey. Hence, there is a need to extend the DEMATEL method with QFD for making better decisions in supplier selection criteria.

Thirty-five participators; from different humanitarian organizations activated in Syria; answered on two questionnaires. These humanitarian responders could submit various approaches because they are working in complex systems of different organizations, mandates, norms and supported by a range of technologies (Van deWalle and Comes, 2014). We selected Syrian case for our empirical research in despite that access to regions that are affected by disasters may put humanitarian researchers at risk and adds a burden to already stressed system. Besides that, the lack of research on conflicts has already been mentioned before. However, even if access to selected sites or responders can be achieved, there are often only few data points are interviewees (Chan and Comes, 2014). Through this study, we oversee on mentioned burdens to reflect realistic results from field. The paper is organized as follows. In Section 2, we review the relevant literature. In Section 3, we determine the supplier's selection-criteria and their priorities from points of views of activated humanitarian organizations in Syria. In Section 4, display search results.

MAIN FOCUS OF THE CHAPTER

After reviewing the literature on selecting suppliers in humanitarian organizations, a four-stage process was used to develop a humanitarian supply partner selection framework, comprising:

Step 1: Data collection for this chapter combined district processes and approaches to gather raw data and measure information, then reach to involved variables in this chapter; which are herein the criteria, attributes, and factors; that could use in potential tool or systemic method to support and optimize suppliers' selection-decision within different stages of humanitarian supply chains.

This chapter reviewed previous involved studies since 1966 until 2016, which pertained with topics of suppliers' selections and involved criteria that used in specific selections. The authors reviewed the studies in context of humanitarian logistics and commercial logistics. Thereafter, the authors gathered involved criteria that will measure in next stages.

The second stage was compromising involved responders in the humanitarian organization WFP, UNICEF, UNHCR, GOPA, OXFAM, ICRC, and St. Ephraim (whom are working in different supply chain functions, from different humanitarian organizations activated in Syria) to comprise appropriate focus group to submit answers that reflect the realistic insights of logisticians on ground.

This chapter used qualitative data collection methods by combining numerical rating scale (NRS) method with closed-ended questionnaires to classify the answers and enable the authors to analysis the data critically. First questionnaire aimed to weigh and scale the priorities of each criteria, while second one aims to evaluate responders' suppliers according to selected criteria. The specific questionnaires allow to the authors to rank the preferences of responders in next stages.

Step 2: Identification the weights of humanitarians' organizations requirements using DEMATEL method. Decision-making trial and evaluation laboratory (DEMATEL) method is a comprehensive method was developed by the Science and Human Affairs Program of the Battelle Memorial Institute of Geneva

(Gabus & Fontela, 1973). In order to find a solution of complex and interlocking problems group (Jerry Ho et al., 2011). DEMATEL method determines the degree of correlation between system components by drawing a diagram of the causal relationships between these components when measuring a problem (Chen-Yi, Ke-Ting, & Gwo-Hshiung, 2007). It portrays a basic concept of contextual relation among the elements of the system by identifying a matrix and related mathematical theories to calculate the cause factors and effect factors (Zolfani and Ghadikolaei, 2013).

DEMATEL has been successfully applied to many research fields including supplier selection in green supply chain (Hsu et al., 2013), evaluating business management process (Bai and Sarkis, 2013), exploring core competencies in IC service industry (Lin et al., 2011), emergency management (Zhou et al., 2011; Li et al., 2014), analysing CSFs of knowledge management (Patil and Kant, 2014), supply chain risk mitigation in electronic supply chain (Rajesh and Ravi, 2015), and to categorise the factors influencing humanitarian supply chains (Yadav and Barve, 2018). Owing to its suitability as an effective technique to comprehensively explore relationships among factors, therefore, authors were motivated to employ DEMATEL. In this study to explore causal relationships among determinants of customer requirements “CRs” (Mar Ephrai, UNHCR, UNICEF, WFP, OXFAM, GOPA, ICRC).

Step 3: Calculate the weights of supplier’s criteria after combined it with weights of humanitarians’ organizations requirements using Quality function method (QFD). The concept of QFD by applying HOQ helps to transform customer voices into technical requirements, improving the company’s ability to understand customer needs and planning its products and services on this basis (Sivasamy et al., 2016). Which are the internal variables (WHAT) on the one hand, and determining the criteria to evaluate and select the suppliers or the process, the external variables (HOW) (Bevilacqua et al., 2006).

Step 4: Supplier evaluation using ELECTRE method. ELECTRE (Elimination and Choice Translating Reality) method, the alternatives are compared in each criterion, which makes it not possible for the calculated standards weights to be compensated for each other (Kadziński & Ciomek, 2016). It includes a systematic analysis of the relationship between the different criteria and different options by building an external relationship and establishing concordance and discordance indices, examining the relative importance of each criterion and evaluating all the outranking relationships (Rogers, Bruen, & Maystre, 2013). This is what distinguishes this method from the rest of MCDM.

To address this concern involving the vagueness of human judgments, an effective method that combines decision-making trial and evaluation laboratory (DEMATEL) and quality function deployment (QFD) is used. Considering the interdependence among factors, this DEMATEL method forms a structural model and then visualizes the causal relationships among factors through a cause-effect relationship diagram. Then according to the results of proposed method, customers' requirements CRs of humanitarian logistics is figured out. Finally, 8 CRs are identified out of 20 influencing factors, and all factors can be achieved in a stepwise way for better promoting the effectiveness and efficiency of Humanitarian logistics suppliers.

Phase One: DEMATEL Method to Weight Customer Requirements (Tzeng et al., 2007; Ranjan et al., 2014)

1.1. Compute the average matrix A.

Each respondent was asked to evaluate the direct influence between any two customers' requirements by an integer score ranging from 0, 1, 2, 3 and 4 representing 'no influence', 'low influence', 'medium influence', 'high influence' and very high influence respectively. For each respondent, and the matrix A is obtained.

1.2. Calculate the normalised initial direct-relation matrix X shown in table 2.

$X=k.A.$

$$k=\frac{1}{\max\limits_{1\leq i\leq n}\left(\sum_{j=1}^{n}a_{ij}\right)},i,j=1,2,\ldots.,n.$$

k=0.0556.

1.3. Determination of the sum of rows and columns of matrix T.

The total-relation matrix T can obtain in table 3, after calculating the normalized direct-relation matrix X and the total relation matrix T can be acquired using the following equation, in which I is the identity matrix, and matrix T reveals the total relationship between each pair of decision variables.

$$T=\left[t_{ij}\right]_{n\times n}.T=X\left(I-X\right)^{-1}.$$

Table 2. The normalised initial direct-relation matrix X

		CR1	CR2	CR3	CR4	CR5	CR6	CR7	CR8
Business domains	CR1	-	-	-	-	-	-	-	-
Technical	CR2	-	-	-	-	-	-	-	-
Capabilities	CR3	0,06	0,17	-	0,17	-	-	-	-
Quality of services	CR4	0,11	0,17	-	-	-	-	-	-
Delivery	CR5	0,17	0,17	0,17	0,17	-	0,11	0,11	0,11
Flexibility	CR6	0,22	0,17	0,17	0,17	-	-	0,06	0,06
Costs	CR7	0,22	0,17	0,06	0,06	-	-	-	-
Geographic spread	CR8	0,22	0,17	0,06	0,06	-	-	0,06	-

Source: Author's Calculation (2020)

Table 3. The total-relation matrix .

	CR1	CR2	CR3	CR4	CR5	CR6	CR7	CR8
CR1	-	-	-	-	-	-	-	-
CR2	-	-	-	-	-	-	-	-
CR3	0,07*	0,19*	-	0,17*	-	-	-	-
CR4	0,11*	0,17*	-	-	-	-	-	-
CR5	0,28*	0,3*	0,2*	0,23*	-	0,11*	0,12*	0,12*
CR6	0,28*	0,25*	0,17*	0,2*	-	-	0,05	0,05
CR7	0,23*	0,19*	0,05	0,06	-	-	-	-
CR8	0,25*	0,2*	0,05	0,068*	-	-	0,05	-

Source: Author's Calculation (2020)

1.4. Calculation of the dispatcher and receiver groups

$$D_i = \left[\sum_{j=1}^{n} t_{ij}\right]_{n\times 1} = \left[t_i\right]_{n\times 1}, i = 1,2\cdots\cdots,n.$$

$$R_i = \left[\sum_{i=1}^{n} t_{ij}\right]_{1\times n} = \left[t_j\right]_{n\times 1}, j = 1,2\cdots\cdots,n.$$

The sum (D + R) shows the total effects given and received. That is, (D + R) indicates the degree of importance that each CR plays in the entire system. On the contrary, the (D - R) depicts the net effect that CR contributes to the system. Specifically, if (D - R) is positive, factor CR is a net cause. When (D - R) is negative, which mean the factor CR is a net receiver or effect. The results of Total cause and net effects for each CR is shown in Table 4.

Table 4. Total causes and effects for each CR

CR	D + R	D - R	Group
CR1	[1.2245]	[-1.2245]	'Effect'
CR2	[1.2902]	[-1.2902]	'Effect'
CR3	[0.9210]	[-0.0506]	'Effect'
CR4	[1.0112]	[-0.4556]	'Effect'
CR5	[1.3612]	[1.3612]	'Cause'
CR6	[1.1280]	[0.9058]	'Cause'
CR7	[0.7776]	[0.3016]	'Cause'
CR8	[0.7980]	[0.4523]	'Cause'

Source: Author's Calculation (2020)

The cause group compiles of Delivery, Flexibility, Costs and Geographic spread. While the effect group composes Business domains, Technical, Capabilities and Quality of services. We observe by looking at the causal diagram of Fig.1, that the customer requirements are separated into cause and effect groups.

It is evident by looking at the causal diagram of Figure, that Delivery, Flexibility, Costs and Geographic spread requirements are the main driving factors Business domains, Technical, Capabilities and Quality of services, because It is located in the positive upper part of causal diagram. This demonstrates the importance of delivery time and flexibility as requirements for humanitarian organizations in their relief distress.

Among these eight CRs, Delivery is recognized as the most significant one because having maximum (D – R) value and it has the maximum intensity of relation to others for others CR. This explains why stocks move from the Delivery CR5 to all other requirements in the fig.2.

On the other hand, Technical factor is having the lowest (D-R) value, for this reason it has much influenced by the other requirements. Which also explains in the fig.2, that the Technical factor receives stocks from all other factors.

Figure 1. DEMATEL causal diagram of CRs. Source: Author's (2020)

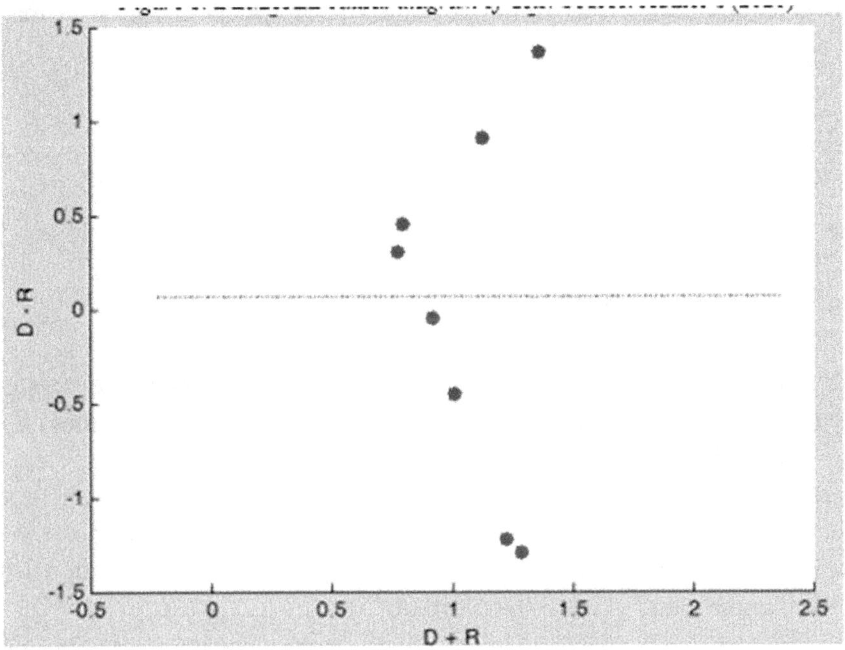

Figure 2. DEMATEL diagraph for supplier selection. Source: Author's (2020)

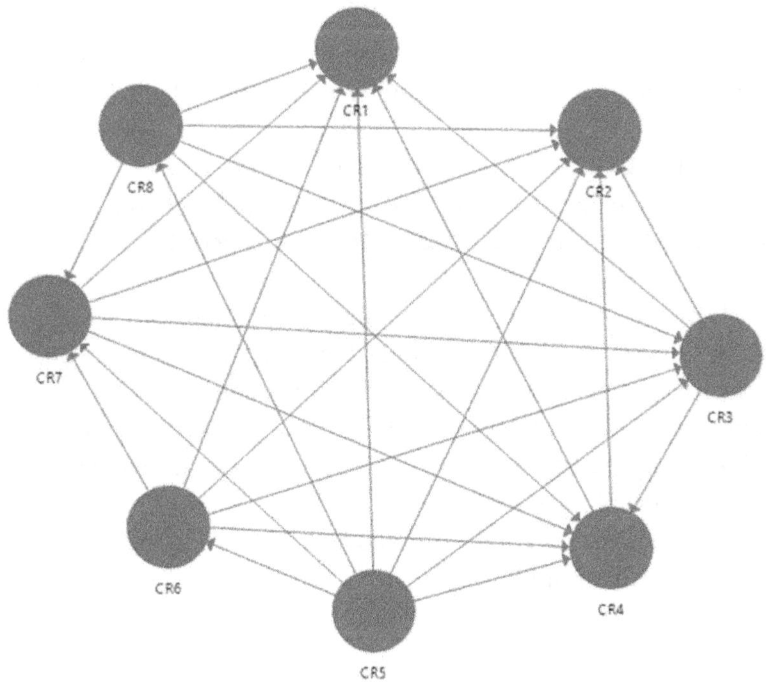

The threshold value (α) was computed by the average of the elements in matrix T. This calculation aimed to eliminate some minor effects elements in matrix T (Yang et al., 2008).

$$\alpha = \frac{\sum_{i=1}^{n}\sum_{j=1}^{n}\left[t_{ij}\right]}{N}.$$

Threshold Alpha: α=0.0665

This digraph represents the contextual and causal relationships between system components that explain the influence of each factor with other factors by using the threshold value.

By referencing, the table of "The total-relation matrix T", each value in this table is higher than the threshold value; an arrow will be drawn from this factor towards the receiving factor. The values are shown as t_{ij}* representing the interaction between two CRs, e.g. the value of t_{31}.(0.07) >α(0.0665).

1.5. Calculation of the weights of the CRs

To calculate the final weights of the CRs that we obtained in Table 6, we normalize the values of the prominence vector (D+ R) of Table 6 with threshold values, and they are shown as the final weights of CRs in Table 7. We find that CR5 "delivery" is the most influencing factor and has a higher weight than other CRs as shown Fig.3.

Phase Two: Figure 3 Represents the Steps that are Followed in a QFD Model by Incorporating the items in the HoQ "House of Quality" as Shown

2.1. A: WHATs matrix, weights of customers' requirements
2.2. B: HOWs matrix by conductting questionnaire to measure the impact of each criteria of supplier selection criteria over the other criteria
2.3. C: relationship matrix between WHATs and HOWs ; shown in table 5
2.4. D: relative importance or weights of WHATs ; shown in table 5
2.5. E: interrelationship between HOWs
2.6. F: weights of HOWs, by conducting questionnaire to determine the performance rating of candidate suppliers.

Figure 3. The customers' requirements weights. Source: Author's (2020)

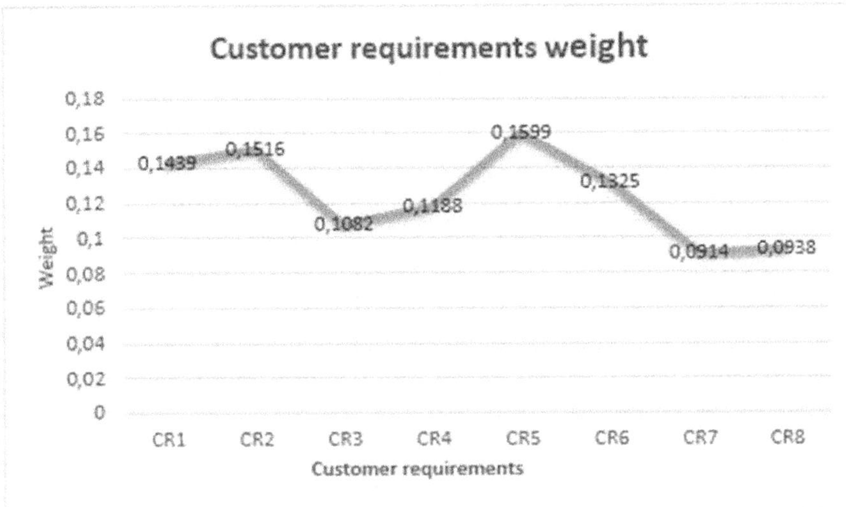

Figure 4. QFD model.

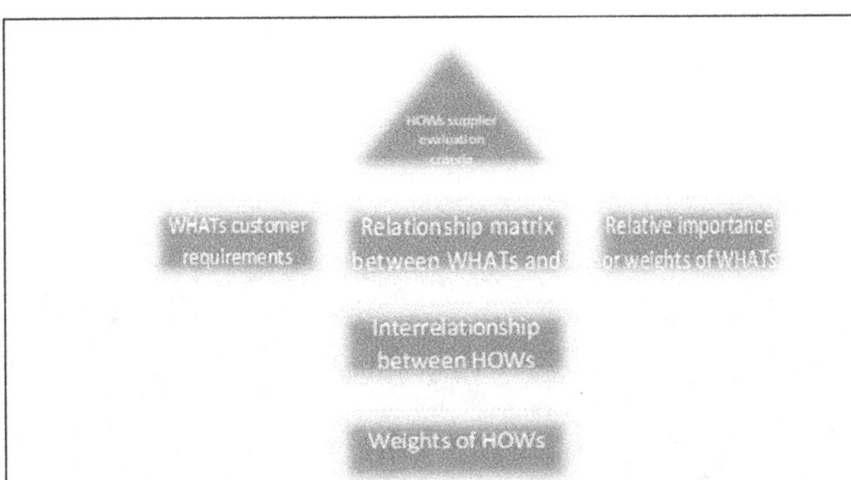

The normalized weights of all criteria for all suppliers are obtained by computed the weights of each supplier selection criteria, which are shown in fig.5. From this fig, we see clear that Environnement criteria which includes (Geographica, Environnement and Green Image) dishonor is the most important supplier selection criterion among others.

Table 5. Supplier selection problem

HOWs (CR)	WHATs (Criteria)						Weight CR
	Suppliers' performance TR1	**Technical & Capability TR2**	**Finance Status TR3**	**Supplier Quality System TR4**	**Cost TR5**	**Environnement TR6**	
CR1	1.0000	1.0000	1.0000	1.0000	6.0000	0	0.1439
CR2	6.0000	6.0000	6.0000	6.0000	6.0000	0	0.1516
CR3	0	3.0000	0	0	6.0000	0	0.1082
CR4	3.0000	3.0000	0	0	0	0	0.1188
CR5	1.0000	1.0000	0	0	0	0	0.1599
CR6	1.0000	1.0000	1.0000	1.0000	1.0000	0	0.1325
CR7	1.0000	0	0	0	0	3.0000	0.0914
CR8	3.0000	3.0000	3.0000	3.0000	3.0000	9.0000	0.0938
Weight TR	2.2062	3.4569	2.7360	2.0620	2.9047	9.0000	22.3657
Normalized criteria weight	0.0986	0.1546	0.1223	0.0922	0.1299	0.4024	1.0000

Source: Author's Calculation (2020)

The last step in QFD, we compose the initial decision matrix by comparing between six criteria for five alternative suppliers. Then we performance ratings of alternative suppliers and criteria weights are integrated.

Figure 5. Supplier selection criteria weight. Source: Author's (2020)

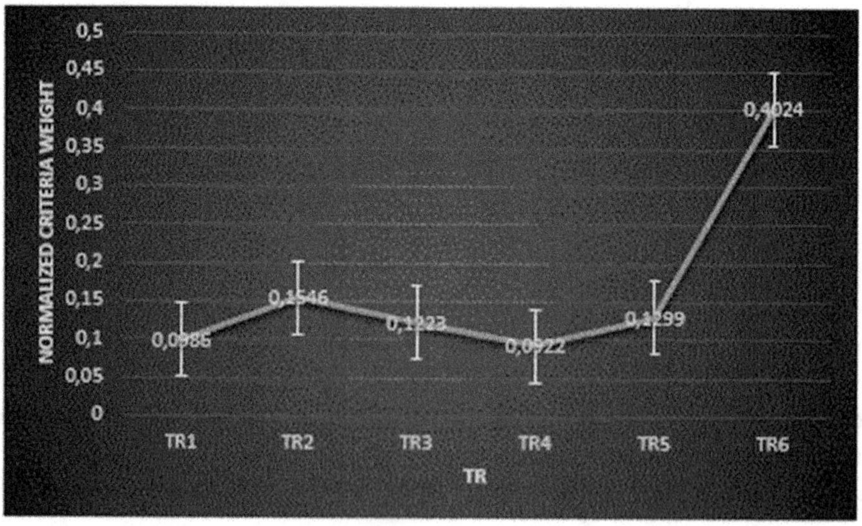

Phase Three: Ranking by the ELECTRE Method

We descaled values of the decision-making matrix by using descaled norms. This matrix is named *N*. Then the Descaled balanced decision-making matrix V will construct by using the initial decision matrix D and the descaled balanced matrix *N* as shown in table 6. (S1 first supplier, S2 second supplier, S3 third supplier, S4 fourth supplier, S5 fifth supplier)

$$V = N \times D_{n\times n}.$$

Table 6. The Descaled balanced decision-making matrix V is shown below:

	S1	S2	S3	S4	S5
S1	0.0466	0.0691	0.0356	0.0412	0.0320
S2	0.0795	0.0691	0.0014	0.0412	0.0655
S3	0.0341	0.0691	0.0189	0.0412	0.0320
S4	0.0080	0.0691	0.0519	0.0412	0.1025
S5	0.0015	0.0691	0.1032	0.0412	0.0024

Source: Author's Calculation (2020)

In this step, all items proportionate to all indices will be evaluated and a set of consistent and inconsistent matrices will be formed. A consistent set of *K* and *I* named $S_{K,I}$ contain all indices within which A_K is more favourable than A_I.

To find this favourability, the positive or negative decision-making indices:

If the index is of a positive aspect: $S_{K,I} = \left\{ j | V_{kj} \geq V_{ij} \right\}, j = 1, \ldots, m$.

If the index of *a* negative aspect: . $S_{K,I} = \left\{ j | V_{kj} \leq V_{ij} \right\}, j = 1, \ldots, m$.

The inconsistent matrix $D_{K,I}$ also contains indices within which A_K is less favoourable than A_I that is $D_{K,I} = \left\{ j | V_{kj} < V_{Ij} \right\}, j = 1, \ldots, m$.

This formula is for positive indices and for negative ones as follows:

$$D_{K,I} = \left\{ j | V_{kj} > V_{Ij} \right\}, j = 1, \ldots, m$$

This criterion measures the ratio of the non-favourability of an inconsistent set of *K* and *I* to the total inconsistency in matrices.

Figure 6. Comparative ranking of supplier. Source: Author's (2020)

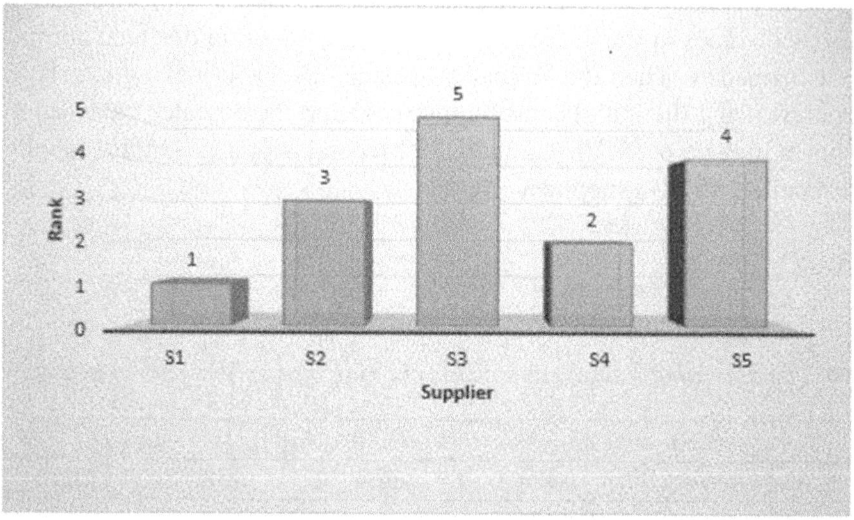

Fig 6 compares each suppliers' rating by the upper and lower net values. The results of the calculation of the net upper values show that S1 has the maximum value, which is the best supplier. According to ELECTRE theory, the optimal supplier selection ranking is S1, S4, S2, S5 and S3.

FUTURE RESEARCH DIRECTIONS

In our study, the authors initially attempted to provide a review of the requirements and criteria for selecting suppliers involved in humanitarian relief work. The study applied in Syria, which includes 35 field and global relief agencies, showed that the handover factor during the war period is the most important requirement of these agencies when selecting suppliers. In addition to the technical factor that plays an important role in the ability of agencies to track suppliers during the delivery period. This makes it easier for humanitarian organizations to search for suppliers and reduce the weaknesses of their suppliers who are partners in this process.

The authors attempt to identify a unique set of criteria for LSP selection for humanitarian relief operations. This was done by analysing literature and having a discussion with the executives of five humanitarian organizations activated in Syria. The outcomes of DEMATEL provide information about the impact each factor has on the whole humanitarian logistics system in Syria. Through analysing and discussing the structural model, we can figure out which of needs of humanitarian organizations are of more fundamental importance for the whole system. Then it will be combined with the supplier's selection criteria to obtain an integrated system that combines

The main objective of this research is to present a model that helps humanitarian organizations solve the issue of classifying suppliers and selecting the best supplier. By incorporating the requirements of these organizations and the standards of your suppliers. Based on the findings related to the study of problem requirements, we provide a recommendation for humanitarian organizations to focus on Delivery, Flexibility, Costs and Geographic When setting supplier standards. Thus, delivery factor plays a very important role in the supplier selection problem, and it has the utmost effect on the others factors. Because it is the most convincing requirement and having maximum (D – R) value.

Where humanitarian organizations can develop a structural model that contributes to making more effective decisions by knowing the humanitarian relief requirements and determining the relative importance of the characteristics of their suppliers. Where relief agencies can follow a specific integrated methodology for selecting the most appropriate supplier by taking into account customer requirements and the basic criteria for suppliers.

Focusing on customer requirements provides a clear picture of suppliers' work, enabling them to develop their performance to suit the needs of the current situation.

CONCLUSION

Supplier selection is one of the most important procedures for outsourcing logistics for providing quicker response to a disaster situation. Supplier selection is important process in humanitarian relief that may highly affect the success of disaster response. One major contribution of this paper is that it realizes the importance of establishing and maintaining close relationships between suppliers and humanitarian organizations, then considers selecting suppliers for providing relief items. By understanding the needs of humanitarian organizations operating in Syria and integrating them with the criteria for selecting suppliers. Whether it is rapid response, delivery, or the ability to reach dangerous locations that may pose a major threat or even cost. A case study of hurricanes in the south eastern United State (especially the Gulf of Mex- ico region) has been conducted to supplier selection. This study demonstrated that supplier selection criteria is beneficial for relief agencies to promote cost-effectiveness, and preventing deceleration in response to the needs of the population in the affected area (Hu and Dong, 2019). Our study contributes to addressing supplier selection decisions for organizations working in humanitarian relief. The proposed model enables the study of the process of selecting suppliers for humanitarian organizations easily in practices for multi-criteria decision-making problems. By analysing the relative importance of each criterion and analysing the causal relationship to the requirements of the current situation. Analysing the problem requirements and suppliers' standards contributes to making clearer decisions based on facts that contribute to evaluating performance among suppliers. The evaluation of supplier performance contributes to improving their performance and ease of communication with the best supplier by analysing the criteria for each supplier and identifying their strengths and weaknesses.

The proposed supplier selection approach enables the DMs in the Humanitarian organizations operating in Syria to better understand the complex relationships of the relevant attributes in the decision-making process, which lead to faster decision making, and improve the reliability this decision. In addition, the selection of suppliers who have special criteria that contribute to the delivery of humanitarian aid under special circumstances and needs. Eventually, this paper will give a depth view of the research on appropriate supplier-selection mechanisms and it will prove useful for managers and academicians for and stimulating further research work in the area by reviewing the requirements of relief organizations and working to provide these requirements in the standards used to improve the work of suppliers.

REFERENCES

Aissaoui, N., Haouari, M., & Hassini, E. (2007). Supplier selection and order lot sizing modeling: A review. *Computers & Operations Research*, *34*(12), 3516–3540. doi:10.1016/j.cor.2006.01.016

Balcik, B., & Ak, D. (2013). Supplier Selection for Framework Agreements in Humanitarian Relief. *Production and Operations Management*, *23*. Advance online publication. doi:10.1111/poms.12098

Balcik, B., Beamon, B., Krejci, C., Muramatsu, K., & Ramirez, M. (2010). Coordination in humanitarian relief chains: Practices, challenges and opportunities. *International Journal of Production Economics*, *126*(1), 22–34. doi:10.1016/j.ijpe.2009.09.008

Bevilacqua, M., Ciarapica, F. E., & Giacchetta, G. (2006). A fuzzy-QFD approach to supplier selection. *Journal of Purchasing and Supply Management*, *12*(1), 14–27. doi:10.1016/j.pursup.2006.02.001

Blecken, A. (2009). *A reference task model for supply chain processes of humanitarian organizations. Universität Paderborn*. Alemanha.

Boltürk, E., Çevik Onar, S., Öztayşi, B., Kahraman, C., & Goztepe, K. (2016). Multi-attribute warehouse location selection in humanitarian logistics using hesitant fuzzy AHP. *International Journal of the Analytic.*

Chan, J., & Comes, T. (2014). Innovative Research Design–A journey into the information typhoon. *Procedia Engineering*, *78*, 52–58. doi:10.1016/j.proeng.2014.07.038

Chen-Yi, H., Ke-Ting, C., & Gwo-Hshiung, T. (2007). FMCDM with Fuzzy DEMATEL Approach for Customers' Choice Behavior Model. *International Journal of Fuzzy Systems*, *9*(4).

Cluster, L. (2015). *Logistics operational guide (LOG): Procurement section*. Available at: https://log.logcluster.org/display/LOG/Procurement

Cozzolino, A. (2012). *Humanitarian logistics: cross-sector cooperation in disaster relief management*. Springer Science & Business Media. doi:10.1007/978-3-642-30186-5

Dickson, G. W. (1966). An analysis of supplier selection system and decision. *J Purch*, *2*(1), 5–17. doi:10.1111/j.1745-493X.1966.tb00818.x

Gabus, A., & Fontela, E. (1973). Perceptions of the world problematique: Communication procedure, communicating with those bearing collective responsibility. Geneva: Battelle Geneva Research Centre. no. 1.

Guha-Sapir, D., & Ph, H. (2015). *Annual disaster statistical review 2014: The numbers and trends*. CRED.

Hancox, M., & Hackney, R. (2000). IT outsourcing: Frameworks for conceptualizing practice and perception. *Information Systems Journal*, *10*(3), 217–237. doi:10.1046/j.1365-2575.2000.00082.x

Heaslip, G. (2013). Services operations management and humanitarian logistics. *Journal of Humanitarian Logistics and Supply Chain Management*, *3*(1), 37–51. doi:10.1108/20426741311328501

Ho, W. R. J., Tsai, C. L., Tzeng, G. H., & Fang, S. K. (2011). Combined DEMATEL technique with a novel MCDM model for exploring portfolio selection based on CAPM. *Expert Systems with Applications*, *38*(1), 16–25. doi:10.1016/j.eswa.2010.05.058

Hu, S., & Dong, Z. S. (2019). Supplier selection and pre-positioning strategy in humanitarian relief. *Omega*, *83*, 287–298. doi:10.1016/j.omega.2018.10.011

Kadziński, M., & Ciomek, K. (2016). Integrated framework for preference modeling and robustness analysis for outranking-based multiple criteria sorting with ELECTRE and PROMETHEE. *Information Sciences*, *352*, 167–187. doi:10.1016/j.ins.2016.02.059

Kaklauskas, A., Zavadskas, E. K., Raslanas, S., Ginevicius, R., Komka, A., & Malinauskas, P. (2006). Selection of low-e windows in retrofit of public buildings by applying multiple criteria method COPRAS: A Lithuanian case. *Energy and Building*, *38*(5), 454–462. doi:10.1016/j.enbuild.2005.08.005

Kim, S., Ramkumar, M., & Subramanian, N. (2019). Logistics service provider selection for disaster preparation: A socio-technical systems perspective. *Annals of Operations Research*, *283*(1-2), 1259–1282. doi:10.100710479-018-03129-3

Kovács, G., & Spens, K. M. (2007). Humanitarian logistics in disaster relief operations. *International Journal of Physical Distribution & Logistics Management*, *37*(2), 99–114. doi:10.1108/09600030710734820

Kunz, N., & Reiner, G. (2012). A meta-analysis of humanitarian logistics research. *Journal of Humanitarian Logistics and Supply Chain Management*, *2*(2), 116–147. doi:10.1108/20426741211260723

Latimer, C., & Swithern, S. (2017). *Global humanitarian assistance report*. Development Initiatives.

Leiras, A., de Brito Jr, I., Queiroz Peres, E., Rejane Bertazzo, T., & Tsugunobu Yoshida Yoshizaki, H. (2014). Literature review of humanitarian logistics research: Trends and challenges. *Journal of Humanitarian Logistics and Supply Chain Management*, *4*(1), 95–130. doi:10.1108/JHLSCM-04-2012-0008

Lukosch, H., & Comes, T. (2019). Gaming as a research method in humanitarian logistics. *Journal of Humanitarian Logistics and Supply Chain Management*.

Min, H. (1994). International supplier selection: A multi-attribute utility approach. *International Journal of Physical Distribution & Logistics Management*, *24*(5), 24–33. doi:10.1108/09600039410064008

Oloruntoba, R., & Gray, R. (2009). Customer service in emergency relief chains. *International Journal of Physical Distribution & Logistics Management*, *39*(6), 486–505. doi:10.1108/09600030910985839

OXFAM. (2019). *Information for suppliers*. Available at: https://www.oxfam.org.uk/what-we-do/about-us/plans-reports-and-policies/information-for-suppliers

Pazirandeh, A. (2011). Sourcing in global health supply chains for developing countries. *International Journal of Physical Distribution & Logistics Management, 41*(4), 364–384. doi:10.1108/09600031111131931

Pérez-Rodríguez, N., & Holguín-Veras, J. (2015). Inventory-allocation distribution models for postdisaster humanitarian logistics with explicit consideration of deprivation costs. *Transportation Science, 50*(4), 1261–1285. doi:10.1287/trsc.2014.0565

Procurement Practice Group. (2010). *Procurement manual*. Available at https://www.unops.org/SiteCollectionDocuments/Procurementdocs/UNOPSprocurementmanualEN.pdf

Ranjan, R., Chatterjee, P., & Chakraborty, S. (2015). Evaluating performance of engineering departments in an Indian University using DEMATEL and compromise ranking methods. *Opsearch, 52*(2), 307–328. doi:10.100712597-014-0186-1

Riloha institute. (2013). *Alexander Blecken (United Nations Office for Project Services), on "Sustainable Procurement and the United Nations"*. Available at: https://www.riloha.org/index.php/component/content/article/86-eve/past/112-11-13-2013-alexander-blecken-united-nations-office-for-project-services-on-sustainable-procurement-and-the-united-nations?Itemid=545

Rogers, M. G., Bruen, M., & Maystre, L. Y. (2013). *Electre and decision support: methods and applications in engineering and infrastructure investment*. Springer Science & Business Media.

Saeyeon, R., & Jang, H. (2018). Strategic Logistics Outsourcing in Humanitarian Supply Chain: A Fuzzy AHP Approach. *Korean Journal of Logistics., 26*(4), 103–113. doi:10.15735/kls.2018.26.4.007

Saksrisathaporn, K. (2015). *A multi-criteria decision support system using knowledge management and project life cycle approach: Application to humanitarian supply chain management* (Doctoral dissertation). Lyon 2.

Salvad6, L. L., Lauras, M., Comes, T., & Van de Walle, B. (2015, May). Towards More Relevant Research on Humanitarian Disaster Management Coordination. ISCRAM.

Shahadat, K. (2003). Supplier choice criteria of executing agencies in developing countries. *International Journal of Public Sector Management, 16*(4), 261–285. doi:10.1108/09513550310480033

Singh, A. (2016). *Supplier Selection and Multi-period Demand Allocation in a Humanitarian Supply Chain*. doi:10.1007/978-81-322-2416-7_14

Sivasamy, K., Arumugam, C., Devadasan, S. R., Murugesh, R., & Thilak, V. M. M. (2016). Advanced models of quality function deployment: A literature review. *Quality & Quantity*, *50*(3), 1399–1414. doi:10.100711135-015-0212-2

Tapia, A. H., Antunes, P., Bañuls, V. A., Moore, K., & Albuquerque, J. P. D. (2016). *Proceedings of the International Conference on Information Systems for Crisis Response and Management*. Academic Press.

Tzeng, G. H., Chiang, C. H., & Li, C. W. (2007). Evaluating intertwined effects in e-learning programs: A novel hybrid MCDM model based on factor analysis and DEMATEL. *Expert Systems with Applications*, *32*(4), 1028–1044. doi:10.1016/j.eswa.2006.02.004

UNICEF. (2019). *Become a supplier*. Available at: https://www.unicef.org/supply/index_become_a_supplier.html

Van deWalle, B., & Comes, T. (2014). *Risk accelerators in disasters. Insights from the typhoon Haiyan response on humanitarian information management and decision support*. Academic Press.

Vandermerwe, S., & Rada, J. (1988). Servitization of business: Adding value by adding services. *European Management Journal*, *6*(4), 314–324. doi:10.1016/0263-2373(88)90033-3

Vega, D., & Roussat, C. (2015). Humanitarian logistics: The role of logistics service providers. *International Journal of Physical Distribution & Logistics Management*, *45*(4), 352–375. doi:10.1108/IJPDLM-12-2014-0309

Wang, X., Fan, Y., Liang, L., De Vries, H., & Van Wassenhove, L. N. (n.d.). Augmenting fixed framework agreements in humanitarian logistics with a bonus contract. *Production and Operations Management*.

Weber, C. A., Current, J. R., & Benton, W. C. (1991). Vendor selection criteria and methods. *European Journal of Operational Research*, *50*(1), 2–18. doi:10.1016/0377-2217(91)90033-R

World Food Programme. Situation Report. (2016). Available at: https://reliefweb.int/sites/reliefweb.int/files/resources/2018%2012%20WFP%20Syria%20Situation%20Report%20%2312.pdf

World Food Programme. (2019). *Do Business With WFP*. Available at: https://www.wfp.org/do-business-with-wfp

Yadav, D. K., & Barve, A. (2018). Segmenting critical success factors of humanitarian supply chains using fuzzy DEMATEL. *Benchmarking*, *25*(2), 400–425. doi:10.1108/BIJ-10-2016-0154

Zolfani, S. H., & Ghadikolaei, A. S. (2013). Performance evaluation of private universities based on balanced scorecard: Empirical study based on Iran. *Journal of Business Economics and Management*, *14*(4), 696–714. doi:10.3846/16111699.2012.665383

Chapter 7
A Memetic Algorithm for Integrated Production Distribution Problem in a Supply Chain

Nihan Kabadayi
https://orcid.org/0000-0003-1950-4877
Istanbul University, Turkey

ABSTRACT

Supply chain is a complex system in which most of the activities are inter-related, and changes in one of these activities can affect the performance of the other processes. Thus, integrated management strategies in a supply chain can yield considerable advantages throughout the system as supply chain members and customers become more integrated. In this study, a memetic algorithm is proposed to solve the integrated production-distribution problem. The objective of the problem is to find optimal production quantity, customer delivery quantity, and schedule to minimize the total system cost, which is composed of production setup cost and variable production cost, inventory holding costs, and distribution cost. The effectiveness of the proposed algorithm is tested on the existing data sets. According to test results, the proposed algorithm is a very effective method to solve integrated production-distribution problems. To assess to benefits and applicability of the method on the real-life problems, a case study is conducted in a Turkish water manufacturing company.

DOI: 10.4018/978-1-7998-3805-0.ch007

INTRODUCTION

Nowadays, firms need to focus on their supply chain success in order to gain a competitive advantage. Supply chain management is the organization of activities between independent companies, from raw material suppliers to the end customers. The main objective of supply chain management is to decrease the total supply chain costs while increasing the customer service level. Inventory and distribution costs are the major costs in the supply chain. It is important to have a well-managed inventory and distribution system in order to minimize the total supply chain costs.

The success of the supply chain depends on the integration of a network of facilities that procure raw materials, transform them into finished products, and deliver the products to the customers through a distribution system in order to meet customer demands. In a supply chain management process, a manager needs to make strategic decisions regarding the procurement of raw materials, production planning, inventory management, and distribution routing in order to reduce overall supply chain costs. These sub-problems have been extensively investigated but they were mostly dealt with separately both in industrial applications and the literature. However, coordinating these sub-problems can induce evidential cost savings in the supply chain as shown in several studies (Ruokokoski et al., 2010). Kellogg and Frito Lay, which are achieved multi-million cost savings by applying integrated planning systems, can be good real-life examples for the successful applications of integrated systems (Adulyasak et al., 2015). Coordination of the two essential planning stages of supply chain (production and distribution), which gets easier with rapid development in communication and information technology, offers an opportunity to reduce firms' operating costs (Thomas & Griffin, 1996; Bank et al., 2020).

Firms can manage their production and distribution operations independently when they have sufficient inventory in their systems. The reason is that inventory can protect the production and distribution systems against unexpected fluctuations in supply and demand. By contrast, high inventory levels negatively affect holding costs and lead times along the supply chain. In today's competitive environment, companies need to provide products/services faster and cheaper than their competitors and need to adequately meet the high customer expectations in order to gain a competitive advantage. Therefore, companies aim to reduce inventory levels and shorten delivery times across the supply chain. Companies that intend to reduce inventory levels need to maintain closer linkages between production and distribution functions in order to ensure sustainable operations through the supply chain. Eventually, companies can obtain cost savings and improve customer service levels by optimizing production and distribution operations in an integrated manner (Shimci-Levi et al. 2004).

The integration of production-distribution operations can yield considerable advantages throughout the supply chain. Recenlty, vendor managed inventory (VMI) replenishment system, wherein the vendor or supplier manages the inventory levels of its customers or retailers has become more prevalent in maintaining an integrated inventory management system in a supply chain (Adulyasak et al., 2015; Yang et al., 2017).

This chapter is organized as follows: Initially, a brief overview on the literature dealing with the integrated production-distribution problem is presented. Secondly, under the main topic of chapter, the importance of the integrated supply chain management is emphasized. Thirdly, the proposed solution methodology is described, and a case study is presented in order to indicate the real-life application of the method. Finally, future research directions and conclusions are discussed.

BACKGROUND

The benefits of coordination of production-distribution decisions were initially investigated by Chandra and Fisher in 1994. They compared the results of solving the production and transportation scheduling problems partially and integrated. They showed that firms can reduce their operation costs about 3-20% by coordinating their production and distribution activities. Fumero and Vercellis (1999) studied a more general problem, which consisted of multiple time periods, and multiple commodities. They showed that the Lagrangian decomposition method outperformed the alternative decomposition method. Lei et al. (2006) investigated an integrated production, inventory, and distribution routing problem in a supply chain with multiple plants. Boudia et al. (2006) examined a multi-period production distribution problem in a two-echelon supply chain, which is very close to the model proposed by Chandra and Fisher (1994). The difference of this approach is limited vehicle capacity and single product. Bard and Nananukul (2008) solved the same problem with a two-phase approach, which was similar to the method developed by Lei et al. (2006). The path relinking method was used to obtain a better solution. According to the computational results, the proposed method can derive 10-20% better solution than the generalized regression analysis and spatial prediction (GRASP) method proposed by Boudia et al. (2006) with more computational effort. Bard and Nananukul (2009a) formulated the inventory routing part of the problem as a mixed integer program for the sake of maximum customer satisfaction. CPLEX, the Tabu search by Bard and Nanakul (2008) and the branch and price algorithm were used to solve the production-distribution problem. Among the relative methods, the branch and price algorithm cab generate better results than the others. However, the results showed that Tabu search outperforms the branch and price algorithm in terms of the computation time. Boudia and Prins (2009) used memetic algorithm with population management (MA/PM) to simultaneously handle production and distribution problems. The proposed algorithm was evaluated in three sets of 30 instances with 50, 100 and 200 customers over 20 time periods. They showed that the memetic algorithm could generate better solutions than the GRASP. Bard and Nananukul (2010) proposed a hybrid methodology that is a combination of the exact method and heuristic procedures within a branch and price framework. It was shown that, while the exact branch and price algorithm is inefficient for relatively small instances, the branch and price heuristic is efficient and can derive highly qualified solutions for the instances with up to 50 customers and eight time periods within a reasonable amount of time. Archetti et al. (2011) developed a hybrid heuristic to solve the integrated production-distribution problem in a two-echelon system, which is composed of a single production plant and a set of customers. They compared the performance of the order-up-to level policy and the maximum level policy in terms of their costs. To test the performance of hybrid heuristic, they proposed small size instances with 14 customers, six time periods, and single vehicle. Their test results showed that hybrid heuristic can derive high quality solutions in a shorter time. Adulyasak et al. (2012) developed an optimization based adaptive large neighborhood search (Op-ALNS) heuristic for integrated production-distribution problem. Adulyasak et al. (2014) considered the production-distribution problem with multiple vehicles and developed two branch-and-cut approaches based on different formulation schemes for the solution of the problem. Adulyasak et al. (2015) represented a comprehensive literature review of solution techniques that have been developed to solve the integrated production-distribution problem. Absi et al. (2015) proposed a two-phase iterative heuristic approach for the production-distribution problem. The proposed algorithm solves the production planning and routing sub-problems in sequence. The experimential test results showed that the proposed iterative solution approach has a good performance in solving the test problems. Boutarfa et al. (2016) presented a Tabu search heuristic to solve an integrated production-distribution problem with clustered retailers. The application results showed that the Tabu list is a critical parameter, which significantly influences the performance of the Tabu search heuristic. Soyali and Sural (2017) developed a multi-phase mathematical programming-based heuristic method for the production-distribution problem. The proposed method formulates and solves the restricted versions of the problem as mixed integer-programs. Kyee and Moin (2018) applied a two-phased approach within a Matmatheuristic framework to solve integrated production-distribution routing problem. They compared the proposed solution methodology with the GRASP method and the results showed that the proposed method outperformed the GRASP method in all samples. Senoussi et al. (2018) applied five heuristic based on a genetic algorithm (GA) method to solve a special case of the production distribution problem. Rafiei et al. (2018) considered an integrated production-distribution planning problem within a four-echelon supply chain with two main objective functions: minimizing the total chain cost and maximizing the service level. Two mixed integer linear programs were developed to solve this problem. Bank et al. (2020) developed a hybrid meta-heuristic method to solve an integrated production and distribution problem in a two-stage supply chain. Moreover, they have extended the classical integrated production problem by adding multiple production companies with different production speeds. The proposed hybrid method combines simulated annealing and GA methods. The performance of the proposed method is compared with the classical GA method. The results of the test study showed that the new hybrid method outperformed the classical GA method in most cases.

The aforementioned literature review reveals that evolutionary algorithms have a successful performance in solving integrated production-distribution problems. In this study, a hybrid MA method developed to solve the integrated production distribution problem. The novel chromosome structure and local search algorithms used in the proposed method contributes to the literature. Moreover, there are a few studies that present a real-life application for the production-distribution problem in the literature. Therefore, another contribution of this chapter is to present a real-life case study for a production-distribution problem.

MAIN FOCUS OF THE CHAPTER

The main contribution of this chapter is to propose a practical and efficient model for supply chain management professionals. Since the proposed method considers production planning, inventory management and distribution planning decisions in an integrated manner, it is able to handle conflicts of interest of among these decision phases. A novel memetic algorithm approach is developed to solve the integrated production-distribution problem. The integrated production-distribution problem is an NP-hard problem since the vehicle routing problem, which is a well-known NP-hard problem, is a part of this problem. The objective of the problem is to simultaneously find optimal production quantity, customer delivery quantity, and schedule in order to minimize the total system cost which consists of production, inventory holding, and distribution costs. The problem aims to find the trade-off between production, inventory, and distribution decisions.

Integrated Supply Chain Management

In the past, companies have been focusing on the success of their operations. However, with the emergence of the concept of supply chain management, this perspective has changed and it has been understood that the success can be achieved through strategies that take into account the overall supply chain success. The main objective of supply chain management is to minimize total operating costs while maximizing the customer value. The supply chain is a complex network that is composed of independent organizations with different goals. The integrated supply chain management aims to determine a common goal in order to eliminate the local optimization and conflicts of interest among these organizations.

There are a number of critical decision phases in a supply chain. Production, inventory management, and routing are three most important of these decision phases. Since there are conflicts of interest among these decision phases, consideration of these decisions in an integrated manner might bring overall success to a supply chain. One of the main objectives of the supply chain is to meet customer requirements at the right time, in the right place, of the right quality, and for the right price. However, it is not an easy task to ensure a flawless movement of the goods in a supply chain because of its complex structure. In a supply chain, having a sufficient amount of inventory can reduce the negative effects of the complexity. Therefore, inventory management is one of the most important decision phases in a supply chain because it has a significant effect on customer satisfaction.

Recently, VMI policy has become popular in the supply chain management by the developments in the information technologies. VMI is an inventory management policy in which vendors (or suppliers) are responsible for managing inventory levels by having access to the demand forecast and inventory records of the firm. The vendor is contractually assigned to maintain the correct inventory level at the demand location and determine delivery routes to minimize total shipping costs (Ramkumar et al., 2011; Schroeder et al., 2017). This policy provides benefits to both suppliers and customers and creates a win-win situation for both parties.

Needless to say that another important issue in the supply chain is to deliver goods to customers economically and on time. Determination of efficient distribution routes can significantly decrease transportation costs while increasing customer satisfaction in a supply chain. The vehicle routing problem deals with finding the most economical routes to deliver products from supply points to demand points. VMI inventory policy requires a complex distribution strategy in which the number of stockouts and distribution costs are minimized simultaneously. The inventory routing problem aims to develop this kind of distribution strategy. The inventory routing problem inquires into the following three basic questions (Campbell et al.,1998; Guimarães et al., 2019).

a) When are the products going to be delivered to the customer?
b) How much product is going to be delivered to the customer when it is served?
c) Which delivery route will be used?

The most important one of the benefits brought by the integrated supply chain is the cost advantage gained through the reduction of inventory levels along the supply chain. In addition to reducing costs by integrating supply chain processes, customer service levels are also being improved.

Many advantages can be achieved through the supply chain integration. However, the creation of an integrated supply chain is not an easy process. Businesses that want to be part of an advanced and integrated supply chain are expected to have an infrastructure that allows a good flow of information and a smooth logistics system. One of the key parts of this infrastructure is the establishment of strong and long-term collaboration among supply chain members (Chen et al., 2017). Additionally, an efficient information system is another main requirements of the integrated supply chain. All the supply chain members should monitor all the activities that are conducted along the supply chain. However, it is a fact that building an effective information system infrastructure in a supply chain would require expensive investments.

Production and distribution decisions should be made on a daily basis in order to find a trade-off among production, stock keeping, and distribution costs. Furthermore, daily production and distribution decisions help to use resources efficiently (Bard & Nananukul, 2009a).

SOLUTION METHODOLOGY

Metaheuristic methods are efficient and effective methods, which are widely used for solving NP-hard problems such as vehicle routing and inventory routing problems. For many years, population-based evolutionary algorithms (EAs) have been successfully applied for solving complicated problems. In the literature, it has been proved that these methods are efficient. Therefore, in this chapter, a memetic algorithm is proposed in order to solve the integrated production-distribution problem.

Memetic Algorithm

Memetic algorithms (MAs) are population-based EAs in which local search plays a significant role. The concept of memetic algorithm was firstly used by Moscato and Norma (1992) and the term of 'meme' is based on the Dawkin' (1989) concept of meme which is described as a unit of information that reproduced itself as people exchange ideas. MAs are developed by adding one or more local search phases to GAs. In this search procedure, the local search phase helps to repair candidate solutions outside of the subspace of optima, which are produced by mutation and recombination (Mekkawy & Liu, 2009; Yadegari et al., 2019).

The search approaches of MAs are similar to those of GAs. However, they are different in terms of their main ideas. While GAs are based on the biological evolution whereas MAs are based on the mimic cultural evolution. The concept of meme refers to a learning or development strategy in the context of heuristic optimization. While, in nature, usually genes are not modified during an individual's lifetime, memes are (Digalakis & Margaritis, 2004). In the literature, alternative names such as hybrid genetic algorithms, genetic local searchers, Lamarckian GAs, Baldwinian GAs, etc. are also used instead of MAs (Krasnogor & Smith, 2005).

In this study, a multi-period production distribution problem is examined in a two-echelon supply chain. The main objective of this problem is to minimize the total supply chain cost (TSCC), comprising production and holding costs. A hybrid MA is introduced to solve this problem. A MA is applied in order to find how much and when to produce goods, how much and when to ship products to customers, and how much of inventory to keep at the plant. And for the routing problem, savings algorithm is embedded in the MA to find optimal delivery routes.

The flowchart of the proposed MA is shown in Figure 1. The proposed MA search starts with the creation of a random initial population of N individuals that might be potential solutions to the problem. Selecting individuals with higher fitness scores creates a mating pool of size N. Local Search I (LSI) is applied to improve each random solution. Then, these individuals are evaluated for their so-called fitness's, i.e. of their corresponding objective function value, Fitness I (FI), which is composed of production and inventory costs. The feasible solutions of that population are duplicated into a new solution pool in which the savings algorithm is applied to solve vehicle routing problem and find a solution which includes production, inventory and distribution decisions simultaneously. Then a Local Search II (LSII) procedure is generated to improve these integrated solutions. Candidate solutions are evaluated in terms of their finesses, which consist of production, inventory holding and vehicle routing costs. The best solution derived after this step is sent to the elitism operator to avoid losing the best solution generated at this phase. Also, classical GA operators, crossover and mutation, are applied to generate new candidate solutions with a better fitness function value.

Representation: This study uses the combined chromosome representation. Each chromosome is coded with a matrix, which is composed of a set of binary and real values representing daily production and order decisions, respectively, for customer. The illustration of the proposed chromosome representation is shown in Table 1. The genetic representation takes the form of a two-dimensional matrix. In the proposed chromosome representation, we consider the production and delivery schedule and leave the vehicle routing part to be solved using the savings algorithm which by Clark and Wright (1964). The production and delivery schedule is represented in the form of a two-dimensional matrix in which each cell in the first part of the matrix

Figure 1. Flowchart of proposed MA

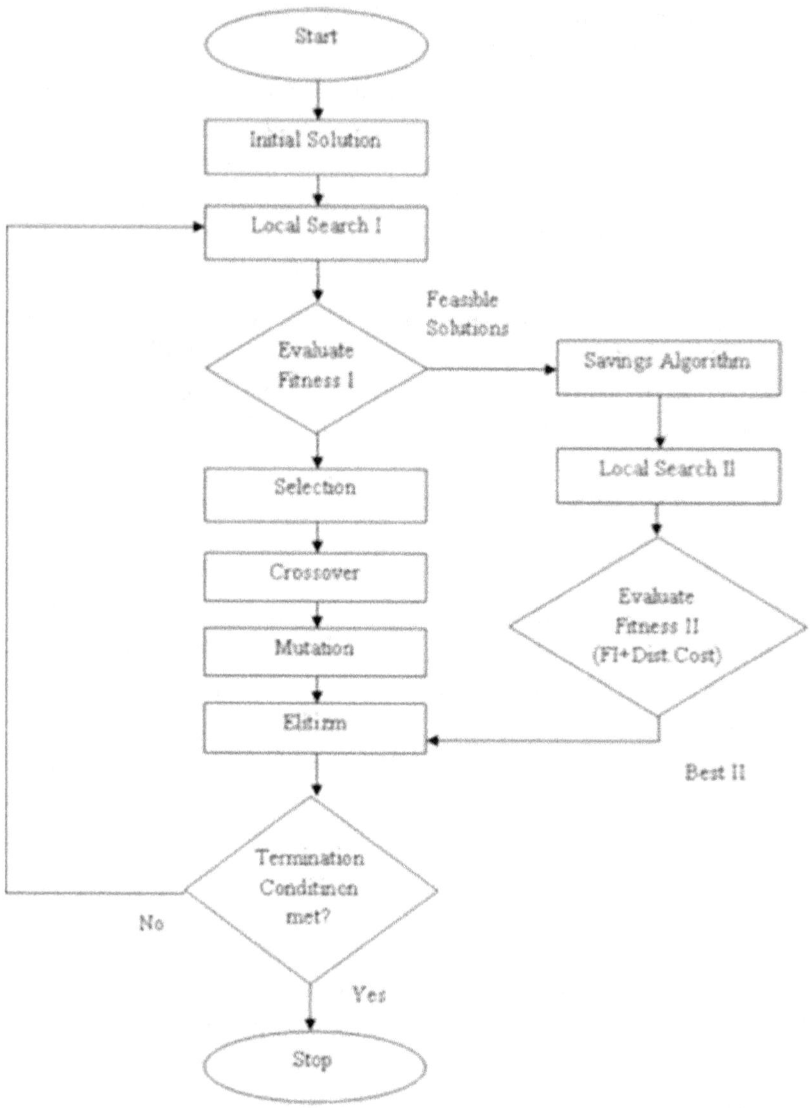

denotes the production day of a relative delivery amount. For example, if there is "1" in the corresponding cell that means this customer's delivery at that period will be supplied form the first day's production. Column P contains the decision of production ("1" if there is production on day t; "0" otherwise) and the rest of the cells contain the delivery schedule for every customer in a given period and amount. Each column in the matrix corresponds to a specific customer beside the

Table 1. Chromosome representation

Period	C1	C2	C3	C4	P	C1	C2	C3	C4
1	1	1	1	1	1	20	19	0	0
2	1	1	1	1	0	0	19	24	0
3	1	1	1	1	0	0	0	0	25
4	1	1	1	1	0	30	38	0	0
5	1	1	1	1	0	0	0	24	0
6	1	1	1	1	0	0	0	0	0

P column, which contains production decisions, and rows represent the planning periods from 1 to T.

Selection: The roulette-wheel selection procedure is used in this study. The aim of the operator is to select parents with high fitness values and pass them to the next generations. In this phase, the candidate solutions with low fitness values are removed from the population.

Crossover: This operator aims to improve the fitness value of solution by combining two candidate solutions (parents). A single point crossover operator is used in this study. A random number between 1 and length of customer (N) is generated to determine a cut point. The parts, which are determined by the cut point, are exchanged between parents and two new offspring are generated during this step.

Mutation: Mutation operator detects a gene from a candidate solution and moves it to a new location with given probability in order to produce a new solution and ensure the diversity of the population. In the first part of the matrix a gene is randomly selected and changed to a number between 1 to M (maximum day of production). For the P column, a gene is randomly selected and if that gene is "1" which, means there is a production takes place at that period, change to "0", thus leading to no production on that day. In the last part of the chromosome, that represents the delivery schedule part, mutation takes place by partially or completely transferring the delivery amount of customer to another scheduled delivery day.

Elitism: Elitism keeps the best solution of the current population in order to prevent loss of this solution with crossover or mutation.

Notation and Mathematical Formulation

In this section a notation is presented that will be used throughout the chapter. We use a mathematical model, which is developed by Adulyasak et al. (2012). The following notation is used in the development of the model.

Sets

T set of l time periods, indexed by $t \in \{1, \ldots, l\}$.

N set of plant and customers, indexed by $i \in \{0, \ldots\ldots n\}$. The plant is denoted by node 0 and $N_c = N / \{0\}$ is the subset of n customers.

K set of m vehicles, indexed by $k \in \{1, \ldots, m\}$.

Decision Variables

p_t production quantity in period t;

I_{it} inventory at node i at the end of the period t;

r_{it} shipment quantity to customer i in period t;

y_t equal to 1 if there is a production setup in period t, 0 otherwise;

z_{it} equal to 1 if customer i is visited in period t, 0 otherwise;

x_{ijkt} equal to 1 if vehicle k travels directly from node i to node j in period t, 0 otherwise;

q_{ikt} quantity delivered to customer i with vehicle k in period t;

Parameters

u unit production cost;

f fixed production setup cost;

h_i unit inventory holding cost at node i;

c_{ij} transportation cost from node i to node j (with assumption $c_{ij} = c_{ji}, \forall (i, j) \in E$);

d_{it} demand at customer i in period t;

C production capacity;

Q vehicle capacity;

L_i storage capacity at node i;

$I_{i,0}$ initial inventory available at node i;

$$M_t = \min \left\{ C, \sum_{j=t}^{l} \sum_{i \in N_c} d_{ij} \right\};$$

$$\dot{M}_{it} = \min \left\{ Q, \sum_{j=t}^{l} d_{ij} \right\}.$$

Objective Function:

$$Min \sum_{t \in T} \left(up_t + fy_t + \sum_{i \in N} h_i I_{it} + \sum_{i \in N} \sum_{j \in N} \sum_{k \in K} c_{ij} x_{ijkt} \right) \tag{1}$$

Subject to:

$$I_{0,t-1} + p_t = \sum_{i \in N_c} r_{it} + I_{0t} \forall t \in T \tag{2}$$

$$I_{i,t-1} + r_{it} = d_{it} + I_{it} \forall i \in N_c, \forall t \in T \tag{3}$$

$$p_t \le M_t y_t \qquad \forall t \in T \tag{4}$$

$$I_{it} \le L_i \qquad \forall i \in N, \forall t \in T \tag{5}$$

$$r_{it} = \sum_{k \in K} q_{ikt} \qquad \forall i \in N_c, \forall t \in T \tag{6}$$

$$q_{ikt} \le \dot{M}_{it} \sum_{j \in N} x_{ijkt} \forall k \in K, \forall i \in N_c, \forall t \in T \tag{7}$$

$$\sum_{i \in N_c} q_{ikt} \le Q \qquad \forall k \in K, \forall t \in T \tag{8}$$

$$\sum_{k \in K} \sum_{j \in N} x_{ijkt} = z_{it} \qquad \forall i \in N_c, \forall t \in T \tag{9}$$

$$\sum_{j \in N} x_{jikt} = \sum_{j \in N} x_{ijkt} \qquad \forall k \in K, \forall i \in N_c, \forall t \in T \tag{10}$$

$$\sum_{i \in N_c} x_{0jkt} \le 1 \qquad \forall k \in K, \forall t \in T \tag{11}$$

$$\sum_{i \in S} \sum_{j \in S} x_{ijkt} \le |S| - 1 \qquad \forall S \subseteq N_c, |S| \ge 2, \forall k \in K, \forall t \in T \tag{12}$$

$$p_t, I_{it}, r_{it}, q_{ikt} \ge 0 \qquad \forall i \in N, \forall k \in K, \forall t \in T \tag{13}$$

$$y_t, z_{it}, x_{ijkt} \in \{0,1\} \qquad \forall i, j \in N, \forall k \in K, \forall t \in T \tag{14}$$

The objective function (1) is to minimize total production-distribution cost which is composed of production setup cost, variable production cost, inventory holding cost and routing cost. Constraints (2) and (3) are inventory balance constraints at the plant and at the customers respectively. Constraint (4) makes sure that the production quantity meet the total demand in the remaining periods and setup variable is "1" if production takes place. Constraint (5) enforces the storage limits both at the plant and customer level. The remaining constraints (6, 7, 8, 9, 10, 11, 12) are the vehicle routing problem constraints. They impose capacitated vehicle routing constraints in the problem.

Performance Evaluation of the Solution Methodology

This section aims to evaluate the performance of the proposed method. Therefore, the test problems in the literature are solved with the proposed method. The developed test problems consider a supply chain, which is composed of one supplier production facility and several retailers located in a given geographic region. The VMI policy is applied in this supply chain. According to this, the supplier is responsible for maintaining inventory levels and determining order quantities for the retailer. Therefore, the requirement of the retailers is produced and distributed by the production company. The problem deals with determining the number of products to be produced, the retailers to be serviced by each vehicle and the amounts to be delivered to retailers. The structure of the considered supply chain model is presented in Figure 2.

The test problems developed by Archetti et al. (2011) are solved in order to evaluate the performance of the proposed algorithm. The corresponding test instances are grouped into three classes according to their sizes. They are A1 with 14 customers, A2 with 50 customers and A3 with 100 customers. Relatively small test problems (A1) with six time periods and 14 customers are considered in this study. There is a single plant with no production capacity and a set of customers with a constant demand. The demands of the relative periods are delivered by a capacitated single vehicle. There is inventory holding cost at the production plant and storage capacity at the customer site and transportation cost is variable and proportional to the distance traveled.

The problem considered in this study is very complex because it contains sub-problems, which are already NP-hard. A novel memetic algorithm approach for solving the integrated production inventory problem is developed. The distribution part of the problem is solved with savings algorithm. The MA is coded in MATLAB.

Figure 2. Structure of the supply chain

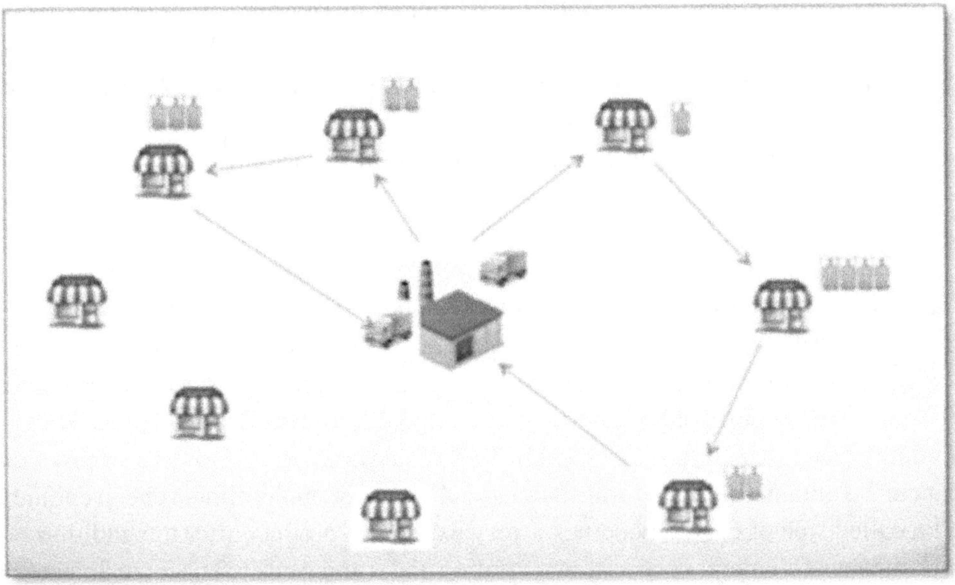

Table 2. Experimental results of the proposed MA

Prob. No.	Optimal	HEURISTIC	Op-ALNS	MA
73.1	26543	26972	26782	26718**
73.2	22692	22971	22800	22806*
73.3	20125	20754	20147	20278*
73.4	24406	24475	24628	24607*
73.5	22889	23281	23149	22987**
74.1	26979	27300	27264	27155**
74.2	23158	23208	23559	23255*
74.3	20190	20866	20282	20392*
74.4	24787	24912	25143	25107*
74.5	23266	24042	24080	23978**
75.1	28558	28652	29489	30163
75.2	23814	23814	24749	24546*
75.3	20763	21267	21190	21306
75.4	-	25912	26777	26508*
75.5	25090	25466	25783	25617*

* Better than one of the exist results
** Better than two of the exist results

During the experiments, the mutation rate and a population size are determined as 0.01 and 80 respectively. The results are presented in Table 2.

According to test results, the proposed MA can be a good alternative solution method for the integrated production-distribution problem. For the future, we are planning to add some different local search operators to improve our MA model and, hence, increase the solution performance of the algorithm.

Case Study

The real-life application of the method is conducted in the water supply industry in which distribution cost has a significant effect on the final prices of the product. Today, most of the people living in big cities of Turkey meet their water needs with 19 liters of HOD-demijohn water due to polluted city waters. Therefore, the HOD-demijohn water market has expanded in Turkey in recent years. However, a product that can be obtained from natural sources such as water and is almost cheap enough to be called free of charge becomes a very expensive product after the addition of important cost elements such as transportation and storage costs. The main objective of this chapter is to provide an efficient model to minimize production, inventory and, distribution costs of HOD-demijohn supply chain of the local company. The company has two HOD-demijohn production lines as shown in Figure 3. When the production decision has been made, the production operations are ongoing 24 hours a day and the production employees are working in one of the three 8-hour shifts. There is a one-hour of setup time before each production process. So, the 24-hour production operations consist of a one-hour setup time and 23 hours of production time. The capacity of each production line is 1,200 carboy bottles/hour, and two employees work in each production line.

Since the carboy bottles are reusable, empty bottles are collected from the dealers every period. The first step of the process is to check the quality of the carboy bottle that brought from the dealers. In this step, if the carboy bottles are worn out and used for another purpose, they are not reused and they are destroyed. The carboy bottles passing the first quality control step successfully are sent to the outer washing process where they are washed with high-pressure water. Following this step, the carboy bottles are sent to the internal washing unit and disinfected with hot water (70 degrees celsius). And then, the carboy bottles are microbiologically disinfected by further internal washing units. In the next step, the carboy bottles are filled with natural spring water after being rinsed out using natural spring water. The filled carboy bottles reach the final control point through the capping, date coding, safety tape fitting, and safety tape sealing processes, consecutively. At the end of

Figure 3. 19 liters HOD-demijohn water production line of the company

the production line, the HOD-demijohn bottles are placed on pallets by a robot as shown in Figure 3.

The total cost of the production consists of unit variable production and setup costs. The unit variable production cost of HOD-demijohn water consists of the carboy bottle, label, pallet, labor, and scrap costs and it is 1.8 TL per unit. Additionally, there is also a production setup cost for each production line since each production line must be cleaned and heated before production starts. The production setup process takes approximately 1 hour to complete and three workers from different departments are on duty for this process. Therefore, it is an important cost and time issue for the company's manufacturing process. The setup cost includes utility (water, gas, electricity), labor, and laboratory costs and it is 400 TL per production run. The unit inventory holding cost of HOD-demijohn water represents the per unit portion of the total cost of warehouse rent, forklift transportation (fuel + labor), and pallet depreciation, and it is calculated to be 0.2 TL per unit. The filled bottles are delivered to three main distribution centers of the company located in Istanbul by a fleet of vehicles. The company's fleet of vehicles including five trucks (960 carboy bottle capacity) and seven lorries (576 carboy bottle capacity).

The supply chain of the company consists of one production facility and five distribution centers. Two of the distribution centers of the company are located on the Anatolian side of Istanbul while three of them on the European side. Figure 4 shows the location of the distribution centers. In the current system, the carboy water bottles produced at the production facilities in Kemerburgaz are transported to the relevant distribution centers by the vehicles, and the HOD-demijohn water retailers around Istanbul travel to the nearest distribution center in order to collect

Figure 4. Location of the company's distribution centers

their demands. The capacity of the vehicle used by the retailers is 100 carboy bottles per vehicle. For this reason, some retailers have to visit the main warehouse in their region several times in a day in order to meet their daily demands.

Each retailer has limited capacity vehicles with an average fuel consumption rate of 50 TL/km. Table 3 shows the number of retailers served by each distribution center. For example, the 22 retailers located around the Sumtas visit this distribution center 32 times a day, and the total length of these visits is 694.38 km/day. Therefore,

Table 3. Number of retailers served by each distribution center

European Side		Asian Side	
Distribution Center	**Number of Retailers**	**Distribution Center**	**Number of Retailers**
Aksu Icme Suları	21	Sumtas	22
Sena	26	Kardelen	25
Sahika	44		

daily and weekly transportation costs of this region are 347.19 TL and 2083.14 TL, respectively.

Table 4. The transportation cost of the current system

Distribution Center	Number of retailer visits	Route lenght (km/ per day)	Daily transportation cost (TL)	Weekly transportation cost (TL)
Sumtas	32	694.38	347.19	2083.14
Kardelen	31	950.81	475.405	2852.43
Sahika	81	1632.47	816.235	4897.41
Sena	40	566.69	283.345	1700.07
Aksu	39	1011.75	505.875	3035.25

Table 4 contains the corresponding information for each of the five distribution centers.

The production capacity at the Kemerburgaz production facility is 1,200 carboy bottles per an hour, and there is 6 production days in a week. As stated before, the production setup cost for each production line and each production day is 400 TL. Therefore, the total weekly production setup cost is 4,800 TL for the current system. Since the produced products are directly sent to the distribution centers, there is no inventory holding cost.

In this case study, an integrated production-distribution plan has been developed for the water production company by using the proposed MA method. This study aims to minimize the company's total supply chain cost. In the current system, the total transportation cost of the supply chain is very high due to the fact that each retailer travels to the distribution center to meet its daily demand. However, an integrated distribution plan can help decrease the total transportation cost of the supply chain. So, an altervative distribution plan is suggested in this study. In the current system, the total transportation cost is very high due to the lack of an integrated distribution plan. For this reason, an integrated model is developed wherein the retailers are served by a fleet of delivery vehicles with a uniform capacity. The new vehicle fleet consists of vehicles each with a capacity of 576 carboy bottles per vehicle and per km of 1.30 TL fuel consumption. The new integrated plan aims to minimize the total supply chain cost by considering production, inventory, and distribution decisions simultaneously. In the new plan, the VMI system is applied, and the retailers are made to hold some amount of inventory in order to reduce the transportation costs.

According to the suggested integrated production-distribution plan, all weekly demands of the retailers can be met by 5 production days. Thus, the number of production days is reduced by the integrated plan and concequently production costs are decreased. The weekly production plan of the company is given in Table 5. The new production plan shows that the total weekly demand for the Sumtas

Table 5. Daily production batch sizes and weekly number of production days

Distribution Center	Daily Production Size (units)	Number of Production Days
Sahika	13,952	3
Sena	6,832	3
Aksu	6,746	3
Kardelen	6,909	2
Sumtas	7,005	2

Table 6. Trasportation Cost of the Integrated Production-Distribution Plan

Distribution Center	Number of tours	Weekly tour distance (km)	Weekly cost of transportation (TL)
Sumtas	16	735.39	956.007
Kardelen	14	956.61	1,243.593
Sahika	26	1,903	2,473.9
Sena	14	758.72	986.336
Aksu	11	1,379.96	1,793.948

distribution center, which is 14,010 bottles, can be met with 7,005 bottles per day and two-day production per week.

Table 6 shows the total transportation cost of the production-distribution plan derived by the proposed method. As mentioned before, in the solution of the proposed method, it is assumed that a new fleet of vehicles will deliver HOD-demijohn bottles

Table 7. Comparison of transportation costs of the solutions

Distribution Center	New Plan's Weekly Transportation Cost (TL)	Previous Weekly Transportation Cost (TL)	Cost Savings (%)
Sumtas	956.007	2,083.14	0.54
Kardelen	1,243.593	2,852.43	0.56
Sahika	2,473.9	4,897.41	0.49
Sena	98.336	1,700.07	0.41
Aksu	1,793.948	3,035.25	0.40
Total	**7,453.784**	**14,568.3**	**0.49**

from the distribution centers to the retailers, and the transportation cost will be 1.30 TL/km.

Table 7 shows that the integrated production-distribution plan developed using the proposed method can help to reduce the total transportation cost by about 50%. Since the number of tours between the retailers and the distribution centers will be

Table 8. Comparison of the total supply chain cost of the new and the current systems

Cost	Current System	New System	Cost Savings (%)
Transportation	14568.3	7453.784	0.49
Production Setup Cost	4800	4000	0.17
Inventory Cost	---	2173	
Total Supply Chain Cost	**19368.3**	**13626.784**	**0.30**

decreased significantly in the new model, the total amount of carbon emission will probably decrease in this operation.

Table 8 shows that the proposed method provides cost savings when it is compared with the current system. In the current system the production facility does not hold inventory, and the inventory cost is zero for the production facility. On the other hand, although the production facility is holding some amount of inventory, the total supply chain cost is decreased in the new system. Since the integrated production-distribution plan helps to find a trade-off between the production, inventory and distribution costs, the total supply chain cost of the proposed model is lower than that of the current system and the total cost savings gained is 30%.

SOLUTIONS AND RECOMMENDATIONS

In this study, an MA developed in order to solve the integrated production-distribution problem. The performance of the proposed method was evaluated by solving the test problems in the literature. The test results proved that the proposed algorithm has a successful performance while solving small and medium-sized problems. Therefore, the proposed method can be an efficient alternative solution method for the current methods existing in the literature. The novel chromosome structure used in the proposed method contributes to the literature as it is successful in modeling the production-distribution method.

A case study is conducted in a HOD-demijohn water manufacturing company to test the performance of the method in real-life problems. The proposed method is applied to minimize the total cost of the HOD-demijohn supply chain, which is composed of production, inventory holding, and transportation costs. In the current supply chain of the company, the production, inventory, and distribution decisions are considered separately, and the retailers collect the final products from the distribution centers individually. According to the results of the study, thanks to the integrated system, transportation costs of the company have been significantly reduced and the limited production capacity usage has become more efficient. Since it can reduce the carbon emission in the system, the integrated system is also beneficial in terms of environmental issues.

FUTURE RESEARCH DIRECTIONS

As a future study, the proposed algorithm's performance can be improved so as to solve more complex problems. Probabilistic demand patterns may be considered in the model to make mimic real-life problems better. Additionally, multiple product variety, heteregoneos vehicle fleet, and multi-echelon supply chain can be considered to improve the model.

CONCLUSION

Nowadays, supply chain management has become a very important issue for the competitive advantage. Due to the globalization and technological developments, transportation distances have increased, the life cycle of the products has shortened, and customer requirements have became more challenging in terms of the price, quality, and delivery time. Supply chain management deals with the coordination of all activities from raw material suppliers to the final customers. A supply chain is a complex system that is composed of independent companies with conflicting objectives. Conflicting objectives may cause operational inefficiency, increased operational costs, and customer dissatisfaction. The integrated supply chain management aims to achieve competitive success by combining the conflicting objectives of supply chain members around a common goal. The coordination of all activities along the supply chain can be beneficial while finding the trade-offs between conflicting objectives within the supply chain.

Production, inventory, and distribution management are three important supply chain decision-making phases. The success of the supply chain hinges on the success of these three phases.Traditionally, these decision phases in the supply chain have been examined independently. However, taking them into account simultaneously these decision phases can significantly reduce total supply chain costs while increasing the efficiency of the overall supply chain.

In the literature, the integrated production-distribution problem generally applied to a two-echelon supply chain where a production facility serves a group of customers spread over a geographic area. The objective of the integrated production-distribution problem is to minimize the total supply chain cost by determining the optimum production batch size, amount of inventory held in the system, and distribution routes. The production-distribution problem can be classified as an NP-hard problem since one of the sub-problems of this problem is the vehicle routing problem, which is a very well-known NP-hard problem. It has been proven in the literature that evolutionary heuristic algorithms are successful in solving NP-hard problems in an acceptable period. The test results showed that the MA is one of the effective evolutionary heuristic algorithms for solving the integrated production-distribution problem.

There are a few studies that present a real-life application for the production-distribution problem in the literature. Therefore, one of the contributions of this chapter is to present a real-life case study for a production-distribution problem. The presented case study results proved that the integrated production-distribution plan could be very beneficial economically and environmentally for the supply chains. This chapter proposes a practical and efficient model for supply chain management professionals and shows the benefits of the integrated production-distribution plan.

REFERENCES

Absi, N., Archetti, C., Dauzère-Pérès, S., & Feillet, D. (2015). A two-phase iterative heuristic approach for the production routing problem. *Transportation Science, 49*(4), 784–795. doi:10.1287/trsc.2014.0523

Adulyasak, Y., Cordeau, J. F., & Jans, R. (2012). Optimization-based adaptive large neighborhood search for the production routing problem. *Transportation Science, 48*(1), 20–45. doi:10.1287/trsc.1120.0443

Adulyasak, Y., Cordeau, J. F., & Jans, R. (2014). Formulations and branch-and-cut algorithms for multivehicle production and inventory routing problems. *INFORMS Journal on Computing, 26*(1), 103–120. doi:10.1287/ijoc.2013.0550

Adulyasak, Y., Cordeau, J. F., & Jans, R. (2015). The production routing problem: A review of formulations and solution algorithms. *Computers & Operations Research, 55*, 141–152. doi:10.1016/j.cor.2014.01.011

Archetti, C., Bertazzi, L., Paletta, G., & Speranza, M. G. (2011). Analysis of the maximum level policy in a production-distribution system. *Computers & Operations Research, 38*(12), 1731–1746. doi:10.1016/j.cor.2011.03.002

Bank, M., Mazdeh, M., & Heydari, M. (2020). Applying meta-heuristic algorithms for an integrated production-distribution problem in a two level supply chain. *Uncertain Supply Chain Management, 8*(1), 77–92. doi:10.5267/j.uscm.2019.8.004

Bard, J. F., & Nananukul, N. (2009a). Heuristics for a multiperiod inventory routing problem with production decisions. *Computers & Industrial Engineering, 57*(3), 713–723. doi:10.1016/j.cie.2009.01.020

Bard, J. F., & Nananukul, N. (2009b). The integrated production–inventory–distribution–routing problem. *Journal of Scheduling, 12*(3), 257–280. doi:10.100710951-008-0081-9

Boudia, M., Louly, M. A. O., & Prins, C. (2007). A reactive GRASP and path relinking for a combined production–distribution problem. *Computers & Operations Research, 34*(11), 3402–3419. doi:10.1016/j.cor.2006.02.005

Campbell, A., Clarke, L., Kleywegt, A., & Savelsbergh, M. (1998). The inventory routing problem. In *Fleet management and logistics* (pp. 95–113). Springer. doi:10.1007/978-1-4615-5755-5_4

Chandra, P., & Fisher, M. L. (1994). Coordination of production and distribution planning. *European Journal of Operational Research, 72*(3), 503–517. doi:10.1016/0377-2217(94)90419-7

Chen, L., Zhao, X., Tang, O., Price, L., Zhang, S., & Zhu, W. (2017). Supply chain collaboration for sustainability: A literature review and future research agenda. *International Journal of Production Economics*, *194*, 73–87. doi:10.1016/j.ijpe.2017.04.005

Clarke, G., & Wright, J. W. (1964). Scheduling of vehicles from a central depot to a number of delivery points. *Operations Research*, *12*(4), 568–581. doi:10.1287/opre.12.4.568

Dawkins, R. (1989). *The Selfish Gene*. Oxford University Press.

Digalakis, J., & Margaritis, K. (2004). Performance comparison of memetic algorithms. *Applied Mathematics and Computation*, *158*(1), 237–252. doi:10.1016/j.amc.2003.08.115

ElMekkawy, T. Y., & Liu, S. (2009). A new memetic algorithm for optimizing the partitioning problem of tandem AGV systems. *International Journal of Production Economics*, *118*(2), 508–520. doi:10.1016/j.ijpe.2009.01.008

Fumero, F., & Vercellis, C. (1999). Synchronized development of production, inventory, and distribution schedules. *Transportation Science*, *33*(3), 330–340. doi:10.1287/trsc.33.3.330

Guimarães, T. A., Coelho, L. C., Schenekemberg, C. M., & Scarpin, C. T. (2019). The two-echelon multi-depot inventory-routing problem. *Computers & Operations Research*, *101*, 220–233. doi:10.1016/j.cor.2018.07.024

Krasnogor, N., & Smith, J. (2005). A tutorial for competent memetic algorithms: Model, taxonomy, and design issues. *IEEE Transactions on Evolutionary Computation*, *9*(5), 474–488. doi:10.1109/TEVC.2005.850260

Kyee, D. L. T., & Moin, N. H. (2018). MatHeuristic Approach for Production-Inventory-Distribution Routing Problem. *Warasan Khana Witthayasat Maha Witthayalai Chiang Mai*, *45*(2), 1145–1160.

Lei, L., Liu, S., Ruszczynski, A., & Park, S. (2006). On the integrated production, inventory, and distribution routing problem. *IIE Transactions*, *38*(11), 955–970. doi:10.1080/07408170600862688

Moin, N. H., Salhi, S., & Aziz, N. A. B. (2011). An efficient hybrid genetic algorithm for the multi-product multi-period inventory routing problem. *International Journal of Production Economics*, *133*(1), 334–343. doi:10.1016/j.ijpe.2010.06.012

Moscato, P., & Norman, M. G. (1992). A memetic approach for the traveling salesman problem implementation of a computational ecology for combinatorial optimization on message-passing systems. *Parallel Computing and Transputer Applications*, *1*, 177-186.

Rafiei, H., Safaei, F., & Rabbani, M. (2018). Integrated production-distribution planning problem in a competition-based four-echelon supply chain. *Computers & Industrial Engineering*, *119*, 85–99. doi:10.1016/j.cie.2018.02.031

Ramkumar, N., Subramanian, P., Narendran, T. T., & Ganesh, K. (2011). A hybrid heuristic for inventory routing problem. *International Journal of Electronic Transport*, *1*(1), 45–63. doi:10.1504/IJET.2011.043113

Ruokokoski, M., Solyali, O. G. U. Z., Cordeau, J. F., Jans, R., & Süral, H. (2010). *Efficient formulations and a branch-and-cut algorithm for a production-routing problem.* GERAD Technical Report G-2010-66.

Schroeder, R. G. (2017). *Operations management in the supply chain decsions and cases*. Irwin/McGraw-Hill.

Senoussi, A., Dauzère-Pérès, S., Brahimi, N., Penz, B., & Mouss, N. K. (2018). Heuristics based on genetic algorithms for the capacitated multi vehicle production distribution problem. *Computers & Operations Research*, *96*, 108–119. doi:10.1016/j.cor.2018.04.010

Simchi-Levi, D., Wu, S. D., & Shen, Z. J. M. (Eds.). (2004). *Handbook of quantitative supply chain analysis: modeling in the e-business era* (Vol. 74). Springer Science & Business Media. doi:10.1007/978-1-4020-7953-5_1

Solyali, O., & Süral, H. (2017). A multi-phase heuristic for the production routing problem. *Computers & Operations Research*, *87*, 114–124. doi:10.1016/j.cor.2017.06.007

Thomas, D. J., & Griffin, P. M. (1996). Coordinated supply chain management. *European Journal of Operational Research*, *94*(1), 1–15. doi:10.1016/0377-2217(96)00098-7

Yadegari, E., Alem-Tabriz, A., & Zandieh, M. (2019). A memetic algorithm with a novel neighborhood search and modified solution representation for closed-loop supply chain network design. *Computers & Industrial Engineering*, *128*, 418–436. doi:10.1016/j.cie.2018.12.054

Yang, Y., Pan, S., & Ballot, E. (2017). Innovative vendor-managed inventory strategy exploiting interconnected logistics services in the Physical Internet. *International Journal of Production Research*, *55*(9), 2685–2702. doi:10.1080/00207543.2016.1275871

ADDITIONAL READING

Bertazzi, L., Coelho, L. C., De Maio, A., & Laganà, D. (2019). A matheuristic algorithm for the multi-depot inventory routing problem. *Transportation Research Part E, Logistics and Transportation Review*, *122*, 524–544. doi:10.1016/j.tre.2019.01.005

Copacino, W. C. (2019). *Supply chain management: The basics and beyond*. Routledge.

Golden, B. L., Raghavan, S., & Wasil, E. A. (Eds.). (2008). *The vehicle routing problem: latest advances and new challenges* (Vol. 43). Springer Science & Business Media. doi:10.1007/978-0-387-77778-8

Gu, W., Archetti, C., Cattaruzza, D., Ogier, M., Semet, F., & Speranza, M. G. (2019, February). A multi-commodity transportation planning problem in supply chain management.

Guimarães, T. A., Coelho, L. C., Schenekemberg, C. M., & Scarpin, C. T. (2019). The two-echelon multi-depot inventory-routing problem. *Computers & Operations Research*, *101*, 220–233. doi:10.1016/j.cor.2018.07.024

Meredith, J. R., & Shafer, S. M. (2019). *Operations and supply chain management for MBAs*. Wiley.

Robeson, J. F. (1994). *Logistics handbook*. Simon and Schuster.

Silver, E. A., Pyke, D. F., & Peterson, R. (1998). *Inventory management and production planning and scheduling* (Vol. 3). Wiley.

Toth, P., & Vigo, D. (Eds.). (2002). *The vehicle routing problem*. Society for Industrial and Applied Mathematics. doi:10.1137/1.9780898718515

KEY TERMS AND DEFINITIONS

Distribution Planning: The planning of distribution processes to deliver goods to different demand points accurately.

HOD-Demijohn Water: It is 19 lt. carboy bottle water to meet home or office water requirements.

Inventory: Physical goods or materials produced or purchased but not used yet are called inventory.

Metaheuristic: A high-level procedure or heuristic to solve complicated optimization problems.

NP-Hard Problem: One of a class of computational problems, which cannot be solved with deterministic methods in polynomial time.

Production Planning: The planning of production activities to align demands with the manufacturing capacity in a company.

Supply Chain: The collection of steps that a company takes to transform raw components into final products and deliver them to customers.

Chapter 8
Mixed Delivery and Pickup Vehicle Routing Problem With Limited Flow and Assignment of Drones in an Urban Network

Hamdi Radhoui
University of Le Havre Normandie, France

Atour Taghipour
Normandy University, France

Beatrice Canel-Depitre
University of Le Havre Normandie, France

ABSTRACT

A new variant of the delivery and pickup transportation problem called mixed delivery and pickup routing problem with unmanned aerial vehicles in case of limited flow is introduced. The objective is to minimize operational costs including total transportation costs and service time at each point. This variant is a solution for the urban congestion, and consequently, it is an improvement of the general transport system. First, the problem is formulated mathematically. It is considered as NP-hard; therefore, the authors proposed an iterated local search algorithm to solve the problem of mixed pickup and delivery without drone. Then, a vehicle first-drone second algorithm is used to solve the mixed delivery and pickup problem with drone. The performance of the method is compared through numerical experiments based on instance derived from the literature as well as on a set of randomly generated instances. Numerical results have shown that proposed metaheuristic method performs consistently well in terms of both the quality of the solution and the computational time when using drone with vehicle.

DOI: 10.4018/978-1-7998-3805-0.ch008

I. INTRODUCTION

The distribution of goods is a very important activity in supply chains. This activity, often managed by third-party logistics companies, can be achieved through different transportation modes including the road, air, rail, etc. The road goods transportation is one of the most flexible means to transport goods since the goods are loaded directly to the truck and transported to the place of destination. Note that in 2015, "*the road freight transportation accounts for 69.6% of the total freight transported between France and EU countries*" (Ministry Of Transition Ecological and Solidarity of France). In the past, goods transportation activities were simple activities of distribution of goods from a distribution center to customers *(Labadi et al., 2008)* or a collection of commercial goods from facility plants to a depot *(Kim et al., 2006)*. In recent years, with an increasing challenge to provide a higher service quality while reducing the operational costs, goods transportation activities have evolved to more complex activities that consist in delivering/picking up goods to/from many customers by means of multiple vehicles from/to a central depot. Freight transportation has received increasing attention of many researchers and has been the source of the enormous work in the literature of the pickup and delivery problems. From the practical point of view, one of the main objectives of industrial companies is to improve the efficiency of their supply chains so that they can organize better service at lower cost as well as the fluidity of the flow of their goods. Habitually, to handle these tasks vehicles have been used. A new method has recently used where unmanned aerial vehicles known as Drones, are chosen to serve small goods. It's important to distinguish between military and non-military use of drones. Michael Toscano, president of the association for Unmanned Vehicle Systems International, is quoted in the Washington Times saying, *"The word [drone] instantly conjures up mental images of large predators firing missiles at hostile targets around the world"*. Until recently, media coverage has focused mainly on military use, coining the term 'drone' and leaving many with negative attitudes towards this new technology. There are many advantages of using drone for distribution: it avoids the congestion of traditional road networks, it can be operated without human being, it has much lower transportation costs per kilometre *(Wohlsen, 2014)*, and it is faster than vehicles. However, it has also disadvantages: drone's flight distance and lifting power are limited because it is powered by batteries.

The purpose of this report is to provide a study to this exciting topic, present use cases from a broad variety of industries, and discuss potential applications in and for the logistics industry. We aim to show the role of the drone in improving the transport service in order to provide a realistic assessment of UAVs. "*German postal and logistics group Deutsche Post DHL recently announced that their Parcelcopter,*

Figure 1. DHL's Parcelcopter (source: dhl.com)

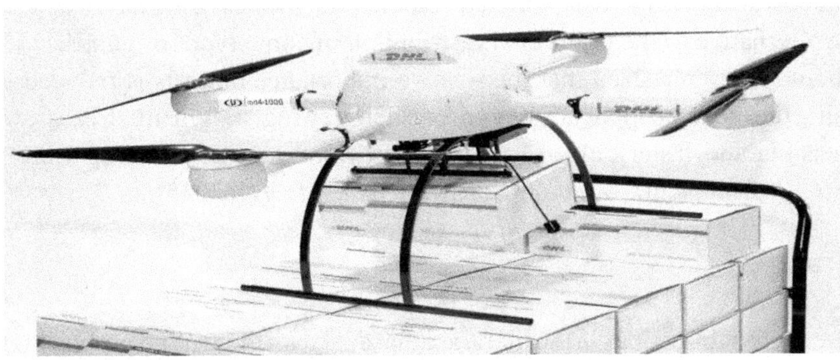

has been authorized to deliver medical supplies to a car-free-island off the coast of Germany" (see Fig.1)*(Bryan, 2014).*

The remainder is organized as follows. An overview of the relevant literature that deals with the general vehicle routing problem with drone and some solution approaches are presented in Section 2. We provide aF definition, a description and a mathematical formulation of the new variant in Section 3. Our metaheuristic solution method is described in Section 4. Section 5 is devoted to a computational study of the method and the numerical results. Finally, the conclusions of our research and some natural extensions for further work are presented in Section 6.

II. RESEARCH BACKGROUND

1 Contribution

This paper aims to define a model in which costs must be minimized by a given decision-maker. This is done in an environment where different types of products can be delivered and requested. At the same time, the company can follow two types of strategies: using just vehicles for transportation between the supplier and the customers or using drones with vehicles in mixed deliver and pickup problem. In the latter case, several constraints such as drone's flight distance and lifting power to take into account.

We will define the corresponding problem and illustrate how the cost differences between the mixed drone-vehicle transport process and the traditional vehicle-based process lead to a partial or total dominance of the former for sufficiently large cost differentials.

The numerical evaluations of the optimization model will be used to illustrate different cost scenarios in which mixed vehicles and drones distribution appears as a viable alternative to the traditional distribution of some types of goods.

It should be emphasized that the relative importance of costs is reduced when examining the medical applications of drone delivery logistics in urban areas, where more feasible and faster deliveries can be provided in case of compelling need *(Thiels, C. A., Aho, J. M., Zietlow, S. P., & Jenkins, D. H. (2015))*.

2 Literature

There are a few publications in the literature that deal with the routing problem related to the vehicle-drone combination on delivery of goods. For a literature review on this category of problems, a new method called "last kilometer delivery with drone", in which the truck transports the drone close to customer locations, thus allowing the drone to serve its customers while remaining in its flight area, thus increasing the usability and making the schedule more flexible for both drones (Banker, 2013). A mixed integer liner programming (MILP) formulation and a heuristic are proposed for the Flying Sidekick Traveling Salesman Problem by (Murray and Chu, 2015). The heuristic is called "Truck First, Drone Second" idea, according to which they build a route for the truck by solving a TSP problem and, then, repeatedly run a relocation procedure to reduce the objective value. The proposed methods are tested only on small-sized instances with up to 10 customers.

A more general problem that use multiple trucks and drones in order to minimize the completion time is introduced by (*Wang et al. 2016)*. They named it "The problem of the circulation of vehicles with drones (VRP-D)". Authors analyzed several worst-case scenarios, from which they propose solutions to save as much time as possible when using drones and trucks instead of trucks only.

a new hybrid genetic algorithm, which supports the cooperation of a land vehicle and several UAVs for efficient delivery of packages has been proposed by *(Peng and al, 2019)*. This routing and scheduling algorithm allows multiple UAVs transported by the vehicle to simultaneously deliver multiple packages to different customers. The results of the performance evaluation show that the proposed algorithm has significant efficiency compared to existing algorithms.

III. PROBLEM STATEMENT AND MATHEMATICAL MODEL

1 Problem Description

The MDPVRP-D consists of carrying an amount of one or more products from a depot to delivery customers and picking up other amount from pickup locations to the depot by a given set of vehicles and Drones starting and ending at a central depot. Vehicles are homogeneous and having a certain capacity. To make a service (delivery/pickup), Drone is launched from the vehicle and later rejoins it at the same location. The objective is to construct routes so that operational cost is minimized. It includes the fixed vehicle/drone cost, the travel cost. The set of vehicles' routes should be Hamiltonian routes, which means that each customer should be visited only once to ensure the pickup or the delivery by either the vehicle or the Drone, when a customer is serviced by the vehicle, this is called a vehicle service VS, while when a customer is serviced by the drone, this is called a drone service DS. There is no splitting of the demand.

2 Problem Definition

The MDPVRP-D can be defined by a complete graph $G=(V,E)$, where $V=\{0,\ldots,n,n+1\}$, and the same depot is represented by the node 0 *and* $n+1$, where 0 *and* $n+1$ both represent the starting and returning points. *E* is the set of arcs $\{i,j\}$, where $\{i,j\}\in V, i\neq j$ Feasible vehicle routes then correspond to paths starting and ending at vertex 0. The set of customers is $N=V\setminus\{0,n+1\}$. Let $V_D \sqsubseteq N$ denote the set of customers served by drone. Without loss of generality, each vertex $i\in N$ represents a customer having a demand $q_{i,p}$ for some products $p\in P$. Note that when $q_{i,p}\geq 0$, the vertex *i* is a pickup customer that provides for one or more of the products *p*, otherwise it is a delivery customer that requires for an amount of products *p*. Each vehicle is characterized by its fixed cost γ and its variable cost per distance unit ω. Each pair of customers *i* and *j* is associated with a distance d_{ij} and their travel cost from vertex *i* to vertex *j* is $c_{ij}=\omega\times d_{ij}$ travelled by the vehicle. Let d_{ij} the distance from *i* to *j* and $c_{ij}^{'}=w_1\times d_{ij}^{'}$ the travel cost by the drone from vertex *i* to vertex *j*. Let s_i denotes the service time at *i* (with S_0=0).

3 Mathematical Formulation

To present the above problem in a mathematical model, we introduce the additional notation. Let

$K = \{1,..., k\}$: the set of available homogeneous vehicles,
$DR = \{1,\ldots, dr\}$: the set of available drones,
$N = \{1, ..., n\}$: the set of customers (pickup and delivery customers), $N = D \cup B$,
D: subsets of delivery (Linehaul) customers,
B: subsets of pickup (Backhaul) customers,
$V = \{0,1, ..., n, n+1\}$: the set of customers including start and end depot node, $V = N \cup \{0, n+1\}$,
V_D: the set of customers served by drone,
$P = \{1,..., p\}$: the set of products,
Q: the capacity of vehicles,
Qd: drone's capacity
F: drone's flight distance
c_{ij}: travelling cost from i to j by vehicle, $\forall i \in V, j \in V, i \neq j$,
C'_{ij} : travelling cost from i to j by drone, $\forall i \in N, j \in N, i \neq j$,
γ: fixed cost of using vehicle,
q_{jp}: amount of product p required by customer j, $\forall p \in P$, $j \in V$,
v_{jp}: amount of product p provided by customer $j, \forall p \in P, j \in V$,
s_i: service time (load or unload time) at customer i, $\forall i \in V \setminus \{n+1\}$,
M: a big number,
t_{ij}: travel time from customer i to customer j by vehicle

$$t_{ij} = \beta \times d_{ij}$$

t'_{ij} : *travel time from customer i to customer j by drone*

$$t'_{ij} = \alpha \times d'_{ij}$$

x_{ijk}: is a binary variable which is equal to one if the arc (i,j) belongs to the route of vehicle k and zero otherwise, $\forall i \in V, j \in V, k \in K$,
y_{ijdr}: is a binary variable equal to one if the arc (i,j) travelled by a drone dr and zero otherwise, $\forall i \in V, j \in V, dr \in DR$,
f_{ijp}: is a non-negative integer indicating the vehicle load of the product p leaving the customer i to the customer $j, \forall i \in V, j \in V, p \in P$,
g_{ijp}: is a non-negative integer indicating the drone load of the product p leaving the customer i to the customer j, $\forall i, j \in V_D, p \in P$

We then state the problem as follows:

$$Min\ \gamma \sum_{j\in V}\sum_{k\in K} x_{ojk} + \sum_{\substack{i\in V\\ i\neq j}}\sum_{j\in V}\sum_{k\in K} c_{ijk}x_{ijk} + \sum_{\substack{i\in V\\ i\neq j}}\sum_{j\in V}\sum_{dr\in DR} c'_{ijdr}y_{ijdr} \tag{1}$$

$$\sum_{i\in V} x_{ijk} - \sum_{i\in V} x_{jik} = 0, \forall j \in N, k \in K \tag{2}$$

$$\sum_{i\in V} y_{ijdr} - \sum_{i\in V} y_{jidr} = 0, \forall j \in N, dr \in DR \tag{3}$$

$$\sum_{\substack{i\in N\\ i\neq j}}\sum_{k\in K} x_{ijk} + \sum_{\substack{i\in N\\ i\neq j}}\sum_{dr\in DR} y_{ijdr} = 1, \forall j \in V_D \tag{4}$$

$$\sum_{i\in V} f_{jip} - \sum_{i\in V} f_{ijp} = q_{jp} \qquad \forall j \in N, p \in P \tag{5}$$

$$\sum_{p\in P} f_{ijp} \leq Q \sum_{k\in K} x_{ijk} \qquad \forall i \in V, j \in V \tag{6}$$

$$\sum_{j\in N} x_{0jk} = 1 \qquad \forall k \in K \tag{7}$$

$$\sum_{j\in N} x_{j,n+1k} = 1 \qquad \forall k \in K \tag{8}$$

$$v_{ip} \leq f_{ijp} \leq Q \forall i \in D \tag{9}$$

$$0 \leq f_{ijp} \leq Q - q_{ip} \forall i \in D \tag{10}$$

$$f_{ijp} + v_{ip} - q_{ip} \leq f_{ijp} + M \times \left(1 - x_{ijkp}\right) \forall i \in V\{0\}, j \in V\{n+1\} \tag{11}$$

$$f_{0jp} = \sum_{i\in D} v_{ip} \sum_{i,j\in N} x_{ijkp} \forall k \in K, p \tag{12}$$

$$g_{ijp} \leq Qd \qquad \forall i, j \in V_D, p \in P \tag{13}$$

$$2 \times t_{ij}^{'} \leq F \qquad \forall i, j \in V_D \tag{14}$$

$$2 \times t_{ij}^{'} \leq t_{ij} \tag{15}$$

$$\sum_{i \in N} y_{ijdr} = 1 \qquad \forall j \in V_D, dr \in DR \tag{16}$$

$$\sum_{j \in V_D} y_{jidr} = 1 \qquad \forall i \in N, dr \in DR \tag{17}$$

$$y_{ijdr} \in \{0,1\}, \forall i, j \in N_0, dr \in DR, p \in P \tag{18}$$

$$x_{ijk} \in \{0,1\}, \forall i, j \in N_0, k \in K, p \in P \tag{19}$$

$$T_i \geq 0, \forall i \in N_0 \tag{20}$$

$$f_{ijp} \geq 0, \forall i, j \in N_0, p \in P \tag{21}$$

$$r_i \geq 0, \forall i \in N_0 \tag{22}$$

In the above formulation, the objective function is to minimize the total routing cost. It includes the fixed cost of using vehicles, the total variable travel cost of vehicles and drones stated by (1). Constraint (2) and (3) is the flow conservation for demands of customers. Constraint (4) state that each customer is visited exactly once. Constraint (5) is the flow conservation for demands of customers. It means that the vehicle load of a particular product should be at least equal to the total quantity of that product that it delivers to demanding locations. Constraint (6) enforces the vehicle capacity restriction.

Constraints (7) - (8) guarantee that a feasible vehicle route starts at vertex 0 and ends at vertex n+1. Constraints (9) and (10) are used to bound vehicle load after pickup (backhaul) and delivery customers, respectively. Constraint (11) concern the successive vehicle loads along a route while for constraint (12) the load of each vehicle when leaving the depot must be equal to the total demand of the delivery customers. Constraint (13) enforces the drone's capacity restriction. Constraints (14) and (15) impose the bounds on the drone's travel distance. Constraints (16) and (17) guarantee that a feasible drone route starts at the node i and ends at it. The definition of decision variables is stated by constraints (18) to (22).

IV. RESOLUTION APPROACH

1 Vehicle-First Drone-second Approach

1.1. Iterative Local Search

1.1.1. Initial Feasible Solution Construction

A constructive algorithm is used to create the initial solution. One route should be first established. The route is initialized with the depot. The remaining un-routed customers are ordered in a decreasing order of their demand for delivery and pickup. If there are some customers that have not appeared in the route, and can be feasibly added to it, we select the customer with the largest demand from them to be added to the route. If the demands of two customers are identic, then, the remaining un-routed (or unvisited) customers are added sequentially based on the least insertion cost method. In fact, each customer with identic demand we evaluate its insertion cost in the correspond route. The customer with the smallest insertion cost is inserted first in the current partial route (Fig. 2) and (Fig.3).

Figure 2. Insertion cost between two customers.

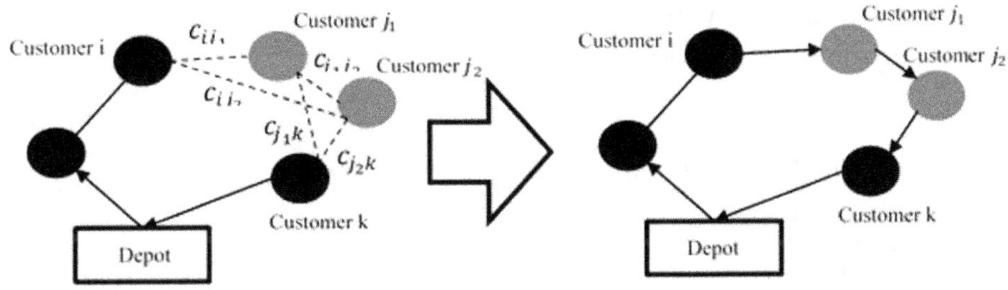

$C_{j_1} = c_{ij_1} + c_{j_1j_2} + c_{j_2k}$ $\qquad C_{j_2} = c_{ij_2} + c_{j_2j_1} + c_{j_1k}$ $\qquad C_{j_1} < C_{j_2}$

Figure 3. Initial solution construction.

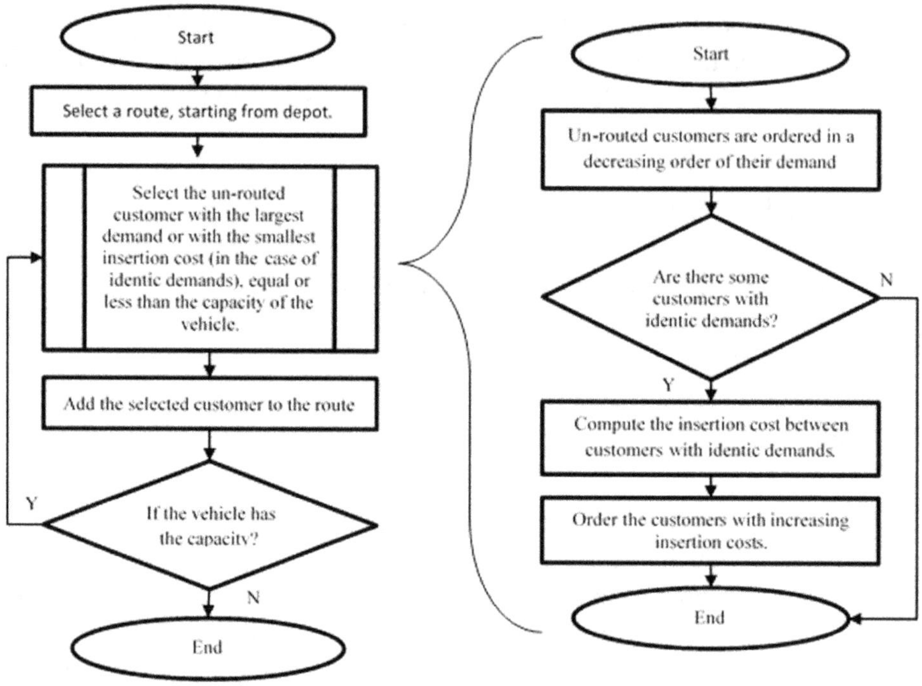

The insertion cost of a customer j_1 is calculated as $C_{j_1} = c_{ij_1} + c_{j_1j_2} + c_{j_2k}$, where c_{ij_1}, $c_{j_1j_2}$ and c_{j_2k} are the costs of the routes between customers i and j_1, j_1 and j_2, j_2 and k, respectively.

If un-routed customers remain, the initialization and insertion procedures are then repeated for other vehicles until all customers are assigned to routes. The aim of selecting the customer with the largest demand from all feasible customers is to increase the probability of constructing a feasible solution.

Table 1. Pseudocode of the iterated local search algorithm

```
S0 ←GenerateInitialSolution();
S´ ←LocalSearch(S0);
fori:=1 to MaxIterILS do
S*←Perturbation(S´, history);
S*´←LocalSearch(S*);
S'←ApplyAcceptanceCriteria(S´, S*´, history);
endfor
end
```

1.1.2. The Metaheuristic Solution Approach

Our algorithm consists of a route construction procedure, intra and inter-route local search and a solution perturbation procedure for just the vehicle without drone. The pseudo-code of the ILS algorithm is shown below. The ILS is described as follows. First, an initial solution is generated in function *GenerateInitialSolution* (). This solution is subsequently improved by the application of a local search in function *LocalSearch*(S_0).

At each iteration *MaxIterILS*, the incumbent solution *S'* is perturbed in the function *Perturbation* (S', history), resulting in a perturbed solution *S**. After the application of the local search to the perturbed solution, the resulting solution *S*´* may either be accepted as new current solution, or not. This is decided in function *ApplyAcceptanceCriterion* (S´, S*´, history).

1.1.3. The Local Search and Neighborhood Structures

The local search is employed until no improvements are found, and all the routes are scanned. For the MDPVRP-D, we consider three move neighborhoods, which are employed respectively, after the initial solution is constructed. The three neighborhood structures are described next. Only feasible moves are admitted. Therefore, during the search process, the algorithm checks if the move is admissible or not. An admissible move is one that does not violate the vehicle capacity (in case of pickup customer) and must satisfy the customer needs (in case of delivery customer). The local search starts by the inter-route neighborhood moves which are the swap and 2-opt moves and then the best admissible move having the lowest cost is determined. In case of an improvement, intra-route neighborhood structures are performed. Two intra-route neighborhood structures are employed: insertion and 2-opt. When a move is applied to the solution, one should consider that only a subset of the solution is modified. So, information about this modified subset of solutions has to be updated (Fig. 4).

Acceptance criterion for the local search determines if the solution is accepted or not. If the solution is accepted, it will be perturbed and will be the initial solution for the next iteration. In this research, the current solution is accepted only if it has a better cost than the starting solution.

a. Swap move

The first inter-route move attempts to swap randomly two neighboring customers b and c from the vehicle route 1 by another two adjacent customers, g and h from another vehicle route (for example vehicle route 2) (Fig. 5).

Figure 4. Flowchart of the Meta-heuristic

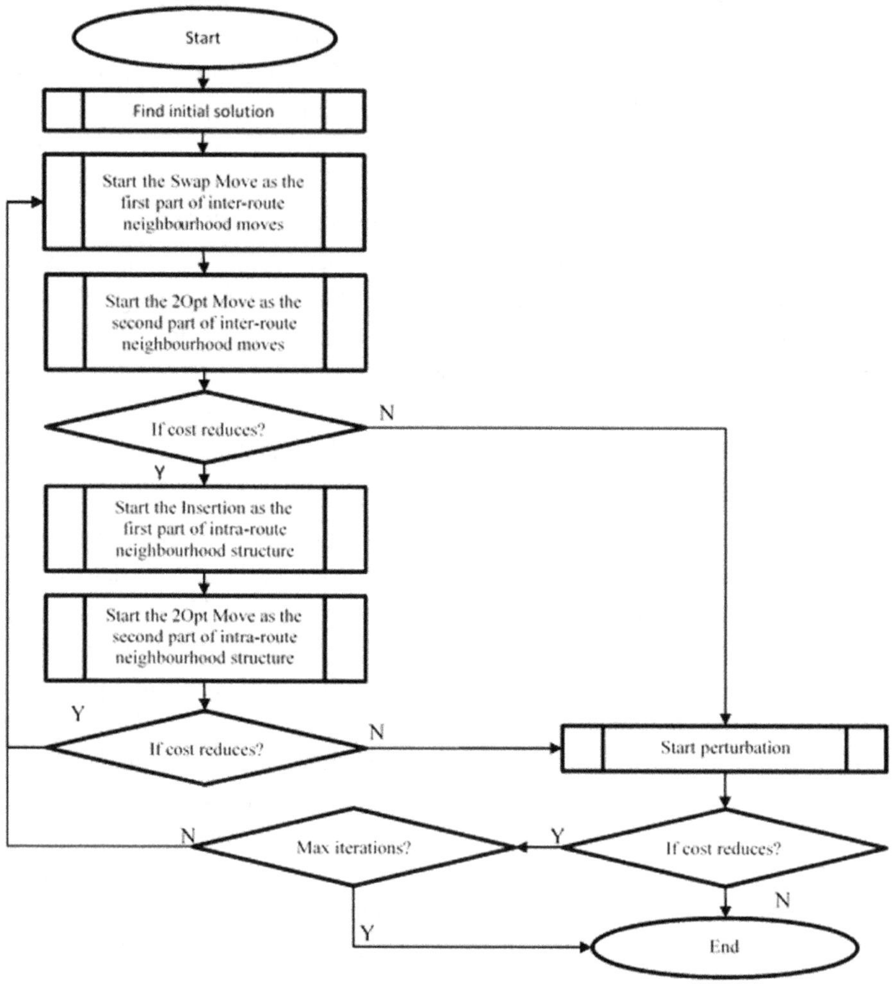

Figure 5. Swap neighborhood structure.

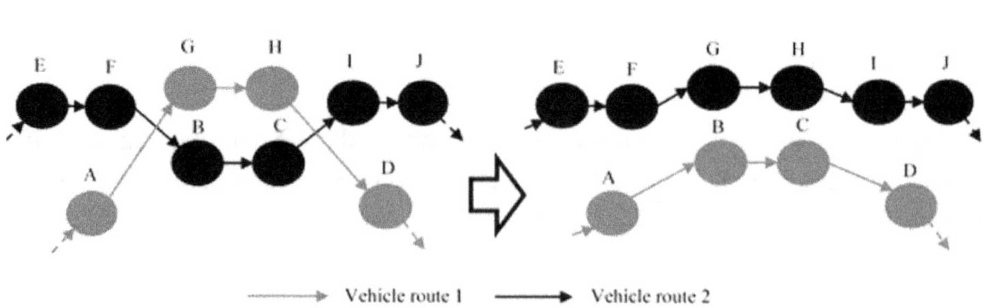

For each swap move inter two routes, we evaluate the cost. The swap cost of the two adjacent customers from a vehicle route by another two neighbouring customers from another vehicle route is calculated as follows:

Let:

$\Delta_{(BC,GH)}$: Swap cost
Cost function: $C \mapsto \mathbb{R}^{+}$ and $x \mapsto C(x)$

$$S_{V1} = Set\ of\ arc\ traveled\ by\ vehicle\ 1 = \{EF, FB, BC, CI, IJ\}$$

$$S_{V2} = Set\ of\ arc\ traveled\ by\ vehicle\ 2 = \{AG, GA, HD\}$$

$$C_{V1} = \sum_{x \in S_{V1}} C(x)$$

$$C_{V2} = \sum_{x \in S_{V2}} C(x)$$

$$\Delta_{GH} = C_{EF} + C_{FG} + C_{GH} + C_{HI} + C_{IJ} - C_{V1}$$

$$\Delta_{BC} = C_{AB} + C_{BC} + C_{CD} - C_{V2}$$

Therefore

$$\Delta_{(BC,GH)} = \Delta_{BC} + \Delta_{GH}$$

Where S_{V1}, S_{V2} are the set of initial arcs constituting each route (V1 and V2), $C_{EF}, C_{FG}, C_{GH}, C_{HI}, C_{IJ}, C_{AB}, C_{BC}, C_{CD}$ are the cost of each arc connecting two customers, and C_{V1}, C_{V2} are the cost of the two routes before the swap move. A swap move is possible if $\Delta_{(BC,GH)} < 0$.

b. Two opt move

The mechanism of this move type is differentiated according to whether it is employed within a route (intra-route), or between a route pair, as illustrated in Figures (6) and (7).

Two opt intra-route move

In this move the algorithm evaluate the possibility of reordering a route by eliminating a cross when the route crosses over itself (Fig. 6).

Figure 6. 2-opt neighborhood structure in one route.

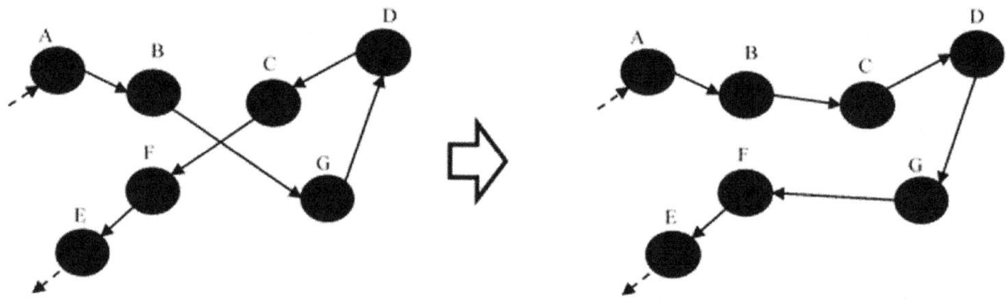

2-Opt intra-route move is calculated as follows:

Let:

$\Delta_{(BG,CF)}$: The 2-opt move cost (intra-route)
Cost function: $C \mapsto \mathbb{R}^+$ and $x \mapsto C(x)$

S_V = Set of arc traveled by vehicle before ordering = $\{AB, BG, GD, DC, CF, FE\}$

$S_{V'}$ = Set of arc traveled by vehicle after ordering = $\{AB, BC, CD, DG, GF, FE\}$

$$C_V = \sum_{x \in S_V} C(x)$$

$$C_{V'} = \sum_{x \in S_{V'}} C(x)$$

Therefore

$$\Delta_{(BG,CF)} = C_{V'} - C_V$$

Where S_V is the set of initial arcs constituting the route V while $S_{V'}$ is the set of arcs constituting this vehicle after the 2-opt move (V'), and $C_V, C_{V'}$ are respectively the costs of the route V before and after the operation of 2- opt. A 2-Opt intra-route move is possible if $\Delta_{(BG,CF)} < 0$. In the case of an intra-route 2-opt, two nonadjacent arcs are deleted and replaced by two others in such a way that a new vehicle route is generated. In figure 5 the arcs (BG) and (CF) are deleted while the arcs (BC) and (GF) are created.

Two opt inter-route move

In this move the algorithm evaluate the possibility of reordering a route by eliminating a cross when the route crosses over another route (Fig. 7).

Figure 7. 2-opt neighborhood structure in two routes.

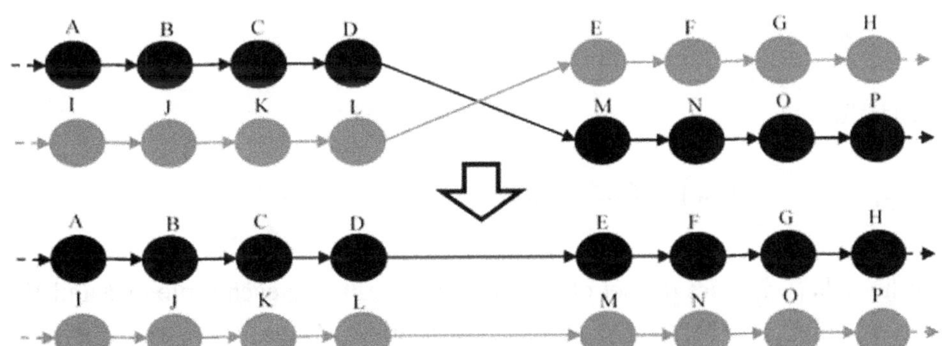

2-Opt inter-route move is calculated as follows:

Let:

$\Delta_{(DM,LE)}$: The 2-opt move cost (inter-route)
Cost function: $C \mapsto \mathbb{R}^+$ and $x \mapsto C(x)$

$$S_{V1} = \{AB, BC, CD, DM, MN, NO, OP\}$$

$$S_{V2} = \{IJ, JK, KL, LE, EF, FG, GH\}$$

$$S_{V1'} = \{AB, BC, CD, DE, EF, FG, GH\}$$

$$S_{V2'} = \{IJ, JK, KL, LM, MN, NO, OP\}$$

$$C_{V1} = \sum_{x \in S_{V1}} C(x)$$

$$C_{V2} = \sum_{x \in S_{V2}} C(x)$$

$$C_{V1'} = \sum_{x \in S_{V1'}} C(x)$$

$$C_{V2'} = \sum_{x \in S_{V2'}} C(x)$$

Therefore:

$$\Delta_{(DM,LE)} = (C_{V1'} - C_{V1}) + (C_{V2'} - C_{V2})$$

Where S_{V1}, S_{V2} are the set of initial arcs constituting each route (V1 and V2) while $S_{V1'}$ $S_{V2'}$ are the set of customers constituting V1 and V2 respectively after the operation of 2-opt $C_{EF}, C_{FG}, C_{GH}, C_{HI}, C_{IJ}, C_{AB}, C_{BC}, C_{CD}$ are the cost of each arc connecting two customers, and C_{V1}, C_{V2} ,$C_{V1'}$ and $C_{V2'}$ are respectively the costs of the two routes V1 and V2 before and after the 2-opt move. A 2-Opt inter-route move is possible if $\Delta_{(DM,LE)} > 0$. In Figure 7, the 2-opt is employed between two routes, the arcs (DM) and (LE) are deleted and the arcs (DE) and (LM) are generated to connect the end of each route to the terminating part.

c. Insertion move

The insertion move is defined as follows: remove the customer C_i at position i from a vehicle route V and insert it to the position j in the same route. In case of $i<j$, $V' = \{C_1, C_2, C_3, ..., C_{i-1}, C_{i+1}, ..., C_j, C_i, C_{j+1}, ..., C_n\}$. In case of $i>j$, we get $V' = \{C_1, C_2, C_3, C_{j-1}, C_i, C_{j,...}, C_{i-1}, Ci_{+1}, ..., C_n\}$. Every possible insertion position is considered. To avoid evaluating an infeasible solution, one should verify if the sum of the pickup demands of the customer (Ci) is less than or equal to the rest of the vehicle capacity, and the quantity requested should be less than or equal to the remaining quantity in the vehicle. Otherwise, it means that moving the customer C_i from a position to the other one is infeasible.

To illustrate the insertion move, the customer D in Figure 7 is re-inserted in other positions in the vehicle route V′ in Fig. 8.

Figure 8. Insertion neighborhood structure in one route.

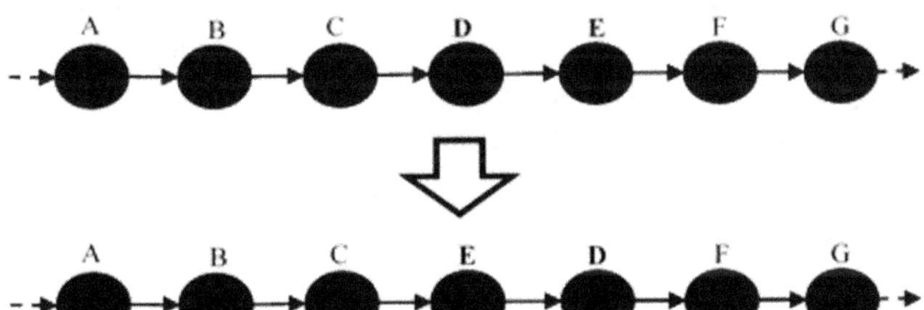

Insertion neighborhood is calculated as follows:

Let:

$\Delta_{(D)}$: The insertion move cost

Cost function: $C \mapsto \mathbb{R}^+$ and $x \mapsto C(x)$

$$S_V = \{AB, BC, CD, DE, EF, FG\}$$

$$S_{V'} = \{AB, BC, CE, ED, DF, FG\}$$

$$C_V = \sum_{x \in S_V} C(x)$$

$$C_{V'} = \sum_{x \in S_{V'}} C(x)$$

Therefore:

$$\Delta_{(D)} = C_{V'} - C_V$$

Where S_V is the set of initial arcs constituting the route V while $S_{V'}$ is the set of arcs constituting this vehicle after the insertion move (V'), and $C_V, C_{V'}$ are the cost of the route V before and after the insertion of customer D in the new position. An insertion is possible if $\Delta_{(D)} < 0$.

1.1.4. Perturbation Procedure

The diversification in the proposed resolution method is controlled by the perturbation of the solution. Larger perturbations and continuing search with an initial solution lead to stronger diversification. The perturbation phase is used in order to escape from local optimum. The pseudo-code of perturbation is presented below.

Table 2. Pseudocode of perturbation

```
i←0;
improve ←FALSE;
repeat
firstCustomer ← Random(n);
secondCustomer ← Random(n);
Exchange firstCustomer with secondCustomer;
Compute the cost savings ΔZ;
if ΔZ<0 then
if the solution is feasible then
improve← TRUE;
else
i:=i+1;
endelse
endif
endif
until (i = MaxIterPert) or (improve = TRUE)
end
```

We apply one intra-route exchange move. Two customers on the same route are selected randomly and then swapped. The algorithm starts with a small perturbation with *MaxIterPert* =2. If the move improves the solution, the perturbation is as soon stopped and the local search techniques are called. If the solution is not improved, the perturbation is increased by one. The perturbation mechanism is applied with a limited number of iterations denoted by *MaxIterPert* (Fig.9).

Figure 9. Perturbation procedure.

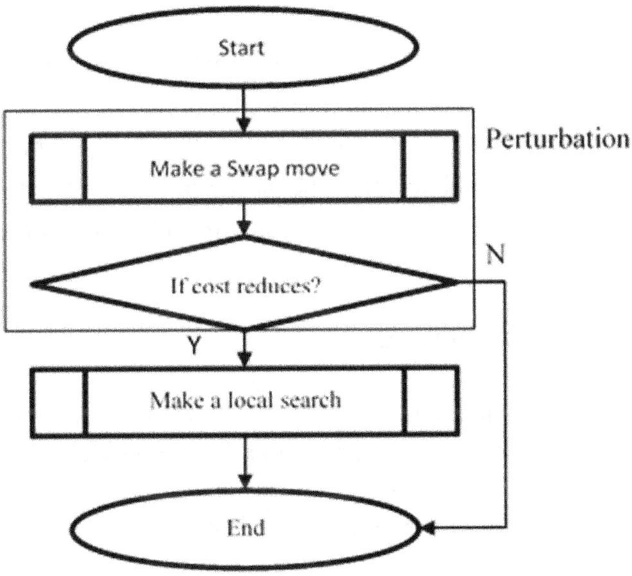

Perturbation cost criteria is calculated as follows:

Let:

$\Delta_{(i,j)}$: The perturbation cost (intra-route)
Cost function: $C \mapsto \mathbb{R}^+$ and $x \mapsto C(x)$

$$S_V = \{ij, \ldots, i_{n-1}j_{n-1}, i_n j_n\}$$

$$S_{V'} = \{ji, \ldots, i_{n-1}j_{n-1}, i_n j_n\}$$

$$C_V = \sum_{x \in S_V} C(x)$$

$$C_{V'} = \sum_{x \in S_{V'}} C(x)$$

Therefore:

$$\Delta_{(i,j)} = C_{V'} - C_V$$

Improve is true when $\Delta_{(i,j)} < 0$ and the solution is feasible, otherwise improve is false $\forall i, j \in S_V, i \neq j$.

Where S_V, is the set of initial arcs constituting the route V while $S_{V'}$ is the set of arcs constituting this vehicle after the perturbation (V'), and $C_V, C_{V'}$ are respectively the costs of the route V before and after the operation of perturbation of the two customers *(i,j)*.

1.2. Assignment - Pprocedure

In order to involve drones in the distribution of goods, the assignment procedure is employed until no possibilities are found, and all the routes are scanned.

The procedure starts by scanning route by route. In ach route, the algorithm search if there is the possibility of assigning a drone to a road.

Table 3. Pseudocode of drone-second

```
Liste_drones ←NULL;
S← { S_1, S_2, . . . , S_n }
s_n← { i, j, . . . , n }
fori:=1 to NumberOfVehiclesUsed do
forj:=1 to NumberOfCustomer do
if distance between two customers i and j ≤ drone's flight distance then
if weight of the goods transported to j ≤ drone's capacity then
Liste_drones←[i, j];
s_n← { i, j, . . . , n }- Liste_drones
else
Liste_drones=0;
Endfor
i:=i+1;
endfor
end
```

V. RESULTS

The results obtained in this study are shown in the following tables:

Table 4. problem's characteristics

Problem	**Number Of nodes (N)**	**Vehicle's capacity (Q)**	**Drone's capacity (Qd)**	**Percentage of delivery customers (%)**	**Percentage of pickup customers (%)**
Ins_1	*50*	*160*	*15*	*60*	*40*
Ins_2	*50*	*100*	*15*	*60*	*40*
Ins_3	*80*	*100*	*15*	*51.25*	*48.75*
Ins_4	*90*	*100*	*15*	*52.2*	*47.7*
Ins_5	*80*	*200*	*15*	*51.25*	*48.75*
Ins_6	*99*	*50*	*15*	*57.58*	*42.42*
Ins_7	*100*	*100*	*15*	*70*	*30*

In this table, the characteristics of each instance are presented.

Table 5. numerical results

Problem	**Time (s) before**	**Time (s) after**	**Number of vehicles used (K)**	**Number of drones used**	**Cost before using drones**	**Cost after using drones**
Ins_1	*15.962*	*11.078*	*4*	*4*	*554.48*	*384.80*
Ins_2	*28.477*	*14.213*	*7*	*7*	*690.30*	*307.90*
Ins_3	*16.986*	*14.852*	*15*	*12*	*1344.83*	*815.75*
Ins_4	*25.859*	*19.064*	*12*	*10*	*1222.80*	*703.55*
Ins_5	*17.363*	*15.847*	*7*	*7*	*878.09*	*477.63*
Ins_6	*18.061*	*21.065*	6	*4*	*13584.39*	*10744.71*
Ins_7	35.059	*38.56*	6	3	*1036,68*	*423.56*
Average	***22,5381429***	***19,2398571***			***2758,79571***	***1979,7***

This table shows that the use of drones and vehicles on practicable roads reduces the total cost. Therefore, it can be said that picking up and delivering some types of goods using the drone is a very important innovation.

In two cases of digital cases, the total service life for the use of drones is higher than when they are not in use. This increase due to the dispersal of customers who seems very distant. Despite this increase, the total cost of transport remains lower.

The difference between the use of just vehicles and the duo vehicle-drone is seen in the following figures:

Figure 10. The difference between the cost of transport with / without the use of the drone

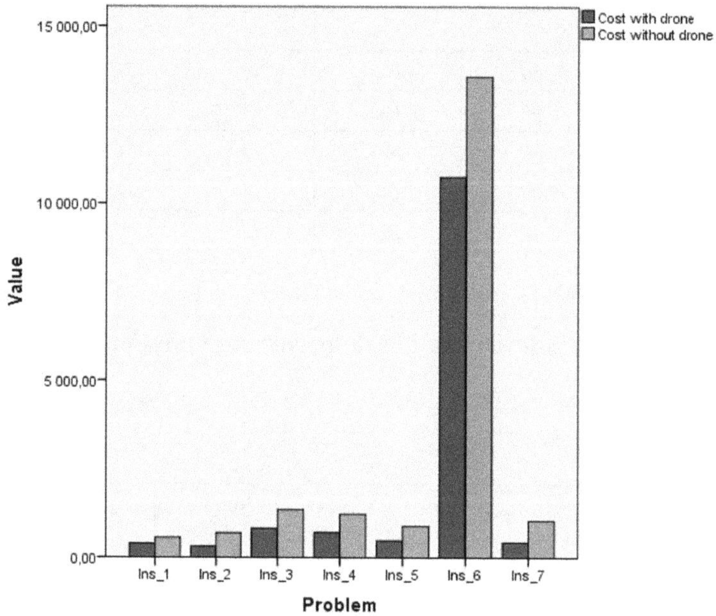

VI. CONCLUSIONS AND RESEARCH PERSPECTIVES

The use of vehicles equipped with drones for the delivery of certain types of goods already exists in some works, but the problem of distribution and pickup with dornes is a new variant.

To solve this problem, we proposed a vehicle-first drone-second algorithm. Considering the fixed and variable cost of vehicle and drone makes the problem more realistic. After analyzing the numerical results found, we have proved the importance of the integration of drones in the reduction of transport costs of some types of products and the avoidance of congestion. This technique of distribution may affect the general transportation system by minimizing the circulation time of goods and the number of vehicles traveling.

Figure 11. A presentation of transportation costs

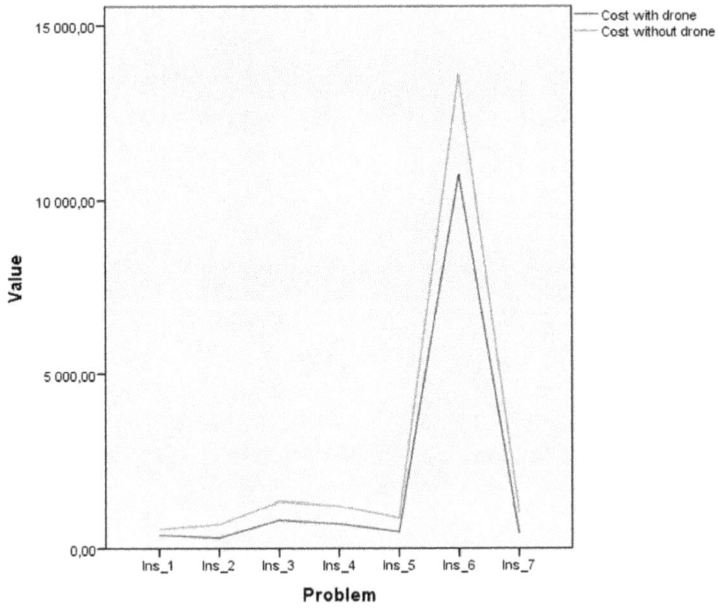

Figure 12. The difference between the execution time with / without the use of the drone

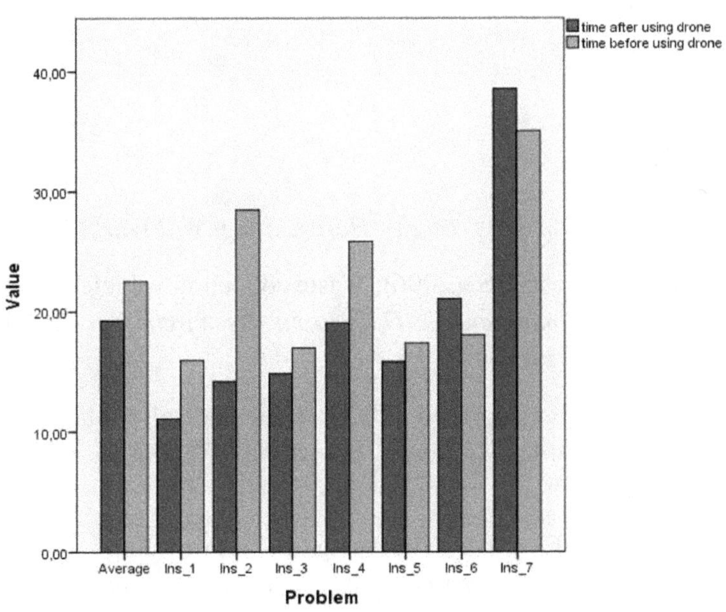

Figure 13. A presentation of the execution time

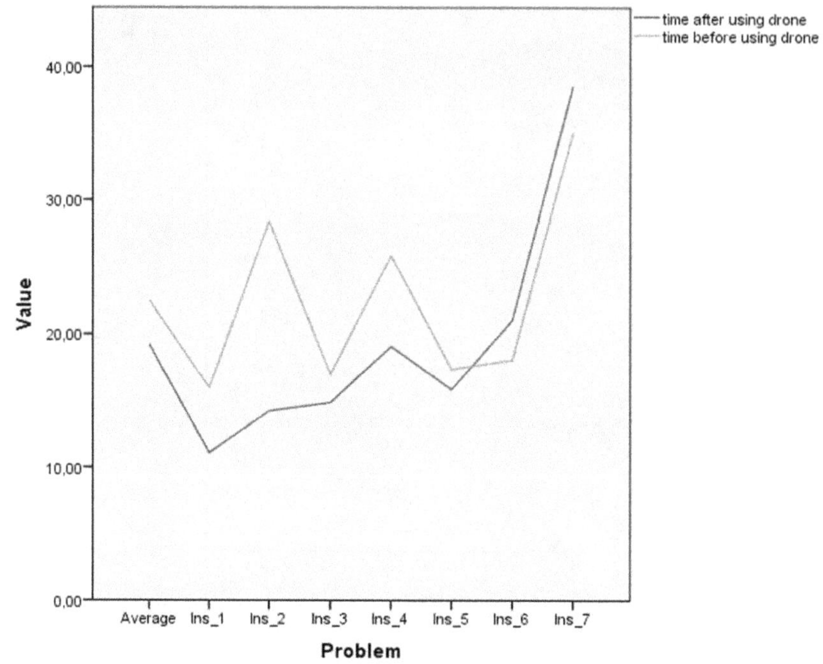

Future research will integrate the drone in the problem of pickup and delivery of some products when late arrival at the customers is allowed conditionally to pay a late penalty.

REFERENCES

Banker, S. (2013). *Amazon and Drones – Here is why it Will Work.* Academic Press.

Kim, B. I., Kim, S., & Sahoo, S. (2006). Waste collection vehicle routing problem with time windows. *Computers & Operations Research*, *33*(12), 3624–3642. doi:10.1016/j.cor.2005.02.045

Labadi, N., Prins, C., & Reghioui, M. (2008). A memetic algorithm for the vehicle routing problem with time windows. *Operations Research*, *42*(3), 415–431. doi:10.1051/ro:2008021

Murray, C. C., & Chu, A. G. (2015). The flying sidekick traveling salesman problem: Optimization of drone-assisted parcel delivery. *Transportation Research Part C, Emerging Technologies*, *54*, 86–109. doi:10.1016/j.trc.2015.03.005

Peng, K., Du, J., Lu, F., Sun, Q., Dong, Y., Zhou, P., & Hu, M. (2019). A hybrid genetic algorithm on routing and scheduling for vehicle-assisted multi-drone parcel delivery. *IEEE Access: Practical Innovations, Open Solutions*, *7*, 49191–49200. doi:10.1109/ACCESS.2019.2910134

Thiels, C. A., Aho, J. M., Zietlow, S. P., & Jenkins, D. H. (2015). Use of unmanned aerial vehicles for medical product transport. *Air Medical Journal*, *34*(2), 104–108. doi:10.1016/j.amj.2014.10.011 PMID:25733117

Wang, X., Poikonen, S., & Golden, B. (2017). The vehicle routing problem with drones: Several worst-case results. *Optimization Letters*, *11*(4), 679–697. doi:10.100711590-016-1035-3

Wohlsen, M. (2014). *The next big thing you missed: Amazon's delivery drones could work—they just need trucks*. http://www. wired. com/2014/06/the-nextbig-thing-you-missed-delivery-drones-launched-from-trucks-are-the-future-ofshipping/

Chapter 9
Forecasting Sales and Return Products for Retail Corporations and Bridging Among Them

Md Mushfique Hasnat Chowdhury
Department of Mechanical and Industrial Engineering, Ryerson University, Canada

Saman Hassanzadeh Amin
Department of Mechanical and Industrial Engineering, Ryerson University, Canada

ABSTRACT

The purpose of this study is to show how we can bridge sales and return forecasts for every product of a retail store by using the best model among several forecasting models. Managers can utilize this information to improve customer's satisfaction, inventory management, or re-define policy for after sales support for specific products. The authors investigate multi-product sales and return forecasting by choosing the best forecasting model. To this aim, some machine learning algorithms including ARIMA, Holt-Winters, STLF, bagged model, Timetk, and Prophet are utilized. For every product, the best forecasting model is chosen after comparing these models to generate sales and return forecasts. This information is used to classify every product as "profitable," "risky," and "neutral," The experiment has shown that 3% of the total products have been identified as "risky" items for the future. Managers can utilize this information to make some crucial decisions.

DOI: 10.4018/978-1-7998-3805-0.ch009

1. INTRODUCTION

Supply Chain Management (SCM) is a very fast-growing and largely studied field of research that is gaining popularity and importance (Meherishi et al., 2019). According to Mentzer et al., (2001), a supply chain is a collection of some elements that are connected by flows of products, information, and/or services. Most organizations focus on cost optimization and maintaining ideal inventory levels to keep consumer's satisfaction particularly in SCM of fresh products. Accurate demand forecasts enable industries to predict demand and maintain the right amount of inventory.

Machine Learning (ML) is a subset of Artificial Intelligence (AI). It enables machines for learning from the past data, experiences, and patterns to have correct forecast. Generally, ML means extracting knowledge about future behaviour from the older data. ML approaches mostly fall into three broad categories depending on the nature of the learning system including Supervised, Unsupervised, and Reinforcement Learning (RL). During a supervised learning, a large amount of labelled input data and desired output are provided for learning in the algorithms. In contrast, an unsupervised learning system uses only "unlabelled" input data for learning. Generally, unsupervised algorithms work with raw data for finding hidden patterns and achieve the best result. Reinforcement Learning (RL) is another subcategory of machine learning. RL interacts with a dynamic environment and utilizes trial and error technique to obtain a human-level performance. Besides of the three-fold categorisation, there is another classification which is called semi-supervised learning. In these algorithms usually small amounts of labelled data and large unlabelled data are utilized together.

Deep Learning is a subfield of ML where algorithms are inspired by the human brain to solve complex problems, learn from large amounts of very diverse, unstructured and inter-connected data sets. These algorithmic approaches have various layers (deep) to enable learning. Deep architectures can be supervised or unsupervised. This biologically-inspired programming paradigm currently provides the best solutions to many real-life problems such as image and video processing, speech recognition, text analysis, natural language processing, and different types of classifiers. Deep learning techniques are novel and useful methods for obtaining accurate forecasts in SCM. However, diverse deep learning techniques perform differently on different types of problems, and some techniques perform better than the others.

In this study, the main aim is to predict the unit sales of thousands of items sold at different chain stores in Ecuador to avoid overstocking, minimize understocking, reduce waste and loss, and increase customer's satisfaction. In this case, good predictions are highly desirable to increase efficiency and determine the prices of products for customers. In this investigation, Corporación Favorita Grocery Sales Forecasting dataset is collected from Kaggle website for forecasting the product sales accurately. Three diverse deep learning methods including Artificial Neural Network (ANN), Convolutional Neural Network (CNN), and Long Short Term Memory (LSTM) are used to build and train the predictive models. In these models, different parameters and weights are used to forecast the unit sales. In this work, some open-source data science tools and Python and packages are used. Furthermore, Mean Squared Error (MSE) and Root Mean Squared Error (RMSE) are adopted as the two indicators for evaluating and comparing the models. The results show that LSTM performs better than ANN and CNN for forecasting the sales units in this case.

This book chapter is structured as follows. Section 2 includes a literature review about some approaches related to this field. Section 3 describes the exploratory analysis of the data, and Section 4 focuses on the systems and the experiment. The obtained results from the experiment are included in Section 5. Finally, conclusions and future research are provided in Section 6. Figure 1(a) represents artificial intelligence, machine learning, and deep learning together. In addition, Figure 1(b) shows the categories of machine learning.

Figure 1. (a) Artificial Intelligence versus Machine Learning versus Deep Learning, (b) the categories of Machine Learning

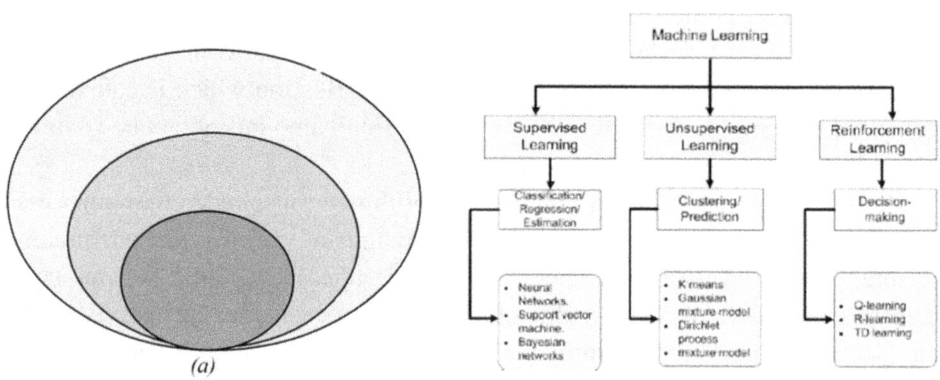

(a) *(b)*

2. LITERATURE REVIEW

Machine and deep learning techniques play important roles in forecasting demands in SCM and logistics fields. This section contains the earlier studies related to this research and an overview of the related articles.

The investigations done by Kohonen (1990), Leung (1995), Kaylani et al. (2010), and Chang et al. (2011) have shown that ANNs have been potentially suitable, very effective, and significantly better for all supply chain forecasting activities. Al-Saba and El-Amin (1999) used ANN for forecasting the annual peak demand for electricity. Chao-ting et al. (2000) used recurrent neural networks for demand forecasting of inventory management to reduce uncertainty and summarized the applications of neural networks in SCM including optimization, prediction modeling, decision support processes, simulation modelling, and management systems. Zhikai and Ge (2002) combined data mining and knowledge discovery, and developed some neural networks forecasting models to investigate the impact of supply chain performance. Choy et al. (2003) showed the importance of selecting proper techniques for forecasting in SCM. Beccali et al. (2004) used an integrated solution of supervised and unsupervised neural networks for the electric energy short or long-term demand forecasting of a residential area. Pai and Lin (2005), and Campbell and Ying (2011) addressed some limitations using a simple neural network, and used combined hybrid models to compare the performances.

Aburto and Weber (2007) developed an integrated intelligent system for demand forecasting which has been combined with neural networks and autoregressive integrated moving average models. They presented an inventory management system for a Chilean supermarket. The results showed improvements in forecasting accuracy including fewer sales failures and lower inventory levels than Chilean supermarket's previous solution. Moreover, the authors proposed a replenishment system.

Kochak and Sharma (2015) presented a new investigation using ANN algorithms (Forward and Backward Propagation NN), and observed the influence and performance of product demand forecasting. In addition, they identified the best training method to predict the next year's consumption. To train the models, the monthly sales data of a fuel filter distributor between 2011 and 2013 have been used as inputs and outputs. They considered the base year data of 2011 in 12th month and 2012 data in 12th month to predict 2012 and 2013 as target data and to calculate the forecasting error and forecasting data of 2014. Their results indicated that the train Levenberg-Marquardt method performed better and was more reliable than the other used methods. They utilized MATLAB 7.0 for simulation. Gaur et al. (2015) introduced a close comparison between Nearest Neighbor method and Bayesian Networks using the confusion matrix as a performance metric. A dataset from Walmart including 1,200 tuples and 35 attributes have been used in this investigation. The authors concluded that the Bayesian Networks technique performed better than K-neighbors in detecting relations in the dataset for demand prediction in the supply chain.

Bousqaoui et al. (2017) examined multiple algorithms of machine learning, and explored their applications for various supply chain processes. Their research started with collecting data from ScienceDirect database using some keywords such as linear regression, machine learning, and deep learning. They selected 42 papers that have been published after 2010. In their paper, Support Vector Machines, Gamma Classifier models, Decision Trees, K-means Algorithms, Random Forests, Linear Regression, Hyperbox Classifier, and Neural Network techniques and the related papers have been examined. Their analysis showed that the most used technique was Neural Network followed by Support Vector Machines and Linear Regression.

There are some limitations in accurate demand forecasting. For instance, it requires a large amount of data to guarantee a correct prediction. In addition, non-linear patterns are difficult to capture, and the estimation of the model parameters can be biased by the outliers. Neural Networks are widely used in demand forecasting because they overcome many of these limitations. Huang and Hou (2017) proposed an ANN model combined with Genetic Algorithm (GA) for demand forecasting in the tourism industry. The GA was used to determine the hidden nodes of a feedforward neural network. The results showed that a reliable prediction has been obtained in that case study.

Three ANN models have been developed for forecasting the demand of different types of parts produced by a gear manufacturing company by Bhadouria and Jayant (2017). They provided a comparative analysis of different ANN models and various traditional forecasting methods like moving average, exponential smoothing, and weighted moving average method based on the obtained results of applying forecasting models. MATLAB 16 and various backpropagation algorithms available in MATLAB ANN toolbox were used for neural network implementation. Their results illustrated that the ANN model with TANSIGMOID transfer function is far better and more accurate than ANN model with LOGSIGMOID and LINEAR and transfer function in terms of Mean Absolute Deviation (MAD), MAPE, and MSE. Kaya and Turkyilmaz (2018) proposed Ad hoc intermittent methods for forecasting demand which considered special intermittent demand features using ANNs, decision tree methods, and support vector regressions. They utilized R programming in this investigation. Based on their study, the Support Vector Machine was the best method among the others in terms of performance.

The closest approach to this book chapter has been proposed by Mupparaju et al., (2008) where they built Factorization Machines, Gradient Boosting, and three variations of Deep Neural Networks (DNN) predictive models to predict demand of grocery items applying Python's deep learning library. In addition, they investigated the impact of categorical embedding layers and sequence-to-sequence type architecture on the forecasted demand. In general, their best neural network model is a final neural network model (NN3) with embedding layers and seq2seq meta, and that model also runs in an acceptable amount of time. Our methods and datasets are different from the mentioned paper.

3. EXPLORATORY ANALYSIS

In this research, the Corporación Favorita Grocery Sales Forecasting dataset for accurately forecasting product sales is collected from Kaggle website (Corporación Favorita Grocery Sales Forecasting, 2019). The data contain the unit sales for thousands of items sold at different Favorita stores located in Ecuador. The data files include test.csv, train.csv, stores.csv, items.csv, transaction.csv, oil.csv, and holidays_events.csv.

The important columns between each data table include (train.csv, Variable:Id, Type:Integer, Description:Identifier defined at the date-store-item-promotion level), (train.csv, Variable:Unit_Sales, Type:Numeric, Description:Sales defined at the date-store-item-promotion level), (transaction.csv, Variable:Date, Type:Date, Description:Date of transaction for an item), (stores.csv, Variable:Store_Nbr, Type:Integer, Description:Store identifier), (items.csv, Variable:Item_Nbr, Type:Integer, Description: Item identifier), (train.csv, Variable:Onpromotion, Type:Boolean, Description:Whether the item is on promotion), (stores.csv, Variable:City, Type:Text, Description:City in which store is located), (stores.csv, Variable:State, Type:Text, Description - State in which store is located), (holidays_events.csv, Variable:Type, Type:Text, Description:internal store categorization), (stores.csv, Variable:Cluster, Type:Integer, Description:internal store clustering), (items.csv, Variable:Family, Type:Text, Description:The family of item), (items.csv, Variable:Class, Type:Text, Description:Class of items), (items.csv, Variable:Perishable, Type:Boolean, Description:Whether the item is perishable). Figure 2 represents the Entity Relationship Diagram (ERD) of the data which is helpful to see the relations at a glance.

3.1. Train and Test

The primary dataset train.csv contains 125 million observations which are the most basic sales data from January 1, 2013 to August 15, 2017. The training data file contains 125,497,040 rows and 6 columns (i.e., row id, date, store number, item number, unit sales, and onpromotion).

Unit sales columns values can be integer or float number, where -1 represents a returned item. The onpromotion column represents whether a particular item is on promotion or not on promotion for a specified date and store_nbr. Since the training set is so large, only 23,808,261 rows among 125,497,040 rows of training.csv file from January 1, 2017 to August 15, 2017 are used for data exploratory analysis and experiment.

Figure 2. Entity Relationship Diagram (ERD)

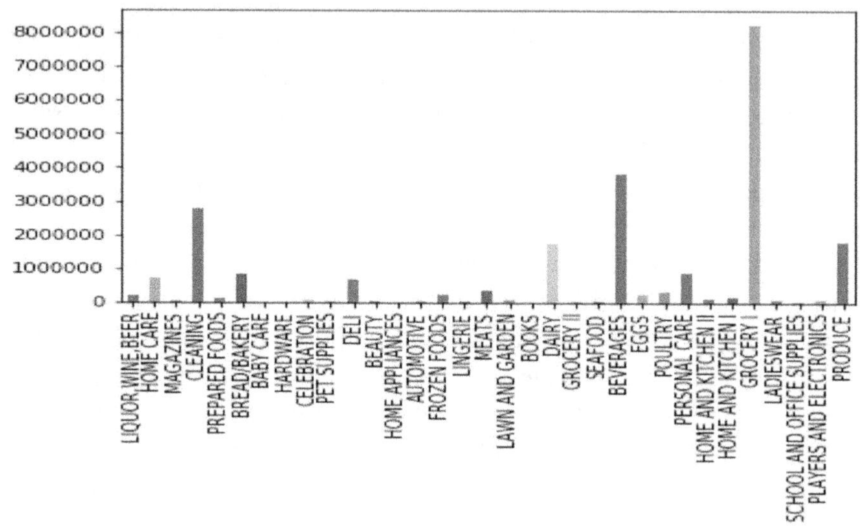

The test.csv file structure is similar to the train dataset; however, the only difference is the lack of unit sales column. The test data is related to July 16 to July 31, 2017 which contains 3,370,464 rows and 5 columns. Figure 3 and Figure 4 show the data structure of train.csv and test.csv data files, respectively.

Figure 3. Data types and columns of train.csv

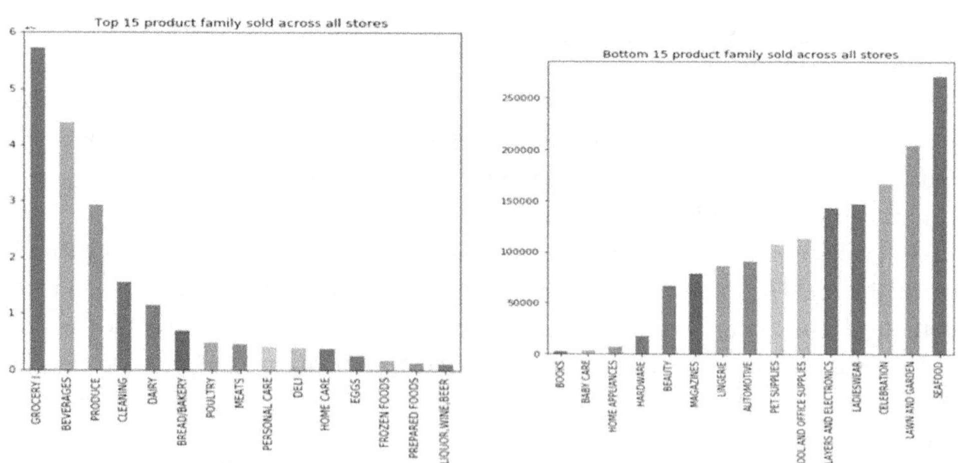

(a) (b)

The columns of training and test are checked for any null or missing values (see Figure 5). Figure 5(a) shows that approximately 17% of the train dataset "onpromotion" variables are missing and shows the NaN values. However, the training dataset of 2017 used in this work has no missing data which is shown in Figure 5(b). In Figure 5(c), it is clear that the test dataset has no missing value.

Figure 4. Data types and columns of test.csv

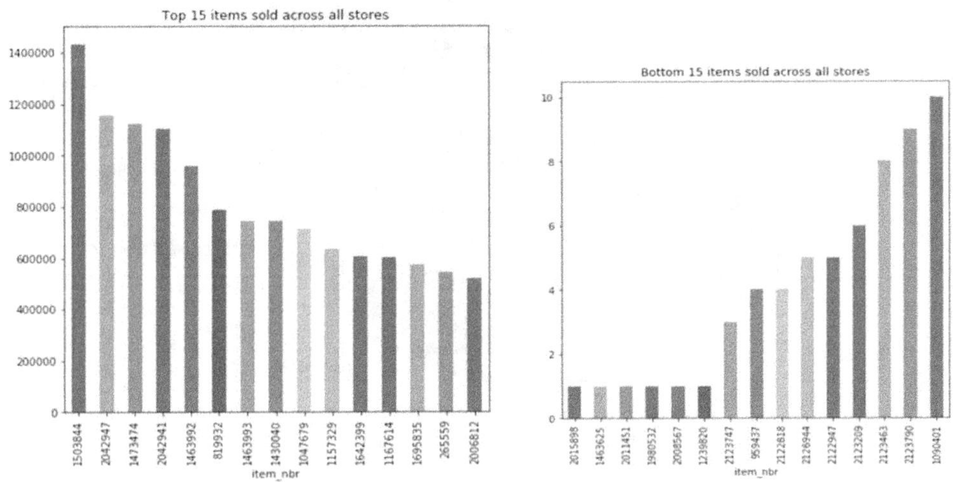

(a) (b)

Figure 6 includes two parts. Figure 6(a) shows how the train observations are distributed by month. The chart is almost uniformly distributed by months of 2017. The maximum observations are in May and July, and the minimum observations are in August. Figure 6(b) represents the train observations distributed by day which is also almost uniformly distributed. The test observations are distributed by year, month, and day in Figure 7.

3.2. Items

In items.csv, there are not too many attributes. The attributes include item id, family, class, and whether the specific item is perishable or not. The "item_nbr" attribute is unique which indicates specific grocery items. Figure 8(a) shows the data structure of items.csv data, and that items file contains 4,100 rows and 4 columns. There is no missing value in the data which is shown in Figure 8(b). In the training dataset, 4,018 unique variety of items are available during 2017 and in the test dataset, the

Figure 5. (a) Full training data, (b) 1 January - 15 August 2017, (c) Null values test

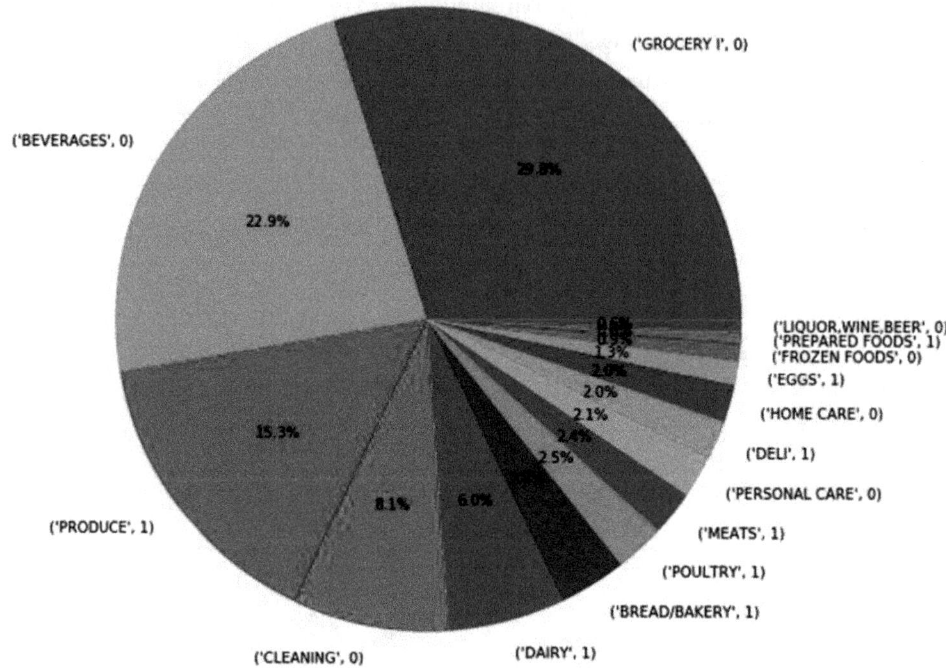

(a)

different types of items are 3,901. After joining the items.csv with the training.csv data, the data structure is visualized in Figure 9.

The available different item families can be visualized in Figure 10. In addition, the top and the bottom 15 sold item families are shown in Figure 11(a) and Figure 11(b), respectively. The top sold product family is "GROCERY I", and the bottom one is "BOOKS".

After joining the items.csv with the training.csv data, the top and the bottom 15 sold items across all stores are shown in Figure 12(a) and Figure 12(b), respectively. The percentages of top and bottom 15 sold items family are visualized respectively in Figure 13(a) and Figure 13(b).

3.3. Stores

From Figure 14, it is found that the stores.csv data file contains 54 rows and 5 columns. There are 54 stores which are presented using a unique attribute "store_nbr" and "cluster" attribute indicating the store groups. There is no missing value in the data.

Figure 6. (a) Train data distribution by month, (b) Train data distribution by day

	store_nbr	city	state	type	cluster
0	1	Quito	Pichincha	D	13
1	2	Quito	Pichincha	D	13
2	3	Quito	Pichincha	D	8
3	4	Quito	Pichincha	D	9
4	5	Santo Domingo	Santo Domingo de los Tsachilas	D	4

Figure 7. (a). The data distribution by year, (b). The data distribution by month, (c) The data distribution by day

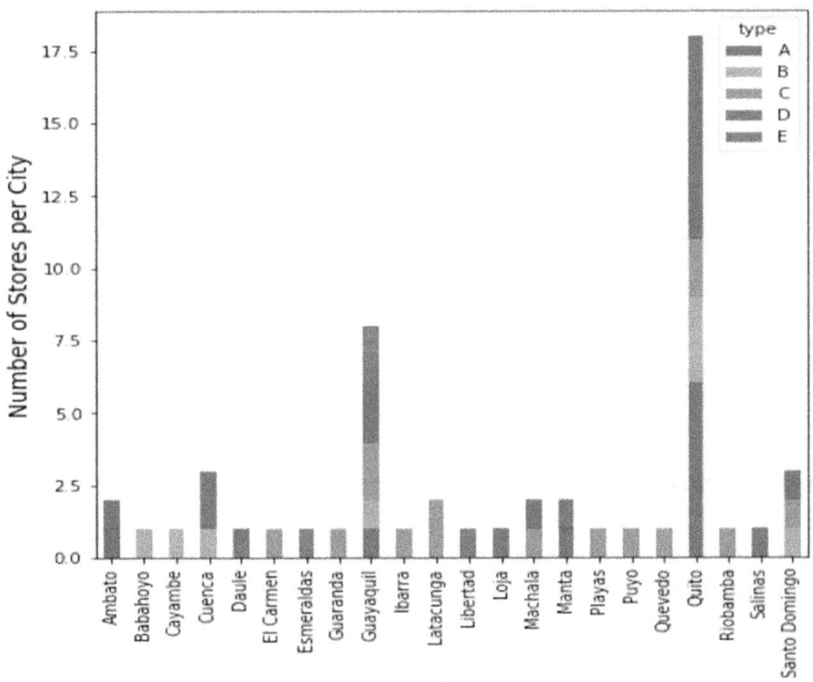

There are five types of stores. Figure 15 and Figure 16 show the store types distributed across different cities and the store types distributed across different states, respectively. Two cities (Guayaquil and Quito) have all the variety of store types as well as the largest counts of store_nbrs attributed in those two cities. Figure 17 shows the relationships between the store types and the clusters. The store type

Figure 8. (a). Data types and columns of items.csv, (b) Items data null values

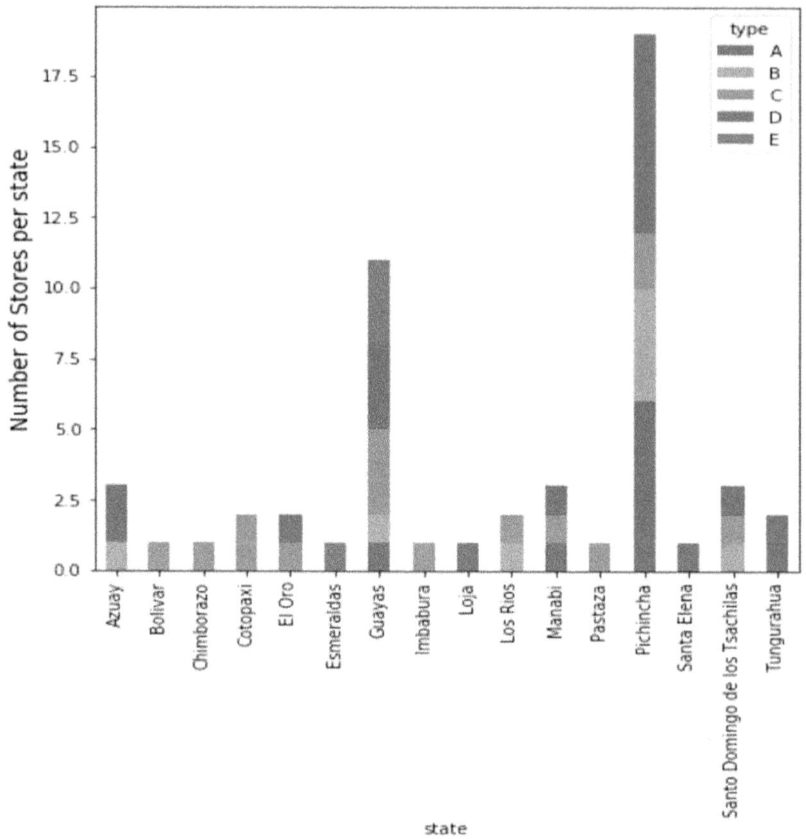

"D" contains a mix of the clusters, whereas only type "E" has a single cluster of Clusters 10.

3.4. Holiday Events

The "holiday_events.csv" file contains the data of the national, regional, and local levels of Ecuador, where the "transferred" column is important. Figure 18 shows the data structure of items.csv file. No missing value is available in the data shown in Figure 19. In Figure 20 and Figure 21, we see that the most of the types of holidays are actually "holiday" followed by "Additional" and "Event". In addition, there are very few "regional" events, and most of the events are not transferred.

Figure 9. Data types and columns after joining the items.csv with the training.csv data

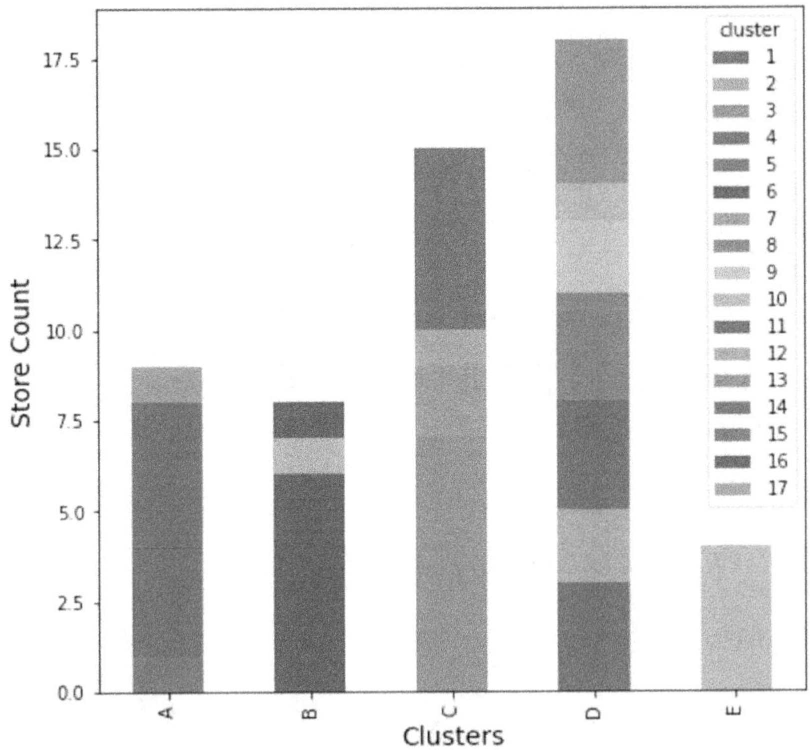

Figure 10. Different item families

	date	type	locale	locale_name	description	transferred
0	2012-03-02	Holiday	Local	Manta	Fundacion de Manta	False
1	2012-04-01	Holiday	Regional	Cotopaxi	Provincializacion de Cotopaxi	False
2	2012-04-12	Holiday	Local	Cuenca	Fundacion de Cuenca	False
3	2012-04-14	Holiday	Local	Libertad	Cantonizacion de Libertad	False
4	2012-04-21	Holiday	Local	Riobamba	Cantonizacion de Riobamba	False

3.5. Oil

Figure 22(a) and Figure 22(b) show the data structure and the missing values of oil. csv data file. In addition, Figure 23 displays the change of oil in price over time, which seems that the oil price has a decreasing trend from January 2013 to July 2017. In the middle of 2014, there was a drastic drop in the price of oil.

Figure 11. (a) Top 15 item families sold, (b) Bottom 15 item families sold

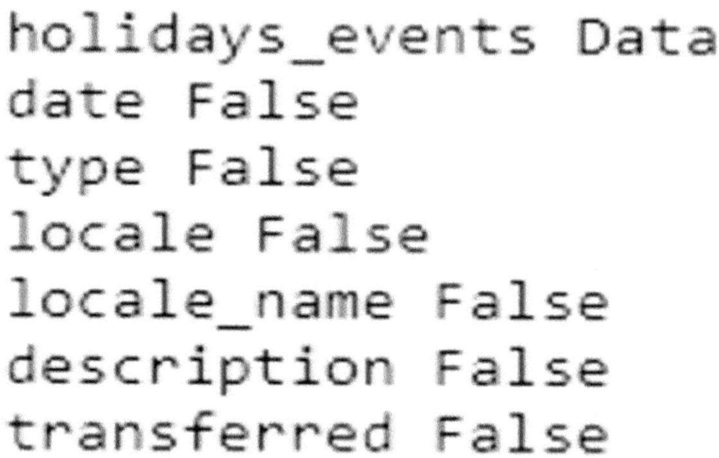

Figure 12. (a) Top 15 sold items, (b) Bottom 15 sold items

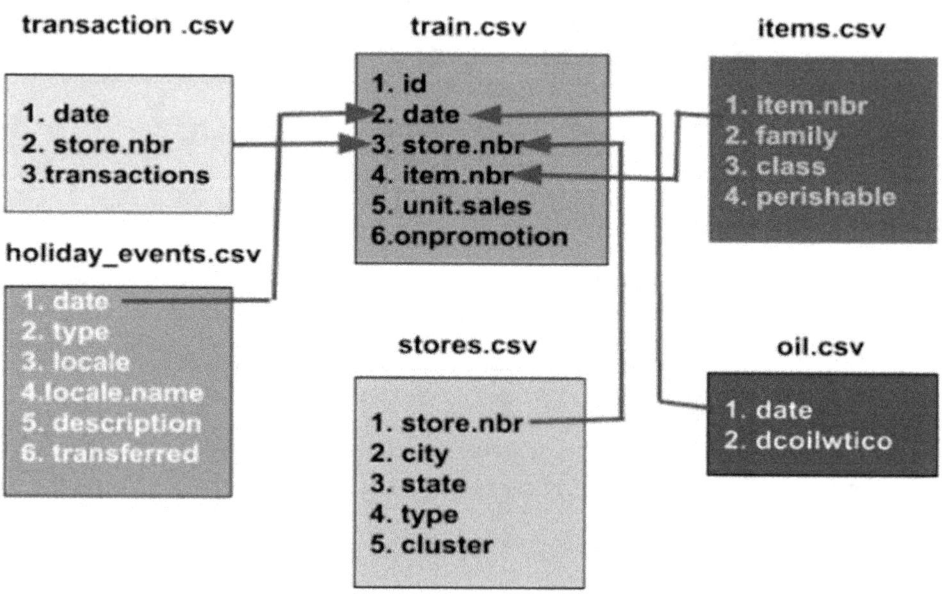

Figure 13. (a) Sold top 15 item family's ratio, (b) Sold bottom 15 item family's ratio

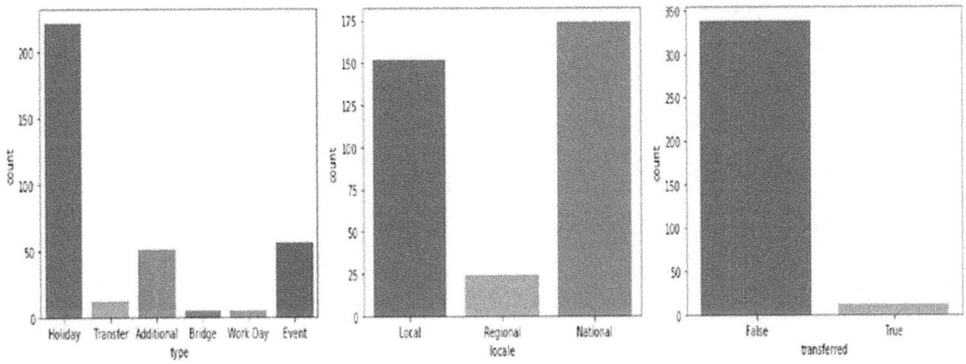

Figure 14. Datatypes and columns of items.csv

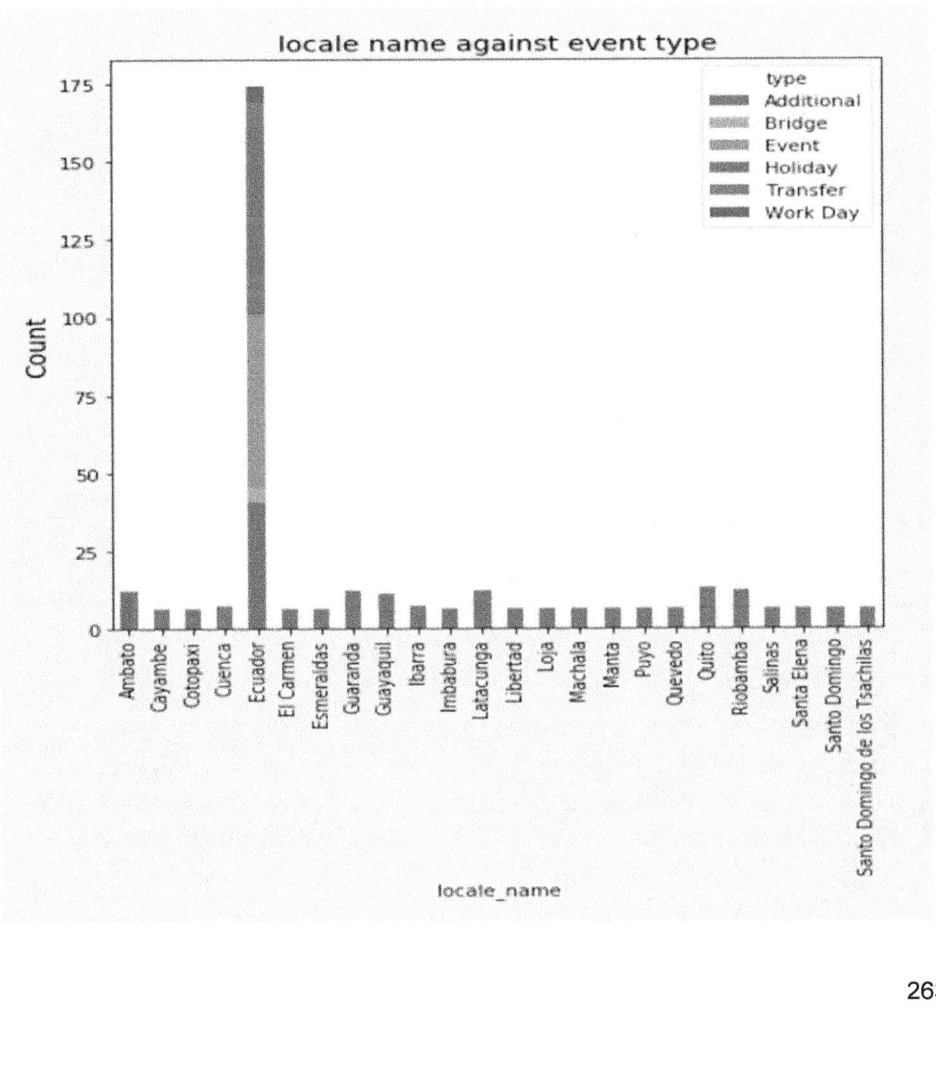

Figure 15. Number of stores and types distributed across different cities

	date	dcoilwtico
0	2013-01-01	NaN
1	2013-01-02	93.14
2	2013-01-03	92.97
3	2013-01-04	93.12
4	2013-01-07	93.20

(a)

```
Oil Data
date False
dcoilwtico True
```

(b)

Figure 16. Number of stores and types distributed across different states

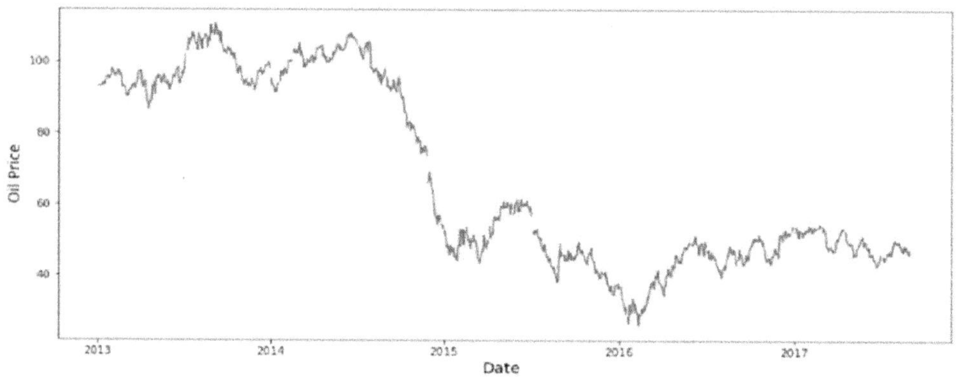

Figure 17. Store types according to the cluster distribution

	date	store_nbr	transactions
0	2013-01-01	25	770
1	2013-01-02	1	2111
2	2013-01-02	2	2358
3	2013-01-02	3	3487
4	2013-01-02	4	1922

(a)

```
transactions Data
date False
store_nbr False
transactions False
```

(b)

Figure 18. Data types and columns of holiday_events.csv

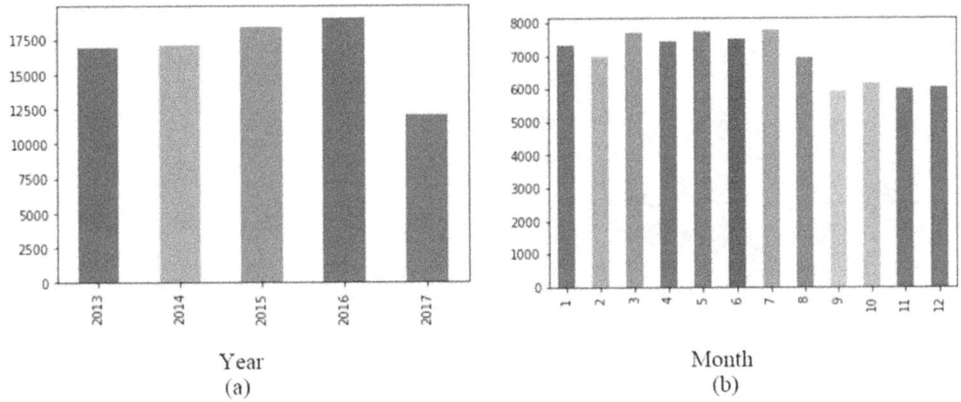

Figure 19. Missing value of holiday_ events.csv

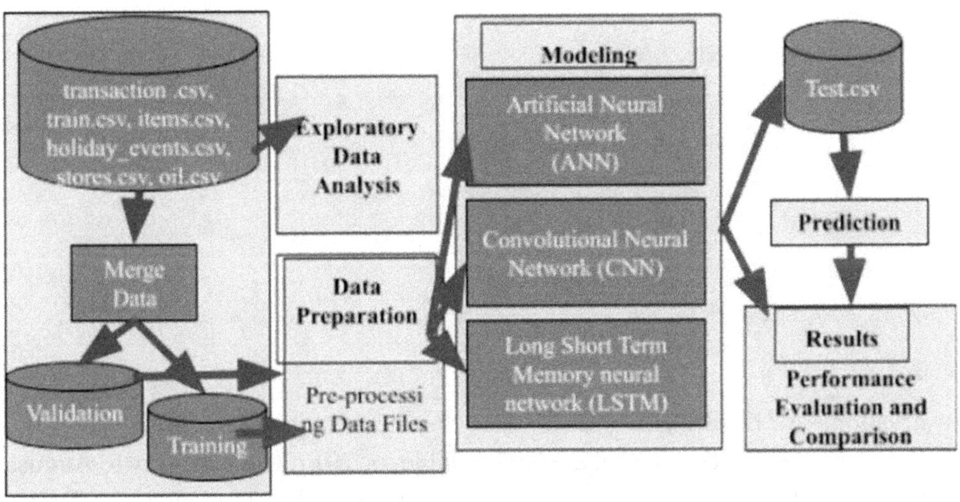

3.6. Transactions

In the transaction.csv file, there are 83,488 observations and three columns (i.e., date, store number, and the number of transactions). Figure 24(a) shows the data structure of the data file. No missing value is available in the data which is shown in Figure 24(b).

The transaction data are only available for the training set which counts the number of transactions in each store in each business day. Figure 25 represents the transactions data distributed by year, month, and day. Figure 25(a) shows that the

Figure 20. Subplot of type, locate, and transferred

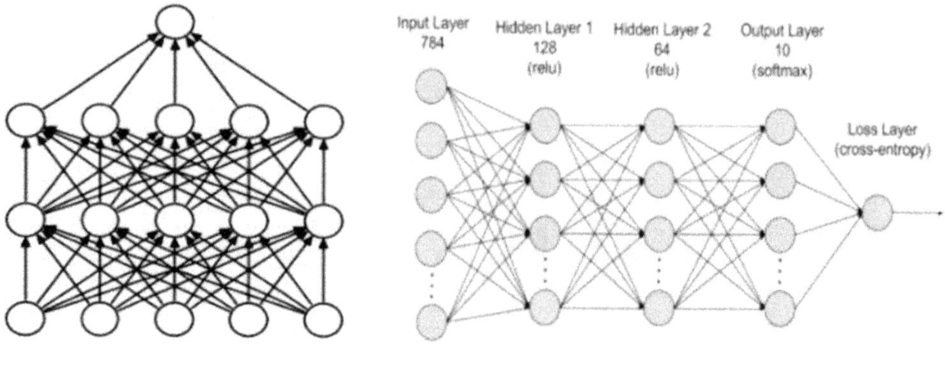

Figure 21. Holiday_events count based on the location

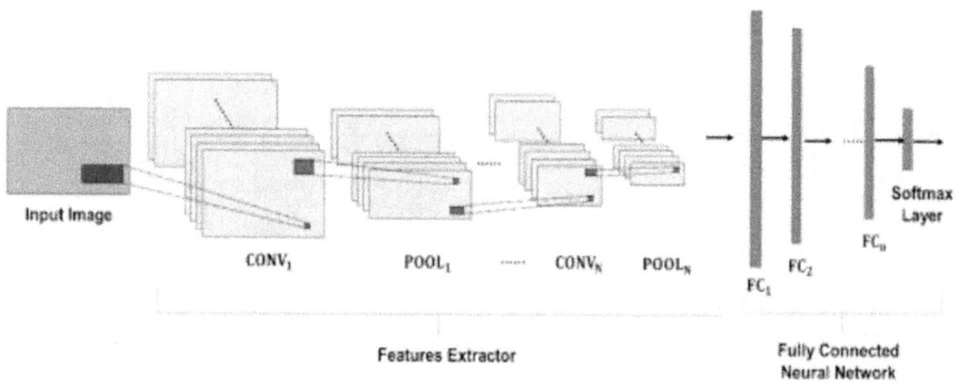

observations are from 2013 to 2017 with the increasing observations except for 2017. It is noticeable that partial data is available for 2017, from January to August. Figure 25(b) illustrates that the transactions are mostly related to January to August rather than the other months of the year which are cooler months. Figure 25(c) displays that the transactions data are distributed by day, which is almost uniformly distributed. The distribution of the observations is low at the 1st and 25th days of the month due to the New Year and Christmas times. Furthermore, 31st days of the month observations are minimum because some months have 31 days.

Figure 22. (a) Data types and columns of oil.csv, (b) Null values of oil.csv

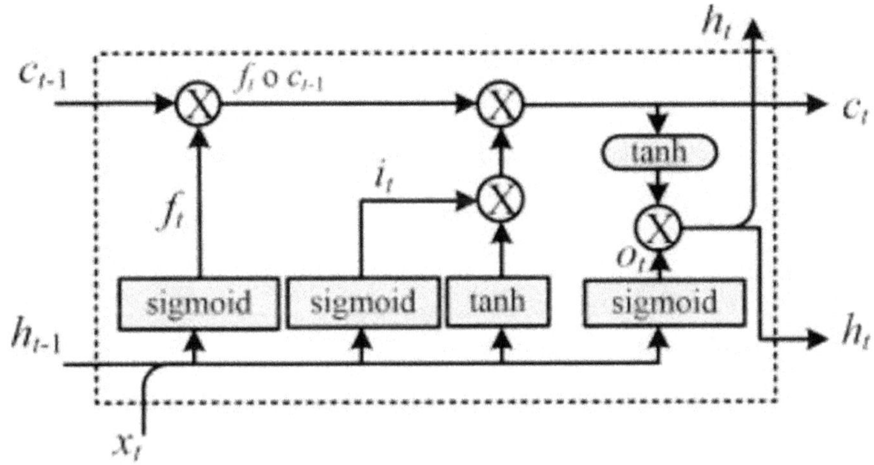

Figure 23. The change of oil price over time

	id	date	store_nbr	item_nbr	unit_sales	onpromotion
0	0	2013-01-01	25	103665	7.0	NaN
1	1	2013-01-01	25	105574	1.0	NaN
2	2	2013-01-01	25	105575	2.0	NaN
3	3	2013-01-01	25	108079	1.0	NaN
4	4	2013-01-01	25	108701	1.0	NaN

4. METHODOLOGY AND EXPERIMENT

The main aim of this research is to forecast the unit sales of thousands of items sold at different chain stores located in Ecuador to avoid overstocking, minimize understocking, reduce waste and loss, and increase customer satisfaction. In this research, good predictions are highly desirable because the chain stores can increase their efficiency and determine the prices of products for customers accurately. The training data is provided where stores, items, and dates information are given including the promoted items and unit sales. Some supplementary information is provided to avoid complexity and enhance the forecasting process.

Figure 24. (a) Data types and columns of transaction, (b) Null values of transaction

```
_________________________________________________________________
Layer (type)                 Output Shape              Param #
=================================================================
dense_30 (Dense)             (None, 64)                256
_________________________________________________________________
dropout_17 (Dropout)         (None, 64)                0
_________________________________________________________________
dense_31 (Dense)             (None, 16)                1040
_________________________________________________________________
dropout_18 (Dropout)         (None, 16)                0
_________________________________________________________________
dense_32 (Dense)             (None, 1)                 17
=================================================================
Total params: 1,313
Trainable params: 1,313
Non-trainable params: 0
_________________________________________________________________
```

Figure 25. (a) Transactions distribution by year, (b) Transactions distribution by month, (c) Transactions distribution by day

```
_________________________________________________________________
Layer (type)                 Output Shape              Param #
=================================================================
conv1d_5 (Conv1D)            (None, 1, 64)             256
_________________________________________________________________
max_pooling1d_2 (MaxPooling1 (None, 1, 64)             0
_________________________________________________________________
flatten_4 (Flatten)          (None, 64)                0
_________________________________________________________________
dense_4 (Dense)              (None, 50)                3250
_________________________________________________________________
dense_5 (Dense)              (None, 1)                 51
=================================================================
Total params: 3,557
Trainable params: 3,557
Non-trainable params: 0
_________________________________________________________________
```

In this study, the explored forecasting models are Artificial Neural Network (ANN), Convolutional Neural Network (CNN), and Long Short Term Memory Neural Network (LSTM). Besides, dropout layer is used for ANN and LSTM to increase the effectiveness and the speed of learning. In this research, a comparative study is performed on the performances of the models based on predictive accuracy, runtime, scalability, and ease of use. The methodology of this experiment is outlined in Figure 26.

Figure 26. The workflow of the experiment

```
Layer (type)                 Output Shape              Param #
=================================================================
lstm_1 (LSTM)                (None, 32)                4608
_________________________________________________________________
dropout_19 (Dropout)         (None, 32)                0
_________________________________________________________________
dense_33 (Dense)             (None, 32)                1056
_________________________________________________________________
dropout_20 (Dropout)         (None, 32)                0
_________________________________________________________________
dense_34 (Dense)             (None, 1)                 33
=================================================================
Total params: 5,697
Trainable params: 5,697
Non-trainable params: 0
_________________________________________________________________
```

4.1. Preliminaries

This research is started by understanding the business's features of real-life problems such as "Oil Price", and "Holidays". The external factors affect the demand of products particularly the perishable goods. The data files of this investigation are pre-processed (e.g., the null values of promotion, holidays, and oil data files are taken care of). The exploratory data analysis has been performed on the data as was described in the previous section. The following subsections provide backgrounds on ANN, LSTM, and CNN.

4.1.1. Artificial Neural Network (ANN)

ANNs are information processing structures that simulate the behavior of the human's brain (Martín and Sanz Molina, 2006). An artificial neural network is a highly connected array of neurons (Park et al., 1991). ANN usually is a network combined of a large number of massively interconnected neurons (simple processors) with each other in an organized fashion by defining weights, and which can operate in parallel and learn from previous examples (Specht, 1991). Simple processors called neurons process input information and convert inputs into reliable outputs (Zhang, 2004). In this research, ANN is proposed for predicting unit sales, as this approach has several advantages for predictive analytics. This technique produces a better and more reliable classification for large volumes of data. In addition, it handles complex underlying relationships, and it is very reliable and not very sensitive to the outliers. Besides, it is very strong for interpolation (Kumar et al., 1995).

Different neural networks have been proposed for different applications. Among them, the feed-forward neural network is the most popular one. A typical neural network involves three layers including input layer, hidden layer, and output layer (Sharma et al., 2013). The input layer comprises independent variables that are used to generate the output layer. It consists of a dependent variable to forecast the sales unit. The network which does not contain any hidden layer is called a single-layer perceptron. Neural networks that include multiple layers for interacting neurons through weighted connections are called Multilayer Perceptron (MLP) networks. A simple architecture of multilayer perceptron is shown in Figure 27.

Figure 27. A simple architecture of Multilayer Perceptron (MLP) (Madan, 2017)

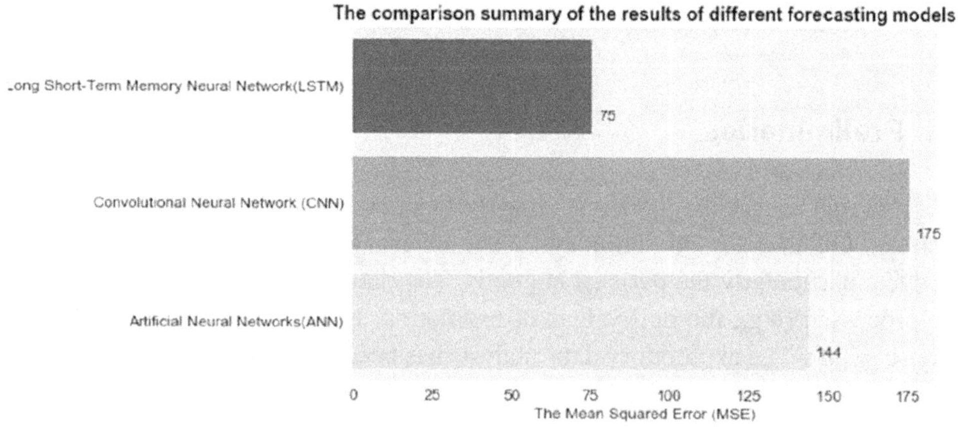

4.1.2. Convolutional Neural Network (CNN)

CNN is a special kind of deep learning method which has been used for processing highly correlated data with a grid topology (LeCun and Bengio, 1995). CNN is effective for dealing with high-dimensional data, and has been successfully applied for the visual image classification, video and text categorization (Bengio et al., 2017). A convolutional neural network architecture has an input, an output, and multiple hidden layers. The hidden layers classically have a series of convolution layers composed by a set of neurons completely independent in a single layer and fully connected to all neurons in the previous layer. The Convo (Convo + RELU) layer is a feature extractor layer where ReLU activation is a popular activation function to make all negative value to zero, followed by additional hidden layers such as pooling layer, fully connected (FC) layer, softmax or logistic layer, and output layer. Figure 28 shows the CNN architecture (Morabito et al., 2019). A pooling

Figure 28. CNN architecture (Morabito et al., 2019)

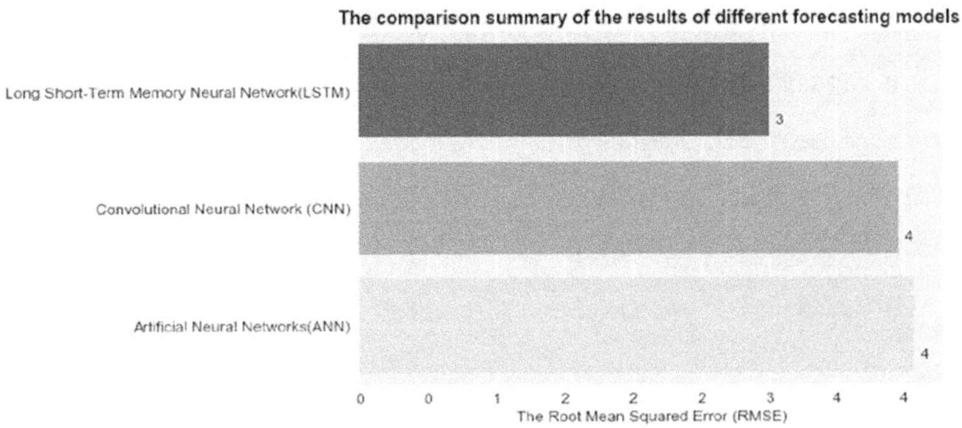

technique is applied to get another version of smaller input than the original size. A new convolutional layer followed by pooling layer steps can be repeated as many times as needed depending on the problem. Finally, when the layers become small enough, the process is completed.

4.1.3. Long Short Term Memory Neural Network (LSTM)

The Long Short Term Memory Neural Network (LSTM) is similar to the Recurrent Neural Network (RNN) which was developed by Hochreiter and Schmidhuber (1997). RNN structure is similar to the Multilayer Perceptron (MLP), but the main difference is that RNN considers feedback connections to reflect the previous states output and the current input to generate the output. The main advantage of LSTM over RNN is to avoid the long-term dependency problem and remove/add information to the units' state over longer periods of time.

The detailed architecture of LSTM is shown in Figure 29. The key idea of LSTM is to regulate the flow of information using different internal mechanisms called gates (e.g., input, forget, and output gates). These gates can carry relevant information throughout the process. They can learn and decide which data in a sequence chain is important to keep or throw away during the training process. Based on Figure 29, the state of each LSTM's cell (ct-1) passes through the LSTM module to generate a state for the next step (ct).

Figure 29. The detailed architecture of LSTM (Jiang et al., 2018)

	id	date	store_nbr	item_nbr	onpromotion
0	125497040	2017-08-16	1	96995	False
1	125497041	2017-08-16	1	99197	False
2	125497042	2017-08-16	1	103501	False
3	125497043	2017-08-16	1	103520	False
4	125497044	2017-08-16	1	103665	False

4.2. Experiment

In this study, we try to keep the algorithm as simple as possible to obtain maximum reproducibility. The multilayer perceptron architecture is utilized which is a fully connected network with two layers. Furthermore, to increase the effectiveness and stability and learning, dropping out units (hidden and visible) are used in the neural network. Because of this process, each hidden layer of the neural network can learn by itself independently from the other layers. The characteristics of the developed neural network are as follow:

- Model type is Sequential.
- Hidden layers have 64 neurons and the other one has 16 with the same activation function - "relu".
- The output layer has 1 neuron for prediction.
- Using "Adam" as the optimizer to change the weights and biases, and MSE as the loss metric.
- Fitting the model with 100 epochs with a batch size of 25.
- Finalizing the model parameters and prediction based on the test data.

The implemented CNN model is a sequential one. The features of this model are as follow:

- Model type is Sequential.
- Adding convolution layer (1-dimensional matrices).
- 64 number of nodes in the first layer.
- The activation function is ReLU or Rectified Linear Activation.
- Three parameters to compile CNN model: optimizer, loss, and metrics.

- The optimizer that adjusts the learning rate throughout training is "Adam".
- Training the model 'fit()' function parameters: training data, target data, validation data, verbose = 2.
- The number of epochs is 5.
- Predicting the test data.

To increase the effectiveness, stability, and learning, dropping out units (hidden and visible) are used for the LSTM model. The LSTM model has the following characteristics:

- Model type is Sequential.
- Adding the LSTM layer with 32 numbers of neurons.
- Adding a dropout layer for preventing data overfitting.
- Adding a dense layer, i.e., the output layer with 1 neuron to predict.
- Using compiler - "Adam" as the optimizer and MSE as the loss metric.
- Fitting the model to run on 5 epochs with a batch size of 512.
- Importing the test data and predicting.

4.3. Experimental Design

The implementation of the models is done on the Corporación Favorita Grocery Sales Forecasting dataset using Tensorflow in Python. The primary dataset (train.csv) contains 125 million observations which are the most basic sales data from January 1, 2013 to August 15, 2017. Among 125,497,040 rows and 6 columns of the training.csv file, 23,808,261 rows are used for this research. The train file is divided to train.csv and validation.csv files, where the validation data contain January 2017 data. The test.csv file has 3,370,464 rows and 5 columns to predict unit sales. The holiday.csv null values are replaced with "no holiday" and promotion.csv, oil.csv. files null values are replaced with 0. All data files are merged with train.csv to build models and test the unit sales.

5. RESULTS AND DISCUSSION

The sales units of the Corporación Favorita Grocery Sales Forecasting dataset are produced using three different deep learning methods including Artificial Neural Network (ANN), Convolutional Neural Network (CNN), and Long Short Term Memory (LSTM) neural network using all data between 01/01/2017 and 08/15/2017. The similarities between all models are feed-forward networks, and the

Figure 30. NN model summary

```
Training Data
id False
date False
store_nbr False
item_nbr False
unit_sales False
onpromotion True
```

(a)

```
Training Data
id False
date False
store_nbr False
item_nbr False
unit_sales False
onpromotion False
```

(b)

```
Test Data
id False
date False
store_nbr False
item_nbr False
onpromotion False
```

(c)

difference between them is related to their structures. Figures 30, 31, and 32 show the comparison of these models.

Mean Squared Error (MSE) is adopted as an indicator for evaluating the models. It measures the average of the squares of errors. MSE is calculated based on Equation (1) where n is the vector of predictions generated from a sample of n data points, and Y is the vector of observed values of the variable being predicted (Wackerly et al., 2014).

$$MSE = \frac{1}{n}\sum_{i=1}^{n}(Y_i - \hat{Y}_i)^2 \tag{1}$$

In this research, Root Mean Squared Error (RMSE) also is utilized as an indicator for evaluating the models. Equation (2) shows the formula. The variables are observed over T times. $\hat{y}_t$ is the prediction value for time t. In addition, y_t is the variable (Hyndman and Koehler, 2006).

$$RMSE = \sqrt{\frac{\sum_{t=1}^{T}(\hat{y}_t - y_t)^2}{T}} \tag{2}$$

The models are built using different parameters and diverse weights. For instance, for the neural network, the MSE for Step 75/100 is 144.02 which is the lowest value. Again, for CNN and LSTM, the lowest MSEs are 175.20 and 75.22, respectively. Table 1 and Table 2 represent the comparison summary of the results of different forecasting models in terms of MSE and RMSE, respectively. Figure 33 and Figure 34 show that the LSTM performs better than the other two models for forecasting the sales units.

Figure 31. CNN model summary

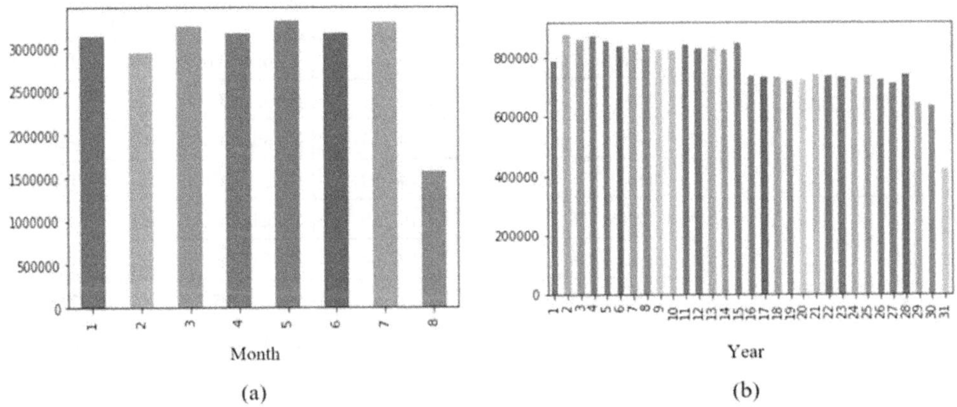

Figure 32. LSTM model summary

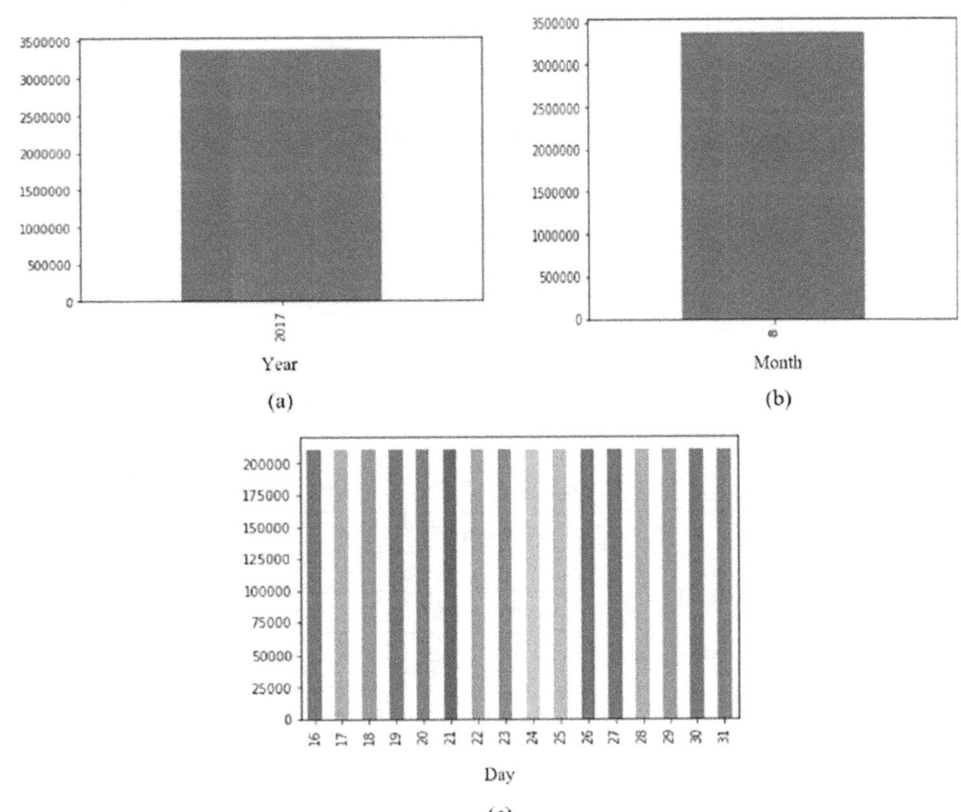

Table 1. The comparison of MSE values

Approach	Training MSE		Validation MSE	
Artificial Neural Networks (ANN)	Step: 0 / 100	148.65	Step: 0 / 100	148.65
	Step: 25 / 100	158.57	Step: 25 / 100	158.57
	Step: 50 / 100	149.17	Step: 50 / 100	149.17
	Step: 75 / 100	**144.02**	Step: 75 / 100	**144.02**
Convolutional Neural Network (CNN)	Epoch 1/5	192.69	Epoch 1/5	233.71
	Epoch 2/5	178.64	Epoch 2/5	241.89
	Epoch 3/5	179.52	**Epoch 3/5**	**215.98**
	Epoch 4/5	175.20	Epoch 4/5	217.25
	Epoch 5/5	172.93	Epoch 5/5	230.60
Long Short-Term Memory Neural Network (LSTM)	**Step4-Epoch 5/5**	**75.2203**	**Step4-Epoch 5/5**	**74.49**
	Step5-Epoch 3/5	88.7221	Step5-Epoch 3/5	87.85
	Step7-Epoch 4/5	279.7268	Step7-Epoch 4/5	279.30
	Step12-Epoch 3/5	170.3472	Step12-Epoch 3/5	169.83
	Step16-Epoch 4/5	458.8012	Step16-Epoch 4/5	463.09

Table 2. The comparison of RMSE values

Approach	Training RMSE		Validation RMSE	
Artificial Neural Networks (ANN)	Step: 0 / 100	4.10	Step: 0 / 100	4.10
	Step: 25 / 100	4.11	Step: 25 / 100	4.11
	Step: 50 / 100	4.08	Step: 50 / 100	4.08
	Step: 75 / 100	**4.07**	**Step: 75 / 100**	**4.07**
Convolutional Neural Network (CNN)	Epoch 1/5	4.498	Epoch 1/5	3.980
	Epoch 2/5	4.115	Epoch 2/5	4.603
	Epoch 3/5	4.261	Epoch 3/5	4.268
	Epoch 4/5	4.147	Epoch 4/5	4.040
	Epoch 5/5	**3.963**	**Epoch 5/5**	**4.363**
Long Short-Term Memory Neural Network (LSTM)	**Step4-Epoch 4/5**	**3.00**	**Step4-Epoch 4/5**	**2.78**
	Step5-Epoch 3/5	3.05	Step5-Epoch 3/5	2.98
	Step7-Epoch 1/5	3.01	Step7-Epoch 1/5	3.11
	Step12-Epoch 3/5	3.08	Step12-Epoch 3/5	2.78
	Step16-Epoch 4/5	4.33	Step16-Epoch 4/5	4.03

Figure 33. Comparison summary of different forecasting models in terms of MSE

	item_nbr	family	class	perishable
0	96995	GROCERY I	1093	0
1	99197	GROCERY I	1067	0
2	103501	CLEANING	3008	0
3	103520	GROCERY I	1028	0
4	103665	BREAD/BAKERY	2712	1

(a)

```
Items Data
item_nbr False
family False
class False
perishable False
```

(b)

Figure 34. Comparison summary of different forecasting models in terms of RMSE

	id	date	store_nbr	item_nbr	unit_sales	onpromotion	family	class	perishable
23808256	125471184	2017-08-15	43	2123839	2.0	False	BEVERAGES	1122	0
23808257	125476599	2017-08-15	45	2123839	1.0	False	BEVERAGES	1122	0
23808258	125484285	2017-08-15	48	2123839	1.0	False	BEVERAGES	1122	0
23808259	125489307	2017-08-15	50	2123839	1.0	False	BEVERAGES	1122	0
23808260	125309124	2017-08-14	8	2011451	1.0	False	GROCERY I	1063	0

6. CONCLUSIONS AND FUTURE RESEARCH

In this research, forecasting the unit sales of thousands of items sold at diverse chain stores located in Ecuador has been investigated using advanced techniques. Three deep learning approaches including Artificial Neural Network (ANN), Convolutional Neural Network (CNN), and Long Short Term Memory (LSTM) have been adopted for reliable and good predictions from the Corporación Favorita Grocery Sales Forecasting dataset collected from Kaggle website. Then, the performances of these methods have been evaluated and compared.

Real data have been utilized in this research. The results show that LSTM has the best performance among the three techniques. In this case, the Mean Squared Error (MSE) is 75.22 for training. For CNN and ANN, the lowest MSE of training is 175.20 and 144.02, respectively.

The key challenge of this research is the resource (memory) limitation of the processor. As the train.csv file is so big, the data processing took a long time to obtain the results. Another challenge is receiving errors in some cases. An important future research direction is exploring more neural network techniques on the same dataset in addition to adding more feature extraction techniques for improvement of the model, and to get more accurate results. Furthermore, it would be interesting to investigate different deep learning techniques on more complex datasets to see there is any improvement in the results.

ACKNOWLEDGMENT

The authors of this chapter would like to recognize Reza Tavakkoli-Moghaddam from the School of Industrial Engineering, College of Engineering, University of Tehran, Iran, who participated in the research and creation of this chapter.

This research has been supported by an NSERC Discovery grant. The authors would like to thank the editor and reviewers for the great comments that improved the quality of this book chapter. In addition, they would like to thank Dr. Ayse Bener who is the Program Director of the MSc program in Data Science and Analytics at Ryerson University. This research was completed as a part of this program.

REFERENCES

Aburto, L., & Weber, R. (2007). Improved supply chain management based on hybrid demand forecasts. *Applied Soft Computing*, *7*(1), 136–144. doi:10.1016/j.asoc.2005.06.001

Al-Saba, T., & El-Amin, I. (1999). Artificial neural networks as applied to long-term demand forecasting. *Artificial Intelligence in Engineering*, *13*(2), 189–197. doi:10.1016/S0954-1810(98)00018-1

Beccali, M., Cellura, M., Brano, V. L., & Marvuglia, A. (2004). Forecasting daily urban electric load profiles using artificial neural networks. *Energy Conversion and Management*, *45*(18-19), 2879–2900. doi:10.1016/j.enconman.2004.01.006

Bengio, Y., Goodfellow, I., & Courville, A. (2017). *Deep learning* (Vol. 1). MIT Press.

Bhadouria, S., & Jayant, A. (2017). Development of ANN models for demand forecasting. *Am. J. Eng. Res*, *6*, 142–147.

Bousqaoui, H., Achchab, S., & Tikito, K. (2017). Machine learning applications in supply chains: An emphasis on neural network applications. In *2017 3rd International Conference of Cloud Computing Technologies and Applications (CloudTech)* (pp. 1-7). IEEE.

Campbell, C., & Ying, Y. (2011). Learning with support vector machines. *Synthesis Lectures on Artificial Intelligence and Machine Learning, 5*(1), 1-95.

Chang, P. C., Fan, C. Y., & Lin, J. J. (2011). Monthly electricity demand forecasting based on a weighted evolving fuzzy neural network approach. *International Journal of Electrical Power & Energy Systems*, *33*(1), 17–27. doi:10.1016/j.ijepes.2010.08.008

Chao-ting, X. U. A. N., Pei-qing, H., & Dong, L. (2000). Applications of Neural Network Technology in Supply Chain Management. *Industrial Engineering and Management, 3*.

Choy, K. L., Lee, W. B., & Lo, V. (2003). Design of an intelligent supplier relationship management system: A hybrid case based neural network approach. *Expert Systems with Applications*, *24*(2), 225–237. doi:10.1016/S0957-4174(02)00151-3

Corporación Favorita Grocery Sales Forecasting. (2019). https://www.kaggle.com/c/favorita-grocery-sales-forecasting/data

Gaur, M., Goel, S., & Jain, E. (2015, March). Comparison between Nearest Neighbours and Bayesian Network for demand forecasting in supply chain management. In *2015 2nd International Conference on Computing for Sustainable Global Development (INDIACom)* (pp. 1433-1436). IEEE.

Hochreiter, S., & Schmidhuber, J. (1997). Long short-term memory. *Neural Computation*, *9*(8), 1735–1780. doi:10.1162/neco.1997.9.8.1735 PMID:9377276

Huang, H. C., & Hou, C. I. (2017). Tourism Demand Forecasting Model Using Neural Network. *International. J. Comput. Sci. Inf. Technol*, *9*, 19–29.

Hyndman, R. J., & Koehler, A. B. (2006). Another look at measures of forecast accuracy. *International Journal of Forecasting*, *22*(4), 679–688. doi:10.1016/j.ijforecast.2006.03.001

Jiang, L., & Hu, G. (2018, November). Day-ahead price forecasting for electricity market using long-short term memory recurrent neural network. In *2018 15th International Conference on Control, Automation, Robotics and Vision (ICARCV)* (pp. 949-954). IEEE. 10.1109/ICARCV.2018.8581235

Kaya, G. O., & Turkyilmaz, A. (2018). Intermittent demand forecasting using data mining techniques. *Applied Computer Science, 14*.

Kaylani, A., Georgiopoulos, M., Mollaghasemi, M., Anagnostopoulos, G. C., Sentelle, C., & Zhong, M. (2010). An adaptive multiobjective approach to evolving ART architectures. *IEEE Transactions on Neural Networks*, *21*(4), 529–550. doi:10.1109/TNN.2009.2037813 PMID:20172827

Kochak, A., & Sharma, S. (2015). Demand forecasting using neural network for supply chain management. *International Journal of Mechanical Engineering and Robotics Research, 4*(1), 96-104.

Kohonen, T. (1990). The self-organizing map. *Proceedings of the IEEE, 78*(9), 1464–1480. doi:10.1109/5.58325

Kumar, A., Rao, V. R., & Soni, H. (1995). An empirical comparison of neural network and logistic regression models. *Marketing Letters*, *6*(4), 251–263. doi:10.1007/BF00996189

LeCun, Y., & Bengio, Y. (1995). Convolutional networks for images, speech, and time series. The Handbook of Brain Theory and Neural Networks, 3361(10), 1995.

Leung, H. C. (1995, June). Neural networks in supply chain management. In *Proceedings for Operating Research and the Management Sciences* (pp. 347–352). IEEE. doi:10.1109/IEMC.1995.524607

Madan, V. (2017). *Introducing Gluon — An Easy-to-Use Programming Interface for Flexible Deep Learning*. https://aws.amazon.com/blogs/machine-learning/introducing-gluon-an-easy-to-use-programming-interface-for-flexible-deep-learning/

Martín del Bío, B., & Sanz Molina, A. (2006). *Neural networks and fuzzy systems*. Editorial RA-MA.

Meherishi, L., Narayana, S. A., & Ranjani, K. S. (2019). Sustainable packaging for supply chain management in the circular economy: A review. *Journal of Cleaner Production*, *237*, 117582. doi:10.1016/j.jclepro.2019.07.057

Mentzer, J. T., DeWitt, W., Keebler, J. S., Min, S., Nix, N. W., Smith, C. D., & Zacharia, Z. G. (2001). Defining supply chain management. *Journal of Business Logistics*, *22*(2), 1–25. doi:10.1002/j.2158-1592.2001.tb00001.x

Morabito, F. C., Campolo, M., Ieracitano, C., & Mammone, N. (2019). Deep Learning Approaches to Electrophysiological Multivariate Time-Series Analysis. In *Artificial Intelligence in the Age of Neural Networks and Brain Computing* (pp. 219–243). Academic Press.

Mupparaju, K., Soni, A., Gujela, P., & Lanham, M. A. (2008). *A Comparative Study of Machine Learning Frameworks for Demand Forecasting*. Academic Press.

Pai, P. F., & Lin, C. S. (2005). A hybrid ARIMA and support vector machines model in stock price forecasting. *Omega*, *33*(6), 497–505. doi:10.1016/j.omega.2004.07.024

Park, D. C., El-Sharkawi, M. A., Marks, R. J., Atlas, L. E., & Damborg, M. J. (1991). Electric load forecasting using an artificial neural network. *IEEE Transactions on Power Systems*, *6*(2), 442–449. doi:10.1109/59.76685

Sharma, A., Panigrahi, D., & Kumar, P. (2013). *A neural network based approach for predicting customer churn in cellular network services*. arXiv preprint arXiv:1309.3945

Specht, D. F. (1991). A general regression neural network. *IEEE Transactions on Neural Networks*, *2*(6), 568–576. doi:10.1109/72.97934 PMID:18282872

Sultan, K., Ali, H., & Zhang, Z. (2018). Big data perspective and challenges in next generation networks. *Future Internet*, *10*(7), 56. doi:10.3390/fi10070056

Wackerly, D., Mendenhall, W., & Scheaffer, R. L. (2014). *Mathematical statistics with applications*. Cengage Learning.

Zhang, G. P. (2004). Business forecasting with artificial neural networks: An overview. In *Neural networks in business forecasting* (pp. 1–22). IGI Global. doi:10.4018/978-1-59140-176-6.ch001

Zhikai, H. Y. L. F. S., & Ge, Z. (2002). Neural Networks Technology for Inventory Management. *Computer Engineering and Applications, 15*.

Compilation of References

Absi, N., Archetti, C., Dauzère-Pérès, S., & Feillet, D. (2015). A two-phase iterative heuristic approach for the production routing problem. *Transportation Science*, *49*(4), 784–795. doi:10.1287/trsc.2014.0523

Aburto, L., & Weber, R. (2007). Improved supply chain management based on hybrid demand forecasts. *Applied Soft Computing*, *7*(1), 136–144. doi:10.1016/j.asoc.2005.06.001

Adulyasak, Y., Cordeau, J. F., & Jans, R. (2012). Optimization-based adaptive large neighborhood search for the production routing problem. *Transportation Science*, *48*(1), 20–45. doi:10.1287/trsc.1120.0443

Adulyasak, Y., Cordeau, J. F., & Jans, R. (2014). Formulations and branch-and-cut algorithms for multivehicle production and inventory routing problems. *INFORMS Journal on Computing*, *26*(1), 103–120. doi:10.1287/ijoc.2013.0550

Adulyasak, Y., Cordeau, J. F., & Jans, R. (2015). The production routing problem: A review of formulations and solution algorithms. *Computers & Operations Research*, *55*, 141–152. doi:10.1016/j.cor.2014.01.011

Aiken, L., Clarke, S., Sloane, D., Sochalski, J., & Silber, J. (2002). Hospital nurse staffing and patient mortality, nurse burnout, and job dissatisfaction. *Journal of the American Medical Association*, *288*(16), 1987–1993. doi:10.1001/jama.288.16.1987 PMID:12387650

Aissaoui, N., Haouari, M., & Hassini, E. (2007). Supplier selection and order lot sizing modeling: A review. *Computers & Operations Research*, *34*(12), 3516–3540. doi:10.1016/j.cor.2006.01.016

Aldunce, P., Beilin, R., Handmer, J., & Howden, M. (2014). Framing disaster resilience: The implications of the diverse conceptualisations of bouncing back. *Disaster Prevention and Management*, *23*(3), 252–270. doi:10.1108/DPM-07-2013-0130

Ali, M. M., Babai, M. Z., Boylan, J. E., & Syntetos, A. A. (2017). Supply chain forecasting when information is not shared. *European Journal of Operational Research*, *260*(3), 984–994. doi:10.1016/j.ejor.2016.11.046

Ali, M. M., & Boylan, J. E. (2011). Feasibility principles for Downstream Demand Inference in supply chains. *The Journal of the Operational Research Society*, *62*(3), 474–482. doi:10.1057/jors.2010.82

Ali, M. M., & Boylan, J. E. (2012). On the effect of non-optimal forecasting methods on supply chain downstream demand. *IMA Journal of Management Mathematics*, *23*(1), 81–98. doi:10.1093/imaman/dpr005

Ali, M. M., Boylan, J. E., & Syntetos, A. A. (2012). Forecast errors and inventory performance under forecast information sharing. *International Journal of Forecasting*, *28*(4), 830–841. doi:10.1016/j.ijforecast.2010.08.003

Alinovi, L., Mane, E., & Romano, D. (2009). Measuring household resilience to food insecurity: application to Palestinian households. In R. Benedetti, M. Bee, G. Espa, & F. Piersimoni (Eds.), *Agricultural Survey Methods*. John Wiley & Sons, Ltd.

Al-Saba, T., & El-Amin, I. (1999). Artificial neural networks as applied to long-term demand forecasting. *Artificial Intelligence in Engineering*, *13*(2), 189–197. doi:10.1016/S0954-1810(98)00018-1

Alsultanny, Y. (2012, April). Successful forecasting for knowledge discovery by statistical methods. In *2012 Ninth International Conference on Information Technology-New Generations* (pp. 584-588). IEEE. 10.1109/ITNG.2012.160

Alwan, L. C., Liu, J. J., & Yao, D. Q. (2003). Stochastic characterization of upstream demand processes in a supply chain. *IIE Transactions*, *35*(3), 207–219. doi:10.1080/07408170304368

Amin-Naseri, M. R., & Tabar, B. R. (2008, May). Neural network approach to lumpy demand forecasting for spare parts in process industries. In *2008 International Conference on Computer and Communication Engineering* (pp. 1378-1382). IEEE. 10.1109/ICCCE.2008.4580831

Anand, K. S., & Goyal, M. (2009). Strategic information management under leakage in a supply chain. *Management Science*, *55*(3), 438–452. doi:10.1287/mnsc.1080.0930

Archetti, C., Bertazzi, L., Paletta, G., & Speranza, M. G. (2011). Analysis of the maximum level policy in a production-distribution system. *Computers & Operations Research*, *38*(12), 1731–1746. doi:10.1016/j.cor.2011.03.002

Arnould, E. J., & Thompson, C. J. (2005). Consumer culture theory (CCT): Twenty years of research. *The Journal of Consumer Research*, *31*(4), 868–882. doi:10.1086/426626

Arshinder, K., Kanda, A., & Deshmukh, S. G. (2011). A Review on Supply Chain Coordination: Coordination Mechanisms, Managing Uncertainty and Research Directions. In *Supply Chain Coordination Under Uncertainty* (pp. 39–82). Springer. doi:10.1007/978-3-642-19257-9_3

Asgari, N., Nikbakhsh, E., Hill, A., & Farahani, R. Z. (2016). Supply chain management 1982–2015: A review. *IMA Journal of Management Mathematics*.

Bachouch, R. B., Guinet, A., & Hajri-Gabouj, S. (2011). A Decision-Making Tool for Home Health Care Nurses' Planning. *Supply Chain Forum: An International Journal, 12*(1), 14-20. doi:10.1080/16258312.2011.11517250

Badot, O., Carrier, C., Cova, B., Desjeux, D., & Filser, M. (2009). L'ethnomarketing: Un élargissement de la recherche en comportement du consommateur à l'ethnologie. [French Edition]. *Recherche et Applications en Marketing, 24*(1), 93–111. doi:10.1177/076737010902400105

Baker, S., & Fradkin, A. (2011). What drives job search? Evidence from Google search data. *Discussion Papers*, 10-020.

Balcik, B., Jahre, M., & Fabbe-Costes, N. (2015). How standards and modularity can improve disaster supply chain responsiveness. *Journal of Disaster Logistics and Supply Chain Management, 3*, 348-386.

Balcik, B., & Ak, D. (2013). Supplier Selection for Framework Agreements in Humanitarian Relief. *Production and Operations Management, 23*. Advance online publication. doi:10.1111/poms.12098

Balcik, B., Beamon, B., Krejci, C., Muramatsu, K., & Ramirez, M. (2010). Coordination in humanitarian relief chains: Practices, challenges and opportunities. *International Journal of Production Economics, 126*(1), 22–34. doi:10.1016/j.ijpe.2009.09.008

Banker, S. (2013). *Amazon and Drones – Here is why it Will Work*. Academic Press.

Bank, M., Mazdeh, M., & Heydari, M. (2020). Applying meta-heuristic algorithms for an integrated production-distribution problem in a two level supply chain. *Uncertain Supply Chain Management, 8*(1), 77–92. doi:10.5267/j.uscm.2019.8.004

Bard, J. F., & Nananukul, N. (2009a). Heuristics for a multiperiod inventory routing problem with production decisions. *Computers & Industrial Engineering, 57*(3), 713–723. doi:10.1016/j.cie.2009.01.020

Bard, J. F., & Nananukul, N. (2009b). The integrated production–inventory–distribution–routing problem. *Journal of Scheduling, 12*(3), 257–280. doi:10.100710951-008-0081-9

Bard, J. F., Shao, Y., & Jarrah, A. I. (2014). A sequential GRASP for the therapist routing and scheduling problem. *Journal of Scheduling, 17*(2), 109–133. doi:10.100710951-013-0345-x

Bard, J. F., Shao, Y., Qi, X., & Jarrah, A. I. (2014). The traveling therapist scheduling problem. *IIE Transactions, 46*(7), 683–706. doi:10.1080/0740817X.2013.851434

Barrera, D., Velasco, N., & Amaya, C. A. (2012). A network-based approach to the multi-activity combined timetabling and crew scheduling problem: Workforce scheduling for public health policy implementation. *Computers & Industrial Engineering, 63*(4), 802–812. doi:10.1016/j.cie.2012.05.002

Beccali, M., Cellura, M., Brano, V. L., & Marvuglia, A. (2004). Forecasting daily urban electric load profiles using artificial neural networks. *Energy Conversion and Management*, *45*(18-19), 2879–2900. doi:10.1016/j.enconman.2004.01.006

Begur, S. V., Miller, D. M., & Weaver, J. R. (1997). An Integrated Spatial DSS for Scheduling and Routing Home-Health-Care Nurses. *Interfaces*, *27*(4), 35–48. doi:10.1287/inte.27.4.35

Benavent, C. (2016). Plateformes. Sites collaboratifs, marketplaces, réseaux sociaux… Comment ils influencent nos choix. FYP editions.

Bengio, Y., Goodfellow, I., & Courville, A. (2017). *Deep learning* (Vol. 1). MIT Press.

Bennett, A. R., & Erera, A. L. (2011). Dynamic periodic fixed appointment scheduling for home health. *IIE Transactions on Healthcare Systems Engineering*, *1*(1), 6–19. doi:10.1080/19488300.2010.549818

Bennett-Milburn, A., & Spicer, J. (2013). Multi-objective home health nurse routing with remote monitoring devices. *Int J Plan Sched*, *1*(4), 242–263. doi:10.1504/IJPS.2013.059677

Bevilacqua, M., Ciarapica, F. E., & Giacchetta, G. (2006). A fuzzy-QFD approach to supplier selection. *Journal of Purchasing and Supply Management*, *12*(1), 14–27. doi:10.1016/j.pursup.2006.02.001

Bhadouria, S., & Jayant, A. (2017). Development of ANN models for demand forecasting. *Am. J. Eng. Res*, *6*, 142–147.

Birkmann, J., Seng, D. C., & Setiadi, N. (2013). Enhancing early warning in the light of migration and environmental shocks. *Environmental Science & Policy*, *27*(1), 76–88. doi:10.1016/j.envsci.2012.04.002

Blecken, A. (2009). *A reference task model for supply chain processes of humanitarian organizations. Universität Paderborn*. Alemanha.

Boltürk, E., Çevik Onar, S., Öztayşi, B., Kahraman, C., & Goztepe, K. (2016). Multi-attribute warehouse location selection in humanitarian logistics using hesitant fuzzy AHP. *International Journal of the Analytic*.

Bosch, R. (2010). Objectivity and Plausibility in the Study of Organizations. *Journal of Management Inquiry*, *19*(4), 383–391. doi:10.1177/1056492610369936

Boudia, M., Louly, M. A. O., & Prins, C. (2007). A reactive GRASP and path relinking for a combined production–distribution problem. *Computers & Operations Research*, *34*(11), 3402–3419. doi:10.1016/j.cor.2006.02.005

Bousqaoui, H., Achchab, S., & Tikito, K. (2017). Machine learning applications in supply chains: An emphasis on neural network applications. In *2017 3rd International Conference of Cloud Computing Technologies and Applications (CloudTech)* (pp. 1-7). IEEE.

Boylan, J. E., & Johnston, F. R. (2003). Optimality and robustness of combinations of moving averages. *The Journal of the Operational Research Society*, *54*(1), 109–115. doi:10.1057/palgrave.jors.2601472

Braman, L. M., van Aalst, M. K., Mason, S. J., Suarez, P., Ait-Chellouche, Y., & Tall, A. (2013). Climate forecasts in disaster management: Red Cross flood operations in West Africa, 2008. *Disasters*, *37*(1), 144–164. doi:10.1111/j.1467-7717.2012.01297.x PMID:23066755

Bräysy, O., & Gendreau, M. (2005). Vehicle Routing Problem with Time Windows, Part II: Metaheuristics. *Transportation Science*, *39*(1), 119–139. doi:10.1287/trsc.1030.0057

Bredström, D., & Rönnqvist, M. (2008). Combined vehicle routing and scheduling with temporal precedence and synchronization constraints. *European Journal of Operational Research*, *191*(1), 19–31. doi:10.1016/j.ejor.2007.07.033

Cachon, G. P., & Fisher, M. (2000). Supply chain inventory management and the value of shared information. *Management Science*, *46*(8), 1032–1048. doi:10.1287/mnsc.46.8.1032.12029

Cachon, G. P., & Lariviere, M. A. (2005). Supply chain coordination with revenue-sharing contracts: Strengths and limitations. *Management Science*, *51*(1), 30–44. doi:10.1287/mnsc.1040.0215

Campbell, C., & Ying, Y. (2011). Learning with support vector machines. *Synthesis Lectures on Artificial Intelligence and Machine Learning, 5*(1), 1-95.

Campbell, A., Clarke, L., Kleywegt, A., & Savelsbergh, M. (1998). The inventory routing problem. In *Fleet management and logistics* (pp. 95–113). Springer. doi:10.1007/978-1-4615-5755-5_4

Cappanera, P., & Scutellà, M. G. (2013). Home Care optimization: Impact of pattern generation policies on scheduling and routing decisions. *Electronic Notes in Discrete Mathematics*, *41*, 53–60. doi:10.1016/j.endm.2013.05.075

Cappanera, P., & Scutellà, M. G. (2015). Joint Assignment, Scheduling, and Routing Models to Home Care Optimization: A Pattern-Based Approach. *Transportation Science*, *49*(4), 830–852. doi:10.1287/trsc.2014.0548

Carter, M. R., Little, P. D., Mogues, T., & Negatu, W. (2004). Shocks, sensitivity and resilience: Tracking the economic impacts of environmental disaster on assets in Ethiopia and Honduras. In *BASIS Research Program on Poverty, Inequality and Development*. US Agency for International Development.

Chandra, P., & Fisher, M. L. (1994). Coordination of production and distribution planning. *European Journal of Operational Research*, *72*(3), 503–517. doi:10.1016/0377-2217(94)90419-7

Chang, P. C., Fan, C. Y., & Lin, J. J. (2011). Monthly electricity demand forecasting based on a weighted evolving fuzzy neural network approach. *International Journal of Electrical Power & Energy Systems*, *33*(1), 17–27. doi:10.1016/j.ijepes.2010.08.008

Chan, J., & Comes, T. (2014). Innovative Research Design–A journey into the information typhoon. *Procedia Engineering*, *78*, 52–58. doi:10.1016/j.proeng.2014.07.038

Chao-ting, X. U. A. N., Pei-qing, H., & Dong, L. (2000). Applications of Neural Network Technology in Supply Chain Management. *Industrial Engineering and Management, 3.*

Charles, A., & Lauras, M. (2011). An enterprise modelling approach for better optimisation modelling: Application to the disaster relief chain coordination problem. *OR-Spektrum*, *33*(3), 815–841. doi:10.100700291-011-0255-2

Charles, A., Lauras, M., Van Wassenhove, L. N., & Dupont, L. (2016). Designing an efficient disaster supply network. *Journal of Operations Management*, *47*(1), 58–70. doi:10.1016/j.jom.2016.05.012

Chen, B., Chen, X., & Kanzow, C. (2000a). A penalized Fischer-Burmeister NCP-function. *Mathematical Programming*, *88*(1), 211–216. doi:10.1007/PL00011375

Chen, F., Drezner, Z., Ryan, J. K., & Simchi-Levi, D. (2000b). Quantifying the bullwhip effect in a simple supply chain: The impact of forecasting, lead times, and information. *Management Science*, *46*(3), 436–443. doi:10.1287/mnsc.46.3.436.12069

Cheng, T. C. E., & Wu, Y. N. (2005). The impact of information sharing in a two-level supply chain with multiple retailers. *The Journal of the Operational Research Society*, *56*(10), 1159–1165. doi:10.1057/palgrave.jors.2601934

Chen, J., & Bell, P. (2011). The impact of customer returns on decisions in a newsvendor problem with and without buyback policies. *International Transactions in Operational Research*, *18*(4), 473–491. doi:10.1111/j.1475-3995.2010.00797.x

Chen, L., Zhao, X., Tang, O., Price, L., Zhang, S., & Zhu, W. (2017). Supply chain collaboration for sustainability: A literature review and future research agenda. *International Journal of Production Economics*, *194*, 73–87. doi:10.1016/j.ijpe.2017.04.005

Chen, Y., Zhao, H., & Yu, L. (2010, August). Demand forecasting in automotive aftermarket based on ARMA model. In *2010 International Conference on Management and Service Science* (pp. 1-4). IEEE. 10.1109/ICMSS.2010.5577867

Chen-Yi, H., Ke-Ting, C., & Gwo-Hshiung, T. (2007). FMCDM with Fuzzy DEMATEL Approach for Customers' Choice Behavior Model. *International Journal of Fuzzy Systems*, *9*(4).

Cheung, K. L., & Lee, H. L. (2002). The inventory benefit of shipment coordination and stock rebalancing in a supply chain. *Management Science*, *48*(2), 300–306. doi:10.1287/mnsc.48.2.300.251

Chiu, T., Fang, D., Chen, J., Wang, Y., & Jeris, C. (2001). A robust and scalable clustering algorithm for mixed type attributes in large database environment. *Proceedings of the seventh ACM SIGKDD international conference on Knowledge discovery and data mining*. 10.1145/502512.502549

Choi, H., & Varian, H. (2009). Predicting initial claims for unemployment benefits. *Google Inc*, 1-5.

Choi, H., & Varian, H. (2012). Predicting the present with Google Trends. *The Economic Record*, *88*, 2–9. doi:10.1111/j.1475-4932.2012.00809.x

Cholez, C., Magrini, M. B., & Galliano, D. (2017). Les contrats de production en grandes cultures. Coordination et incitations par les coopératives. *Économie rurale. Agricultures, alimentations, territoires*, (360), 65-83.

Choy, K. L., Lee, W. B., & Lo, V. (2003). Design of an intelligent supplier relationship management system: A hybrid case based neural network approach. *Expert Systems with Applications*, *24*(2), 225–237. doi:10.1016/S0957-4174(02)00151-3

Chu, C. L., & Leon, V. J. (2008). Power-of-two single-warehouse multi-buyer inventory coordination with private information. *International Journal of Production Economics*, *111*(2), 562–574. doi:10.1016/j.ijpe.2006.12.063

Chu, F. L. (2009). Forecasting tourism demand with ARMA-based methods. *Tourism Management*, *30*(5), 740–751. doi:10.1016/j.tourman.2008.10.016

Ciancimino, E., Cannella, S., Bruccoleri, M., & Framinan, J. M. (2012). On the bullwhip avoidance phase: The synchronised supply chain. *European Journal of Operational Research*, *221*(1), 49–63. doi:10.1016/j.ejor.2012.02.039

Cissé, M., Yalçındağ, S., Kergosien, Y., Şahin, E., Lenté, C., & Matta, A. (2017). OR problems related to Home Health Care: A review of relevant routing and scheduling problems. *Operations Research for Health Care*, *13-14*, 1–22. Advance online publication. doi:10.1016/j.orhc.2017.06.001

Clarke, G., & Wright, J. W. (1964). Scheduling of vehicles from a central depot to a number of delivery points. *Operations Research*, *12*(4), 568–581. doi:10.1287/opre.12.4.568

Cluster, L. (2015). *Logistics operational guide (LOG): Procurement section*. Available at: https://log.logcluster.org/display/LOG/Procurement

Comes, T. (2016). Cognitive biases in disaster sensemaking and decision-making lessons from field research. *2016 IEEE International Multi-Disciplinary Conference on Cognitive Methods in Situation Awareness and Decision Support (CogSIMA)*, 56-62. 10.1109/COGSIMA.2016.7497786

Comes, T., Wijngaards, N., & Van de Walle, B. (2015). Exploring the future: Runtime Scenario Selection for Complex and Time-Bound Decisions. *Technological Forecasting and Social Change*, *97*(1), 29–46. doi:10.1016/j.techfore.2014.03.009

Corporación Favorita Grocery Sales Forecasting. (2019). https://www.kaggle.com/c/favorita-grocery-sales-forecasting/data

Counter, S. (2017). Search engine market share worldwide. *StatCounter 1997 –2017.*

Courtin, G. (2013). *Supply chain and the future of applications*. Research Report October 2013 by SCM World.

Cozzolino, A. (2012). *Humanitarian logistics: cross-sector cooperation in disaster relief management*. Springer Science & Business Media. doi:10.1007/978-3-642-30186-5

Croson, R., Donohue, K., Katok, E., & Sterman, J. (2014). Order stability in supply chains: Coordination risk and the role of coordination stock. *Production and Operations Management*, *23*(2), 176–196. doi:10.1111/j.1937-5956.2012.01422.x

Dawkins, R. (1989). *The Selfish Gene*. Oxford University Press.

Day, J. M., Melnyk, S. A., Larson, P. D., Davis, E. W., & Whybark, D. C. (2012). Humanitarian and Disaster Relief Supply Chains: A Matter of Life and Death. *The Journal of Supply Chain Management*, *48*(2), 21–36. doi:10.1111/j.1745-493X.2012.03267.x

Delish, E. (2018). *America's Most Delish.* https://www.delish.com/food/a23117553/america-most-delish-grocery-items-2018/

Di Domenica, N., Mitra, G., Valente, P., & Birbilis, G. (2007). Stochastic programming and scenario generation within a simulation framework: An information systems perspective. *Decision Support Systems*, *42*(4), 2197–2218. doi:10.1016/j.dss.2006.06.013

Dickson, G. W. (1966). An analysis of supplier selection system and decision. *J Purch*, *2*(1), 5–17. doi:10.1111/j.1745-493X.1966.tb00818.x

Dieckhaus, D., Heigh, I., Gomez-Tagle Leonard, N., Jahre, M., & Navangul, K. A. (2011), Predicting the Unpredictable – Demand Forecasting in International Disaster Response. IFRC Global Logistics Service Annual Report.

Digalakis, J., & Margaritis, K. (2004). Performance comparison of memetic algorithms. *Applied Mathematics and Computation*, *158*(1), 237–252. doi:10.1016/j.amc.2003.08.115

Disney, S. M., & Towill, D. R. (2002). A discrete transfer function model to determine the dynamic stability of a vendor managed inventory supply chain. *International Journal of Production Research*, *40*(1), 179–204. doi:10.1080/00207540110072975

Djalante, R., Holley, C., & Thomalla, F. (2011). Adaptive governance and managing resilience to natural hazards. *International Journal of Disaster Risk Science*, *2*(4), 1–14. doi:10.100713753-011-0015-6

Dudek, G., & Stadtler, H. (2005). Negotiation-based collaborative planning between supply chains partners. *European Journal of Operational Research*, *163*(3), 668–687. doi:10.1016/j.ejor.2004.01.014

Dupačová, J., Consigli, G., & Wallace, S. W. (2000). Scenarios for Multistage Stochastic Programs. *Annals of Operations Research*, *100*(1), 25–53. doi:10.1023/A:1019206915174

Eckhaus, E. (2010). *Consumer Demand Forecasting: Popular Techniques, Part 1: Weighted and Unweighted Moving Average*. Academic Press.

ElMekkawy, T. Y., & Liu, S. (2009). A new memetic algorithm for optimizing the partitioning problem of tandem AGV systems. *International Journal of Production Economics*, *118*(2), 508–520. doi:10.1016/j.ijpe.2009.01.008

Erdem, M., & Bulkan, S. (2017). A Two-Stage Solution Approach for the Large-Scale Home Healthcare Routeing and Scheduling Problem. *South African Journal of Industrial Engineering, 28*(4), 133-149.

Ervural, B. C., Beyca, O. F., & Zaim, S. (2016). Model estimation of ARMA using genetic algorithms: A case study of forecasting natural gas consumption. *Procedia: Social and Behavioral Sciences, 235*, 537–545. doi:10.1016/j.sbspro.2016.11.066

Fawcett, S. E., Osterhaus, P., Magnan, G. M., Brau, J. C., & McCarter, M. W. (2007). Information sharing and supply chain performance: The role of connectivity and willingness. *Supply Chain Management, 12*(5), 358–368. doi:10.1108/13598540710776935

Ferris, E., Petz, D., & Stark, C. (2013). The year of recurring disasters: A review of natural disasters in 2012. The Brookings Institution – London School of Economics – Project on Internal Displacement.

Fikar, C., & Hirsch, P. (2017). Home health care routing and scheduling: A review. *Computers & Operations Research, 77*, 86–95. doi:10.1016/j.cor.2016.07.019

Forslund, H., & Jonsson, P. (2007). The impact of forecast information quality on supply chain performance. *International Journal of Operations & Production Management, 27*(1), 90–107. doi:10.1108/01443570710714556

Frigg, R., & Hartmann, S. (2012). Models in Science. The Stanford Encyclopedia of Philosophy, 23.

Fumero, F., & Vercellis, C. (1999). Synchronized development of production, inventory, and distribution schedules. *Transportation Science, 33*(3), 330–340. doi:10.1287/trsc.33.3.330

Gabus, A., & Fontela, E. (1973). Perceptions of the world problematique: Communication procedure, communicating with those bearing collective responsibility. Geneva: Battelle Geneva Research Centre. no. 1.

Galindo, G., & Batta, R. (2013). Review of recent developments in OR/MS research in Humanitarian Logistics. *European Journal of Operational Research, 230*(2), 201–211. doi:10.1016/j.ejor.2013.01.039

Gamst, M., & Jensen, T. S. (2012). A branch-and-price algorithm for the long-term home care scheduling problem. In D. Klatte, H.-J. Lüthi, & K. Schmedders (Eds.), *Operations Research Proceedings 2011: Selected Papers of the International Conference on Operations Research (OR 2011)* (pp. 483-488). Berlin: Springer Berlin Heidelberg. 10.1007/978-3-642-29210-1_77

Gaur, M., Goel, S., & Jain, E. (2015, March). Comparison between Nearest Neighbours and Bayesian Network for demand forecasting in supply chain management. In *2015 2nd International Conference on Computing for Sustainable Global Development (INDIACom)* (pp. 1433-1436). IEEE.

Gaur, V., Giloni, A., & Seshadri, S. (2005). Information Sharing in a Supply Chain under ARMA Demand. *Management Science, 51*(6), 961–969. doi:10.1287/mnsc.1050.0385

Giannoccaro, I., & Pontrandolfo, P. (2004). Supply chain coordination by revenue sharing contracts. *International Journal of Production Economics*, *89*(2), 131–139. doi:10.1016/S0925-5273(03)00047-1

Gilbert, K. (2005). An ARIMA supply chain model. *Management Science*, *51*(2), 305–310. doi:10.1287/mnsc.1040.0308

Ginsberg, J., Mohebbi, M. H., Patel, R. S., Brammer, L., Smolinski, M. S., & Brilliant, L. (2009). Detecting influenza epidemics using search engine query data. *Nature*, *457*(7232), 1012–1014. doi:10.1038/nature07634 PMID:19020500

Gittell, J. H., & Weiss, L. (2004). Coordination networks within and across organizations: A multi-level Framework. *Journal of Management Studies*, *41*(1), 127–153. doi:10.1111/j.1467-6486.2004.00424.x

Goel, S., Hofman, J. M., Lahaie, S., Pennock, D. M., & Watts, D. J. (2010). Predicting consumer behavior with Web search. *Proceedings of the National Academy of Sciences of the United States of America*, *107*(41), 17486–17490. doi:10.1073/pnas.1005962107 PMID:20876140

Gong, W. (2010, August). ARMA-GRNN for passenger demand forecasting. In *2010 Sixth International Conference on Natural Computation* (Vol. 3, pp. 1577-1581). IEEE. 10.1109/ICNC.2010.5583711

Google Trends. (2019). https://trends.google.com/trends

Gordon, G., & Tibshirani, R. (2012). Karush-kuhn-tucker conditions. *Optimization, 10*(725/36), 725.

Graves, S. C. (1999). A single-item inventory model for a nonstationary demand process. *Manufacturing & Service Operations Management*, *1*(1), 50–61. doi:10.1287/msom.1.1.50

Guha-Sapir, D., & Ph, H. (2015). *Annual disaster statistical review 2014: The numbers and trends*. CRED.

Guimarães, T. A., Coelho, L. C., Schenekemberg, C. M., & Scarpin, C. T. (2019). The two-echelon multi-depot inventory-routing problem. *Computers & Operations Research*, *101*, 220–233. doi:10.1016/j.cor.2018.07.024

Gustavsson, P., & Nordström, J. (2001). The impact of seasonal unit roots and vector ARMA modelling on forecasting monthly tourism flows. *Tourism Economics*, *7*(2), 117–133. doi:10.5367/000000001101297766

Guzman, G. (2011). Internet search behavior as an economic forecasting tool: The case of inflation expectations. *Journal of Economic and Social Measurement*, *36*(3), 119–167. doi:10.3233/JEM-2011-0342

Ha, A. Y., Tong, S., & Zhang, H. (2011). Sharing demand information in competing supply chains with production diseconomies. *Management Science*, *57*(3), 566–581. doi:10.1287/mnsc.1100.1295

Hair, J. F., Black, W. C., Babin, B. J., Anderson, R. E., & Tatham, R. L. (2006). *Multivariate data analysis* (Vol. 6). Pearson Prentice Hall.

Hancox, M., & Hackney, R. (2000). IT outsourcing: Frameworks for conceptualizing practice and perception. *Information Systems Journal, 10*(3), 217–237. doi:10.1046/j.1365-2575.2000.00082.x

Hansen, P., & Mladenovic, N. (2002). Developments of Variable Neighborhood Search. In C. C. Ribeiro & P. Hansen (Eds.), *Essays and Surveys in Metaheuristics* (1st ed., pp. 415–439). doi:10.1007/978-1-4615-1507-4_19

Hansen, P., Mladenović, N., Brimberg, J., & Pérez, J. A. M. (2010). Variable Neighborhood Search. In M. Gendreau & J.-Y. Potvin (Eds.), *Handbook of Metaheuristics* (pp. 61–86). Springer US. doi:10.1007/978-1-4419-1665-5_3

Hays, C. L. (2004). What Wal-Mart knows about customers' habits. *The New York Times,* 14.

Health, M. o. (2015). *Ministry of Health* (960). Ankara: Türkiye Sağlıklı Yaşlanma Eylem Planı ve Uygulama Programı 2015-2020. Retrieved from http://sbu.saglik.gov.tr/Ekutuphane/Yayin/508

Heaslip, G. (2013). Services operations management and humanitarian logistics. *Journal of Humanitarian Logistics and Supply Chain Management, 3*(1), 37–51. doi:10.1108/20426741311328501

Henderson, J. (2018). *Supply Chain Digital.* https://www.supplychaindigital.com/scm/nine-automakers-share-supply-chain-data

Hertz, A., & Lahrichi, N. (2009). A patient assignment algorithm for home care services. *The Journal of the Operational Research Society, 60*(4), 481–495. doi:10.1057/palgrave.jors.2602574

Hiermann, G., Prandtstetter, M., Rendl, A., Puchinger, J., & Raidl, G. R. (2015b). *Appendix of: Metaheuristics for Solving a Multimodal Home-Healthcare Scheduling Problem.* Retrieved from https://www.ac.tuwien.ac.at/research/problem-instances/

Hiermann, G., Prandtstetter, M., Rendl, A., Puchinger, J., & Raidl, G. (2015a). Metaheuristics for solving a multimodal home-healthcare scheduling problem. *Central European Journal of Operations Research, 23*(1), 89–113. doi:10.100710100-013-0305-8

Hirschkind, N., Mollick, S., Pari, J., & Khim, J. (2019). Convolutional Neural Network. *BRILLIANT.* https://brilliant.org/wiki/convolutional-neural-network/

Hochreiter, S., & Schmidhuber, J. (1997). Long short-term memory. *Neural Computation, 9*(8), 1735–1780. doi:10.1162/neco.1997.9.8.1735 PMID:9377276

Hosoda, T., & Disney, S. M. (2006). On variance amplification in a three-echelon supply chain with minimum mean square error forecasting. *Omega, 34*(4), 344–358. doi:10.1016/j.omega.2004.11.005

Ho, W. R. J., Tsai, C. L., Tzeng, G. H., & Fang, S. K. (2011). Combined DEMATEL technique with a novel MCDM model for exploring portfolio selection based on CAPM. *Expert Systems with Applications, 38*(1), 16–25. doi:10.1016/j.eswa.2010.05.058

Huang, H. C., & Hou, C. I. (2017). Tourism Demand Forecasting Model Using Neural Network. *International. J. Comput. Sci. Inf. Technol, 9*, 19–29.

Hu, S., & Dong, Z. S. (2019). Supplier selection and pre-positioning strategy in humanitarian relief. *Omega, 83*, 287–298. doi:10.1016/j.omega.2018.10.011

Hyndman, R. J., & Koehler, A. B. (2006). Another look at measures of forecast accuracy. *International Journal of Forecasting, 22*(4), 679–688. doi:10.1016/j.ijforecast.2006.03.001

Ireland, R. K., & Crum, C. (2005). *Supply chain collaboration: How to implement CPFR and other best collaborative practices*. J. Ross Publishing.

Jahre, M., & Fabbe-Costes, N. (2015). How standards and modularity can improve disaster supply chain responsiveness: The case of emergency response units. *Journal of Disaster Logistics and Supply Chain Management, 5*(3), 348–386.

Jain, A. K., Mao, J., & Mohiuddin, K. M. (1996). Artificial neural networks: A tutorial. *Computer, 29*(3), 31–44. doi:10.1109/2.485891

Jain, A., Seshadri, S., & Sohoni, M. (2011). Differential pricing for information sharing under competition. *Production and Operations Management, 20*(2), 235–252. doi:10.1111/j.1937-5956.2010.01161.x

Jiang, L., & Hu, G. (2018, November). Day-ahead price forecasting for electricity market using long-short term memory recurrent neural network. In *2018 15th International Conference on Control, Automation, Robotics and Vision (ICARCV)* (pp. 949-954). IEEE. 10.1109/ICARCV.2018.8581235

Jin, B. (2006). Performance implications of information technology implementation in an apparel supply chain. *Supply Chain Management, 11*(4), 309–316. doi:10.1108/13598540610671752

Johnston, F. R., Boyland, J. E., Meadows, M., & Shale, E. (1999). Some properties of a simple moving average when applied to forecasting a time series. *The Journal of the Operational Research Society, 50*(12), 1267–1271. doi:10.1057/palgrave.jors.2600823

Jolliffe, I. (2002). *Principal component analysis*. John Wiley & Sons, Ltd.

Jun, S. P., Park, D. H., & Yeom, J. (2014). The possibility of using search traffic information to explore consumer product attitudes and forecast consumer preference. *Technological Forecasting and Social Change, 86*, 237–253. doi:10.1016/j.techfore.2013.10.021

Kadziński, M., & Ciomek, K. (2016). Integrated framework for preference modeling and robustness analysis for outranking-based multiple criteria sorting with ELECTRE and PROMETHEE. *Information Sciences, 352*, 167–187. doi:10.1016/j.ins.2016.02.059

Kaggle. (2019). https://www.kaggle.com/manjeetsingh/retaildataset

Kaklauskas, A., Zavadskas, E. K., Raslanas, S., Ginevicius, R., Komka, A., & Malinauskas, P. (2006). Selection of low-e windows in retrofit of public buildings by applying multiple criteria method COPRAS: A Lithuanian case. *Energy and Building*, *38*(5), 454–462. doi:10.1016/j.enbuild.2005.08.005

Kalaoglu, Ö. İ., Akyuz, E. S., Ecemiş, S., & Eryuruk, S. H., Sümen, H., & Kalaoglu, F. (2015). Retail demand forecasting in clothing industry. *Tekstil ve Konfeksiyon*, *25*(2), 172–178.

Kamble, S. S., Gunasekaran, A., & Gawankar, S. A. (2020). Achieving sustainable performance in a data-driven agriculture supply chain: A review for research and applications. *International Journal of Production Economics*, *219*, 179–194. doi:10.1016/j.ijpe.2019.05.022

Kandananond, K. (2012). Consumer product demand forecasting based on artificial neural network and support vector machine. *World Academy of Science, Engineering and Technology*, *63*, 372–375.

Kapgate, D. (2014). Weighted moving average forecast model based prediction service broker algorithm for cloud computing. *International Journal of Computer Science and Mobile Computing*, *3*(2), 71–79.

Karimi, I., & Hüllermeier, E. (2007). Risk assessment system of natural hazards: A new approach based on fuzzy probability. *Fuzzy Sets and Systems*, *158*(9), 987–999. doi:10.1016/j.fss.2006.12.013

Kaya, G. O., & Turkyilmaz, A. (2018). Intermittent demand forecasting using data mining techniques. *Applied Computer Science, 14*.

Kaylani, A., Georgiopoulos, M., Mollaghasemi, M., Anagnostopoulos, G. C., Sentelle, C., & Zhong, M. (2010). An adaptive multiobjective approach to evolving ART architectures. *IEEE Transactions on Neural Networks*, *21*(4), 529–550. doi:10.1109/TNN.2009.2037813 PMID:20172827

Kim, B. I., Kim, S., & Sahoo, S. (2006). Waste collection vehicle routing problem with time windows. *Computers & Operations Research*, *33*(12), 3624–3642. doi:10.1016/j.cor.2005.02.045

Kim, S., Ramkumar, M., & Subramanian, N. (2019). Logistics service provider selection for disaster preparation: A socio-technical systems perspective. *Annals of Operations Research*, *283*(1-2), 1259–1282. doi:10.100710479-018-03129-3

Klein, R., Rai, A., & Straub, D. W. (2007). Competitive and cooperative positioning in supply chain logistics relationships. *Decision Sciences*, *38*(4), 611–646. doi:10.1111/j.1540-5915.2007.00172.x

Klibi, W., & Martel, A. (2012). Scenario-based supply chain network risk modelling. *European Journal of Operational Research*, *223*(3), 644–658. doi:10.1016/j.ejor.2012.06.027

Kochak, A., & Sharma, S. (2015). Demand forecasting using neural network for supply chain management. *International Journal of Mechanical Engineering and Robotics Research, 4*(1), 96-104.

Kohonen, T. (1990). The self-organizing map. *Proceedings of the IEEE, 78*(9), 1464–1480. doi:10.1109/5.58325

Kourentzes, N., Barrow, D. K., & Crone, S. F. (2014). Neural network ensemble operators for time series forecasting. *Expert Systems with Applications, 41*(9), 4235–4244. doi:10.1016/j.eswa.2013.12.011

Kovács, G., & Spens, K. M. (2007). Disaster HL in disaster relief operations. *International Journal of Physical Distribution & Logistics Management, 37*(2), 99–114. doi:10.1108/09600030710734820

Krasnogor, N., & Smith, J. (2005). A tutorial for competent memetic algorithms: Model, taxonomy, and design issues. *IEEE Transactions on Evolutionary Computation, 9*(5), 474–488. doi:10.1109/TEVC.2005.850260

Kumar, A., Rao, V. R., & Soni, H. (1995). An empirical comparison of neural network and logistic regression models. *Marketing Letters, 6*(4), 251–263. doi:10.1007/BF00996189

Kunz, N., & Reiner, G. (2012). A meta-analysis of humanitarian logistics research. *Journal of Humanitarian Logistics and Supply Chain Management, 2*(2), 116–147. doi:10.1108/20426741211260723

Kyee, D. L. T., & Moin, N. H. (2018). MatHeuristic Approach for Production-Inventory-Distribution Routing Problem. *Warasan Khana Witthayasat Maha Witthayalai Chiang Mai, 45*(2), 1145–1160.

Labadi, N., Prins, C., & Reghioui, M. (2008). A memetic algorithm for the vehicle routing problem with time windows. *Operations Research, 42*(3), 415–431. doi:10.1051/ro:2008021

Laguna Salvad6, L., Lauras, M., & Comes, T. (2015). Towards More Relevant Research on Disaster Disaster Management Coordination. *Proceedings of the 12th Information Systems for Crisis Response And Management (ISCRAM) Conference.* http://idl.iscram.org

Laguna Salvad6, L., Lauras, M., & Comes, T. (2016). Towards a Monitoring System for American IFRC Logistics Network. *Proceedings of the 13th Information Systems for Crisis Response And Management (ISCRAM) Conference.* http://idl.iscram.org

Lambert, D. M., & Cooper, M. C. (2000). Issues in supply chain management. *Industrial Marketing Management, 29*(1), 65–83. doi:10.1016/S0019-8501(99)00113-3

Larsen, T. S., Thernoe, C., & Andresen, C. (2003). Supply chain collaboration: Theoretical perspective and empirical evidence. *International Journal of Physical Distribution & Logistics Management, 33*(6), 531–549. doi:10.1108/09600030310492788

Latimer, C., & Swithern, S. (2017). *Global humanitarian assistance report.* Development Initiatives.

Lea, B. R., & Fredendall, L. D. (2002). The impact of management accounting, product structure, product mix algorithm, and planning horizon on manufacturing performance. *International Journal of Production Economics, 79*(3), 279–299. doi:10.1016/S0925-5273(02)00253-0

LeCun, Y., & Bengio, Y. (1995). Convolutional networks for images, speech, and time series. The Handbook of Brain Theory and Neural Networks, 3361(10), 1995.

Lee, H. H., Zhou, J., & Hsu, P. H. (2015). The role of innovation in inventory turnover performance. *Decision Support Systems*, *76*, 35–44. doi:10.1016/j.dss.2015.02.010

Lee, H. L., So, K. C., & Tang, C. S. (2000). The value of information sharing in a two-level supply chain. *Management Science*, *46*(5), 626–643. doi:10.1287/mnsc.46.5.626.12047

Lee, H. L., & Whang, S. (2000). Information sharing in a supply chain. *International Journal of Manufacturing Technology and Management*, *1*(1), 79–93. doi:10.1504/IJMTM.2000.001329

Lei, L., Liu, S., Ruszczynski, A., & Park, S. (2006). On the integrated production, inventory, and distribution routing problem. *IIE Transactions*, *38*(11), 955–970. doi:10.1080/07408170600862688

Leiras, A., de Brito Jr, I., Queiroz Peres, E., Rejane Bertazzo, T., & Tsugunobu Yoshida Yoshizaki, H. (2014). Literature review of humanitarian logistics research: Trends and challenges. *Journal of Humanitarian Logistics and Supply Chain Management*, *4*(1), 95–130. doi:10.1108/JHLSCM-04-2012-0008

Lemoine, J. F. (2003). Vers une approche globale de l'atmosphère du point de vente. *Revue française du marketing*, (194), 83.

Leung, H. C. (1995, June). Neural networks in supply chain management. In *Proceedings for Operating Research and the Management Sciences* (pp. 347–352). IEEE. doi:10.1109/IEMC.1995.524607

Li, C. (2013). Controlling the bullwhip effect in a supply chain system with constrained information flows. *Applied Mathematical Modelling*, *37*(4), 1897–1909. doi:10.1016/j.apm.2012.04.020

Li, L. (2002). Information sharing in a supply chain with horizontal competition. *Management Science*, *48*(9), 1196–1212. doi:10.1287/mnsc.48.9.1196.177

Lin, T., Guo, T., & Aberer, K. (2017). Hybrid Neural Networks Over Time Series For Trend Forecasting. *Proceedings of the Twenty-Sixth International Joint Conference on Artificial Intelligence*. 10.24963/ijcai.2017/316

Liouville, J. (2011). Enchères électroniques inversées et confiance dans les relations B to B. *REDACTION: Brahim BENABDESLEM Directeur Général de le revue Boualem ALIOUAT Rédacteur en chef*, *1*(1), 68.

Liu, H. (2015, April). Forecasting Model of Supply Chain Management Based on Neural Network. In *2015 International Conference on Automation, Mechanical Control and Computational Engineering*. Atlantis Press. 10.2991/amcce-15.2015.32

Liu, J., Zhang, S., & Hu, J. (2005). A case study of an inter-enterprise workflow-supported supply chain management system. *Information & Management*, *42*(3), 441–454. doi:10.1016/j.im.2004.01.010

Li, Y., Xu, X., Zhao, X., Yeung, J. H. Y., & Ye, F. (2012). Supply chain coordination with controllable lead time and asymmetric information. *European Journal of Operational Research*, *217*(1), 108–119. doi:10.1016/j.ejor.2011.09.003

Lukosch, H., & Comes, T. (2019). Gaming as a research method in humanitarian logistics. *Journal of Humanitarian Logistics and Supply Chain Management.*

Lv, F., Ma, S., & Guan, X. (2015). The implication of capacity reservation contracts in assembly system with asymmetric demand information. *International Journal of Production Research, 53*(18), 5564–5591. doi:10.1080/00207543.2015.1036150

Madan, V. (2017). *Introducing Gluon — An Easy-to-Use Programming Interface for Flexible Deep Learning.* https://aws.amazon.com/blogs/machine-learning/introducing-gluon-an-easy-to-use-programming-interface-for-flexible-deep-learning/

Malone, T. W., & Crowston, K. (1990, September). What is coordination theory and how can it help design cooperative work systems? In *Proceedings of the 1990 ACM conference on Computer-supported cooperative work* (pp. 357-370). 10.1145/99332.99367

Martín del Bío, B., & Sanz Molina, A. (2006). *Neural networks and fuzzy systems.* Editorial RA-MA.

Martins, C. L., & Pato, M. V. (2019). Supply chain sustainability: A tertiary literature review. *Journal of Cleaner Production, 225*, 995–1016. doi:10.1016/j.jclepro.2019.03.250

Mason, A. N., & Villalobos, J. R. (2015). Coordination of perishable crop production using auction mechanisms. *Agricultural Systems, 138*, 18–30. doi:10.1016/j.agsy.2015.04.008

Matta, A., Chahed, S., Sahin, E., & Dallery, Y. (2014). Modelling home care organisations from an operations management perspective. *Flexible Services and Manufacturing Journal, 26*(3), 295–319. doi:10.100710696-012-9157-0

Mattke, S., Klautzer, L., Mengistu, T., Garnett, J., Hu, J., & Wu, H. (2010). *Health and Well-Being in the Home: A Global Analysis of Needs, Expectations, and Priorities for Home Health Care Technology.* https://www.rand.org/pubs/occasional_papers/OP323.html

Maya Duque, P. A., Castro, M., Sörensen, K., & Goos, P. (2015). Home care service planning. The case of Landelijke Thuiszorg. *European Journal of Operational Research, 243*(1), 292–301. doi:10.1016/j.ejor.2014.11.008

medicare.gov. (2016). *What's home health care?* Retrieved from https://www.medicare.gov/what-medicare-covers/home-health-care/home-health-care-what-is-it-what-to-expect.html

Meherishi, L., Narayana, S. A., & Ranjani, K. S. (2019). Sustainable packaging for supply chain management in the circular economy: A review. *Journal of Cleaner Production, 237*, 117582. doi:10.1016/j.jclepro.2019.07.057

Mendelson, H. (2000). Organizational architecture and success in the information technology industry. *Management Science, 46*(4), 513–529. doi:10.1287/mnsc.46.4.513.12060

Mendonca, D., Beroggi, G. E., Van Gent, D., & Wallace, W. A. (2006). Designing gaming simulations for the assessment of group decision support systems in emergency response. *Safety Science, 44*(6), 523–535. doi:10.1016/j.ssci.2005.12.006

Mentzer, J. T., DeWitt, W., Keebler, J. S., Min, S., Nix, N. W., Smith, C. D., & Zacharia, Z. G. (2001). Defining supply chain management. *Journal of Business Logistics*, *22*(2), 1–25. doi:10.1002/j.2158-1592.2001.tb00001.x

Merz, M., Hiete, M., Comes, T., & Schultmann, F. (2013). A composite indicator model to assess natural disaster risks in industry on a spatial level. *Journal of Risk Research*, *16*(9), 1077–1099. doi:10.1080/13669877.2012.737820

Min, H. (1994). International supplier selection: A multi-attribute utility approach. *International Journal of Physical Distribution & Logistics Management*, *24*(5), 24–33. doi:10.1108/09600039410064008

Mladenovic, N., & Hansen, P. (1997). Variable neighborhood search. *Computers & Operations Research*, *24*(11), 1097–1100. doi:10.1016/S0305-0548(97)00031-2

Moin, N. H., Salhi, S., & Aziz, N. A. B. (2011). An efficient hybrid genetic algorithm for the multi-product multi-period inventory routing problem. *International Journal of Production Economics*, *133*(1), 334–343. doi:10.1016/j.ijpe.2010.06.012

Montgomery, D. C., Jennings, C. L., & Kulahci, M. (2015). *Introduction to time series analysis and forecasting*. John Wiley & Sons.

Morabito, F. C., Campolo, M., Ieracitano, C., & Mammone, N. (2019). Deep Learning Approaches to Electrophysiological Multivariate Time-Series Analysis. In *Artificial Intelligence in the Age of Neural Networks and Brain Computing* (pp. 219–243). Academic Press.

Moscato, P., & Norman, M. G. (1992). A memetic approach for the traveling salesman problem implementation of a computational ecology for combinatorial optimization on message-passing systems. *Parallel Computing and Transputer Applications*, *1*, 177-186.

Müller, R., & Turner, J. R. (2005). The impact of principal–agent relationship and contract type on communication between project owner and manager. *International Journal of Project Management*, *23*(5), 398–403. doi:10.1016/j.ijproman.2005.03.001

Mupparaju, K., Soni, A., Gujela, P., & Lanham, M. A. (2008). *A Comparative Study of Machine Learning Frameworks for Demand Forecasting*. Academic Press.

Murray, C. C., & Chu, A. G. (2015). The flying sidekick traveling salesman problem: Optimization of drone-assisted parcel delivery. *Transportation Research Part C, Emerging Technologies*, *54*, 86–109. doi:10.1016/j.trc.2015.03.005

Nagurney, A. Y. M., & Qiang, Q. (2012). *Multiproduct Humanitarian Healthcare Supply Chains: A Network Modeling and Computational Framework.* Paper presented at the the 23rd Annual POMS Conference, Chicago, IL. 10.2139srn.1636294

NAHC. (2010). *Basic Statistics About Home Care*. Retrieved from www.nahc.org/assets/1/7/10hc_stats.pdf

NAHC. (2015). *Foundation for Hospice and Homecare and NAHC Hold Press Conference on Miles Traveled Each Year By Home Care Nurses*. Retrieved from http://www.nahc.org/NAHCReport/nr151215_1/

Ndille, R., & Belle, J. A. (2014). Managing the Limbe floods: Considerations for disaster risk reduction in Cameroon. *International Journal of Disaster Risk Science*, *5*(2), 147–156. doi:10.100713753-014-0019-0

Nickel, S., Schröder, M., & Steeg, J. (2012). Mid-term and short-term planning support for home health care services. *European Journal of Operational Research*, *219*(3), 574–587. doi:10.1016/j.ejor.2011.10.042

Oloruntoba, R., & Gray, R. (2006). Disaster aid: An agile supply chain? *Supply Chain Management*, *11*(2), 115–120. doi:10.1108/13598540610652492

Oloruntoba, R., & Gray, R. (2009). Customer service in emergency relief chains. *International Journal of Physical Distribution & Logistics Management*, *39*(6), 486–505. doi:10.1108/09600030910985839

OXFAM. (2019). *Information for suppliers*. Available at: https://www.oxfam.org.uk/what-we-do/about-us/plans-reports-and-policies/information-for-suppliers

PAHO. (2001). *Humanitarian Supply Management and Logistics in the Health Sector, Pan American Health Organization*. PAHO.

Pai, P. F., & Lin, C. S. (2005). A hybrid ARIMA and support vector machines model in stock price forecasting. *Omega*, *33*(6), 497–505. doi:10.1016/j.omega.2004.07.024

Pappas, S. S., Ekonomou, L., Karampelas, P., Karamousantas, D. C., Katsikas, S. K., Chatzarakis, G. E., & Skafidas, P. D. (2010). Electricity demand load forecasting of the Hellenic power system using an ARMA model. *Electric Power Systems Research*, *80*(3), 256–264. doi:10.1016/j.epsr.2009.09.006

Park, D. C., El-Sharkawi, M. A., Marks, R. J., Atlas, L. E., & Damborg, M. J. (1991). Electric load forecasting using an artificial neural network. *IEEE Transactions on Power Systems*, *6*(2), 442–449. doi:10.1109/59.76685

Pazirandeh, A. (2011). Sourcing in global health supply chains for developing countries. *International Journal of Physical Distribution & Logistics Management*, *41*(4), 364–384. doi:10.1108/09600031111131931

Peng, K., Du, J., Lu, F., Sun, Q., Dong, Y., Zhou, P., & Hu, M. (2019). A hybrid genetic algorithm on routing and scheduling for vehicle-assisted multi-drone parcel delivery. *IEEE Access: Practical Innovations, Open Solutions*, *7*, 49191–49200. doi:10.1109/ACCESS.2019.2910134

Peres, E. Q., Brito, I. Jr, Leiras, A., & Yoshizaki, H. (2012). Disaster logistics and disaster relief research: trends, applications, and future research directions. *Proceedings of the 4th International Conference on Information Systems, Logistics and Supply Chain*, 26-29.

Pérez-Rodríguez, N., & Holguín-Veras, J. (2015). Inventory-allocation distribution models for postdisaster humanitarian logistics with explicit consideration of deprivation costs. *Transportation Science*, *50*(4), 1261–1285. doi:10.1287/trsc.2014.0565

Prandtstetter, M., Raidl, G. R., & Misar, T. (2009). A Hybrid Algorithm for Computing Tours in a Spare Parts Warehouse. In C. Cotta & P. Cowling (Eds.), *Evolutionary Computation in Combinatorial Optimization: 9th European Conference, EvoCOP 2009* (pp. 25-36). Berlin: Springer Berlin Heidelberg. 10.1007/978-3-642-01009-5_3

Procurement Practice Group. (2010). *Procurement manual*. Available at https://www.unops.org/SiteCollectionDocuments/Procurementdocs/UNOPSprocurementmanualEN.pdf

Python Software Foundation. (2016). *Pytrends*. https://pypi.org/project/pytrends/1.1.3/

Qi, L., & Sun, D. (1999). A survey of some nonsmooth Equations and smoothing Newton methods. In Progress in optimization (pp. 121-146). Springer.

Qian, Y., Chen, J., Miao, L., & Zhang, J. (2012). Information sharing in a competitive supply chain with capacity constraint. *Flexible Services and Manufacturing Journal*, *24*(4), 549–574. doi:10.100710696-011-9102-7

Rafiei, H., Safaei, F., & Rabbani, M. (2018). Integrated production-distribution planning problem in a competition-based four-echelon supply chain. *Computers & Industrial Engineering*, *119*, 85–99. doi:10.1016/j.cie.2018.02.031

Raghunathan, S. (2001). Information sharing in a supply chain: A note on its value when demand is nonstationary. *Management Science*, *47*(4), 605–610. doi:10.1287/mnsc.47.4.605.9833

Raghunathan, S. (2003). Impact of demand correlation on the value of and incentives for information sharing in a supply chain. *European Journal of Operational Research*, *146*(3), 634–649. doi:10.1016/S0377-2217(02)00365-X

Ramkumar, N., Subramanian, P., Narendran, T. T., & Ganesh, K. (2011). A hybrid heuristic for inventory routing problem. *International Journal of Electronic Transport*, *1*(1), 45–63. doi:10.1504/IJET.2011.043113

Ramos, A. F. T., Lizarazo, E. H. A., Rubiano, L. S. R., & Araújo, C. L. Q. (2014). *Mathematical Model for the Home Health Care routing and scheduling problem with multiple treatment and time windows*. Paper presented at the Mathematical Methods in Science and Engineering, Athens, Greece.

Ranjan, R., Chatterjee, P., & Chakraborty, S. (2015). Evaluating performance of engineering departments in an Indian University using DEMATEL and compromise ranking methods. *Opsearch*, *52*(2), 307–328. doi:10.100712597-014-0186-1

Rasmussen, M. S., Justesen, T., Dohn, A., & Larsen, J. (2012). The Home Care Crew Scheduling Problem: Preference-based visit clustering and temporal dependencies. *European Journal of Operational Research*, *219*(3), 598–610. doi:10.1016/j.ejor.2011.10.048

Richardson, D. C., Dale, R., & Kirkham, N. Z. (2007). The art of conversation is coordination. *Psychological Science*, *18*(5), 407–413. doi:10.1111/j.1467-9280.2007.01914.x PMID:17576280

Riloha institute. (2013). *Alexander Blecken (United Nations Office for Project Services), on "Sustainable Procurement and the United Nations"*. Available at: https://www.riloha.org/index.php/component/content/article/86-eve/past/112-11-13-2013-alexander-blecken-united-nations-office-for-project-services-on-sustainable-procurement-and-the-united-nations?Itemid=545

Rogers, M. G., Bruen, M., & Maystre, L. Y. (2013). *Electre and decision support: methods and applications in engineering and infrastructure investment*. Springer Science & Business Media.

Ruokokoski, M., Solyali, O. G. U. Z., Cordeau, J. F., Jans, R., & Süral, H. (2010). *Efficient formulations and a branch-and-cut algorithm for a production-routing problem*. GERAD Technical Report G-2010-66.

Saeyeon, R., & Jang, H. (2018). Strategic Logistics Outsourcing in Humanitarian Supply Chain: A Fuzzy AHP Approach. *Korean Journal of Logistics.*, *26*(4), 103–113. doi:10.15735/kls.2018.26.4.007

Sahin, F., & Robinson, E. P. Jr. (2005). Information sharing and coordination in make-to-order supply chains. *Journal of Operations Management*, *23*(6), 579–598. doi:10.1016/j.jom.2004.08.007

Saksrisathaporn, K. (2015). *A multi-criteria decision support system using knowledge management and project life cycle approach: Application to humanitarian supply chain management* (Doctoral dissertation). Lyon 2.

Salvadó, L. L., Lauras, M., Comes, T., & Van de Walle, B. (2015, May). Towards More Relevant Research on Humanitarian Disaster Management Coordination. ISCRAM.

Sanders, N. R. (2008). Pattern of information technology use: The impact on buyer–suppler coordination and performance. *Journal of Operations Management*, *26*(3), 349–367. doi:10.1016/j.jom.2007.07.003

Sanders, N. R., & Manrodt, K. B. (1994). Forecasting practices in US corporations: Survey results. *Interfaces*, *24*(2), 92–100. doi:10.1287/inte.24.2.92

Sanders, N. R., & Manrodt, K. B. (2003). Forecasting software in practice: Use, satisfaction, and performance. *Interfaces*, *33*(5), 90–93. doi:10.1287/inte.33.5.90.19251

Schroeder, R. G. (2017). *Operations management in the supply chain decsions and cases*. Irwin/McGraw-Hill.

Senoussi, A., Dauzère-Pérès, S., Brahimi, N., Penz, B., & Mouss, N. K. (2018). Heuristics based on genetic algorithms for the capacitated multi vehicle production distribution problem. *Computers & Operations Research*, *96*, 108–119. doi:10.1016/j.cor.2018.04.010

Shahadat, K. (2003). Supplier choice criteria of executing agencies in developing countries. *International Journal of Public Sector Management*, *16*(4), 261–285. doi:10.1108/09513550310480033

Shao, Y., Bard, J. F., & Jarrah, A. I. (2012). The therapist routing and scheduling problem. *IIE Transactions*, *44*(10), 868–893. doi:10.1080/0740817X.2012.665202

Sharma, A., Panigrahi, D., & Kumar, P. (2013). *A neural network based approach for predicting customer churn in cellular network services.* arXiv preprint arXiv:1309.3945

Shimshoni, Y., Efron, N., & Matias, Y. (2009). *On the predictability of search trends. Technical report.* Google.

Shumway, R. H., & Stoffer, D. S. (2011). ARIMA models. In *Time Series Analysis and Its Applications* (pp. 83–171). Springer New York. doi:10.1007/978-1-4419-7865-3_3

Silver, E. A., Pyke, D. F., & Peterson, R. (1998). *Inventory management and production planning and scheduling* (Vol. 3). Wiley.

Simchi-Levi, D., Wu, S. D., & Shen, Z. J. M. (Eds.). (2004). *Handbook of quantitative supply chain analysis: modeling in the e-business era* (Vol. 74). Springer Science & Business Media. doi:10.1007/978-1-4020-7953-5_1

Singh, A. (2016). *Supplier Selection and Multi-period Demand Allocation in a Humanitarian Supply Chain.* doi:10.1007/978-81-322-2416-7_14

Sinha, S., & Sarmah, S. P. (2008). An application of fuzzy set theory for supply chain coordination. *International Journal of Management Science and Engineering Management*, *3*(1), 19–32. doi:10.1080/17509653.2008.10671033

Sivasamy, K., Arumugam, C., Devadasan, S. R., Murugesh, R., & Thilak, V. M. M. (2016). Advanced models of quality function deployment: A literature review. *Quality & Quantity*, *50*(3), 1399–1414. doi:10.100711135-015-0212-2

Skymind, A. I. Wiki. (2019). *The Artificial Intelligence Wiki.* https://skymind.ai/wiki/

Solyali, O., & Süral, H. (2017). A multi-phase heuristic for the production routing problem. *Computers & Operations Research*, *87*, 114–124. doi:10.1016/j.cor.2017.06.007

Sorensen, D. C. (1985). Analysis of pairwise pivoting in Gaussian elimination. *IEEE Transactions on Computers*, *C-34*(3), 274–278. doi:10.1109/TC.1985.1676570

Sosa, P. M. (2018). *Twitter Sentiment Analysis using Combined LSTM-CNN Models.* http://konukoii.com/blog/2018/02/19/twitter-sentiment-analysis-using-combined-lstm-cnn-models/

Specht, D. F. (1991). A general regression neural network. *IEEE Transactions on Neural Networks*, *2*(6), 568–576. doi:10.1109/72.97934 PMID:18282872

StackExchange. (2018). *Structure of LSTM RNNs.* https://ai.stackexchange.com/questions/6961/structure-of-lstm-rnns

Su, B. C. (2008). Characteristics of consumer search on-line: How much do we search? *International Journal of Electronic Commerce*, *13*(1), 109–129. doi:10.2753/JEC1086-4415130104

Sultan, K., Ali, H., & Zhang, Z. (2018). Big data perspective and challenges in next generation networks. *Future Internet, 10*(7), 56. doi:10.3390/fi10070056

Taghipour, A., & Frayret, J. M. (2013). Dynamic mutual adjustment search for supply chain operations planning co-ordination. *International Journal of Production Research, 51*(9), 2715–2739. doi:10.1080/00207543.2012.737952

Tapia, A. H., Antunes, P., Bañuls, V. A., Moore, K., & Albuquerque, J. P. D. (2016). *Proceedings of the International Conference on Information Systems for Crisis Response and Management.* Academic Press.

Tatham, P., Oloruntoba, R., & Spens, K. (2012). Cyclone preparedness and response: An analysis of lessons identified using an adapted military planning framework. *Disasters, 36*(1), 54–82. doi:10.1111/j.1467-7717.2011.01249.x PMID:21702893

Thiels, C. A., Aho, J. M., Zietlow, S. P., & Jenkins, D. H. (2015). Use of unmanned aerial vehicles for medical product transport. *Air Medical Journal, 34*(2), 104–108. doi:10.1016/j.amj.2014.10.011 PMID:25733117

Thomas, D. J., & Griffin, P. M. (1996). Coordinated supply chain management. *European Journal of Operational Research, 94*(1), 1–15. doi:10.1016/0377-2217(96)00098-7

Tietje, O. (2005). Identification of a small reliable and efficient set of consistent scenarios. *European Journal of Operational Research, 162*(2), 418–432. doi:10.1016/j.ejor.2003.08.054

Tliche, Y., Taghipour, A., & Canel-Depitre, B. (2019). Downstream Demand Inference in decentralized supply chains. *European Journal of Operational Research, 274*(1), 65–77. doi:10.1016/j.ejor.2018.09.034

Trapero, J. R., Kourentzes, N., & Fildes, R. (2012). Impact of information exchange on supplier forecasting performance. *Omega, 40*(6), 738–747. doi:10.1016/j.omega.2011.08.009

Trautsamwieser, A., & Hirsch, P. (2014). A Branch-Price-and-Cut approach for solving the medium-term home health care planning problem. *Networks, 64*(3), 143–159. doi:10.1002/net.21566

Trkman, P., Groznik, A., & Koohang, A. (2006). Measurement of supply chain integration benefits. *Interdisciplinary Journal of Information, Knowledge & Management, 1.*

Tveiten, C. K., Albrechtsen, E., Wærø, I., & Wahl, A. M. (2012). Building resilience into emergency management. *Safety Science, 50*(10), 1960–1966. doi:10.1016/j.ssci.2012.03.001

Tzeng, G. H., Chiang, C. H., & Li, C. W. (2007). Evaluating intertwined effects in e-learning programs: A novel hybrid MCDM model based on factor analysis and DEMATEL. *Expert Systems with Applications, 32*(4), 1028–1044. doi:10.1016/j.eswa.2006.02.004

UNDP. (2004). *Reducing Disaster Risk: A Challenge for Development–A Global Report.* UN Press.

UNESCAP. (2008). *Building Community Resilience to Natural Disasters through Partnership: Sharing Experience and Expertise in the Region.* UN Press.

UNICEF. (2019). *Become a supplier.* Available at: https://www.unicef.org/supply/index_become_a_supplier.html

UNISDR. (2009). *Terminology on Disaster Risk Reduction.* UN Press.

Vaillancourt, A., Tatham, P., Wu, Y., & Haavisto, I. (2018). Humanitarian health project supply chain costs. *Supply Chain Forum: An International Journal, 19*(1), 70-80. doi:10.1080/16258312.2017.1394775

Van de Walle, B., & Comes, T. (2015). On the nature of information management in complex and natural disasters. *Procedia Engineering, 107*(1), 403–411. doi:10.1016/j.proeng.2015.06.098

van der Laan, E., van Dalen, J., Rohrmoser, M., & Simpson, R. (2016). Demand forecasting and order planning for disaster logistics: An empirical assessment. *Journal of Operations Management, 45*(1), 114–122. doi:10.1016/j.jom.2016.05.004

Van deWalle, B., & Comes, T. (2014). *Risk accelerators in disasters. Insights from the typhoon Haiyan response on humanitarian information management and decision support.* Academic Press.

Vandenberghe, L., & Boyd, S. (1996). Semidefinite programming. *SIAM Review, 38*(1), 49–95. doi:10.1137/1038003

Vandermerwe, S., & Rada, J. (1988). Servitization of business: Adding value by adding services. *European Management Journal, 6*(4), 314–324. doi:10.1016/0263-2373(88)90033-3

Vargas, J., Rojas, J., Inga, A., Mantilla, W., Añasco, H., Basurto, M. F., Campos, R., Sánchez, J., & Checa, P. I. (2016). Towards Reliable Recurrent Disaster Forecasting Methods: Peruvian Earthquake Case. *Proceedings of the 13th Information Systems for Crisis Response And Management (ISCRAM) Conference.* http://idl.iscram.org

Vargas, J., Lauras, M., Okongwu, U., & Dupont, L. (2015). A decision support system for robust disaster facility location. *Engineering Applications of Artificial Intelligence, 46*(1), 326–335. doi:10.1016/j.engappai.2015.06.020

Vega, D., & Roussat, C. (2015). Humanitarian logistics: The role of logistics service providers. *International Journal of Physical Distribution & Logistics Management, 45*(4), 352–375. doi:10.1108/IJPDLM-12-2014-0309

Vickery, S. K., Jayaram, J., Droge, C., & Calantone, R. (2003). The effects of an integrative supply chain strategy on customer service and financial performance: An analysis of direct versus indirect relationships. *Journal of Operations Management, 21*(5), 523–539. doi:10.1016/j.jom.2003.02.002

Vitoriano, B., de Juan, J. M., & Ruan, D. (2013). *Decision aid models for disaster management and emergencies.* Springer Science & Business Media. doi:10.2991/978-94-91216-74-9

Vosooghidizaji, M., Taghipour, A., & Canel-Depitre, B. (2019). Supply chain coordination under information asymmetry: A review. *International Journal of Production Research*, 1–30.

Wackerly, D., Mendenhall, W., & Scheaffer, R. L. (2014). *Mathematical statistics with applications*. Cengage Learning.

Wang, X., Fan, Y., Liang, L., De Vries, H., & Van Wassenhove, L. N. (n.d.). Augmenting fixed framework agreements in humanitarian logistics with a bonus contract. *Production and Operations Management*.

Wang, J. W., & Cheng, C. H. (2007, August). Information fusion technique for weighted time series model. In *2007 International Conference on Machine Learning and Cybernetics* (Vol. 4, pp. 1860-1865). IEEE. 10.1109/ICMLC.2007.4370451

Wang, X., Poikonen, S., & Golden, B. (2017). The vehicle routing problem with drones: Several worst-case results. *Optimization Letters, 11*(4), 679–697. doi:10.100711590-016-1035-3

Weber, C. A., Current, J. R., & Benton, W. C. (1991). Vendor selection criteria and methods. *European Journal of Operational Research, 50*(1), 2–18. doi:10.1016/0377-2217(91)90033-R

Weichselgartner, J. (2001). Disaster mitigation: The concept of vulnerability revisited. *Disaster Prevention and Management: An International Journal, 10*(2), 85–95. doi:10.1108/09653560110388609

Wenxia, X., Feijia, L., Shuo, L., Kun, G., & Guodong, L. (2015, August). Design and application for the method of dynamic weighted moving average forecasting. In *2015 Sixth International Conference on Intelligent Systems Design and Engineering Applications (ISDEA)* (pp. 278-280). IEEE. 10.1109/ISDEA.2015.77

WGCEP. (2007). *The Uniform California Earthquake Rupture Forecast*. U.S. Geological Survey Open-File Report and California Geological Survey Special Report. https://pubs.usgs.gov/of/2007/1091/

WHO. (2013). *A Universal Truth: No Health Without a Workforce*. Retrieved from https://www.who.int/workforcealliance/knowledge/resources/hrhreport2013/en/

Wijnhoven, F., & Plant, O. (2017). Sentiment Analysis and Google Trends Data for Predicting Car Sales. *Thirty Eighth International Conference on Information Systems*.

Wirnitzer, J., Heckmann, I., Meyer, A., & Nickel, S. (2016). Patient-based nurse rostering in home care. *Operations Research for Health Care, 8*, 91–102. doi:10.1016/j.orhc.2015.08.005

Wisner, B., Blaikie, P., Cannon, T., & Davis, I. (2004). At risk. Natural people's vulnerability and disasters. Routledge.

Wohlsen, M. (2014). *The next big thing you missed: Amazon's delivery drones could work—they just need trucks*. http://www. wired. com/2014/06/the-nextbig-thing-you-missed-delivery-drones-launched-from-trucks-are-the-future-ofshipping/

World Food Programme. (2019). *Do Business With WFP*. Available at: https://www.wfp.org/do-business-with-wfp

World Food Programme. Situation Report. (2016). Available at: https://reliefweb.int/sites/reliefweb.int/files/resources/2018%2012%20WFP%20Syria%20Situation%20Report%20%2312.pdf

Wright, G., Cairns, G., & Goodwin, P. (2009). Teaching scenario planning: Lessons from practice in academe and business. *European Journal of Operational Research*, *194*(1), 323–335. doi:10.1016/j.ejor.2007.12.003

Xie, J., Liang, L., Liu, L., & Ieromonachou, P. (2017). Coordination contracts of dual-channel with cooperation advertising in closed-loop supply chains. *International Journal of Production Economics*, *183*, 528–538. doi:10.1016/j.ijpe.2016.07.026

Xu, H., Yao, N., & Tong, S. (2013). Sourcing under cost information asymmetry when facing time-sensitive customers. *International Journal of Production Economics*, *144*(2), 599–609. doi:10.1016/j.ijpe.2013.04.023

Xu, H., Zhang, K., Shen, J., & Li, Y. (2010). Storm surge simulation along the US East and Gulf Coasts using a multi-scale numerical model approach. *Ocean Dynamics*, *60*(6), 1597–1619. doi:10.100710236-010-0321-3

Yadav, D. K., & Barve, A. (2018). Segmenting critical success factors of humanitarian supply chains using fuzzy DEMATEL. *Benchmarking*, *25*(2), 400–425. doi:10.1108/BIJ-10-2016-0154

Yadegari, E., Alem-Tabriz, A., & Zandieh, M. (2019). A memetic algorithm with a novel neighborhood search and modified solution representation for closed-loop supply chain network design. *Computers & Industrial Engineering*, *128*, 418–436. doi:10.1016/j.cie.2018.12.054

Yalçındağ, S., Cappanera, P., Grazia Scutellà, M., Şahin, E., & Matta, A. (2016). Pattern-based decompositions for human resource planning in home health care services. *Computers & Operations Research*, *73*, 12–26. doi:10.1016/j.cor.2016.02.011

Yang, Y., Pan, S., & Ballot, E. (2017). Innovative vendor-managed inventory strategy exploiting interconnected logistics services in the Physical Internet. *International Journal of Production Research*, *55*(9), 2685–2702. doi:10.1080/00207543.2016.1275871

Ye, F., Li, Y., & Yang, Q. (2018). Designing coordination contract for biofuel supply chain in China. *Resources, Conservation and Recycling*, *128*, 306–314. doi:10.1016/j.resconrec.2016.11.023

Yin, Y., Bu, X., & Yu, F. (2008, October). Adaptive neural network in logistics demand forecasting. In *2008 International Conference on Intelligent Computation Technology and Automation (ICICTA)* (Vol. 1, pp. 168-172). IEEE. 10.1109/ICICTA.2008.73

Yu, Z., Yan, H., & Cheng, T. C. E. (2002). Modelling the benefits of information sharing-based partnerships in a two-level supply chain. *The Journal of the Operational Research Society*, *53*(4), 436–446. doi:10.1057/palgrave.jors.2601255

Yu, Z., Yan, H., & Edwin Cheng, T. C. (2001). Benefits of information sharing with supply chain partnerships. *Industrial Management & Data Systems*, *101*(3), 114–121. doi:10.1108/02635570110386625

Zhang, G. P. (2004). Business forecasting with artificial neural networks: An overview. In *Neural networks in business forecasting* (pp. 1–22). IGI Global. doi:10.4018/978-1-59140-176-6.ch001

Zhang, K., Li, Y., Liu, H., Xu, H., & Shen, J. (2013). Comparison of three methods for estimating the sea level rise effect on storm surge flooding. *Climatic Change, 118*(2), 487–500. doi:10.100710584-012-0645-8

Zhang, X. (2004). Evolution of ARMA demand in supply chains. *Manufacturing & Service Operations Management, 6*(2), 195–198. doi:10.1287/msom.1040.0042

Zhao, H. F., & Zhu, C. (2017, June). Service supply chain coordination contract considering advertising level. In *2017 International Conference on Service Systems and Service Management* (pp. 1-5). IEEE. 10.1109/ICSSSM.2017.7996143

Zhao, Y., & Zhao, X. (2015). On human decision behavior in multi-echelon inventory management. *International Journal of Production Economics, 161*, 116–128. doi:10.1016/j.ijpe.2014.12.005

Zhikai, H. Y. L. F. S., & Ge, Z. (2002). Neural Networks Technology for Inventory Management. *Computer Engineering and Applications, 15.*

Zolfani, S. H., & Ghadikolaei, A. S. (2013). Performance evaluation of private universities based on balanced scorecard: Empirical study based on Iran. *Journal of Business Economics and Management, 14*(4), 696–714. doi:10.3846/16111699.2012.665383

About the Contributors

Atour Taghipour is an Associate professor and the head of two international management master programs at Normandy University (Le Havre) in France. He holds a PhD in Industrial Engineering from the Polytechnic School of Montreal in Canada. He received two masters' degrees, one in Management, Logistics & Strategy and other in Industrial Engineering. He has more than ten years of experiences as a manager in automobile industries. He has published four books and many research papers in international journals. His areas of research are supply chain and operations management.

* * *

Serol Bulkan received his bachelor's degree in Management Engineering from Istanbul Technical University in 1986 and his master's degree in 1989, and his second master's degree in Operations Research from the Florida Institute of Technology in 1991 and his Ph.D. in Industrial Engineering from Cleveland State University in 1989. He is currently a faculty member in the Department of Industrial Engineering at Marmara University.

Béatrice Canel-Depitre is a Senior Lecturer in Management Sciences at Le Havre Normandy University. She has published different books and many research papers in international journals. Her research areas are business management, strategic management and marketing.

Md Mushfique Chowdhury is currently working as "IP Planner" in Freedom Mobile (Telecom Operator) in Toronto, Canada. During working, he has completed M.Sc in Data Science & Analytics and also MEng in Computer Networks. Prior to coming in Canada, he worked in telecom sectors for 10 years. His research interest includes computer networks, prediction analysis, etc.

Tina Comes is Associate Professor and Delft Technology Fellow on Designing Resilience. She is Full Professor ICT at the University of Agder, Norway, Senior Research Fellow at the Harvard Humanitarian Initiative and Visiting Professor at Université Dauphine in Paris. Tina serves as Scientific Co-Director of the 4TU Center on Resilience Engineering. Tina's research focuses on decision-making under uncertainty and the collaborative and informational aspects of resilient societies.

Mehmet Erdem received his Ph.D, M.Sc. and B.Sc. degrees in industrial engineering from Marmara University, Gazi University and Başkent University, respectively. He is a faculty member in the Department of Industrial Engineering Department of Ondokuz Mayıs University. His primary research interests are in vehicle routing, scheduling, heuristics, and data mining.

Saman Hassanzadeh Amin is an Assistant Professor at the Department of Mechanical and Industrial Engineering, Ryerson University in Toronto, Ontario, Canada. Prior joining Ryerson University, he was an Assistant Professor of Supply Chain Management at Cape Breton University in Nova Scotia. Dr. Amin's research interests include Supply Chain Management, Operations Management, Operations Research, Optimization, Information Technology, and Decision Support Systems. He has published several journal papers in well-known journals such as "International Journal of Production Research" and "Expert Systems with Applications". His publications have received several citations. Dr. Amin's research is supported by internal grants in addition to external grants such as NSERC Discovery Grant, NSERC Engage Grant, and SSHRC Insight Development Grant. He has received some awards such as Honorable Mention Award from ASAC in 2016. Dr. Amin has supervised several graduate and undergraduate students.

Asma Husna's received her M.Sc. in Computer Science and M.Sc. in Data Science and Analytics, both from Ryerson University, Canada. Her research interests include Supply Chain Management, Information Technology, Machine Leaning and Decision Support Systems. She has significant programming skills in Object-Oriented programming (OOP) and good knowledge in machine learning and R & python program.

Nihan Kabadayi is an Assistant Professor in the School of Business at Istanbul University (Istanbul, Turkey) where she has been a faculty member since 2005. She received her Ph.D. in Supply Chain Management from Istanbul University in 2013. Her research interest includes supply chain management, healthcare operations management, quality management, and multi-criteria decision making.

Matthieu Lauras is Full-Professor and Deputy-Head of the Industrial Engineering Center at IMT Mines Albi (France). He is also research Adjunct-Professor at the Physical Internet Center of ISyE - Georgia Institute of Technology (USA) and at the School of Economics and Management - Beijing Jiaotong University (China). His research works develop contributions to support collaborative networks' stakeholders to better make their decisions in uncertain and/or disruptive environments. His research activities concern both industrial management systems and crisis management systems.

Jomana Mahfod is a Ph.D. candidate in Management Science in NIMEC laboratory at Le Havre University in France. She received master degree in management sciences. Teacher in management at the University of Le Havre.

Hamdi Radhoui is currently PhD student at the University of Le Havre, France. He holds a master of research degree in Logistics & Transportation. His areas of research are supply chain and operations management.

Bharat Shah is a professor at Ted Rogers School of Management, Ryerson University. He has published several papers pertaining to information technology management and is co-author of the book How to Manage a Successful Software Project. His research interests include Information Technology Strategy, Operations Management, and Supply Chain Management.

Reza Tavakkoli-Moghaddam is a Professor of Industrial Engineering at the College of Engineering, University of Tehran in Iran. He obtained his Ph.D., M.Sc. and B.Sc. degrees in Industrial Engineering from Swinburne University of Technology in Melbourne (1998), University of Melbourne in Melbourne (1994), and Iran University of Science and Technology in Tehran (1989), respectively. He serves as the Editor-in-Chief of Journal of Industrial Engineering published by the University of Tehran and the Editorial Board member of 10 reputable journals. He is the recipient of the 2009 and 2011 Distinguished Researcher Awards and the 2010 and 2014 Distinguished Applied Research Awards at University of Tehran. He has been selected as the National Iranian Distinguished Researcher in 2008 and 2010 by the MSRT (Ministry of Science, Research, and Technology) in Iran. He has obtained the outstanding rank as the top 1% scientist and researcher in the world elite group since 2014. Also, he received the Order of Academic Palms Award as a distinguished educator and scholar for the insignia of Chevalier dans l'Ordre des Palmes Academiques by the Ministry of National Education of France in 2019. He has published 5 books, 24 book chapters, and more than 1000 journal and conference papers.

Youssef Tliche is a PhD student in Management Sciences at the University of Le Havre in France. He holds an engineering diploma in statistics and information analysis from the higher school of statistics and information analysis in Tunis in Tunisia, and a master's degree in actuarial science and mathematical engineering in finance and insurance from the University of Le Havre in France.

Md Rokon Uddin is currently a graduate student in the Data Science and Analytics (MSc) program at Ryerson University in Toronto, Ontario, Canada. He received his Bachelor's degree in Computer Science and Engineering from the University of Dhaka in Dhaka, Bangladesh. His research interests include Artificial Intelligence (AI) in Supply Chain Management, Operations Management, Optimization, and Information Technology. His professional career reflects his interests.

Jorge Vargas-Florez is a Professor of Engineering Department at Pontifical Catholic University of Peru (PUCP). He leads the research group about the Crisis and Disaster Management at PUCP. He got his Ph.D. in Industrial Systems from IMT Mines Albi, in 2014. His research works develop contributions to support humanitarian and sustainable supply chains. He published on more than a dozen international conferences and journal articles in this domain.

Guoqing Zhang, Ph.D., PEng, is a Professor in Industrial Engineering, the director of supply chain and logistics optimization research center, at Department of Mechanical, Automotive & Materials Engineering, University of Windsor. He received the Ph.D. degree in management sciences from City University of Hong Kong in 2000. His recent research interests include operations research, algorithms design and development, supply chain management and optimization, logistics, warehouse management, data driven optimization, and intelligent decision support systems. He has published over 60 articles on those areas in journals such as Operations Research, Computational Optimization and Applications, IIE Transactions, European Journal of Operational Research, Omega, IJPE, IJPR, Computers and Operations Research, and so on. Dr. Zhang has provided consulting to several world leading companies on Automotive, Energy, Airline, and Foods industries. Dr. Zhang and his team won the first place in the Canadian Operations Research Society's Practice Prize competition in 2015. He is an associate editor of INFOR.

Index

L

M

N

O

P

R

S

T

V

W

www.ingramcontent.com/pod-product-compliance
Lightning Source LLC
LaVergne TN
LVHW081339300926
849161LV00008B/2014